alfred kazin / the open form

ESSAYS FOR OUR TIME

For Bowdoin College Library
Lawrence Sargent Hall

HARCOURT, BRACE & WORLD, INC.

NEW YORK / BURLINGAME

contents

IV

V

introduction

the essay as a modern form

Of the twenty-nine authors represented in this anthology of contemporary essays, twenty-five are still alive. Malcolm Bradbury, the young English novelist and essayist who writes here with such pleasant irony about the "beats," is still in his twenties; the well-known American novelists Truman Capote and James Baldwin are still in their thirties. More significant, perhaps, some of the most vital essays in the book, like Saul Bellow's commentary on our affluent society, Elizabeth Hardwick's barbed comments on Boston as a "lost ideal," and D. W. Brogan's amazingly fresh reappraisal of the Civil War, have appeared only very recently in American or English periodicals. In several cases —C. P. Snow's "The Two Cultures" and Bruno Bettelheim's "The Real Lesson of the Concentration Camps"—I have drawn upon books only very recently published. My aim throughout has been to present the possibilities of the essay as a form for our time—and in order to show students just how sensitively and brilliantly the essay form can be handled, it has seemed to me important to demonstrate this through the work of those who are "living" writers in the true sense—alive in the words they use, alive to the real issues of man's destiny today.

So often, in making up an anthology of essays for college use, editors feel that they have to choose between the traditional essay, such as was written by Montaigne or Hazlitt or Emerson, and the timely but journalistic article of today. What I have tried to do in *The Open Form* is to show that the essay as a literary form, and the "article" in its relevance to contemporary issues, can and indeed must be the same.

So here are essays on mass culture and our technological age; on the television "quiz show" scandals and the ineradicable memory of the Second World War; on the problem of being a Negro in America and on the "beats"; on the look of the Soviet Union today and on Russia as it was; on the irresistible drive of scientific knowledge and the unhappy division between literature and science; on the real or fancied menace of the organization man, on the new science of the sea, and on the problem of Belief. Since there is nothing more contemporary than a great work of literature that has significance to our age, here as well are essays on *Leaves of Grass,* on *Moby-Dick* and *Huckleberry Finn.* But not one of these essays has been selected merely for its topicality; not one could have appeared in a Sunday magazine section or in the *Reader's Digest* under the title, "Youth Wants To Know," or "Whither The U.N.?" Each selection has been chosen because its vitality and precision as a piece of writing are clearly related to the sensitiveness of its concern with human experience today.

II

What I have looked for in each selection has been not just the discussion of "current problems," but the essayist's ability to make us see the hidden issue, the deeper issue, the unexpected issue pressing for our awareness—the issue that really *is* an issue to the individual writing the essay. Large and abstract considerations like "conformity" are not issues; all we can say of "conformity," as of sin, is that we are against it. The difference is startling between the usual warning against "conformity," such as one can read every week and every month in the American press, and a thoughtful and provocative essay such as Saul Bellow's "The Sealed Treasure" or Harold Rosenberg's "The Orgamerican Phantasy," which lays bare the clichés of thinking that we are actually conforming to. Usually, it is the run-of-the-mill article, the kind of article that is thought up by editors or that has been watered down by editors from the writer's manuscript, that talks about "conformity" in the abstract. Such articles can go nowhere, for they start from the expected conclusion that "conformity"—whatever that is—is bad. But the genuine essayist, as one can see from Saul Bellow's unexpected conclusion that perhaps it is the very rapidity with which we are accomplishing a revolution of plenty that now dismays us, is the writer who thinks his way through the essay—and so comes out where perhaps he did not wish to. Such a writer is prepared to meet contemporary experience on its own terms. He uses the essay as an open form—as a way of thinking things out for himself, as a way of discovering *what* he thinks.

But to do this for oneself, to show students what this can mean, one must present the deeper issues of our time as they have been discovered and *lived* by the more thoughtful writers of our time. Students still do not look enough to the best contemporary writers to illuminate their own lives. Instead, they're asked to face "big topics" that are too large and abstract for them to handle, and about which, as they understandably feel, *they* can do nothing. Surely the real issues, for students and teachers alike, are not to be found in the questions that are always put to us by public opinion polls, newspapers, and advertisers—*What Should We Do About The Underdeveloped Nations?* The true issues are those that we discover in our personal experience, upon which in some sense our lives depend, issues that we know we have to do something about—if only by thinking hard and clearly. Once we make such issues our own, we can connect them to the public questions that so often seem external to students, merely imposed on them by an older generation.

Take an essay like James Baldwin's brilliant and tumultuous "Notes Of A Native Son." This is not an essay on "the Negro problem," but a report of what it means to be James Baldwin. The power and brilliance of this essay come from Baldwin's ability to confront his own experience, to make us see the incidents, associations, loyalties, anguish, doubts, of a life like James Baldwin's. "Notes Of A Native Son" should encourage the student to see his own and perhaps vastly different experience *as* an experience; it should help to break up the generalities and abstractions, the empty repetitions and the resounding slogans that are constantly offered to us as "reality" by the newspapers, television, movies and advertising. It is my deepest hope for this book that the student who so often tends to distrust his own individual reactions to things, who cannot help feeling that he is "small" in contrast to the "big" issues that make up the headlines and our anxieties, will remember that each of the writers in this book is only an individual, too, as human and as "small" as anyone else. Perhaps the student who tends to distrust his own individual reactions to contemporary life, who has been discouraged by the charge that he is "apathetic" to the issues, may learn from some of these brilliant and direct essays that he has never been apathetic at all—he has been merely bored by public issues that just are not very real to him.

If the student is ever to discuss the issues as he has discovered them, in the shape presented by his own experience, he must begin by accepting the fact that an essay like Elizabeth Hardwick's on Boston is not meant to be the "whole truth," the sociological truth, the abstract and neutral truth about a great city in which live over 800,000 people. No writer can do justice to the experience of so many people in one essay; let him not even try. But the essay, "the open form," as I have been calling it, is an attempt to do justice at least to one person's experience. The subject is in a sense *someone's* relationship to certain things and not all things at once. There is the source of the close-packed power that comes when, like Elizabeth Hardwick on Boston or Robert Lowell in his more native and ironic perspective on the same city, the subject is *someone's*. Then the thoughts that cluster around the subject are also someone's, and someone's honesty, freshness, someone's intensity of observation (rather than intensity of emotion), becomes fundamental.

We are dealing here with a form, the essay, that is peculiarly personal. It is personal not because it is necessarily *about* the self, but because it is an expression of the self thinking. The beauty of the form is that it allows the writer, as himself, the freedom to discover and to develop his individual statement on things. This is the freedom to find out what one really wants to say and *has* to say. In a novel or play, even in a "personal" and lyric poem, an imagined individual speaks; but it is in the name that is signed to an essay, the name of the author himself, that the essayist speaks. He starts from the fact that is himself, and there is nothing that he can say about himself that is more personal than what he thinks. The essay, as a form, is open enough to allow the writer to find the run of his argument. That is why the essay is so peculiarly modern a form, for it expresses the individual's wholly undetermined and freely discovered point of view. Imagination, in the pure sense, is much older; but newer in history and actually less familiar is the kind of literally self-conscious individuality that made the essay possible. As a form, it is relatively new. New too is the individual thinking about himself as an individual.

It is this quality, not even of pure thought but of the thinker identifying himself with his thought, that gives the essay as a form its special quality. Poetry works on us by the power of language which somehow awakens the most instinctive and profound forces in us. A novel may contain characters and situations that are more real to us than our own lives. A work of philosophy must convince us by the pure logic of its argument. But an essay, though it also must "convince" us, can do this only if the individual voice that we hear in every true essay—the voice of the writer ruminating, describing, thinking, remembering—is wholly consonant with the subject; only if the self writing and the argument become one and the same. The oldest and perhaps the deepest forms of literature, like poetry, somehow depend on the writer's ability to reveal the almost consecrational beauty of something that existed before the voice of the poet was heard in its praise. But the value of the essay as a form is that it succeeds not for the sake of the argument, as philosophy does; not for the sake of the writer's "personality," as character does, but because the writer has succeeded in *sharing* his meditations with us. In an essay, it is not the thought that counts but the experience we get of the writer's thought; not the self, but the self thinking. And above all, it is not the "subject" that counts with us, for this subject might have been arrived at by any-one—it is the subject as arrived at by the writer, as it has grown in his thought, as it has been done justice to by himself alone.

ALFRED KAZIN

New York
November, 1960

I

saul bellow

---

the sealed treasure

Saul Bellow was born in Canada in 1915, grew up in Chicago, and is for many readers the most exciting American novelist who has emerged since the Second World War. His most famous novel, *The Adventures of Augie March* (1953), was instantly recognized as a triumph of style— of the easy, defiant, tough and common literary style that we identify with modern American writing.

In the present selection, originally published as an article in the London *Times Literary Supplement,* Bellow's gift of style—the easy, low-slung, familiar style—is very striking. Perhaps because the subject of his essay is the deadening, homogenizing, flattening effect of our super-prosperity—"Pig Heaven," as they say in parts of Illinois—producing the shallow sameness that we have learned to associate with mass society and mass culture, Bellow's own writing here is full of rapid strokes, quick and original images. Only a born writer would describe the new American cars as "glossy cars in giddy colors," would compare them to "ships from outer space." Only a man with an unusual eye and a particularly ironic imagination would single out the Negro woman, her head wrapped in an old-fashioned bandanna, flashing by in a blue Packard with a Boston bull terrier affectionately seated on her shoulder.

Details like these, founded on the writer's instinctive sense of the contrasting, the ironic, the unexpected, give vitality to this piece of personal writing. Yet Bellow's artful and deliberate manner supports a subtle thesis. Everyone knows the dangers of conformity; not many people have noticed the dangers of "living it up." Even the artist and the novelist, when they do tend to notice them, tend to react with disgust.

This is the point at which so many critics of our society stop. Bellow goes on to make the interesting point that the "big change" we are witnessing just now, the change to unlimited material satisfaction, has perhaps checked the literary impulse because the rapidity of so many new developments has itself dazzled and exhausted us. As Harold Rosenberg notes in "The Orgamerican Phantasy" (p. 324), this is a time full of lament and nostalgia for a time of scarcity. We tend to underrate the revolution taking place before our eyes. Or as Bellow puts it: "We are temporarily miracle-sodden and feeling faint." We may be seeing more than we can take in. "Was it possible," he asks, "that what people complained of as boredom might in fact be an unbearable excitement caused by the greatness of the change?"

A few years ago I traveled through the state of Illinois to gather material for an article. It was brilliant fall weather, the corn was high and it was intersected by straight, flat roads over which it was impossible not to drive at top speed. I went from Chicago to Galena and then south through the center of the state to Cairo and Shawneetown. Here and there, in some of the mining counties and in the depopulated towns along the Mississippi there were signs of depression and poverty, but these had the flavor of the far away and long ago, for the rest of the state was dizzily affluent. "Pig Heaven," some people said to me. "Never nothing like it." The shops were filled with goods and buyers. In the fields were the newest harvesting machines; in the houses washers, dryers, freezers and refrigerators, air conditioners, vacuum cleaners, Mixmasters, Waringblenders, television and stereophonic high-fi sets, electrical can openers, novels condensed by the *Reader's Digest* and slick magazines. In the yards, glossy cars in giddy colors, like ships from outer space.

Down in Egypt, as the narrow southern end of the state is called, a Negro woman, her head wrapped in an old-fashioned bandanna, flashed by in her blue Packard with a Boston bull terrier affectionately seated on her shoulder. Here at least was some instinct for the blending of old and new. For the most part, everything was as new as possible. Churches and supermarkets had the same modern design. In the skies the rich farmers piloted their own planes. The workers bowled in alleys of choice hardwood where fouls were scored and pins reset by electronic devices. Fifty years ago the Illinois poet Vachel Lindsay had visited these towns preaching the Gospel of Beauty and calling on the people to build the New Jerusalem.

Except for the main stem, the streets were boringly empty, and at night even the main stem was almost deserted. Restless adolescents gathered in the ice-cream parlors or loitered before the chain saws, vibrators, outboard motors and garbage disposal units displayed in shop windows. These, like master spirits, ruled the night in silence.

Some important ingredients of life were conspicuously absent.

I had been asked to write about Illinois, but how was I to distinguish it from Indiana, Michigan, Iowa or Missouri? The houses were built and furnished in the same style, the cows were milked by the

THE SEALED TREASURE: From the *Times Literary Supplement* (London), July 1, 1960, Copyright © 1960 by The Times Publishing Company, Limited. Reprinted by permission of the author.

same machines, the programs broadcast by C.B.S. and N.B.C. were alike in Rockford, Illinois, and Danbury, Connecticut, and Salt Lake City, Utah. The magazines, the hair styles, the salad dressings, the film stars were not merely American but international. What but slight differences in the menu and the cut of the clothes distinguished the comfortable life of middle-class Illinois from that of Cologne or Frankfurt?

I asked, "What do people do, hereabouts?" "They work." "And when they don't work?" "They watch TV. They play a little poker or canasta or gin." "What else?" "They go to club meetings. Or to the drive-in movie. They pitch a little. They raise a little hell. They bowl. They drink some. They tinker around the place, fool with power-tools. They teach the kids baseball in the Little League. They're Den Mothers over at the Cub Scouts." "Yes, but what do they *do?*" "Well, mister, I'm telling you what they do. What are you getting at?" "You see, I'm writing an article on life here." "Is *that so!* Gosh, you're barking up the wrong tree. There ain't nothing here to write about. There's nothing doing here, or anywhere in Ellenois. It's boring." "You can't have millions of people and nothing doing." "I tell you, you want to write about Hollywood or Las Vegas or New York or Paris. That's where they've got excitement."

I had a score of conversations like this one.

Was the vitality of these people entirely absorbed by the new things? Had a superior inventive and productive power taken them over, paralyzing all the faculties it did not need? Or had the old understanding of reality been based on the threat of hunger and on the continual necessity for hard labor? Was it possible that what people complained of as boredom might in fact be an unbearable excitement caused by the greatness of the change?

I went to the libraries and was not surprised to learn that good books were very much in demand, and that there were people in central Illinois who read Plato, Tocqueville, Proust and Robert Frost. I had expected this. But what I did not understand was what use these isolated readers were making of the books they borrowed. With whom did they discuss them? At the country club, the bowling league, sorting mail at the post office or in the factory, over the back fence, how did they bring up Plato's Justice or Proust's Memory? Ordinary life gave them little opportunity for such conversation. "You can't have millions of people and nothing doing." I was dead sure of that. But the intelligence or cultivation of a woman in Moline, Illinois, would necessarily be her secret, almost her private vice. Her friends at the bridge club would think it very odd of her to think such things. She might not reveal them to her sister, nor perhaps even to her husband. They would be her discovery, her treasure ten times sealed, her private source of power.

"The language, the dress, and the daily actions of men in democracies are repugnant to ideal conceptions," said Tocqueville. He said more, but this is text enough for the moment. Let us set beside it the fact that these men, or some of them, will read *The Divine Comedy, The Tempest* and *Don Quixote*. What will they make of these works? They will, some of them, mix them up with television productions. Others will scale them down. Our understanding of them (it is time to drop the third person) will certainly be faulty. Nevertheless, they move us. That is to say, human greatness can still be seen by us. And it is not a question of the gnat who sees the elephant. We are not members of a different species. Without a certain innate sympathy we could not read Shakespeare and Cervantes. In our own contemporary novels this power to understand the greatest human qualities appears to be dispersed, transformed or altogether buried. A modern mass society has no open place for such qualities, no vocabulary for them and no ceremony (except in the churches) which makes them public. So they remain private and are mingled with other private things which vex us or of which we feel ashamed. But they are not lost. The saleswoman in Moline, Ill., *will* go to the library and borrow *Anna Karenina*. This society with its titanic products conditions but cannot absolutely denature us. It forces certain elements of the genius of our species to go into hiding. In America they take curiously personal, secret forms. Sometimes they corrupt people; sometimes they cause them to act with startling generosity. On the whole they are not to be found in what we call our Culture.

They are not in the streets, in the stores, at the movies. They are the missing ingredients.

The greatest danger, Dostoevsky warned in *The Brothers Karamazov*, was the universal ant-hill. D. H. Lawrence believed the common people of our industrial cities were like the great slave populations of the ancient empires. Joyce was apparently convinced that what happened to the ordinary modern man, his external life, was not interesting enough to chronicle. James Stephens in his preface to *Solitaria* by the Russian philosopher Rozanov said that novelists were trying to keep alive by artificial means feelings and states of being which had died out of the modern world, implying that we were only flattering the dwarfs by investing them with the passions of dead giants.

Mind manipulation, brainwashing and social engineering are only the newest developments in an evolution long understood by writers of the civilized world. When we read the best nineteenth and twentieth-century novelists we soon realize that they are trying in a variety of ways to establish a definition of human nature, to justify the continuation of life as well as the writing of novels. Like it or not, says Dostoevsky, it is our nature to be free, and under the sting of suffering to choose between good and evil. And Tolstoy says of human nature that it contains a need for truth which will never allow it to rest permanently in falsehood or unreality.

I think the novelists who take the bitterest view of our modern condition make the most of the art of the novel. "Do you think," Flaubert replies to a correspondent who has complained of *Madame Bovary,*

> that this ignoble reality, so disgusting to you in reproduction, does not oppress my heart as it does yours? If you knew me better you would know that I abhor ordinary existence. Personally, I have always held myself as aloof from it as I could. But aesthetically I desired this once—and only once—to plumb its very depths.

The writer's art appears to be a compensation for the hopelessness or meanness of existence. *He* by some method has retained the feelings and the ideal conceptions of which no sign remains in ordinary existence. Some novelists, the naturalists, have staked everything on ordinary existence in their desire to keep their connection with the surrounding world. Many of these have turned themselves into recording instruments at best, and at worst they have sucked up to the crowd, disgustingly. But the majority of modern novelists have followed the standard of Flaubert, the aesthetic standard. The shock caused by the loss of faith, says Professor Heller in *The Disinherited Mind,* made Burckhardt adopt an aesthetic view of history. If he is right, a sharp sense of disappointment and aestheticism go together. Flaubert complained that the exterior world was "disgusting, enervating, corruptive and brutalizing. . . . I am turning towards a kind of aesthetic mysticism," he wrote.

I am sticking to Flaubert because the connection between Yonville in Normandy and Galesburg, Illinois, (and London and Chicago) is constantly growing closer; because Flaubert believed that the writer by means of imagery and style must supply the human qualities that the exterior world lacks; and because we have all been schooled in his method—we are like the isolated lady in Moline whose sensitivity is her ten times sealed treasure.

Disappointment with its human material is built into the contemporary novel. It is assumed that society cannot give the novelist suitable themes and characters. Therefore the important humanity of the novel must be the writer's own. His force, his virtuosity, his powers of poetry, his reading of fate are at the center of his book. The reader is invited to bring his sympathies to the writer rather than the characters, and this makes him something of a novelist too.

The insistent aesthetic purpose in novelists like Flaubert and Henry James and Virginia Woolf and James Joyce is tyrannical at times. It over-conditions the situation of the characters. We are greatly compensated with poetry and insight, but it often seems as though the writer were deprived of all power except the power to see and to despair. In reality, however, he has a very great power. Is it likely that Westerns, thrillers, movies, soap-operas and True Confessions can usurp that power and permanently replace it? Not unless human nature is malleable without limits and can be conditioned to do without its ancient bread and meat.

A work of fiction consists of a series of moments during which we are willingly engrossed in the experiences of others. Or, as a recent article in the *Hudson Review* puts it, "the exuberant conviction that the individual life of *somebody else* holds all human truth and human potentiality" must be shared by the novelist and his reader. Let us say, putting it as mildly as possible, that modern society does not often inspire this exuberant conviction. We must not lie to ourselves about this. We must not lie. The Americans are softly optimistic and do lie about the love they bear one another. My informant in Illinois was telling the truth when he said his life was boring, but he would have turned awfully pious if I had asked him whether he loved his neighbor. Then he would have stood on the creed and answered that he felt a boundless love for him.

The matter was put as strongly as possible by D. H. Lawrence. "The sympathetic heart is broken," he said. "We stink in each other's nostrils." That is, we cannot easily accept our own creaturely existence or that of others. And that is the fault of modern civilization, he tells us. We must in part agree, but the matter is so serious that we should be careful not to exaggerate. Our lives depend on it. Yes, there are good reasons for revulsion and fear. But revulsion and fear impair judgment. Anxiety destroys scale and suffering makes us lose perspective.

One would have to be optimistic to the point of imbecility to raise the standard of pure Affirmation and cry, "Yea, Yea," shrilly against the deep background of "Nays." But the sympathetic heart is sometimes broken, sometimes not. It is reckless to say "broken"; it is nonsense to say "whole and unimpaired." On either side we have the black and white of paranoia.

As for the novelist, it would become him to proceed with care and modesty. He should deplore no general evil on purely literary grounds. The world owes him nothing, and he has no business to be indignant with it on behalf of the novel. He must not expect life to bind itself to be stable for his sake or to accommodate his ambitions. If he must, let him, like Flaubert, "abhor ordinary existence." But he should not fall into despair over trifles. One of his legacies from Romanticism is a sensitivity to banality and ugliness in which originates much of the small change of modern fiction—the teeth that are crooked, the soiled underclothes, the clerk with carbuncles. From this comes a conventional unearned wretchedness, a bitterness about existence which is mere fashion. One of his legacies from Humanism is an idea of dignity which makes him think a great deal of what he sees about him absurd.

The enormous increases in population seem to have dwarfed the individual. So have modern physics and astronomy. But we may be somewhere between a false greatness and a false insignificance. At least we can stop misrepresenting ourselves to ourselves and realize that the only thing we can be in this world is human. We are temporarily miracle-sodden and feeling faint.

louis kronenberger

america and art

Louis Kronenberger was born in Cincinnati, Ohio, in 1904, and since 1938 has been drama editor of *Time* magazine. He has been a visiting professor at several American universities, is currently professor of theatre arts at Brandeis University, and he has written novels and plays as well as many works in cultural and literary criticism. As a scholar, he has specialized in the eighteenth century, and although he writes for an enormous public, he delights in the practiced elegance of eighteenth-century style, with its balanced sentences and practical antitheses.

This combination of learning and a highly polished literary wit makes Kronenberger a formidable critic of contemporary American culture. The present selection is the first chapter of a witty but intensely serious inquiry into the present state of American culture, *Company Manners;* in developing his thesis that Americans are not really "an artistic people," Kronenberger first startles his readers, then goes on to persuade them. The chief skill in a piece of writing like this is the writer's ability to reason with us, to carry us along on an argument that we may not have been prepared to make. In order to do this, Kronenberger has not only to convince us that Americans are *not* an artistic nation, but also that perhaps it does not matter whether we are artistic or not! "The compelling fact about art in America is that it is not organic. . . . the American bent, the American genius, has honestly moved in other directions. Like the Romans and the Germans, we are not an artistic people."

Kronenberger makes it easier for us to accept this point by a witty simile—"French women owe their chic, I would think, to their general lack of girlish beauty." Although it is never easy for us to accept the fact that we Americans are not first in everything, Kronenberger reconciles us to the fact by telling us something about ourselves that we did not know before. Perhaps there is a subtle flattery for us in being told that "We . . . go on binges with Beauty because it is no part of our daily life—and we somehow think the extent of the undertaking will make up for the quality. . . . our aging plutocrats leave a spendthrift order for art like the flashy sports who buy their women ten dozen American Beauty roses."

The compelling fact about art in America is that it is not organic. [1] It has almost no share in shaping our life; it offers, rather, compensation for the shapelessness. And just because we prescribe a certain amount of art for ourselves as a kind of corrective—being "deficient" in art as we might be in calcium or iron—we regard it less as ordinary nourishment than as a tonic, something we gulp rather than sip, regard with esteem and yet suspicion, and either require to be made up with a pleasant taste or exult in because it tastes unpleasant. The American feeling, or lack of feeling, for art has been immemorially easy to satirize, whether at the one extreme of Babbittry or at the other of Bohemia. All the same, for whatever reasons, such feeling has long been part of the American character—which is to say that the American bent, the American genius, has honestly moved in other directions. Like the Romans and the Germans, we are not an artistic people. This may be partly the result of our so long being able to reach out, rather than having to turn inward; of our possessing a vast continent to traverse, subdue, explore, develop, grow rich on, so that there was no husbanding or skilled handling of resources, no modifying what we started with or were saddled with into something gracious and expres-

sive. A race, like an individual, develops a style in part through what
it has uniquely, in part through what it has too little of. French prose
owes its dry, neat lucidity to the same things that produced a general
lack of magic in French poetry; French women owe their chic, I would
think, to their general lack of girlish beauty. Americans have suffered
from over-abundance—from not needing to substitute art for nature,
form for substance, method for materials. At the very point where a
patina might begin to appear, or mellowness to suffuse, we have abandoned what we made for something newer, brisker, shinier; and with
each such act we have become a little less "artistic" in our approach.
But of course there is more to it than that. An artistic people—the
French, the Chinese, the ancient Greeks—is one whose necessities are
made the comelier by its dreams, but whose dreaming is equally
controlled by its necessities: the two are integrated, are never so
harshly at odds that the dreaming must serve as a lurid compensation.
With an artistic people a kind of good sense regulates both its acquisitive side and its aspiring one; and from deprecating excess on a large
scale, it eventually does so in small ways as well. Hence the design of
existence stands forth more powerfully than the décor; and because
design, unlike décor, affects a whole society, the national traits and instincts and responses get beyond cost or size or class, and equally char-
acterize the rich and the poor, the cultivated and the unlettered. There
is always a sense of bone structure about an artistic people—think of
the Spaniards—a touch of severity, of economy. There is, I suppose,
something rather classic than romantic—a sense of the ancestor as well
as the individual.

An artistic people need not (and very likely will not) be profoundly
poetic or mystical, as the English and the Germans are. It is plainly
because the English and the Germans lead such double lives, because
one extreme must almost atone for the other, because dreaming grows
out of repressions or helps to stamp out reality, that two nations so
given to vulgar instincts and material aims should be capable of such
splendid intensities—intensities which, for all that, do constitute excesses. And we too, as a people, are driven to compensate; are so excessively aspiring for being so excessively acquisitive; come back to
God through guilt or satiety; go on binges with Beauty because it is
no part of our daily life—and we somehow think the extent of the undertaking will make up for the quality. Our magnates are always
giving away millions not too shiningly acquired; our aging plutocrats
leave a spendthrift order for art like the flashy sports who buy their
women ten dozen American Beauty roses. Nothing amuses or appalls
us more than a gangster's funeral with its carloads of flowers and

wreaths; and nothing teaches us less. The gangster's funeral is actually the model for Broadway's supermusicals, for the murals on civic architecture, for Florida's luxury resorts; and the gangster's funeral is itself a late development, the descendant of the Newport "cottage"—the only difference being that at Newport conspicuous waste was confined to living, where in Chicago it specialized in death.

But it is not just the excesses born of wealth that have failed to make us an artistic people. After all, corsairs and conquistadors are the ancestors of *most* cultures; and French châteaux and Italian *palazzi* of even the best periods stress sheer display quite as much as they stress beauty. We may just come near enough to being an artistic people to explain why we *are* not and perhaps *cannot be* one. We are an inventive and adaptive people; and thus our whole effort, our whole genius, is to modify rather than mold, to make more efficient rather than more expressive. We are dedicated to improvement—to improving our minds and our mousetraps, our inventions and our diets. We are so dedicated to improvement that we neither ask nor care whether a thing needs to be improved, is able to be improved, or, qualifying as an improvement, will necessarily seem a benefit. We never seem to wonder whether we may not be complicating things by simplifying them, or making them useless by so constantly making them over. But the ability to invent, the desire to improve, may partly spring from our having got so much later a start than other civilizations—from our being at a log-cabin and homespun stage when Europe had long achieved silks and marble, and then lagging for so long behind them. We first were made competitive from a sense of our marked inferiority to others; we then became, from our sense of our natural wealth and resources, competitive among ourselves; and we are now, of course, inventive *because* we are competitive: last year's model must be disparaged so that this year's model can be sold. But no matter how genuine was the original impulse, or how sheerly commercial it is today, inventiveness has become ingrained in our practice, and our source of constant pride; and even among the best of us— unless we are extremely vigilant—it is now an influence on our taste. Abroad, avant-gardism expressed the crying need among old cultures for new forms and feelings; here, we often seem to be breaking with tradition before establishing it; here, experiment has a gadget air, a will-to-invent about it, as often as a sense of rebellion or release.

This gadget aspect crops up everywhere, in the most unexpected places. Thus our highbrow criticism is constantly inventing and amending a vocabulary—one that somehow will seem a special, up-to-the-minute possession for critics, exactly as the latest models in cars or television sets will seem a special, up-to-the-minute possession of prosperous businessmen. The actual character, too, of our present-day literary jargon—so much of it psychiatric and sociological—is that of a profoundly inartistic, indeed, an aesthetically quite barbarous, yet irrepressibly inventive people. Take just one simple example. In the entire language I doubt whether there exists an uglier word, or one less needed for the use it has been put to, than the word *sensitivity*. One special and particular meaning could be allowed it—the sensitivity, let us say, of a photographic plate to light. But even among critics with a historical sense and a cultivated ear, it has almost completely ousted the two words that for centuries so happily shouldered, and so neatly divided, the burden: *sensibility* and *sensitiveness*. But the whole highbrow vocabulary, the whole need for new spring-and-fall models in literary language—*subsume* one year, *mystique* the next, *exfoliate* the year after—exhibits our national need to adapt and amend and apply at any cost, with no great concern for the urgency, and perhaps even less for the rightness, of the words themselves. And even more indicative than their original "coinage" is the indecent speed with which they become almost unbearable clichés; even more, also, than their coinage itself is the fact that they are so uniformly pretentious, so very rarely picturesque. If only critics would read Dr. Johnson for his wisdom and not for his unhappier choices in words. We are inartistic, indeed, in our very approach to art.

We have never as a people regarded art as something to live with, to freely delight in, to call by its first name. Perhaps this derives from something beyond an inventive streak that keeps us restless, or an awe that makes us uncomfortable: perhaps had we had more opportunity to live with art, we might have acquired a more relaxed attitude toward it. It has never been on our doorstep; we have had to go in search of it, go doubly in search—as much to discover what it is as where it is. The journeys have had a little of the air of pilgrimages; the works of art, a great deal of the sanctity of shrines. The whole burden of our criticism, our constant cultural plaint, is how scant, and impure, and imperfect, and isolated, art in America has been—which, inevitably, has conditioned our approach to it. We insist on strong, emphatic, unmistakable reactions; we either swoon or snub, analyze at tedious length or dismiss with a mere wave of the hand. We got at art, in other words, not like casual, cultivated shoppers, but like a race of antique-shop dealers for whom everything is either magnificently authentic or the merest fake; and the result—though of course there are other reasons, too—is that we cannot take art in our stride. So belated and uneasy an approach has made us about art what Prohibition made my whole generation about wine: either frank, unblushing ignoramuses or comically solemn snobs. Different levels of Americans reveal very different attitudes toward art; but what is perhaps most significant is that they all reveal one marked kind of attitude or another. They either tend to hold back lest they commit howlers; or to go into raptures lest they be taken for clods; or to pooh-pooh the whole business lest they seem longhaired and sissified; or to purse their lips and utter pronunciamentos lest they seem just vulgarly susceptible or humanly responsive.

If classifying them as fence-straddlers or as poseurs or as philistines or as prigs is to simplify and even travesty the matter, it may yet help account for the fact that we are not a people for whom, at any level, art is just a natural and congenial aspect of existence. The very "uslessness" of it—the fact that art, like virtue, is its own reward; again, the very magic of it—the fact that it cannot be reduced to a formula or equation; the utter arrogance of it—the fact that money cannot buy it nor American salesmanship or elbow grease achieve it: these are, at the very outset, reasons for mystification and distrust. *Its* kind of arrogance, of refusal to be won on extrinsic terms—as of a high-mettled, beautiful girl whom no suitor can win on the strength of his bank account, his family background, or his sober, industrious habits—seems improper, even unethical, to a people who can respect putting a high price on something, who can approve and enjoy a hard tussle till things are won, but who can no more understand than they can approve that something is beyond negotiations, is just not to be bought. Art to their minds is not a high-mettled girl, but an extremely unreasonable woman. Art's kind of magic again—art's refusal to be achieved through laboratory methods, through getting up charts or symposiums or sales conferences, through looking at smears under the microscope—its magic seems behind the times, almost downright retarded, to a people with a genius for the synthetic. Art's kind of uselessness, finally—its non-vitamin-giving health, its non-pep-you-up modes of pleasure, its non-materialistic enrichment—quite genuinely confuses a people who have been educated to have something to show for their efforts, if only a title or a medal or a diploma. Art, for most Americans, is a very queer fish—it can't be reasoned with, it can't be bribed, it can't be doped out or duplicated; above all, it can't be cashed in on.

Someone, Max Beerbohm perhaps, once defined a Bohemian as a person who uses things for what they're not intended—a window drapery, let us say, for a ball dress, or a goldfish bowl for a soup tureen. And this just a little defines the American sense of the artistic. We must endow everything with a new twist, an added value, an extra function. We literally cannot let well enough alone; hence we very often make it worse—and never more, perhaps, than when we also make it better. The new element, the new effect, the new use to which an art form is put, very often has to do with achieving something more tractable or palatable or painless or time- or labor-saving; with offering, at the very least, old wine in new bottles, and much more to our satisfaction, old wine in plastic containers or ice cream cones. Thus we have Somerset Maugham re-edit and abridge the classics; we get a present-day version of Buckingham's *The Rehearsal*, a Negro *Juno and the Paycock*, a *Cherry Orchard* laid in Mississippi; we have Mr. Orson Welles telescoping five of Shakespeare's plays into one; we have something written for the piano performed on the violin, something intended for men taken over by women. We're not, to be sure, the only nation that does such things, but I think we're the only nation that feels a compulsive urge to do them. Where the Germans have a particular genius for ersatz, for substitutions, we have one for new twists and gimmicks, new mixtures and combinations. We simply *have* to tamper: if we don't cut the words, we must add to the music; if we don't change the story, we must shift the locale. Nowhere else, surely, can there be such a compulsion to make plays out of books, musicals out of plays, *Aida's* into *My Darlin' Aida's*; to insert scenes, delete characters, include commentators; to turn gas stations into cathedrals, or churches into dance halls. Out of Plato and Berkeley we get Transcendentalism; out of Transcendentalism we concoct Christian Science; and then, almost immediately, Jewish Science out of Christian. Many nations have discovered the devil in dancing, but we are perhaps the first to find God through calisthenics.

And no doubt we create, from all this, the illusion that we are notably experimental in the arts, ever seeking news forms, contriving new functions, establishing new perspectives. But, even ignoring the material or commercial side of it all, our contrivance of so many artful blends and twists and variants is really our avoidance of art itself, exactly as our craving for sensations argues a distaste or fear of experiences. Our whole artistic effort, if it does not parallel, at least involves our genius for concocting the mixed drink and for putting the packaging ahead of the product. The result—from which almost all of us suffer more than we realize—is a kind of vulgarization, and one that can take place at high levels no less than at low ones. Our stressing significance in art rather than intensity, our present search for symbolic figures and concealed meanings and multiple levels: isn't this part of our compulsion to introduce something new, add something extra, offer something unprecedented? Does it not bear witness, also, to our intellectual ingenuity rather than our aesthetic responsiveness? Hasn't the new multi-

level *Pierre* or *Confidence Man* a kinship with the new split-level
house, or the concealed meanings with the concealed plumbing, or the
indirect approach with the indirect lighting, or the taste for knotty
problems with the taste for knotty pine? I do not think I am being anti-
intellectual when I say that in America the intellect itself is being
overused and misused in the world of art, where—after all—the most
thoughtful elucidation avails nothing without the right, pure, instinctive response; for in art the reverse of Wordsworth's saying is also true
and immensely important: in art, there are tears that do often lie too
deep for thoughts.

Given our inventiveness, such endless and manifold vulgarization is
inevitable. No race can make an idea go farther than we can. We get
the last ounce of derivable income from it; we carry it, indeed, to distances that virtually obscure the original starting point. From the
classic sandwich made with bread we evolve the triple-decker made
with ice cream; from the first motel, that could hardly have competed
with a bathhouse, we are now contriving structures that will outdo—if
not soon outmode—the Ritz. And quite beyond our double-barreled
desire to make things profitable as well as attractive, all this technical
skill and inventive cleverness must in the end conspire as much against
our creative instincts as against our artistic ones. A nation that can so
marvelously concoct must less and less feel any need to create. We are
developing a genius for rewrite at the expense of one for writing, for
stage directors who shall do the work of dramatists, for orchestrators,
who shall do the work of composers. Everything today must carefully
and exactly conform to public taste, yet offer a new wrinkle into the
bargain—we insist on what might be called a kind of Murphy-bed of
Procrustes.

The effect of this vulgarization is almost sure to be pervasive and permanent. There is something disarming, often inded unnoticeable,
about vulgarization itself. Sheer vulgarity quickly stands self-con-
demned, hence tends quickly to correct itself. Or where it persists—
as representing something congenial to a particular social milieu or
human type—it is so blatant as to isolate itself and proclaim its own quarantine. So long as what is "wrong" can be quickly spotted, and there-
after vividly contrasted with what is "right," whether or not it continues to exist, it can no longer triumph. The most insidious aspect of
vulgarity, I would think, concerns not those to whom its appeal is obvious and immediate, but those, rather, whom it gradually and imperceptibly manages to win over, those who in the beginning are partly
superior to it and who only by habituation sink to its level. A vulgarity
that can thus contaminate won't often, it seems clear, be of a primitive

or glaring sort; it will be, rather, a worm in the apple, a sort of Greek bearing gifts. In the world of art, such vulgarity may boast that it does far more good than it does harm, that it makes many people respond to what they might otherwise pass by. I'm not speaking of the out-and-out popularization, but rather of such things as the movie version of *Henry V* or Stokowski's arrangements of Bach—of things offered under the auspices of culture and aimed at reasonably cultured people. This form of vulgarization will by no means altogether misrepresent or even too greatly discolor. And though a severe taste may resist or reject it at once, a fairly sensitive taste—what I suppose is most conveniently called a middlebrow taste that, if left alone, might come to appreciate Bach or Shakespeare "neat"—will not resist or reject the adulteration, will soon, in fact, come to prefer and eventually to require it.

Vulgarization isn't always a matter of making things pleasanter to the taste, or easier to swallow; it can also consist—which can constitute the highbrow maneuver—in making them more difficult and abstruse, rather resembling the homely girl who goes out of her way to accentuate her homeliness. It is as possible to defeat the primary end of art, the sense of beauty, by minimizing it as by rouging it up. Short cuts represent one kind of vulgarization, labyrinths represent another. The highbrow procedure, if we were to raid the vocabulary that accompanies it, might be called countervulgarization. It constitutes, in any case, no cure or corrective for the middlebrow ailment, but rather a different kind of disease; and though its very lack of cheap allure will cause it to render art far less of a disservice than the rouge-and-syrup process, it is yet equally a barrier to our becoming an artistic people. What with art being something, on the one side, that slides smoothly down our gullets and, on the other, something to be chewed long after any flavor is left, we can seldom any longer, I think, get the fine, sharp, vivid, simple first experience of art that must be the preliminary to any more complex one. Something is always doused over it or drained out of it, hiding the flavor or heightening it, removing gristle or adding lumps; or the thought or look of the thing, before we even bite into it, conditions us. A man can no longer even read, let us say, the "Ode to a Nightingale" without the slightly guilty or, at any rate, self-conscious feeling that it is "romantic poetry."

As a result of the vulgarizing effort to make things palatable, and of a countervulgarization that renders things parched, there is being beggared out of existence a high yet workable ideal, a climate in which a *sense* of art can flourish. And it seems to me that the lack of a proper climate for art is a much more serious shortcoming in America than the actual number of works of art themselves. Culture—in the old-fashioned, well-rounded sense of something civilized and civilizing alike —has not simply failed as a reality in America, but is fast fading as an ideal. Such a culture stands in relation to formal education as good wine to the grape: it is a fermentation, a mellowing, a very special and at the same time wholly characterizing element; and it permeates society in terms of its sensibilities no less than its art. One can, of course, all too easily exalt such a culture as a way of disparaging much that is essential and even healthful in modern life; and one can sigh for it on a sentimental basis, in standpat terms. All the same, any way of life that lacks its best qualities can scarcely be looked upon as cultivated at all; at any rate, no amount of education or knowledge or skill can begin to mean the same thing. And actually the climate I desiderate is no more than a salubrious, breeze-swept temperate zone; it is not forbidding, nor oppressively patrician, nor strenuously democratic. A cool, dry judgment is mingled there with gusto and generous appreciation; the people there are no more mired in the past than running wild in the present; its tone is altogether urbane without being even faintly genteel; it boasts neither untouchables nor sacred cows; it displays a constant corrective irony and perhaps not overmuch virtue; and everyone there is just sufficiently wrongheaded and prejudiced and inconsistent to be attractively human.

2

Being a curiously inartistic and ingenious people; being, also, too serious-minded to look on pleasure bare, and so commercialized as to put a price tag on Beauty, we approach art by many routes, but never by the most direct. Most frequently vulgarization sets in, the point of the story is sacrificed to the plot, Shakespeare is streamlined or Chekhov fattened up. Among the overserious there is often a process of dehydration, with only such fluid retained as has medicinal properties; or the work of art is converted from thoroughbred to packhorse and forced to stagger under a heavy sociological and psychiatric load.

Although what frankly seem to me the most delightful and rewarding qualities of art are precisely these that are slighted in many highbrow ranks today, I must admit that it is not done altogether without reason. The slighting constitutes a form of dissociation, even of protest. The sight of panders everywhere must inevitably call forth the prig; the sight of art being everywhere rouged and perfumed, groomed and tricked out for harlotry, must inspire a violent contrary wish—a wish to have art, like an orthodox Jewish bride, shorn of her locks and made as unalluring as possible. Middlebrow adulteration, its slight softening of every texture, its faint sweetening of every taste, have clearly had a hand in creating the current highbrow distrust of charms and graces. This isn't to say there need be an abundance of such qualities or that, in an age like ours, there can be. In this unquiet age, an age not even of scars but of outright wounds, clearly very little that is charming or delightful will seem central or germane. Yet though there is truth in such a statement, there is also cant. It is perhaps not necessary to dance on the edge of volcanoes; but need one ignore, or even disapprove of, the sunset because the sky may soon grow dark with bomber planes? Again, is shaving off the hair an answer to overroughing the cheeks, or a desert the corrective to a swamp? Even so, one might agree that one kind of excess tends, not unprofitably, to breed another—did not highbrow criticism, in the very act of professing to probe the tensions of contemporary life, seem so pedagogically remote from them. Art is not something marketable but neither is it something mummified; and indeed, if it is not chiefly and most palpably a form of transcendence and release, pray then what is? If the impress of style, the vivid air of distinction, the artist's ability to be uniquely expressive and intense—if these do not invite, do not indeed impose, some immediate, electrical response, can the result—however rich in cerebral or moral mineral matter—really have much to do with art itself?

I was not surprised, reading an Inquiring Reporter column on "What Is Charm?" to find a sculptor identifying charm with the prettier examples of eighteenth-century painting. It was to be assumed that charm's status would be relatively low, its character rigorously limited; that it would be equated with Sir Joshua Reynolds' children or, by extension, with Sir James M. Barrie's grownups; that it would at most signify Watteau and Fragonard, minuets and romantic ballets, Hans Andersen or Charles Lamb. No doubt the word itself has acquired vapid and even repellent connotations; and plainly writers who spray charm about without discretion are like women who mistreat an atomizer. Moreover, charm can be a strong ally of gentility and a quite conscienceless weapon of fraud: we usually do right, I think, to ask to see its credentials. But that is very far from trying to have it deported; and to suggest that, because many writers misuse charm, there is no virtue to fragrance is to come closer, I would think, to the gospel of unyielding naturalism than to any goal of truth. Ignoring such obvious charmers as Poulenc or Dufy or Walter de la Mare, if contemporary artists so unlike as Picasso, E. E. Cummings and Marianne Moore haven't, among other things, a very decided charm, what have they? Art, today, sometimes seems in danger of acquiring all the vices of science without any of the virtues. What with being anthropology's field worker and psychiatry's receptionist, art is quite prevented from cultivating its own garden.

Charm is by now too ambiguous, too merely decorative a word to be made the symbol of my own dissatisfaction. But it is clear that all the old, traditional, taken-for-granted "surface" qualities of art—distinction, fragrance, elegance, gaiety, style: those things for which we prize a Mendelssohn or a Vermeer, a Tennyson or a Congreve—such qualities, it is clear, are being slighted or ignored. No doubt *The Tempest* can be profitably viewed as something more than a masque; but to interpret it as something quite other, to regard it as principally a study in expiation, seems to me to make Shakespeare very much of an age—and an age, moreover, not his own. Possibly we are falling into the shallowness of despising the "shallow." He was the mightiest of Puritans no less than of philistines who first insisted that beauty is only skin deep. Depth, and its step-daughter Complexity, and its handmaiden Symbolism, are so much revered today, so much courted and curtsied to, as almost to obscure the fact of exactly what we mean by them, or whether —on the terms set—they aren't properly associated with philosophy rather than art. Perhaps the greatest of all our critics remarked that "poetry gives most pleasure when only generally and not perfectly understood," and he offered it as a principle to honor, not as a puzzle to resent. But so pressing now has become the critical obligation to explain or reinterpret that it is almost mandatory to pitch on something either obscure enough to need explaining or misunderstood enough by all previous critics to need to be straightened out. And since no one can burrow deep where the author happens to be shallow, we must make canyons out of moleholes; we must everywhere find size and significance, those idols so much less of art than of America; and more and more our criticism suggests the tread of elephants approaching a temple.

Given our feeble artistic sense, the whole present tendency isn't too hard to grasp. Anything journalistic must be outlawed—which could be a virtue; but outlawed in terms of the pedagogical, which is almost always a vice. Everywhere people reappraise some simple classic for the small ingenious theory that isn't worth the paper that is written on it. All too frequently the creative is turned into the intellectual, soaring is replaced by delving; while art, which has always constituted the highest and noblest form of release, is more and more tinged with something so gnawing and anxious as to seem more like remorse. But surely one very great characteristic of any inherently artistic people is a sense of play—play of mind, most of all, not mere prankishness—and a natural sense of irony. The reigning current mood has quite ousted all sense of play and exhibits no working sense of irony. To be sure, irony is a much approved and discussed and dissected quality in today's approach to literature, and wherever possible, and perhaps sometimes where not, critics isolate and decipher it; but it doesn't seem very contagious.

Mr. Richard Chase, in his recent book on Emily Dickinson, deplores what he calls the rococo element in her poetry—the minor, dainty, toy-like, *bibelot* aspect. And in anyone who at her best is so deeply imaginative and intense an artist as Emily Dickinson, the persistence of this merely whimsical and fanciful streak causes real injury, becomes a real misfortune. We could similarly wish that the English Metaphysicals had indulged in much fewer conceits, or that Sterne, or even Shakespeare himself—but I needn't dig for other examples. Yet where the superior artist is harmed by not rising above what we may call, with Mr. Chase, the rococo, a nation is very often harmed by not reaching up to it. The artist can dispense with the small forms of beauty, but the public cannot. The artist can function largely in a world of his own making—too much culture is perhaps even "weakening" for genius, and beautiful material objects may in a sense be the enemy of beauty. But nonartists, noncreative people, the world at large, need the atmosphere, the ornaments, the décor of culture. A predominantly *bibelot*-like culture could only, of course, be frivolous, dilettantish, effeminate. But a purely functional, no-nonsense, always-abreast-of-the-times culture, where in one's bookcase Toynbee leans only on Schweitzer and Schweitzer leans only on Freud—does this bespeak anything temperamental or personal, or is it only a part of the times? It's not a question of Old Guard and avant-garde, or whether a Canaletto print does more for a home than a Mexican primitive, or oldish things made of mahogany more than brand-new things made of metal, but whether there are not amenities and graces of the spirit; whether there are not cultures, as well as cups, that cheer. I don't contend that Jung or Margaret Mead or Frank Lloyd Wright aren't more central to our time than Osvald Siren or Sir Charles Singer; or that in order to be cultured, or well adjusted, or happy, one need be able to distinguish R. L. from G. B. Hobson, A. W. from A. F. Pollard, Oliver from André Simon, Vincent from Gertrude, or Gertrude from T. E., or T. E. from W. W., or W. W. from W. J., or W. J. from D. H. Lawrence. But for every ten educated people who have read Margaret Mead, is there one who knows which Hobson was the great authority on bindings and which on Chinese art?

Much of our own antirococoism stems, I think, from something Puritan in us. We are only given to a kind of love of the graces, a feeling for the charming in culture, when the wind is blowing from Europe; and it hasn't blown steadily from there since the 1920s. The '20s, of course, have latterly been as much romanticized as they were formerly run down. The mood of the '20s was made up of many things—not least, of that sense of promise in life, and of profusion in literature, that made us emotionally both spendthrift and carefree. But upstart and disordered and excessive though the '20s were, they were in impulse genuinely antibourgeois, antipuritan, antipedagogical: they reacted to the creative, they relished the creative, they aspired passionately to create. We lacked, then, the measure and control, the ability to select, delete, hew to the line, that constitute an artistic people; but we had, at any rate, the capacity to absorb and participate, to feel release and indulge in appreciation. We lacked the discipline, but we had the positive qualities that needed disciplining. The mood of the '20s had to pass, Depression or not; while, granted the Depression, the mood of the '30s had to be what it was. But the enduring significance of the '30s is less the purpose and propaganda that writers put into their work than the high spirits they took out of it. For the propaganda has been long discredited, but the joyousness has never been restored.

The present age is in the strong grip of cultural authoritarianism and of the most dogmatic kind. For great natural cultural lawgivers of Dr. Johnson's type there is much to be said, though even here "there is much to be said on both sides." And of course today there are not only all those who would legislate and lead, there are all the many more who hunger to be led, who crave to cry "Master." Lionel Trilling has rather chided E. M. Forster—in an age so generally contrariwise—for his "refusal to be great." One knows what Mr. Trilling means, one knows what is valid in what he means—whether with Forster specifically or with intellectuals and artists in general. A "refusal to be great" can mask a certain evasion of moral responsibility, of final decisions and allegiances. It can reflect too a certain self-consciousness, on the refuser's part, that is mere vanity; it can constitute a special, perhaps quite extreme, form of egoism. And Forster himself seems at times not merely casual but playful and frivolous. All the same, whatever personal shortcomings or debatable human traits may lodge with this attitude, it yet seems the backbone of a very notable, a very much honored, tradition—of that indeed very great tradition of skeptical humanism. It is a tradition that having said *Thus I think* next always asks *What do I know?*, a tradition that forces the very bringer of light to assay the light he brings as sharply as the darkness he dispels. In the history of thought and culture the dark nights have perhaps in some ways cost mankind less grief than the false dawns, the prison houses in which hope persists less grief than the Promised Lands where hope expires. Skeptical humanism is no enemy of positive values or even of resolute action; but men bred to that tradition will continue to feel that their values must be exhibited, warts and all, and must in the end be made to speak for themselves. About any other method, including the acceptance of greatness, there is always at least a touch of *force majeure* and perhaps even a drop or two of patent medicine. Today anyone's refusal to be great seems the more formulated for being so out of line with prevailing thought. The Great Men, the Strong Men, of literature today are men of fierce passions and strong convictions, men playing the role of prophet, teacher, moralist, martyr, saint, sinner, seer—the Melvilles, Nietzsches, Kierkegaards, the Gides, Dostoevskys, D. H. Lawrences. Some of these men are as individual, one or two are now and then as skeptical, as Forster; but the real point is to what degree have they encouraged independence, individualism, skepticism, the relaxed will, in others?

If only because the tide has been running strong against the old humanist attitude, the Forsters with their relaxed wills and their refusals to be great must take on a special value. The tradition of Socrates, of Montaigne and Erasmus, of Hume and of the Enlightenment, all the more because it never flourishes *below* the cultured classes, is immensely vital to them, is what we might almost call their claim to culture. It seems to me an absolutely essential tradition for societies and nations in need of something equable as well as affirmative, in need of lasting daylight as well as glowing dawns. It is a tradition that has never really established itself in America—a corollary, I think, to our being an inartistic people; it is a tradition, at any rate, at variance with a people who love the *idea* of greatness, who love panaceas, and formulas, and solutions, and absolutions, and reassuring answers. To a nation that worships God and Mammon both there must be something profoundly uncongenial in an attitude that blindly worships nothing. From the failure of the humanist tradition to participate fully or to act decisively, civilization may perhaps crumble or perish at the hands of barbarians. But unless the humanist tradition itself in some form survives, there can really be no civilization at all.

anonymous

---

tv in the world of letters

This excellent little spoof on the television industry's uneasy relationship to American intellectuals was published anonymously in *The American Scholar,* the national organ of Phi Beta Kappa. So uneasy, indeed, are relations between television and American teachers, scholars, writers! Although television, which reaches into almost every American home, constantly protests its concern with culture, it does not really take seriously any intellectual concern that cannot immediately be sold to millions of people. Television pays lip-service to our cultural ideals, but even on the rare occasions when it tries to present "the great books" or "the great ideas of mankind," it pays little or nothing to scholars who give lectures or who participate in television discussions. Somehow the television industry assumes that scholars should be grateful just to be asked.

It is this air of being nice to culture, the pompousness with which the television industry patronizes the intellectual life in America, that our anonymous author has satirized so well. What he has caught distinctly is the pious and mechanical language, the "line," that gets into the language of people so much concerned with "selling" things to others, with "projecting an image." When the scholar declines to cut his book in order to read it to a non-existent audience early on Sunday morning, the television producer replies—". . . I am sorry that you adopt an uncooperative line about editing which is all too common among writers, and which shows that you do not appreciate the exigencies of the new and powerful medium which is TV."

Compare these clichés with the weary and dignified reply—"I am only trying to show you the gap between your large professions and your meager performance." Television, in regard to "culture" and the "intellectual life," *is* full of "large professions." And for once, in this essay, the victim strikes back, man bites the dog, the much-abused American highbrow at last has his say. "Fortunately for public service, writers are so besotted that the millions they sometimes dream of are readers, not dollars. Hence the custom which makes it low and shameful to cadge a consultation from a doctor or lawyer, but normal and proper to ask a writer or lecturer to do something for the sole delight of being asked."

D EAR MR. AIGHED:

January 5, 1960

As you may know, the FOB network has steadily endeavored to increase its public service function by offering in non-sponsored time programs of lasting intellectual value. On one of these programs, "Sit and Think," it has been customary to have notable authors read an article of theirs on some issue currently under discussion.

We have just come across your provocative essay in *Foreign Affairs* entitled "Disciplines for Diplomats," and we should like to feature it as soon as practicable on "Sit and Think." Since the program occupies a 15-minute spot, from 7:15 to 7:30 on Sunday morning, the reading time available is 13½ minutes, and this in turn means that your article will have to be somewhat shortened. You may want to do this yourself, or we will gladly have one of our experienced editors here in the office suggest the necessary cuts for your approval. The tape can be made at your home or in our studio, at your convenience.

Hoping for the pleasure of hearing from you soon and favorably,

Sincerely yours,

DOUGLAS DOISTER
Director of Public Service Programs

January 11, 1960

DEAR MR. DOISTER:

I am touched by your kind interest in my recent article on the training of diplomats and I wish I could accept your invitation to read it over the air.

But I must point out that it runs to 4,500 words, which would take about 35 minutes to read. When therefore you speak of "cutting" it to fit into 13½ minutes, you really mean discarding nearly two-thirds of the substance. Having just reread the piece, I cannot persuade myself that it is too long for what I have to say, though I could with some effort omit, say, 500-600 words and thus shorten the reading time by four or five minutes.

Any reduction such as you require would call for a complete rewriting from scratch.

Yours faithfully,

ARNOLD AIGHED

January 15, 1960

DEAR MR. AIGHED:

I would not presume to argue with you over the contents of your essay. You no doubt know best how long it should be. But I am sorry that you adopt an uncooperative line about editing which is all too common among writers, and which shows that you do not appreciate the exigencies of the new and powerful medium which is TV.

Surely you want your ideas to reach millions of people rather than the few thousands who read the specialized magazine for which you wrote your article. If I add that we will make an exception in your case and print for free distribution your article *in full,* will you not reconsider and allow us to extract the 13½ essential minutes?

Hoping for the pleasure of your prompt and favorable reply,

Yours sincerely,

DOUGLAS DOISTER

Director of Public Service Programs

January 27, 1960

DEAR MR. DOISTER:

I am sorry to persist in my refusal and even more sorry that I did not succeed in conveying to you the grounds of it.

In declining to be excerpted as you wish, I am not "adopting a line." The reason for my response, which I am not surprised to hear is common in writers, is simply that I understand the exigencies of an old and powerful medium known as expository prose. These exigencies you apparently fail to appreciate. Instead you think it a public service to present an incomplete or disjointed argument, expecting the listener (I suppose) to sit and think it out.

You say that I surely want to reach millions of people. That depends on whether the emphasis is put on "reach" much more than on "millions." I will not, by the way, try to guess how many millions are likely to be awake at 7:15 on Sunday morning. Let me only remark that to all appearances your good deed is being done by stealth, as enjoined by the Scriptures.

Please understand that I am not telling you indirectly what you should do: I am only trying to show you the gap between your large professions and your meager performance.

Yours sincerely,

ARNOLD AIGHED

February 10, 1960

DEAR MR. AIGHED:

When George Baker introduced us the other day he said something about your high sales resistance to TV and told me not to bring up the subject, least of all socially. Well, you remember, I didn't. But right now I'm sure I've got a proposition that will make you feel quite different about the whole subject.

You've probably never heard of "Talkfest." It's new. But I'm sure that when I explain it you'll fall for it. At long last it's the program we've all been waiting for, where people who can talk and people who like to hear *and see* good talk can get together by means of the new and powerful medium which is TV.

"Talkfest" gives you all the freedom of a real conversation. It starts at 2 p.m. on Saturday and goes on, free and uninhibited, till Sunday midnight. The people on the show any weekend wander in freely any time they want, and wander out again when they like—just as the listeners do, or for that matter the denizens of an old-world *salon*.

Same with the subject—anything goes. I'm on the show merely to put in the plugs for my sponsors every half hour and to ask a question or two when things look like they're beginning to flag. I do not m.c. or moderate. My job comes ahead of time, in making the right mixture, I mean inviting the people who'll catalyze each other—and then you're off!

Now think it over and give me a ring to say which weekend you'll go on. George told me how busy you are with your new book, on foreign policy, is it? Well, I promise you "Talkfest" is an experience that won't set you back. It will give you a lift. And when the time comes it'll do your book a lot of good. So spare us even just a Sunday. We'd want you to come about noon sharp so as to be able to wander in about 1:30, after a little briefing by my assistant, Miss Chorio. That way there's no strain.

I'm asking you first so I can line up the others. The balance I have in mind for you would be perfect: as a heavy, thoughtful type and not likely to go off the handle, you need someone vivacious, unpredictable—a woman, preferably an actress-type or even an actress. We might ask Diana Cecily. And then, just for kicks and to keep the audience guessing, someone with a bit of mystery and a man-about-town flavor. There is a Prince Detropoff you probably know, who claims he is a grandnephew of the Tsar. He has great personality.

You see the pains I'm taking over you and your prejudice against TV. Say you'll come; all you have to do is tell me when.

As ever yours,

RALPH ROISTER

P.S. Of course, it's none of my business, but let me just add that it would be great if when I get you three together you could spend a good bit of your time discussing the future of the arts in America.

February 19, 1960

DEAR MR. AIGHED:

Excuse my delay in answering your letter of last month about what you called the exigencies of writers, which you think I do not appreciate.

I am sure I appreciate them as fully as you do. I was a writer once myself, and an editor after that, and my experience suggests that every writer who is worth his salt takes a very humble view of his work and knows he can be improved by competent editing.

In fact—and I say it to you without offense—I think that adapting to the format of a TV show, long or short, is for any writer a wonderful discipline. I know it is not usual in your line of work, where there is plenty of time to read and plenty of paper and print to expend on scholarly subjects. But we live in a dynamic world, and in TV especially, where broadcast time is expensive, it's bound to be short. That is why it must be used with the utmost efficiency, no matter what older habits may permit elsewhere.

Accordingly, I am sorry we cannot see eye to eye about your article which we liked so much in this office, but I send you good wishes all the same. Should you ever change your mind about "Sit and Think," please let me know.

Yours sincerely,
DOUGLAS DOISTER
Director of Public Service Programs

February 29, 1960

DEAR MR. ROISTER:

You are kind to invite me to appear on "Talkfest" in such distinguished company.

It is true that I like conversation and would do almost anything to obtain it, but I am afraid that the absence of limits which is the main feature of "Talkfest" would unnerve me to the point where I might wander out freely whenever my fellow-participants began to open their mouths, returning only when I had something to say. Even if this should prove acceptable to you as an attractive novelty, I could not undertake to keep it up faithfully from about noon sharp to midnight more or less.

The truth is that in any public performance in which I am to take part I want a moderator, with a gavel and a watch, to open and close the proceedings. Besides, I am occasionally vivacious too, and I may need to be called to order. It is only when required to talk about the future of the arts in America that my spirits droop, and then I need a moderator to cut me off *before* the audience notices it. For these few public services I would willingly give up all the half-hour interruptions of sponsor-worship.

My best to George when you see him.

Yours faithfully,
ARNOLD AIGHED

· *February 29, 1960*

DEAR MR. DOISTER:

One final word in reply to your last, in which you chose to turn our difference of opinion into an argument against writers and scholars as represented by my unworthy self.

In so doing you abandoned your case, for I remind you that it was you who sought me out, not I who submitted my work to you. I have never objected to editing; I did and do object to abridgement by two-thirds. You are the one who claimed to perform a public service; I merely pointed out, when challenged, that garbling ideas is not a service. You put the word "Think" into a program so scheduled that it might better be called "Came the Dawn." I contented myself with showing that you do not understand the proper conditions either of thought or of its reception by the general public.

There is one further point I have not yet touched on. If Gibbon had just published the first volume of *The Decline and Fall,* you would doubtless ask him to whittle it down to the essential 13½ minutes. To which he would reply: "I can indeed furnish a text on my subject which will occupy these few moments, but that entails a fresh piece of work for which I must be paid."

This would not be naïveté on Gibbon's part, for how could he know that the public service which sheds luster on the great networks must rest on a broad base of unpaid talent? It would be necessary to explain to him that broadcasting time is expensive enough as it is without adding a charge that might well stop the world from being dynamic. Fortunately for public service, writers are so besotted that the millions they sometimes dream of are readers, not dollars. Hence the custom which makes it low and shameful to cadge a consultation from a doctor or lawyer, but normal and proper to ask a writer or lecturer to do something for the sole delight of being asked.

These are but a few points to sit and think about.

Yours faithfully,
ARNOLD AIGHED

April 1, 1960

DEAR MR. AIGHED:

We have been looking at the copy of your new book, which has just come from your publishers. We think it is a wonderful book, the kind our listeners I am sure would enjoy hearing thoroughly discussed.

That's why I am asking you to give us the pleasure of attending the session of "Take the Rap," which will be devoted to your work, one week from next Thursday at 11 p.m. in our studios. I hope to greet you there myself.

As you know the "critics" on this program, now in its sixth year, are not all professionals. The layman, who is so important in a democracy, is represented also, usually by one businessman, one housewife and one teen-ager. This will be particularly appropriate for your book, since foreign policy is something which closely concerns all these occupations and age groups.

Our regular critic and moderator, John DeTester, will unfortunately be on a lecture tour, but we have a promise from Mr. Kurt Erfloh, the dance critic of *Terpsichore,* that he will be delighted to stand in for John.

We look forward to your call accepting the date, as well as to meeting you and having you autograph our office copy of your marvelous book.

> Cordially,
>
> (MRS.) SUSAN ROISTER-DOISTER

April 5, 1960

DEAR MRS. ROI . . .

lawrence s. hall

eyeless in wonderland

Lawrence S. Hall, born in 1915, is a professor of English at Bowdoin College in Maine, a novelist and short-story writer—and at one time shared an office in Columbia College with a young instructor named Charles Van Doren.

Perhaps no case of corruption in high places has saddened American scholars and intellectuals quite so much as the "Van Doren case." As a leading contestant on one of the now-defunct television quiz shows, Van

Doren was privately given the questions in advance, then publicly pretended to answer them honestly. When he finally confessed to the deception before a Congressional committee, Van Doren said that he had agreed to it, in part, in order not to let down the American intellectual community.

Professor Hall's sharp and bristling analysis of young Van Doren's "service" to the intellectual community was originally delivered as a talk at Bowdoin and reprinted in *The Reporter*. It is the kind of polemic that one almost never reads in America today, for it combines closeness of reasoning with intense emotion, and the result is bracing in its moral power. "It has been a painful chore to come to grips with this case," writes Professor Hall, and indeed it has been for many intellectuals. But it is not only his pain but his feeling for the essential issue that comes through when he writes, in balanced rhythms that might have come out of the eighteenth century— ". . . as if the burden of the honor of his profession were not being carried by thousands of the relatively obscure, conscientious men who were his colleagues, who were and still are discharging their responsibilities to the intellectual life undeceiving and undeceived, and whose honor could neither be upheld nor despoiled by any one man."

Ο ne snowy December afternoon in 1955 a tall young man with a cultivated and ingratiating manner came into an office I was occupying at Columbia College. He tossed his green-cloth book satchel on the table, and without removing his coat sat down and looked at me with shining eyes.

"It's wonderful!" he exclaimed with equal obscurity and charm, as though the mere feeling of wonder were in itself what was important and not the thing, whatever it may have been, that caused it. "It's wonderful . . . !"

Not being addicted to this sort of mesmerism, I said: "What's wonderful?"

"The mind of man. You know," he said, "it's wonderful what you can learn from people. I'm editing an anthology of famous love letters, and it's incredible how much I've learned. I tell my students what my father always does: they aren't in class to learn from me; we're all there to learn from each other. And I have as much to learn from them, if not more." Notable events have occurred which now lead me to speculate with alarm on what in fact it was that Charles Van Doren's students taught him and he taught them.

EYELESS IN WONDERLAND: Reprinted from *The Reporter*, December 10, 1959. Copyright © 1959, The Reporter Magazine Company. By permission of the author.

Today in 1959 he tells us in his own words: "I have learned a lot in those three years, especially in the last three weeks. I've learned a lot about life."

In spite of the freshman-theme idiom, we grant that this is a considerable lesson, and we ask him what it is he has learned about life, and find him saying: ". . . the truth is the only thing with which a man can live."

Again we grant the premise and ask what truth he has learned, and hear him say: "I've learned a lot about myself. . . ."

Now we put it to him: What truth has he learned about himself? And this is what he says:

"I was involved, deeply involved, in a deception. The fact that I, too, was very much deceived cannot keep me from being the principal victim of that deception, because I was its principal symbol. . . . There may be a kind of justice in that. I don't know."

Well, here is obviously something he has *not* learned: he doesn't know whether what has happened to him is just or not. But beyond this, when he describes himself as being "very much deceived" and the "victim" of a deception, by whom or what does he think he was deceived? From his own testimony certainly not by producer Albert Freedman, who told him he could not possibly go on the quiz program "Twenty-One" without collaborating in the deceit that had been so undeceitfully proposed in the privacy of Freedman's bedroom.

The only deception of which Van Doren is certainly the victim is his own self-deception. He has been made aware, with the great help of external pressures, of the more obvious phases of this self-deception. He knows, for example, that you do not do "a great service to the intellectual life, to teachers, and to education," of which he says he believes "nothing is more vital to our civilization," by performing mental stunts, even when they are honest; though it comes hard to imagine how, with his high intelligence, the best of education, and training and experience in the profession of the intellect, he could have avoided realizing this from the beginning.

But I myself do not see that he recognizes any of those acts of deception which have not been made forcibly obvious to him, because he is still practicing them.

While he was preparing his statement to the House subcommittee, he told a *Time* correspondent: "I've been getting just wonderful letters from wonderful people. I put the good letters in one pocket and the *bad* [italics mine] in another. When I looked I had thirty-nine good letters in one pocket and there was only one bad one in the other pocket. I've been getting so much love from so many people that I just wish I could return it all. People are wonderful."

Here is material for another volume of love letters, of which the young man can this time be both editor and recipient. Of one of these letters Charles Van Doren says to a committee of Congress: "In the end, it was a small thing that tipped the scales. A letter came to me. . . . It was from a woman, a complete stranger, who had seen me on the Garroway show and who said she admired my work there. She told me that the only way I could ever live with myself, and make up for what I had done . . . was to admit it, clearly, openly, truly. Suddenly I knew she was right, and this way, which had seemed for so long the worst of all possible alternatives, suddenly became the only one. . . . In the morning I telephoned my attorney and told him my decision."

This is an extraordinary piece of self-hypnosis. On October 14, two days prior to receiving the quoted letter, Mr. Van Doren was served with a subpoena that he had by his own statement been forced to invite. At any stage of the three years preceding that moment he had been free to *decide* to tell the truth, but from this point on it became impossible for him to make a decision because he had left no real choice. To the very end he never did perform the ethical free act of making up his mind, and to the very end of his hearing he had not learned that vital fact about himself. At the very end he still speaks of "possible alternatives" as though circumstances, as inexorably as in a work of fiction, had not closed every one of them off. Van Doren did not *decide* to tell the truth; what he did was adapt himself to the finally inescapable necessity of telling it. The "way" he talks about finding, with the help of his correspondent who did not know he was no longer a free moral agent, was to blur the stark and damning distinction between these two actions.

"I spent the rest of the week [before the hearing]," he says, "trying hopelessly to seek a way out. There was no way, but even though my mind knew there was none, I could not face the prospect emotionally." Van Doren frankly did not have the emotional strength to face what he had done or what he was; and from the necessity, moral and practical, of facing this, he did at the zero hour find a way, as he inadvertently puts it, "out." By means of the little packet of letters in his pocket he was able to lay down a smoke screen of love and devotion which clouded the issue so that all distinctions could be miraged.

Any man must struggle for the image he needs of himself to make life supportable, regardless of what that image is, in the best way he can. If camouflage is indispensable to Van Doren, then in all humanity I am willing it should do him as much grace as possible. I would do better than forgiveness, which as Shaw once pointed out has an element of condescension in it; I would forget him and let him rescue what felicity he is able to as a private man. But it is not as a private man that I am concerned with him, because he himself calls himself a symbol. And it is by this symbol, in all its pretentious deceptiveness, that I am repelled and alarmed.

There have been men throughout history who have regarded themselves as symbols; some of them have been good and some have not. But all are dangerous if they are not seen to be what they are. There is always megalomania in a man who regards himself as symbol, as Eliot's Archbishop Becket saw when he rejected the fourth and ultimate temptation of martyrdom. There is certainly megalomania in a man who says he could not act honestly without betraying the hope and faith of millions of people—as if the hope and faith of all these millions hung on him alone; who further says, "I felt that I carried the whole burden of the honor of my profession"—as if the burden of the honor of his profession were not being carried by thousands of the relatively obscure, conscientious men who were his colleagues, who were and still are discharging their responsibilities to the intellectual life undeceiving and undeceived, and whose honor could neither be upheld nor despoiled by any one man.

What Van Doren is asking us to believe here is that he sacrificed his personal need for honesty to his larger duty to all those people whose symbol he saw himself as being. So as not to fail in his larger duty, he martyred himself to the fatal obligation of deceiving them into believing he was the symbol he knew he was not. Van Doren told an interviewer for *Newsweek:* "Oedipus's reaction was to pluck out his eyes in order to see a strange paradox. Well, some explosion had taken place in me, too." When I read this I realized to my utter amazement that this young man sees himself as a hero in a Greek tragedy.

But in spite of his talk about his inner explosion, the record will show that from beginning to end Van Doren has learned nothing of himself, from himself or from others. He has indeed, though in a very different way from Oedipus, plucked his eyes out. There is a pitiful circular consistency in his behavior. His performance on "Twenty-One" and his performance before the House sub-committee with its nation-wide gallery are of a piece. Let me quote him again:

"I have deceived my friends, and I had millions of them. Whatever their feelings for me now, my affection for them is stronger today than ever before. I am making this statement *because of them* [italics again mine]. I hope my being here will serve them well and lastingly." The symbol, alas, is still pathetically deceiving its believers, chief among whom is Van Doren himself.

Van Doren has taken his medicine only after, by a specious alchemy, he has converted it to an elixir—a love potion. He bowed out still representing himself as the loving martyred servant of these wonderful people who will be saved by his hapless example from being beguiled by worldly wickedness.

The shortest sane response to all this is, How noble can you get? Well, pretty noble, I'm afraid, if you set sail on the befogged sea of schmaltz in Van Doren's beautiful pea-green boat. And the alarming thing is that so many members of this culture are doing just that. We have the spectacle of four members of the House subcommittee commending this young man, and the chairman actually God-blessing him as if he had done something heroic, for a confession which he was driven into.

We have another spectacle of the students, who learned from him and from whom he learned, petitioning Columbia to restore to his intellectual duties a man they described as a "conscientious and brilliant teacher."

But this is not a brilliant and conscientious teacher; this is a cruelly and pitiably confused young man who by exuding and receiving indiscriminate compassion, playing footsie with the public to the end, had made himself a rallying point, a national hero of the similarly confused. They do not help one another; they compound each other's difficulties. This is far more dangerous to a culture than crooked television with its rigged quizzes and its shows of murder and rape for which Van Doren thought he was atoning by being, he imagined, "the only person" to read seventeenth-century poetry on a TV network program. Crookedness, murder, and rape are among those evils he had alluded to which appear to be clearly what they are. But so far neither he nor his sympathizers have learned to detect the other kind, which lurks, among other places, behind the easy safeguards of the sacred slogan.

The supreme fraud in this whole sordid and sick affair lies in concealing under piously reflexive formulas—"poetry," "kind heart," "truth," "gentle soul," "contrition," "fellow sinner," "forgiveness," "love"—the most maudlin and promiscuous ethical whoredom the soap-opera public has yet witnessed. The time can come, if it has not already come, when wanton pity for human weakness will betray the equally pitiable but uninfatuated fidelity to its strength.

Nor is this kicking a man when he's down, because this young man is anything but down, a fact he realized well in advance of most when he said (*Newsweek*): "Will I have the guts to withstand this if they come up with new attractive possibilities? I don't know." He will have many chances to find out. Among other things, he has already been offered, in the movie *Wake Me When It's Over,* the role of prosecutor in which, if he chooses, he can duplicate the histrionic subterfuge with which as unawakened defendant he delivered his lines before a committee of Congress and the nation.

It has been a painful chore to come to grips with this case, which has in it many of the authentic Conradian tensions between judgment and sympathy. But in defense of what may seem to be and indeed may be harshness, I offer this paradox. If judgment without sympathy is monstrous, sympathy without judgment is also monstrous. Every sound judgment has behind it the injunction: Judge not, that ye be not judged. But this does not mean, as the misguided compassionate think, Don't judge at all, because you too are guilty. It means, Don't judge in a way that assumes you are not open to the same judgment. The first enjoins chaos, the second understanding. We have to judge where we are required to, though we may already ourselves have defaulted, or we perpetuate our defections in others from a sympathetic fear of denouncing our own.

What I have really indicted here, at the expense of Charles Van Doren, is an attitude, a cultural soft spot. In this connection I have indicted also Van Doren's commenders, his condoners, his publicizers—all those who are his creators and the creators of others like him.

I would say a final word about the man who, behind all the rest—the self-pity, self-delusion, self-devotion, and self-destruction—is the same as we all are, as all men have been and will be. Not the symbol, not the tragic hero publicly pronouncing "Troubles bring you closer together," "I found myself again," "Everything came too easy," "Maybe this is all a farce, too, part of the masquerade," "This is a phenomenal thing that has happened to me—I don't think it happens to most men." Not this man but the one whose genuine private torture shows now and then amid these tortuous and phony clichés.

The man I would finally speak about is the one you get only an insufficient faltering glimpse of now and then, as I did that wintry day four years ago when I forbore to tell him directly what I thought of his philosophy of education. It is the man who pitifully told the reporter for *Newsweek:* "I've been acting a role for ten or fifteen years, maybe all my life. It's a role of thinking that I've done far more than I've done, accomplished more than I've accomplished, produced more than I've produced. It has, in a way, something to do with my family, I suppose. I don't mean just my father, there are other people in my family. But I've been running . . ."

c. p. snow

the two cultures

"It just happened to be an unusual experience," C. P. Snow writes in this essay. "By training I was a scientist: by vocation I was a writer. That was all. It was a piece of luck, if you like, that arose through coming from a poor home." The unpretentious, deliberately casual tone of this is typical of Snow's writing. Yet "The Two Cultures" is in the great British tradition of pamphleteering that seeks to dramatize a pressing contemporary situation, to locate a cause and to change our minds, to exhort us to imaginative human effort in a new direction. Snow believes that the scientific community and the literary world are hopelessly cut off from each other. The scientists remain obdurately ignorant of literary creation; and perhaps even more serious, the literary men, by remaining illiterate in science, are missing out on the great new advance for humanity that can result only through the advancement of scientific knowledge and its immediate offspring, the technological revolution.

C. P. Snow (now Sir Charles Percy Snow) , was born in Leicester, England in 1905. With his series of novels, *Strangers and Brothers,* he has become one of the most widely read of contemporary novelists. But he took a Ph.D. in Physics at Cambridge University, and was knighted for his work during the war as a director of scientific personnel. Snow, to use his revealing and characteristic phrase, was "privileged to have a ringside view" of modern physics in its exciting creative upsurge in the 1920's, and during the Second World War, he had a ringside view of the work done on radar and the atomic bomb. His writing has both the authority that comes from such experience and the suppleness of an extremely alert intelligence. The little book from which this selection is taken, *The Two Cultures and the Scientific Revolution,* originally the 1959 Rede Lecture at Cambridge University, has put at the center the whole question of how much science is to determine our future. In many ways it is one of the most suggestive discussions of a topic which dominates our concern today. Yet at the same time it is not just a

pamphlet for propaganda purposes. Much as Snow feels the crying need
for a wider dissemination of the scientific point of view, his essay is
essentially the work of an expert writer and a sensitive humanist. He
believes that our civilization will perish unless it applies to everyone's
well-being what science alone can teach us, but only a writer could put
the case so well. Nowhere is this better seen than in the moving passage
where Snow contrasts the limited hopes of the individual human being,
whose life is inescapably tragic, and the *social* possibilities for mankind
at large.

It is about three years since I made a sketch in print of a problem
which had been on my mind for some time.[1] It was a problem I could
not avoid just because of the circumstances of my life. The only
credentials I had to ruminate on the subject at all came through those
circumstances, through nothing more than a set of chances. Anyone
with similar experience would have seen much the same things and
I think made very much the same comments about them. It just happened to be an unusual experience. By training I was a scientist: by
vocation I was a writer. That was all. It was a piece of luck, if you like,
that arose through coming from a poor home.

But my personal history isn't the point now. All that I need say is
that I came to Cambridge and did a bit of research here at a time of
major scientific activity. I was privileged to have a ringside view of
one of the most wonderful creative periods in all physics. And it
happened through the flukes of war—including meeting W. L. Bragg
in the buffet on Kettering station on a very cold morning in 1939,
which had a determining influence on my practical life—that I was
able, and indeed morally forced, to keep that ringside view ever since.
So for thirty years I have had to be in touch with scientists not only
out of curiosity, but as part of a working existence. During the same
thirty years I was trying to shape the books I wanted to write, which
in due course took me among writers.

There have been plenty of days when I have spent the working
hours with scientists and then gone off at night with some literary
colleagues. I mean that literally. I have had, of course, intimate
friends among both scientists and writers. It was through living
among these groups and much more, I think, through moving regu-

1 'The Two Cultures', *New Statesman*. 6 October 1956.

THE TWO CULTURES: From *The Two Cultures and the Scientific Revolution* by
C. P. Snow. © 1959 by C. P. Snow. Published by The Syndics of the Cambridge
University Press. Used by permission of the Cambridge University Press, New York.

larly from one to the other and back again that I got occupied with the problem of what, long before I put it on paper, I christened to myself as the 'two cultures'. For constantly I felt I was moving among two groups—comparable in intelligence, identical in race, not grossly different in social origin, earning about the same incomes, who had almost ceased to communicate at all, who in intellectual, moral and psychological climate had so little in common that instead of going from Burlington House or South Kensington to Chelsea, one might have crossed an ocean.

In fact, one had traveled much further than across an ocean—because after a few thousand Atlantic miles, one found Greenwich Village talking precisely the same language as Chelsea, and both having about as much communication with M.I.T. as though the scientists spoke nothing but Tibetan. For this is not just our problem; owing to some of our educational and social idiosyncrasies, it is slightly exaggerated here, owing to another English social peculiarity it is slightly minimized; by and large this is a problem of the entire West.

By this I intend something serious. I am not thinking of the pleasant story of how one of the more convivial Oxford greats dons—I have heard the story attributed to A. L. Smith—came over to Cambridge to dine. The date is perhaps the 1890's. I think it must have been at St. John's, or possibly Trinity. Anyway, Smith was sitting at the right hand of the President—or Vice-Master—and he was a man who liked to include all round him in the conversation, although he was not immediately encouraged by the expressions of his neighbors. He addressed some cheerful Oxonian chit-chat at the one opposite to him, and got a grunt. He then tried the man on his own right hand and got another grunt. Then, rather to his surprise, one looked at the other and said, 'Do you know what he's talking about?' 'I haven't the least idea.' At this, even Smith was getting out of his depth. But the President, acting as a social emollient, put him at his ease, by saying, 'Oh, those are mathematicians! We never talk to *them*.'

No, I intend something serious. I believe the intellectual life of the whole of western society is increasingly being split into two polar groups. When I say the intellectual life, I mean to include also a large part of our practical life, because I should be the last person to sug-gest the two can at the deepest level be distinguished. I shall come back to the practical life a little later. Two polar groups: at one pole we have the literary intellectuals, who incidentally while no one was looking took to referring to themselves as 'intellectuals' as though there were no others. I remember G. H. Hardy once remarking to me in mild puzzlement, some time in the 1930's: 'Have you noticed how the word "intellectual" is used nowadays? There seems to be a new definition which certainly doesn't include Rutherford or Eddington or Dirac or Adrian or me. It does seem rather odd, don't y' know.'[2]

Literary intellectuals at one pole—at the other scientists, and as the most representative, the physical scientists. Between the two a gulf of mutual incomprehension—sometimes (particularly among the young) hostility and dislike, but most of all lack of understanding. They have a curious distorted image of each other. Their attitudes are so different that, even on the level of emotion, they can't find much common ground. Non-scientists tend to think of scientists as brash and boastful. They hear Mr. T. S. Eliot, who just for these illustrations we can take as an archetypal figure, saying about his attempts to revive verse-drama, that we can hope for very little, but that he would feel content if he and his co-workers could prepare the ground for a new Kyd or a new Greene. That is the tone, restricted and constrained, with which literary intellectuals are at home: it is the subdued voice of their culture. Then they hear a much louder voice, that of another archetypal figure, Rutherford, trumpeting: 'This is the heroic age of science! This is the Elizabethan age!' Many of us heard that, and a good many other statements beside which that was mild; and we weren't left in any doubt whom Rutherford was casting for the role of Shakespeare. What is hard for the literary intellectuals to understand, imaginatively or intellectually, is that he was absolutely right.

And compare 'this is the way the world ends, not with a bang but a whimper'—incidentally, one of the least likely scientific prophecies ever made—compare that with Rutherford's famous repartee, 'Lucky fellow, Rutherford, always on the crest of the wave.' 'Well, I made the wave, didn't I?'

The non-scientists have a rooted impression that the scientists are shallowly optimistic, unaware of man's condition. On the other hand, the scientists believe that the literary intellectuals are totally lacking in foresight, peculiarly unconcerned with their brother men, in a deep sense anti-intellectual, anxious to restrict both art and thought to the existential moment. And so on. Anyone with a mild talent for invective could produce plenty of this kind of subterranean back-chat. On each side there is some of it which is not entirely baseless. It is all destructive. Much of it rests on misinterpretations which are danger-

---

[2] This lecture was delivered to a Cambridge audience, and so I used some points of reference which I did not need to explain. G. H. Hardy, 1877-1947, was one of the most distinguished mathematicians of his time, and a picturesque figure in Cambridge both as a young don and on his return in 1931 to the Sadleirian Chair of Mathematics.

ous. I should like to deal with two of the most profound of these now, one on each side.

First, about the scientists' optimism. This is an accusation which has been made so often that it has become a platitude. It has been made by some of the acutest non-scientific minds of the day. But it depends upon a confusion between the individual experience and the social experience, between the individual condition of man and his social condition. Most of the scientists I have known well have felt—just as deeply as the non-scientists I have known well—that the individual condition of each of us is tragic. Each of us is alone: sometimes we escape from solitariness, through love or affection or perhaps creative moments, but those triumphs of life are pools of light we make for ourselves while the edge of the road is black: each of us dies alone. Some scientists I have known have had faith in revealed religion. Perhaps with them the sense of the tragic condition is not so strong. I don't know. With most people of deep feeling, however high-spirited and happy they are, sometimes most with those who are happiest and most high-spirited, it seems to be right in the fibres, part of the weight of life. That is as true of the scientists I have known best as of anyone at all.

But nearly all of them—and this is where the color of hope genuinely comes in—would see no reason why, just because the individual condition is tragic, so must the social condition be. Each of us is solitary: each of us dies alone: all right, that's a fate against which we can't struggle—but there is plenty in our condition which is not fate, and against which we are less than human unless we do struggle.

Most of our fellow human beings, for instance, are underfed and die before their time. In the crudest terms, *that* is the social condition. There is a moral trap which comes through the insight into man's loneliness: it tempts one to sit back, complacent in one's unique tragedy, and let the others go without a meal.

As a group, the scientists fall into that trap less than others. They are inclined to be impatient to see if something can be done: and inclined to think that it can be done, until it's proved otherwise. That is their real optimism, and it's an optimism that the rest of us badly need.

In reverse, the same spirit, tough and good and determined to fight it out at the side of their brother men, has made scientists regard the other culture's social attitudes as contemptible. That is too facile: some of them are, but they are a temporary phase and not to be taken as representative.

I remember being cross-examined by a scientist of distinction. 'Why do most writers take on social opinions which would have been thought distinctly uncivilized and démodé at the time of the Plantagenets? Wasn't that true of most of the famous twentieth-century writers? Yeats, Pound, Wyndham Lewis, nine out of ten of those who have dominated literary sensibility in our time—weren't they not only politically silly, but politically wicked? Didn't the influence of all they represent bring Auschwitz that much nearer?'

I thought at the time, and I still think, that the correct answer was not to defend the indefensible. It was no use saying that Yeats, according to friends whose judgment I trust, was a man of singular magnanimity of character, as well as a great poet. It was no use denying the facts, which are broadly true. The honest answer was that there is, in fact, a connection, which literary persons were culpably slow to see, between some kinds of early twentieth-century art and the most imbecile expressions of anti-social feeling.[3] That was one reason, among many, why some of us turned our backs on the art and tried to hack out a new or different way for ourselves.[4]

But though many of those writers dominated literary sensibility for a generation, that is no longer so, or at least to nothing like the same extent. Literature changes more slowly than science. It hasn't the same automatic corrective, and so its misguided periods are longer. But it is ill-considered of scientists to judge writers on the evidence of the period 1914-50.

Those are two of the misunderstandings between the two cultures. I should say, since I began to talk about them—the two cultures, that is—I have had some criticism. Most of my scientific acquaintances think that there is something in it, and so do most of the practising artists I know. But I have been argued with by non-scientists of strong down-to-earth interests. Their view is that it is an over-simplification, and that if one is going to talk in these terms there ought to be at least three cultures. They argue that, though they are not scientists themselves, they would share a good deal of the scientific feeling. They would have as little use—perhaps, since they knew more about it, even less use—for the recent literary culture as the scientists themselves. J. H. Plumb, Alan Bullock and some of my American sociological friends have said that they vigorously refuse to be corralled in a cultural box with

[3] I said a little more about this connection in *The Times Literary Supplement*, 'Challenge to the Intellect', 15 August 1958. I hope some day to carry the analysis further.

[4] It would be more accurate to say that, for literary reasons, we felt the prevailing literary modes were useless to us. We were, however, reinforced in that feeling when it occurred to us that those prevailing modes went hand in hand with social attitudes either wicked, or absurd, or both.

people they wouldn't be seen dead with, or to be regarded as helping to produce a climate which would not permit of social hope.

I respect those arguments. The number 2 is a very dangerous number: that is why the dialectic is a dangerous process. Attempts to divide anything into two ought to be regarded with much suspicion. I have thought a long time about going in for further refinements: but in the end I have decided against. I was searching for something a little more than a dashing metaphor, a good deal less than a cultural map: and for those purposes the two cultures is about right, and subtilizing any more would bring more disadvantages than it's worth.

At one pole, the scientific culture really is a culture, not only in an intellectual but also in an anthropological sense. That is, its members need not, and of course often do not, always completely understand each other; biologists more often than not will have a pretty hazy idea of contemporary physics; but there are common attitudes, common standards and patterns of behavior, common approaches and assumptions. This goes surprisingly wide and deep. It cuts across other mental patterns, such as those of religion or politics or class.

Statistically, I suppose slightly more scientists are in religious terms unbelievers, compared with the rest of the intellectual world—though there are plenty who are religious, and that seems to be increasingly so among the young. Statistically also, slightly more scientists are on the Left in open politics—though again, plenty always have called themselves conservatives, and that also seems to be more common among the young. Compared with the rest of the intellectual world, considerably more scientists in this country and probably in the U.S. come from poor families.[5] Yet, over a whole range of thought and behavior, none of that matters very much. In their working, and in much of their emotional life, their attitudes are closer to other scientists than to non-scientists who in religion or politics or class have the same labels as themselves. If I were to risk a piece of shorthand, I should say that naturally they had the future in their bones.

They may or may not like it, but they have it. That was as true of the conservatives J. J. Thomson and Lindemann as of the radicals Einstein or Blackett: as true of the Christian A. H. Compton as of the materialist Bernal: of the aristocrats Broglie or Russell as of the proletarian Faraday: of those born rich, like Thomas Merton or Victor Rothschild, as of Rutherford, who was the son of an odd-job handy-

[5] An analysis of the schools from which Fellows of the Royal Society come tells its own story. The distribution is markedly different from that of, for example, members of the Foreign Service or Queen's Counsel.

man. Without thinking about it, they respond alike. That is what a culture means.

At the other pole, the spread of attitudes is wider. It is obvious that between the two, as one moves through intellectual society from the physicists to the literary intellectuals, there are all kinds of tones of feeling on the way. But I believe the pole of total incomprehension of science radiates its influence on all the rest. That total incomprehension gives, much more pervasively than we realize, living in it, an unscientific flavor to the whole 'traditional' culture, and that unscientific flavor is often, much more than we admit, on the point of turning anti-scientific. The feelings of one pole become the anti-feelings of the other. If the scientists have the future in their bones, then the traditional culture responds by wishing the future did not exist.[6] It is the traditional culture, to an extent remarkably little diminished by the emergence of the scientific one, which manages the western world.

This polarization is sheer loss to us all. To us as people, and to our society. It is at the same time practical and intellectual and creative loss, and I repeat that it is false to imagine that those three considerations are clearly separable. But for a moment I want to concentrate on the intellectual loss.

The degree of incomprehension on both sides is the kind of joke which has gone sour. There are about fifty thousand working scientists in the country and about eighty thousand professional engineers or applied scientists. During the war and in the years since, my colleagues and I have had to interview somewhere between thirty to forty thousand of these—that is, about 25 per cent. The number is large enough to give us a fair sample, though of the men we talked to most would still be under forty. We were able to find out a certain amount of what they read and thought about. I confess that even I, who am fond of them and respect them, was a bit shaken. We hadn't quite expected that the links with the traditional culture should be so tenuous, nothing more than a formal touch of the cap.

As one would expect, some of the very best scientists had and have plenty of energy and interest to spare, and we came across several who had read everything that literary people talk about. But that's very rare. Most of the rest, when one tried to probe for what books they had read, would modestly confess, 'Well, I've *tried* a bit of Dickens', rather as though Dickens were an extraordinarily esoteric, tangled and dubiously rewarding writer, something like Rainer Maria Rilke. In fact that is exactly how they do regard him: we thought that discovery,

---

[6] Compare George Orwell's *1984*, which is the strongest possible wish that the future should not exist, with J. D. Bernal's *World Without War*.

that Dickens had been transformed into the type-specimen of literary incomprehensibility, was one of the oddest results of the whole exercise.

But of course, in reading him, in reading almost any writer whom we should value, they are just touching their caps to the traditional culture. They have their own culture, intensive, rigorous, and constantly in action. This culture contains a great deal of argument, usually much more rigorous, and almost always at a higher conceptual level, than literary persons' arguments—even though the scientists do cheerfully use words in senses which literary persons don't recognize, the senses are exact ones, and when they talk about 'subjective', 'objective', 'philosophy' or 'progressive',[7] they know what they mean, even though it isn't what one is accustomed to expect.

Remember, these are very intelligent men. Their culture is in many ways an exacting and admirable one. It doesn't contain much art, with the exception, an important exception, of music. Verbal exchange, insistent argument. Long-playing records. Color-photography. The ear, to some extent the eye. Books, very little, though perhaps not many would go so far as one hero, who perhaps I should admit was further down the scientific ladder than the people I've been talking about—who, when asked what books he read, replied firmly and confidently: 'Books? I prefer to use my books as tools.' It was very hard not to let the mind wander—what sort of tool would a book make? Perhaps a hammer? A primitive digging instrument?

Of books, though, very little. And of the books which to most literary persons are bread and butter, novels, history, poetry, plays, almost nothing at all. It isn't that they're not interested in the psychological or moral or social life. In the social life, they certainly are, more than most of us. In the moral, they are by and large the soundest group of intellectuals we have; there is a moral component right in the grain of science itself, and almost all scientists form their own judgments of the moral life. In the psychological they have as much interest as most of us, though occasionally I fancy they come to it rather late. It isn't that they lack the interests. It is much more that the whole literature of the traditional culture doesn't seem to them relevant to those interests. They are, of course, dead wrong. As a result, their imaginative understanding is less than it could be. They are self-impoverished.

---

[7] *Subjective,* in contemporary technological jargon, means 'divided according to subjects'. *Objective* means 'directed towards an object'. *Philosophy* means 'general intellectual approach or attitude' (for example, a scientist's 'philosophy of guided weapons' might lead him to propose certain kinds of 'objective research'). A 'progressive' job means one with possibilities of promotion.

But what about the other side? They are impoverished too—perhaps more seriously, because they are vainer about it. They still like to pretend that the traditional culture is the whole of 'culture', as though the natural order didn't exist. As though the exploration of the natural order was of no interest either in its own value or its consequences. As though the scientific edifice of the physical world was not, in its intellectual depth, complexity and articulation, the most beautiful and wonderful collective work of the mind of man. Yet most non-scientists have no conception of that edifice at all. Even if they want to have it, they can't. It is rather as though, over an immense range of intellectual experience, a whole group was tone-deaf. Except that this tone-deafness doesn't come by nature, but by training, or rather the absence of training.

As with the tone-deaf, they don't know what they miss. They give a pitying chuckle at the news of scientists who have never read a major work of English literature. They dismiss them as ignorant specialists. Yet their own ignorance and their own specialization is just as startling. A good many times I have been present at gatherings of people who, by the standards of the traditional culture, are thought highly educated and who have with considerable gusto been expressing their incredulity at the illiteracy of scientists. Once or twice I have been provoked and have asked the company how many of them could describe the Second Law of Thermodynamics. The response was cold: it was also negative. Yet I was asking something which is about the scientific equivalent of: *Have you read a work of Shakespeare's?*

I now believe that if I had asked an even simpler question—such as, What do you mean by mass, or acceleration, which is the scientific equivalent of saying, *Can you read?*—not more than one in ten of the highly educated would have felt that I was speaking the same language. So the great edifice of modern physics goes up, and the majority of the cleverest people in the western world have about as much insight into it as their neolithic ancestors would have had.

Just one more of those questions, that my non-scientific friends regard as being in the worst of taste. Cambridge is a university where scientists and non-scientists meet every night at dinner.[8] About two years ago, one of the most astonishing experiments in the whole history of science was brought off. I don't mean the sputnik—that was admirable for quite different reasons, as a feat of organization and a triumphant use of existing knowledge. No, I mean the experiment at Columbia by Yang and Lee. It is an experiment of the greatest beauty

[8] Almost all college High Tables contain Fellows in both scientific and non-scientific subjects.

and originality, but the result is so startling that one forgets how beautiful the experiment is. It makes us think again about some of the fundamentals of the physical world. Intuition, common sense— they are neatly stood on their heads. The result is usually known as the contradiction of parity. If there were any serious communication between the two cultures, this experiment would have been talked about at every High Table in Cambridge. Was it? I wasn't here: but I should like to ask the question.

There seems then to be no place where the cultures meet. I am not going to waste time saying that this is a pity. It is much worse than that. Soon I shall come to some practical consequences. But at the heart of thought and creation we are letting some of our best chances go by default. The clashing point of two subjects, two disciplines, two cultures—of two galaxies, so far as that goes—ought to produce creative chances. In the history of mental activity that has been where some of the breakthroughs came. The chances are there now. But they are there, as it were, in a vacuum, because those in the two cultures can't talk to each other. It is bizarre how very little of twentieth-century science has been assimilated into twentieth-century art. Now and then one used to find poets conscientiously using scientific expressions, and getting them wrong—there was a time when 'refraction' kept cropping up in verse in a mystifying fashion, and when 'polarized light' was used as though writers were under the illusion that it was a specially admirable kind of light.

Of course, that isn't the way that science could be any good to art. It has got to be assimilated along with, and as part and parcel of, the whole of our mental experience, and used as naturally as the rest.

I said earlier that this cultural divide is not just an English phenomenon: it exists all over the western world. But it probably seems at its sharpest in England, for two reasons. One is our fanatical belief in educational specialization, which is much more deeply ingrained in us than in any country in the world, west or east. The other is our tendency to let our social forms crystallize. This tendency appears to get stronger, not weaker, the more we iron out economic inequalities: and this is specially true in education. It means that once anything like a cultural divide gets established, all the social forces operate to make it not less rigid, but more so.

The two cultures were already dangerously separate sixty years ago; but a prime minister, Lord Salisbury, could have his own laboratory at Hatfield, and Arthur Balfour had a somewhat more than amateur interest in natural science. John Anderson did some research in organic chemistry in Würzburg before passing first into the Civil Service, and incidentally took a spread of subjects which is now impossible.[9] None of that degree of interchange at the top of the Establishment is likely, or indeed thinkable, now.[10]

In fact, the separation between the scientists and non-scientists is much less bridgeable among the young than it was even thirty years ago. Thirty years ago the cultures had long ceased to speak to each other: but at least they managed a kind of frozen smile across the gulf. Now the politeness has gone, and they just make faces. It is not only that the young scientists now feel that they are part of a culture on the rise while the other is in retreat. It is also, to be brutal, that the young scientists know that with an indifferent degree they'll get a comfortable job, while their contemporaries and counterparts in English or History will be lucky to earn 60 per cent as much. No young scientist of any talent would feel that he isn't wanted or that his work is ridiculous, as did the hero of *Lucky Jim,* and in fact, some of the disgruntlement of Amis and his associates is the disgruntlement of the under-employed arts graduate.

There is only one way out of all this: it is, of course, by rethinking our education. In this country, for the two reasons I have given, that is more difficult than in any other. Nearly everyone will agree that our school education is too specialized. But nearly everyone feels that it is outside the will of man to alter it. Other countries are as dissatisfied with their education as we are, but are not so resigned.

The U.S. teach out of proportion more children up to eighteen than we do: they teach them far more widely, but nothing like so rigorously. They know that: they are hoping to take the problem in hand within ten years, though they may not have all that time to spare. The U.S.S.R. also teach out of proportion more children than we do: they also teach far more widely than we do (it is an absurd western myth that their school education is specialized) but much too rigorously.[11] They know that—and they are beating about to get it right. The Scandinavians, in particular the Swedes, who would make a more sensible job of it than any of us, are handicapped by their practical need to devote an inordinate amount of time to foreign languages. But they too are seized of the problem.

9 He took the examination in 1905.

10 It is, however, true to say that the compact nature of the managerial layers of English society—the fact that 'everyone knows everyone else'—means that scientists and non-scientists do in fact know each other as people more easily than in most countries. It is also true that a good many leading politicians and administrators keep up lively intellectual and artistic interests to a much greater extent, so far as I can judge, than is the case in the U.S. These are both among our assets.

11 I tried to compare American, Soviet and English education in 'New Minds for the New World', *New Statesman,* 6 September 1956.

Are we? Have we crystallized so far that we are no longer flexible at all?

Talk to schoolmasters, and they say that our intense specialization, like nothing else on earth, is dictated by the Oxford and Cambridge scholarship examinations. If that is so, one would have thought it not utterly impracticable to change the Oxford and Cambridge scholarship examinations. Yet one would underestimate the national capacity for the intricate defensive to believe that that was easy. All the lessons of our educational history suggest we are only capable of increasing specialization, not decreasing it.

Somehow we have set ourselves the task of producing a tiny *élite*—far smaller proportionately than in any comparable country—educated in one academic skill. For a hundred and fifty years in Cambridge it was mathematics: then it was mathematics or classics: then natural science was allowed in. But still the choice had to be a single one. It may well be that this process has gone too far to be reversible. I think it is a disastrous process for the purpose of a living culture. I also think it is nearly fatal if we are to perform our practical tasks in the world.

II

rachel carson

---

the surface of the sea

Rachel Carson was born in Pennsylvania in 1907, and says of herself that "I grew up inland, without a glimpse of the sea until I had graduated from college. Among my earliest conscious memories, however, are two things: a feeling of absolute fascination for everything relating to the ocean, and a determination that I would some day be a writer."

There are few writer-scientists today who have Miss Carson's particular gift for explaining technical matters to the layman in language that is lucid, vivid and graceful. Miss Carson is a marine biologist who writes with the quiet intensity of someone thoroughly absorbed in and committed to her subject. She describes technical matters in a prose that glows with excitement at what she can see and reach.

The following selection, Chapter II of the book that instantly made her famous, *The Sea Around Us*, is a particularly good example of her modulated prose. Her writing succeeds because her rhythms are so intensely human, because the reader is aware of her arousal to the subject. Her phrases are always concrete and evocative. Miss Carson speaks of "the fierce uncompromisingness of sea life," a phrase that only a true writer would ever think of using. Perhaps it is because she has so many personal, and deeply human, associations with the sea that she finally brings home to us the final strangeness of the sea. She uses adjectives the way a painter emphasizes an object with an unexpected stroke of color. Above all, she has the writer's passion—the desire to make the reader *see*. "From the deck of a vessel you may look down, hour after hour, on the shimmering discs of jellyfish, their gently pulsating bells dotting the surface as far as you can see."

> *There is, one knows not what sweet mystery about this sea, whose gently awful stirrings seem to speak of some hidden soul beneath.*
>
> HERMAN MELVILLE

Nowhere in all the sea does life exist in such bewildering abundance as in the surface waters. From the deck of a vessel you may look down, hour after hour, on the shimmering discs of jellyfish, their gently pulsating bells dotting the surface as far as you can see. Or one day you may notice early in the morning that you are passing through a sea that has taken on a brick-red color from billions upon billions of microscopic creatures, each of which contains an orange pigment granule. At noon you are still moving through red seas, and when darkness falls the waters shine with an eerie glow from the phosphorescent fires of yet more billions and trillions of these same creatures.

And again you may glimpse not only the abundance but something of the fierce uncompromisingness of sea life when, as you look over the rail and down, down into water of a clear, deep green, suddenly there passes a silver shower of finger-long fishlets. The sun strikes a metallic gleam from their flanks as they streak by, driving deeper into the green depths with the desperate speed of the hunted. Perhaps you never see the hunters, but you sense their presence as you see the gulls hovering, with eager, mewing cries, waiting for the little fish to be driven to the surface.

Or again, perhaps, you may sail for days on end without seeing anything you could recognize as life or the indications of life, day after day of empty water and empty sky, and so you may reasonably conclude that there is no spot on earth so barren of life as the open ocean. But if you had the opportunity to tow a fine-meshed net through the seemingly lifeless water and then to examine the washings of the net, you would find that life is scattered almost everywhere through the surface waters like a fine dust. A cupful of water may contain millions upon millions of diatoms, tiny plant cells, each of them far too small to be seen by the human eye; or it may swarm with an infinitude of animal creatures, none larger than a dust mote, which live on plant cells still smaller than themselves.

If you could be close to the surface waters on the ocean at night, you would realize that then they are alive with myriads of strange creatures never seen by day. They are alive with the moving lamps of small shrimplike beings that spend the daylight hours in the gloom of deep water, and with the shadowy forms of hungry fish and the dark shapes of squid. These things were seen, as few men have seen them, by the Norwegian ethnologist Thor Heyerdahl in the course of one of the most unusual journeys of modern time. In the summer of 1947 Heyerdahl and five companions drifted 4300 miles across the Pacific on a raft of balsa logs, to test a theory that the original inhabitants of Polynesia might have come from South America by raft. For 101 days and nights these men lived practically on the surface of the sea, driven by the trade wind, carried on the strong drift of the Equatorial Current, as much a part of the inexorable westward movement of wind and water as the creatures of the sea. Because of his enviable opportunity to observe the life of the surface while living as an actual part of it for so many weeks, I asked Mr. Heyerdahl about some of his impressions, especially of the sea at night, and he has written me as follows:

'Chiefly at night, but occasionally in broad daylight, a shoal of small squids shot out of the water precisely like flying fish, gliding through the air as much as up to six feet above the surface, until they lost the speed accumulated below water, and fell down helplessly. In their gliding flight with flaps out they were so much like small flying fish at a distance, that we had no idea we saw anything unusual until a live squid flew right into one of the crew and fell down on deck. Almost every night we found one or two on the deck or on the roof of the bamboo hut.

'It was my own definite impression that the marine life in general went deeper down in the daytime than during the nights, and that the darker the night was, the more life we had around us. At two different occasions, a snake-mackerel, Gempylus, never before seen by man except as skeletal remains washed ashore on South America and the Galapagos, came jumping clear out of the water and right up on the raft (once right into the hut). To judge from the huge eyes and the fact that the fish has never before been observed, I am inclined to suspect that it is a deep-sea fish that comes to the surface only at night.

'On dark nights we could see much marine life which we were unable to identify. They seemed to be deep-sea fishes approaching the surface at night. Generally we saw it as vaguely phosphorescent bodies, often the size and shape of a dinner plate, but at least one night in the shape of three immense bodies of irregular and changing shape and dimensions which appeared to exceed those of the raft (KON-TIKI measured about 45 by 18 feet). Apart from these greater bodies, we observed occasionally great quantities of phosphorescent plankton, often containing illuminating copepods up to the size of a millimeter or more.'

With these surface waters, through a series of delicately adjusted, interlocking relationships, the life of all parts of the sea is linked. What happens to a diatom in the upper, sunlit strata of the sea may well determine what happens to a cod lying on a ledge of some rocky canyon a hundred fathoms below, or to a bed of multicolored, gorgeously plumed seaworms carpeting an underlying shoal, or to a prawn creeping over the soft oozes of the sea floor in the blackness of mile-deep water.

The activities of the microscopic vegetables of the sea, of which the diatoms are most important, make the mineral wealth of the water available to the animals. Feeding directly on the diatoms and other groups of minute unicellular algae are the marine protozoa, many crustaceans, the young of crabs, barnacles, sea worms, and fishes. Hordes of the small carnivores, the first link in the chain of flesh eaters, move among these peaceful grazers. There are fierce little dragons half an inch long, the sharp-jawed arrowworms. There are gooseberry-like comb jellies, armed with grasping tentacles, and there are the shrimp-like euphausiids that strain food from the water with their bristly appendages. Since they drift where the currents carry them, with no power or will to oppose that of the sea, this strange community of creatures and the marine plants that sustain them are called 'plankton,' a word derived from the Greek, meaning 'wandering.'

From the plankton the food chains lead on, to the schools of plankton-feeding fishes like the herring, menhaden, and mackerel; to the fish-eating fishes like the bluefish and tuna and sharks; to the pelagic squids that prey on fishes; to the great whales who, according to their species but not according to their size, may live on fishes, on shrimps, or on some of the smallest of the plankton creatures.

Unmarked and trackless though it may seem to us, the surface of the ocean is divided into definite zones, and the pattern of the surface water controls the distribution of its life. Fishes and plankton, whales and squids, birds and sea turtles, all are linked by unbreakable ties to certain kinds of water—to warm water or cold water, to clear or turbid water, to water rich in phosphates or in silicates. For the animals higher in the food chains the ties are less direct; they are bound to water where their food is plentiful, and the food animals are there because the water conditions are right.

The change from zone to zone may be abrupt. It may come upon us unseen, as our ship at night crosses an invisible boundary line. So Charles Darwin on H.M.S. *Beagle* one dark night off the coast of South America crossed from tropical water into that of the cool south. Instantly the vessel was surrounded by numerous seals and penguins, which made such a bedlam of strange noises that the officer on watch was deceived into thinking the ship had, by some miscalculation, run close inshore, and that the sounds he heard were the bellowing of cattle.

To the human senses, the most obvious patterning of the surface waters is indicated by color. The deep blue water of the open sea far from land is the color of emptiness and barrenness; the green water of the coastal areas, with all its varying hues, is the color of life. The sea is blue because the sunlight is reflected back to our eyes from the water molecules or from very minute particles suspended in the sea. In the journey of the light rays into deep water all the red rays and most of the yellow rays of the spectrum have been absorbed, so when the light returns to our eyes it is chiefly the cool blue rays that we see. Where the water is rich in plankton, it loses the glassy transparency that permits this deep penetration of the light rays. The yellow and brown and green hues of the coastal waters are derived from the minute algae and other micro-organisms so abundant there. Seasonal abundance of certain forms containing reddish or brown pigments may cause the 'red water' known from ancient times in many parts of the world, and so common is this condition in some enclosed seas that they owe their names to it—the Red Sea and the Vermilion Sea are examples.

The colors of the sea are only the indirect signs of the presence or absence of conditions needed to support the surface life; other zones, invisible to the eye, are the ones that largely determine where marine creatures may live. For the sea is by no means a uniform solution of water; parts of it are more salty than others, and parts are warmer or colder.

The saltiest ocean water in the world is that of the Red Sea, where the burning sun and the fierce heat of the atmosphere produce such rapid evaporation that the salt content is 40 parts per thousand. The Sargasso Sea, an area of high air temperatures, receiving no inflow of river water or melting ice because of its remoteness from land, is the saltiest part of the Atlantic, which in turn is the saltiest of the oceans. The polar seas, as one would expect, are the least salty, because they are constantly being diluted by rain, snow, and melting ice. Along the Atlantic coast of the United States, the salinity range from about 33 parts per thousand off Cape Cod to about 36 off Florida is a difference easily perceptible to the senses of human bathers.

Ocean temperatures vary from about 28° F. in polar seas to 96° in the Persian Gulf, which contains the hottest ocean water in the world. To creatures of the sea, which with few exceptions must match in their own bodies the temperature of the surrounding water, this range is tremendous, and change of temperature is probably the most important single condition that controls the distribution of marine animals.

The beautiful reef corals are a perfect example of the way the inhabitable areas for any particular class of creatures may be established by temperatures. If you took a map of the world and drew a line 30° north of the Equator and another 30° south of it, you would have outlined in general the waters where reef coals are found at the present time. It is true that the remains of ancient coral reefs have been discovered in arctic waters, but this means that in some past ages the climate of these northern seas was tropical. The calcareous structure of the coral reef can be fashioned only in water at least as warm as 70° Fahrenheit. We would have to make one northward extension of our map, where the Gulf Stream carries water warm enough for corals to Bermuda, at 32° north latitude. On the other hand, within our tropical belt, we would have to erase large areas on the west coasts of South America and Africa, where upwelling of cold water from lower ocean levels prevents the growth of corals. Most of the east coast of Florida has no coral reefs because of a cool inshore current, running southward between the coast and the Gulf Stream.

As between tropical and polar regions, the differences in the kinds and abundance of life are tremendous. The warm temperatures of the tropics speed up the processes of reproduction and growth, so that many generations are produced in the time required to bring one to maturity in cold seas. There is more opportunity for genetic mutations to be produced within a given time; hence the bewildering variety of tropical life. Yet in any species there are far fewer individuals than in the colder zones, where the mineral content of the water is richer, and there are no dense swarms of surface plankton, like the copepods of the Arctic. The pelagic, or free-swimming forms of the tropics live deeper than those of the colder regions, and so there is less food for large surface-feeders. In the tropics, therefore, the sea birds do not compare in abundance with the clouds of shearwaters, fulmars, auks, whalebirds, albatrosses, and other birds seen over far northern or far southern fishing grounds.

In the cold-water communities of the polar seas, fewer of the animals have swimming larvae. Generation after generation settle down near the parents, so that large areas of bottom may be covered with the descendants of a very few animals. In the Barents Sea a research vessel once brought up more than a ton of one of the siliceous sponges at a single haul, and enormous patches of a single species of annelid worm carpet the east coast of Spitsbergen. Copepods and swimming snails fill the surface waters of the cold seas, and lure the herring and the mackerel, the flocks of sea birds, the whales, and the seals.

In the tropics, then, sea life is intense, vivid, and infinitely varied. In cold seas life proceeds at a pace slowed by the icy water in which it exists, but the mineral richness of these waters (largely a result of seasonal overturn and consequent mixing) makes possible the enormous abundance of the forms that inhabit them. For a good many years it has been said categorically that the total productivity of the colder temperate and polar seas is far greater than the tropical. Now it is becoming plain that there are important exceptions to this statement. In certain tropical and subtropical waters, there are areas where the sheer abundance of life rivals the Grand Banks or the Barents Sea or any antarctic whaling ground. Perhaps the best examples are the Humboldt Current, off the west coast of South America, and the Benguela Current, off the west coast of Africa. In both currents, upwelling of cold, mineral-laden water from deeper layers of the sea provides the fertilizing elements to sustain the great food chains.

And wherever two currents meet, especially if they differ sharply in temperature or salinity, there are zones of great turbulence and unrest, with water sinking or rising up from the depths and with shifting eddies and foam lines at the surface. At such places the richness and abundance of marine life reveals itself most strikingly. This changing life, seen as his ship cut across the pathways of the great currents of the Pacific and the Atlantic, was described with vivid detail by S. C. Brooks:

'Within a few degrees of the equator, the scattered cumulus clouds become thicker and grayer, a confused swell makes up, rain squalls come and go, and birds appear. At first there is only a greater abundance of storm petrels, with here and there petrels of other kinds hunting along utterly indifferent to the ship, or small groups of tropic birds flying along with the ship, off to one side or high overhead. Then scattered groups of various petrels appear, and finally for an hour or two there are birds on every hand. If one is not too far from land, a few hundred miles perhaps, as in the case of the south equatorial drift north of the Marquesas, one may also see multitudes of sooty or crested terns. Occasionally one sees the grayish blue form of a shark gliding along, or a big purplish-brown hammerhead lazily twisting around as though trying to get a better view of the ship. Flying fish, while not so closely localized as the birds, are breaking the water every few seconds, and bewitch the beholder by their myriad sizes, shapes, and antics, and their bewildering patterns and shades of deep brown, opal blue, yellow and purple. Then the sun comes out again, the sea takes on its deep tropical blue, the birds become more and more scarce, and gradually, as the ship moves on, the ocean resumes its desert aspect.

'If it were daylight all the time, this same sequence might be seen in a more or less striking fashion twice or perhaps even three or four times. Inquiry soon reveals that this sequence marks the time of passing the edge of one of the great currents . . .

'In the North Atlantic ship lanes the same play is staged with different actors. Instead of the equatorial currents there are the Gulf Stream and its continuation, the North Atlantic Drift, and the Arctic Current; instead of confused swell and squalls of rain there are slicks and fogs. Tropic-birds are replaced by jaegers and skuas; and different species of the petrel group, usually here spoken of as shearwaters and fulmars, are flying or swimming about, often in great flocks . . . Here, too, perhaps, one sees less of sharks and more of porpoise racing with the cut-water or doggedly hurrying, school after school, toward some un-guessable objective. The flashing black and white of the young orcas, or the distant sudden spurt and lazy drift of a whale's spouting, lend life to the water, as do the antics of flying fish, distant though they be from their traditional home in the tropics . . . One may pass from the blue water of the Stream, with floating gulf weed (Sargassum), and perhaps here and there the iridescent float of a Portuguese man-of-war, into the gray-green water of the Arctic Current with its thousands of jelly fish, and in a few hours back again into the Stream. Each time, at the margin, one is likely to see the surface display of that abundance of life which has made the Grand Banks one of the great fisheries of the world.'*

The mid-ocean regions, bounded by the currents that sweep around the ocean basins, are in general the deserts of the sea. There are few birds and few surface-feeding fishes, and indeed there is little surface plankton to attract them. The life of these regions is largely confined to deep water. The Sargasso Sea is an exception, not matched in the anticyclonic centers of other ocean basins. It is so different from any other place on earth that it may well be considered a definite geographic region. A line drawn from the mouth of Chesapeake Bay to Gibraltar would skirt its northern border; another from Haiti to Dakar would mark its southern boundary. It lies all about Bermuda and extends more than halfway across the Atlantic, its entire area being roughly as large as the United States. The Sargasso, with all its legendary terrors for sailing ships, is a creation of the great currents of the North Atlantic that encircle it and bring into it the millions of tons of floating sargassum weed from which the place derives its name, and all the weird assemblage of animals that live in the weed.

The Sargasso is a place forgotten by the winds, undisturbed by the strong flow of waters that girdle it as with a river. Under the seldom-clouded skies, its waters are warm and heavy with salt. Separated widely from coastal rivers and from polar ice, there is no inflow of fresh water to dilute its saltiness; the only influx is of saline water from the adjacent currents, especially from the Gulf Stream or North Atlantic Current as it crosses from America to Europe. And with the little, inflowing streams of surface water come the plants and animals that for months or years have drifted in the Gulf Stream.

The sargassum weeds are brown algae belonging to several species.

* From *The Condor*, vol. 36, no. 5, Sept.-Oct. 1934, pp. 186-7.

Quantities of the weeds live attached to reefs or rocky outcroppings off the coasts of the West Indies and Florida. Many of the plants are torn away by storms, especially during the hurricane season. They are picked up by the Gulf Stream and are drifted northward. With the weeds go, as involuntary passengers, many small fishes, crabs, shrimps, and innumerable larvae of assorted species of marine creatures, whose home had been the coastal banks of sargassum weed.

Curious things happen to the animals that have ridden on the sargassum weed into a new home. Once they lived near the sea's edge, a few feet or a few fathoms below the surface, but never far above a firm bottom. They knew the rhythmic movements of waves and tides. They could leave the shelter of the weeds at will and creep or swim about over the bottom in search of food.

Now, in the middle of the ocean, they are in a new world. The bottom lies two or three miles below them. Those who are poor swimmers must cling to the weed, which now represents a life raft, supporting them above the abyss. Over the ages since their ancestors came here, some species have developed special organs of attachment, either for themselves or for their eggs, so that they may not sink into the cold, dark water far below. The flying fish make nests of the weed to contain their eggs, which bear an amazing resemblance to the sargassum floats or 'berries.'

Indeed, many of the little marine beasts of the weedy jungle seem to be playing an elaborate game of disguise in which each is camouflaged to hide it from the others. The Sargasso sea slug—a snail without a shell—has a soft, shapeless brown body spotted with dark-edged circles and fringed with flaps and folds of skin, so that as it creeps over the weed in search of prey it can scarcely be distinguished from the vegetation. One of the fiercest carnivores of the place, the sargassum fish Pterophryne, has copied with utmost fidelity the branching fronds of the weed, its golden berries, its rich brown color, and even the white dots of encrusting worm tubes. All these elaborate bits of mimicry are indications of the fierce internecine wars of the Sargasso jungles, which go on without quarter and without mercy for the weak or the unwary.

In the science of the sea there has been a long-standing controversy about the origin of the drifting weeds of the Sargasso Sea. Some have held that the supply is maintained by weeds recently torn away from coastal beds; others say that the rather limited sargassum fields of the West Indies and Florida cannot possibly supply the immense area of the Sargasso. They believe that we find here a self-perpetuating community of plants that have become adapted to life in the open sea, needing no roots or hold-fasts for attachment, and able to propagate vegetatively. Probably there is truth in both ideas. New plants do come in each year in small numbers, and now cover an immense area because of their very long life once they have reached this quiet central region of the Atlantic.

It takes about half a year for the plants torn from West Indian shores to reach the northern border of the Sargasso, perhaps several years for them to be carried into the inner parts of this area. Meanwhile, some have been swept onto the shores of North America by storms, others have been killed by cold during the passage from offshore New England across the Atlantic, where the Gulf Stream comes into contact with waters from the Arctic. For the plants that reach the calm of the Sargasso, there is virtual immortality. A. E. Parr of the American Museum has recently suggested that the individual plants may live, some for decades, others for centuries, according to their species. It might well be that some of the very weeds you would see if you visited the place today were seen by Columbus and his men. Here, in the heart of the Atlantic, the weed drifts endlessly, growing, reproducing vegetatively by a process of fragmentation. Apparently almost the only plants that die are the ones that drift into unfavorable conditions around the edges of the Sargasso or are picked up by outward-moving currents.

Such losses are balanced, or possibly a little more than balanced, by the annual addition of weeds from distant coasts. It must have taken eons of time to accumulate the present enormous quantities of weed, which Parr estimates as about 10 million tons. But this, of course, is distributed over so large an area that most of the Sargasso is open water. The dense fields of weeds waiting to entrap a vessel never existed except in the imagination of sailors, and the gloomy hulks of vessels doomed to endless drifting in the clinging weed are only the ghosts of things that never were.

alfred north whitehead

dialogues as recorded
by lucien price

Alfred North Whitehead (1861-1947), the great English philosopher and mathematician, was over sixty when he came to Harvard University in 1924 as professor of philosophy. He was already famous for his scientific and mathematical works, but at Harvard he flowered into a kind of universal savant, and in a series of works developing out of his lectures—the most famous of which is *Science and the Modern World* (1926)—he applied his profound originality of thought to social and even literary topics.

Whitehead's charm in conversation and his capacity for developing fresh points of view on the most unexpected topics are here displayed in the "dialogues" with Whitehead conducted by a Boston newspaperman, Lucien Price. The book from which they are taken, *Dialogues of Alfred North Whitehead* (1954), is one of the most engaging books of this sort that we have had in recent years. There have been many records of the conversation of great men—Dr. Johnson's as taken down by Boswell, Goethe's as taken down by Eckermann—and in many respects Whitehead is in the same class with these seminal minds. "Great conversation" of this kind depends on the ability of the great man to approach everything freshly, to communicate new lines of thought, to suggest unexpected factors and combinations. He cannot dogmatize, he must suggest; he must be an influence, not a commander; and perhaps above all, he must be shown to us (as Socrates was presented by Plato and Dr. Johnson by Boswell) as a figure of great charm, selflessly giving his life to an intellectual passion.

It is not only Whitehead's conversation that is so charming in these selections; it is also Lucien Price's staging of the old English professor in his American setting and in his talk. Ultimately, however, the talk charms us because of Whitehead's gentle detachment, because of his always evident ability to make us see the nature of things. A great philosopher like Whitehead, despite all rumors to the contrary, is distinguished by his common sense—or to put it in another way, by the fact that he can be thoughtful about everything and anything.

This interest in anything which philosophy can illuminate is really what philosophy means. It is typical of Whitehead, for example, that in one selection here he speaks of writing in an historical perspective that almost no one else in this book can capture. Unlike D. H. Lawrence, who in his essay, "Why The Novel Matters" (p. 81), sets the highest possible value on one kind of literature as the only repository of value, Whitehead says here that "Writing only brings out comparatively superficial experiences. Man has had it a relatively short time—shall we say about four thousand years? . . . Now for ages before that you had immense quantities of human experience accumulating in men's bodies. The body itself was, and still is, an immense experience . . . it far outweighs the scope of the written word."

This point of view is rare today. Whitehead as a writer had a singular capacity for going straight to the point (as if he were still a mathematician concerned with pure forms) and then finding words for these new concepts. Price tends to humanize and to familiarize Whitehead's speculative originality, and the result is that we get just enough of the man's patient, comprehensive and lucid intelligence to realize that, as is true with only the greatest figures, depth of thought and the nobility of character are alive in the same man.

It was two days after the undeclared attack by the Japanese on our *December 10, 1941*

fleet at Pearl Harbor. After dinner at the Faculty Club with Louis Lyons, who had just returned from Washington with a budget of not-very-cheerful news (he is curator of the Nieman Foundation at Harvard), I telephoned to ask the Whiteheads if I could come and call for half an hour.

By good luck no one else was there. Since our minds had been full of nothing else but Pearl Harbor for the past two days, there was a tacit agreement to keep off that subject.

Mr. Whitehead sat with an envelope containing the whole sheaf of my typescripts thus far. He wore his spectacles and dipped into the pages for some correction here and there.

"It is very unusual," he said, "to get authentic records of conversation from the past."

"None occur to me at the moment," I replied, "except Boswell's *Johnson,* and Eckermann's with Goethe, and Eckermann's are seldom general conversation so much as monologues by Goethe, valuable though they are."

"The novelists," said he, "don't help us much here, for they must always be getting on with their story; although occasionally a mediocre

DIALOGUES AS RECORDED BY LUCIEN PRICE: From *Dialogues of Alfred North Whitehead* ed. by Lucien Price, by permission of Little, Brown & Co. Copyright 1954 by Lucien Price.

novelist like Anthony Trollope does bring back exactly the kind of talk I heard amongst my father's friends when I was a small boy, the provincial clergy with an occasional dean and archbishop."

"Later than that," said she. "It was still going on when I arrived at your house. I remember it well."

"The letters of authors seldom give it to you," said he, "for they always know, whether they admit it or not, that their letters will be printed. What posterity really want to know is what people talked about when they got together, and there's very little of it. I should think these pages of yours might be more valuable a hundred years from now than they are now."

"Before they can be printed," said Mrs. Whitehead, smiling, "there will have to be a few 'demises,' including our own. We talk with you completely off guard."

"I know that, and therefore nobody has seen them except my sister, who typed them. She has said that they make an 'Introduction to Whitehead'—that abstract ideas which the average reader might find it difficult to get from your published works, here come out in casual conversation, quite easy to grasp. Most of the matter, it seems to me, is new. I don't remember much, if any, of it in your books."

"No, it is not in any of them. . . . I was trying to think of the name of that Roman banker to whom Cicero wrote letters, Atticus. There you have a semblance of conversation from the ancient world—at least the topics in which educated men were interested; and you get some of it in Plato, though of course not even the educated man of Athens was up to Plato all, or even most, of the time."

"Occasionally, though, you do get a bit in Plato that must have come straight out of life. I am thinking," said I, "of that comic anecdote in the *Laches* about a naval battle where a marine, fighting with a scythe-spear, stuck it into the rigging of the other vessel and couldn't pull it out again; and so as the two vessels wore past each other he ran along his own ship hanging to the end of the scythe handle till he had to let go. The crews of both ships knocked off fighting to laugh and applaud the act. His scythe-spear was waving in the air on the other vessel. It was evidently a yarn that went all over Athens."

"You get those homely touches in the earlier *Dialogues*," said Whitehead, pleasantly reminiscent, and cited one or two more, but he resumed:

"Writing only brings out comparatively superficial experiences. Man has had it a relatively short time—shall we say about four thousand years?—first in the form of chipping pieces of stone for the decrees and boasts of monarchs; then on papyrus. For only about three thousand years, or less, have men written down their thoughts; let us say from Homer's time. Now for ages before that you had immense quantities of human experience accumulating in men's bodies. The body itself was, and still is, an immense experience; the sheer harmony of its properly functioning organs gives us a flood of unconscious enjoyment. It is quite inarticulate, and doesn't need to be articulate. But in bulk, and perhaps in significance, it far outweighs the scope of the written word. That, by comparison, is most trivial."

"Even with the very greatest masters of the written word," I remarked, "Dante, Goethe, Aeschylus . . . one is left aware of how pale the statement is in comparison with the experience itself; Goethe can only suggest the misery and horror of the Gretchen tragedy; Dante's *Inferno* can be only a shadow of what he imagined; or the murder of Agamemnon, and the agony which came before it and after. What perhaps the written word *can* do is recall to us our own experiences, or give us intimations of experiences which we are likely to have. But since you say the written word is comparatively superficial, what is it that does come first as conscious experience, after these floods of sheer bodily self-enjoyment?"

"The moral values, I should say," he replied, after a longish pause for reflection. "Even dogs have them, in the form of simple-minded affection and loyalty."

"Even that 'subtle-soul'd psychologist,' William James," said I, "was immensely interested in the behavior of dogs and touched by their affection. He sometimes used them as illustrations when he was lecturing."

"Dogs do better than cats," observed Mrs. Whitehead. "Have you noticed how people divide in their likings, the one sort for cats, the other for dogs? Cats are selfish and self-centered," she added, leaving the inference to be drawn, but he supplied it, smiling:

"If a dog jumps up into your lap, it is because he is fond of you; but if a cat does the same thing, it is because your lap is warmer."

"Are you ever aware of human beings having a predominance of 'cat qualities' or of 'dog qualities'—canine personalities as distinct from feline personalities? Among the felines I would class the person who 'doesn't like people.' Precisely what does that phrase signify?" I asked.

"Self-centeredness," suggested Mrs. Whitehead, "and a nature that broods over 'never having had its due.' One, I should think, produces the other."

"After the moral values developing in early men (since we are speculating on origins), what," I asked, "would you say came next?"

"The aesthetic," said Whitehead. "When a nightingale sits up all night singing to his wife, and singing very well, too, you can't make me believe that aesthetic values of a very high order are not present."

"Tell him about our poor nightingale in Surrey," prompted Mrs. Whitehead. As he looked a little at a loss for the episode, she supplied the setting:

"We had a cottage in Surrey in the early spring, and, believe it or not, on the first of May, after the nightingales had arrived, there was a fall of snow. The poor dear caught cold, but went right on singing; and he never did get back to proper pitch all that summer."

"Yes," said Whitehead, smiling, "we had the experience of hearing a nightingale sing out of tune."

"I would rather hear a performance with heart in it," said I, "than an impeccable technique."

"And mind you," said Whitehead, "the same holds for personalities; they make their effect more by what they are than by anything they say. Even when you are using words effectively, they gain a great deal from the physical presence of the speaker; warmth, accent, emphasis, are emanations from body and spirit."

"Of course the very best writing is an attempt to convey in printed words some of those overtones which are sounded by the voice and emanated from the physical personality."

"Yes," said he, "and occasionally with surprising success. That is a property of the very best writing."

"In what you have just said, you 'countenance' me in a perception toward strangers of which I have been aware for years," said I. "It is not necessarily an intuitive perception of beauty or goodness, although it often takes that form; rather, it seems to be an unconscious emanation from the face and body and spirit of a total stranger which one's wireless somehow picks up and signals that, in one sort or another, there is interest and vitality in that person."

"There is nothing surprising in it to me," said Mrs. Whitehead. "We have just been reading Mrs. Margaret Deland's autobiography (it's there on the little stand at your elbow) and—did you know her?"

"No. I wasn't so fortunate. She was one of my mother's favorite contemporary authors. Didn't she and her husband stand a little aside from social Boston?"

"That is what I meant," said she, ". . . their taking into their home unmarried mothers, to save them from suicide and degradation and steady them by letting them reorganize their lives around the love for the child until they would get on their feet. *There* you have that sense of the interest and worth of a stranger even under a cloud." And she went on to speak of an experience she had had rescuing a beautiful girl, ". . . with that hectic glow of the consumptive. I drove to eleven places in London before I found one that would take her in. First, a Church of England home. 'We don't take second offenders' . . . and so on till we came to—what do you suppose?"

"The Salvation Army?"

"Right. We were received as long-awaited friends and taken in as if we were week-end guests. I asked how much it would cost to maintain her there. 'Nothing,' was the answer. 'If you can afford to pay, of course we shall expect you to do so, but only so that we can take in someone else.' The girl stayed there fifteen months of her own choice and was quite happy."

"What finally became of her?"

"She married a greengrocer, but being consumptive, she died young."

"How good a rating would you give the Salvation Army as Christians?" I asked Whitehead.

"Excellent," said he; "they take their Christianity simply."

"As simply as Francis of Assisi?"

"Oh, much more simply than he. They aren't nearly as encumbered with a bad theology."

"You *do* consider the theology a bad one, then?" I baited him.

"The trouble," said he, "comes from intellectualizing upon a religion. Jesus was not very intellectual; what he had was a profound insight. Humanity in the Eastern Mediterranean between 500 B.C. and 200 A.D. began to write down their intimate thoughts and a great age resulted. I am speaking of course of the exceptionally gifted men who wrote down their thoughts. Paul comes as quite a drop from Jesus, and although his followers included many estimable persons, their idea of God, to my mind, is the idea of the devil."

"How about Buddhism?"

"It is a religion of escapism. You retire into yourself and let externals go as they will. There is no determined resistance to evil. Buddhism is not associated with an advancing civilization."

July 27, 1943

After a busy and hot day in the city, it was a refreshment to go over to Cambridge and dine with the Whiteheads at six-thirty. No one else was there. A breeze had sprung up and was drawing pleasantly through their open windows five stories up and overlooking lawns and trees.

There had been joking about the dinner. Mrs. Whitehead had said:

"I'm not sure we can give you enough to eat. We ourselves dine on five butterflies and find it quite sufficient." I told her three butterflies would be enough for me in warm weather.

Professor Whitehead was in his study, so we went in there. Being dressed in white and without his coat (I was invited to shed mine, and did) he looked cool and uncommonly fit. Mussolini had just fallen, and I remembered that two summers before in this very room, Whitehead had said to me, "Machiavelli has written the rules of a short-term success, say from fifteen to twenty years." Also that there was an old Roman who had been legate of Upper Germany under the Emperor Domitian, and who though ill and racked by pain, clung to life "so that I can survive that brigand for one day at least." I said it was some satisfaction to have seen Mussolini go down.

"It is *good!*" said Whitehead.

" 'Brigand' for him!" said she. "He is a foul scorpion!"

I asked Mr. Whitehead if he was writing anything.

"No," said he, "but I have been reading what you have been writing."

At first I could not think what he meant, for I have written little daily journalism since April; then it occurred to me that the *Atlantic* for August, which was just out, contained my "Eye of the Hurricane."

There had been a conference between several headmasters of New England preparatory schools and members of the *Globe* editorial staff on the plight of liberal education in wartime as it affected boys below the conscription age of eighteen. The danger was of their education being abandoned, if not entirely to the military sciences, certainly to science at the expense of the humanities. There was no knowing how long the war would last, and if several successive crops of adolescents were denied their only access to general education and to those civilian habits of mind on which our society had depended for the transmission of its liberal traditions, our war might be a Mississippi steamboat race, stoking the furnaces with cargo and cabin furnishings to end with a victory won by a hulk empty of everything but its industrial boilers and military engines.

"You raise all of the right questions," said Whitehead, "but I could not agree with all of your conclusions. If in America, unlike England and some of the European continental countries, you undertake to give a good education not to a few but to all your people, the form it takes will need to be modified. I would be inclined to require universal education up to, say, the age of sixteen; then, between sixteen and nineteen, infuse it with the elements of practicality. After that there would need to be the widest possible access to opportunity for further study, both in institutions and outside of them, as by university extension lecturers, so that people could satisfy their curiosity about all sorts of subjects and find their special aptitudes. Their reading, too, would be enlivened by personal association with the lecturers. I would make some of this advanced education compulsory, and keep up the process of education to the age of ninety." This last he said smilingly; but all the same, he meant it. "Mind you," he resumed, "I doubt if these great universities with their high concentrations of specialized learning and societies of scholars so shut off from the daily lives of average people are altogether a good thing."

"The same idea has occurred to me, and repeatedly," said I. "My own phrase for it is that they grow intellectually dandified."

"There are numerous groups of professional people in this, in any city, whose instruction would be quite as valuable to the public as that of university lecturers," (we had been called to dinner and were walking out to the table) "and one of these groups are the newspaper men. They ought to lecture more than they do."

"One of the puzzles to me," (I had decided to come out with it) "is that after three centuries of Harvard's pumping supposedly and often really educated men into the city of Boston, more hasn't come of it. Oughtn't the city to have done much better than it has?"

"It *has* done well, uncommonly well," he replied with emphasis. "Will you name me an American city which has done better? Your professional people maintain, on the whole, a very high standard, especially the medical profession. What do you expect of it?"

"A steady blaze of genius, I suppose, is all that would satisfy me; and also, perhaps I know too much of the city's seamy side."

We sat at a beautiful little Duncan Phyfe mahogany table set for three, the late-afternoon yellow of sunshine filtering in from the west through the slightly tilted shutters of the Venetian blinds, which, a few minutes later, the sun having set behind the tower of Memorial Hall, Mrs. Whitehead raised, letting in the still strong and clear but paler light of the afterglow, which fell full upon the philosopher's serene face. The "five butterflies" for dinner was certainly understatement, for we dined, I thought, sumptuously (though Mrs. Whitehead said "simply"), with glasses of a chilled sauterne beside our plates. She explained how the fowl, the salad, and the apple pie had been done; the "sumptuousness" came from skillful touches in the cookery. She told me what they were, adding:

"Cookery is one of those tasks which are insupportable unless done for people one loves. But for that, I myself would be willing to live on bread and cheese and would vastly prefer to."

"People are unlikely to get good food, no matter how many cooks they have, or how much they pay for them," said Whitehead, "unless the cooks love the people for whom they cook."

I said the two best cooks I had ever known, one a Yorkshire woman, the other Irish, did come exactly in that classification, in addition to which they were both devout, one a Protestant, the other Catholic.

"Cooking," replied Whitehead demurely, "is one of those arts which most requires to be done by persons of religious nature."

"And a good cook," added his wife, "cooks to the glory of God."

We lingered at the table in the fading afterglow. By now the breeze which drew in at the large window was deliciously cool and refreshing. In that tranquil light it was one of those summer evenings which seem like a pleasant eternity.

We shifted scene to the living room. Whitehead was saying that his leaving Cambridge at fifty and going up to London was one of the determinants in his development: "It plunged me into the *practicalities* of education. At Cambridge I had had experience in political work and organization, but the actualities of life in London were much broader." He told many of the things he had to do and how they carried him amongst all classes. "Our polytechnical schools," said he, "are a specimen of the kind of thing I meant when earlier in the evening we were discussing universal education. I know the system of popular education in London has been criticized as inadequate, but from close association with it, I think it is admirable. It gives all sorts of people access to studies useful to them in practical life and also in the arts; and you find people of all classes and all ages haunting them."

"As showing their 'classlessness,'" said Mrs. Whitehead, "a young man we knew, who was enormously wealthy, and had had the best instruction in painting on the Continent that money could buy, found on coming home the best instruction he had found anywhere was in one of these London polytechnics."

"I am hearing, again, a partial explanation of something which has puzzled me about you two ever since I have known you. Pickled in donnish society though you have been pretty much all your lives, you are the least donnish of dons."

"In what way do you notice it?" asked Mrs. Whitehead.

"Understanding of common life. Restrict the case to your sympathy with the working class: that is something which experience had taught me not to take for granted with the average college professor, at Harvard or anywhere else. Here and there a specialist? Yes, in sociology perhaps. They have limbered up somewhat in the past few years, possibly because their own security has been affected."

"One of the great fallacies of American thinking," said Whitehead, "is that human worth is constituted by a particular set of aptitudes which lead to economic advancement. This is not true at all. Two thirds of the people who can make money are mediocre; and at least one half of them are morally at a low level. As a whole, they are vastly inferior to other types who are not animated by the economic motives; I mean the artists, and teachers, and professional people who do work which they love for its own sake and earn about enough to get along on. This habitual elevation of the type of ability that leads to economic advancement is one of the worst mistakes in your American thinking and needs to be unceasingly corrected by people who speak to the public, as you do."

Some of it, I said, was a hangover from our pioneering days when the subduing of this continent did take courage and ability.

"Yes," said Mrs. Whitehead, "but even there, a fine distinction must be drawn. The swollen fortunes were seldom made by the pioneers; they were made by the men who came after."

"The mischief of elevating the type that has aptitude for economic advancement," said Whitehead, "is that it denies the superior forms of aptitude which exist in quite humble people. Who shall say that to live kindly and graciously and meet one's problems bravely from day to day is not a great art, or that those who can do it are not great artists? Aesthetics are understood in too restricted a sense. People who can live beautifully in humble environments have a most advanced understanding of aesthetics—compared with which the ability to paint pictures on canvas," (he did so in dumb show) "delightful as that may be, is a rudimentary form."

"You confirm me in a glow I often feel when meeting my neighbors on the village street, the carpenter, the postman, the lobster fisherman—their goodness and geniality warm me to my marrow, and I smile inwardly, thinking, 'Life comes before literature.' "

"Fifty thousand years ago," said Whitehead, "or five hundred thousand—I don't know how long—when man, perhaps suddenly, took a turn of development which produced his faculty of enjoyment, he produced something whose possibilities are infinite. A human being— you, Evelyn, I—has certain capacities for enjoyment developed, partly because inherent, partly by training. There is a good deal of luck in it. You, for example, besides your enjoyment of literature have the faculty and training for the enjoyment of music. Some have the faculty for enjoying mathematics, but it is latent, and has to be brought out by study. We aren't *born* with the faculty of enjoying mathematics. Others, though born with the latent faculty of enjoying music, either as listeners or as performers, aren't *born* as either performers or highly intelligent listeners; both must be developed. The range of our faculties for enjoyment is enormous and has been explored hardly beyond a fringe. Even the insects must have it, though I don't know enough about them to surmise what their forms of enjoyment are. . . . Now the singular part is that man, in his social systems, has so far given so little scope to the development of our faculties of enjoyment. There have been various fortunate periods. Turbulent as the Italian cities in the Renaissance were, they did occasionally have rulers with acute perceptions for various and new forms of human enjoyment, and the rulers of certain small German principalities in the late eighteenth and early nineteenth centuries, too, were successful in fostering certain forms, principally music and the theatre. Small states, I think, do it better than large ones. The small German states were able to produce excellent provincial opera throughout the nineteenth century, while the French Government, though it maintained an excellent theatre, tended to rigidity of classicism. There was little experiment, and ideas always require adventure."

"That 'time lag' between the individual and his social system throws me back upon your remark of last year about the relationship between man's infinite possibilities, and the limitations of finite form. States concern themselves with the organization of material existence, which is a very finite thing. You may remember how once, when you lived out in the Blue Hills, we talked about the fact that there has never been, except incidentally, a Culture State, only Power States with a little creativity on the side; and you remarked that you doubted whether the state was best competent to foster the creative arts."

"When big states attempt it," said he, "they tend to formularize men's faculties of enjoyment and creativity. That tends toward rigidity. I doubt if state supervision would be good for the arts in America. The vitality of thought is in adventure. That is what I have been saying all my life, and I have said little else. Ideas won't keep. Something must be done about them. The idea must constantly be seen in some new aspect. Some element of novelty must be brought into it freshly from time to time; and when that stops, it does. The meaning of life is adventure."

"It is an adventure to be born," said Mrs. Whitehead, gravely, "and a very dangerous one."

She spoke standing. Behind her was the wall tinted its peculiar shade just off black; she wore a black gown with white embroidery at the throat; her hair is white, and there in the tranquil summer twilight her aspect was that of a striking portrait canvas by some eminent painter. The glimpse was only instantaneous, the moment of pause required to deliver her remark, then she turned away to go into the dining room.

"How about the adventurers," I asked, "whose adventures are, for all their good will, mistaken and mischievous?"

"They are damned fools," said Whitehead emphatically. "That is where learning comes in. Adventurers must use their reason and must know the past, so as not to go on repeating the mistakes of history. One of my anxieties about this war has been lest a rigid system be imposed on mankind and that fragile quality, his capacity for novel ideas, for novel aspects of old ideas, be frozen and he go on century after century, growing duller, more formularized until he and his society reach the static level of the insects. Asia has known something of this sort. Good things no doubt were being said in China a thousand years ago, but for at least two thousand years, each century was a little less interesting than the century before; and when people want to tell me what civilization owes to India they have to start back at about 500 B.C. You may have wondered at my coolness, not to John Dewey personally, whom I respect as a man and certain aspects of whose work I admire, but to his thought. The reason is that the emphasis of his thought is on security. But the vitality of man's mind is in adventure. The Egyptians in 500 B.C. obviously had an enormous history behind them, yet there was no adventure in it. Contrast with it the little they have bequeathed to Western man with the much in aesthetics and morals that we have inherited from the Greeks and the Hebrews."

"I was doing so as you spoke. That old Egyptian priest in Plato's story was unconsciously recognizing some contrast of the sort when he told Solon, 'You Hellenes are never anything but boys. . . . In mind you are all young.'—The boy is adventurous."

"My hope is," replied Whitehead, "that out of this war, America will take the leadership of humanity. America, as I see it, is the only hope. There is adventure here, and a welcome for novelty. You could do for the future of humanity what Greece and Judaea did for the modern world as against Asia and Europe. The Jews had certain moral ideas but these would not have come to much without the Greeks."

"What would you say was the contribution of the Greeks?"

"The aesthetic view of life."

"I noticed a moment ago when you used those two words, 'aesthetics' and 'morals,' in connection with Hellas and Israel, that 'aesthetics' came first."

"Properly so," said he.

"Beauty is 'a wider and more fundamental notion than truth'?"

"Yes. Apart from beauty, truth is neither good nor bad."

"That was how the Puritans tumbled overboard," said Mrs Whitehead, who had returned during the discussion. "They cast out beauty.

They began well, by believing they were made in the image of God. They ended by making God in their own image."

"And how fast such cream can curdle: it is less than a century from the Plymouth Colony and William Bradford to Cotton Mather."

"The idea," said Whitehead, "was losing its vitality. It had ceased to adventure. The inheritors of it inherit the idea without inheriting the fervor. Their progenitors would have gone to the stake for it, and some of them did. Perhaps there was no longer any stake for its inheritors to go to; they knew how strongly their forebears believed, felt that they ought to feel the old fervor and tried to or pretended to, and so gave the impression of being hypocrites."

"Your own parents," Mrs. Whitehead reminded him, "didn't believe as strongly as they thought they did."

"They *thought* they still believed strongly," he took it up, "and *their* parents had been strong believers; but by the time mine came along, the idea had cooled off to a point where, today, the attitude of my parents might have been regarded as hypocritical. Mind you, I don't say it was. They were quite sincere. Only, the attitude had changed, and they represented their religion to us chiefly as a means of keeping order—order in the family and order in society. But that is something quite different from religious conviction."

"One sees a similar change in the Cathedral of Strassburg," I remarked. "Nobody had prepared me for it and it was a great surprise. The nave and aisles are late Gothic, light and graceful in its elegant logical perfection; the older parts at the chancel end are Romanesque from an age of strong belief, and their effect is so powerful that they dim the force of the nave, beautiful though it is."

"Architecture," said Whitehead, "is a good illustration of the life cycle in adventures of ideas. It happens that it is one of the art-forms in which I am most interested. Let me take English Gothic. You start with early Norman, Romanesque, and go on century by century through, roughly, the four successive styles to the fifteenth century when it comes to an end. What was happening in those four successive centuries was that the new aspects of the idea were being discovered and developed; successive elements of novelty were being introduced and explored—the abundant fenestration, the height of the piers, beauty of tracery, possibilities of novel aspect had been used up, the Gothic idea comes to a full stop, and you get a complete break. They go back to the architecture of Greece and Rome, adapt it to the changed world of the Renaissance, and you get, instead of a Gothic abbey, St. Paul's. But the classic style of ancient architecture brought into the modern world has, I think, this peculiarity: although it does lend itself admirably to a host of purposes and can generally, in the hands of a good craftsman, be made to look well, it lacks that . . . that final something . . . What shall I call it? . . ."

"Transcendence," suggested Mrs. Whitehead.

"Yes," he accepted the word, "that final 'transcendence.' I mean that it doesn't produce the building which I would take a four-hour railway journey to see. A new material, as well as a new way of looking at the idea, may give it the happy turn," he resumed, "as when your early New England settlers brought the English house to these shores but had to build it of wood. It was the same style but with fresh and delightful modifications. With your stone houses I doubt if you have done so well. . . ."

"We hardly got round to them until the 1840's and 1850's, 'Gothic revival'; and you know how short a time that lasted. . . ."

"I don't think they are considered very successful."

"It was an attempt to return to the Gothic style without the Gothic tradition."

"The greatness of Lawrence Lowell included this perception of the difficulty in keeping an idea vital," Whitehead suddenly opened his own idea into a novel aspect, "and this form of his greatness is not yet generally appreciated. He had seen that what is wanted is a certain period of systematized instruction for young men, then that they be allowed to explore for themselves, with or without professional guidance, various areas of learning or achievement. To this he saw the need of adding the oldest form of entertainment and instruction known to the human race; namely, conversation. If you will notice, his foundation of the Junior Fellows is on these principles. They are chosen as nearly as possible for merit from all over this continent and their pursuits are as varied as the arts and sciences. They have had a certain amount of systematized training and some achievement to their credit. Their association is so organized that they meet to dine and spend an evening together at least once a week in conversation with one another and with a wide variety of notable guests drawn from all the professions. There is no 'departmentalism.' The men studying literature are at elbows with men studying biology or mathematics. In the Harvard faculty itself I notice a good deal of departmentalism. You would think the men in one department had nothing to learn from their colleagues in another, or else that"—his eyes twinkled roguishly —"they were protecting themselves from contamination. I consider it a monstrous presumption that university lecturers should think themselves competent to go on talking year after year to young men, students, while holding themselves aloof from the opportunity of learning from eager youth, which is one of the most valuable things on earth. . . ."

"Lecturers," observed Mrs. Whitehead, "are licensed to brag!"

"When you use the expression, 'eager youth' as 'one of the most valuable things on earth,' will you explain more explicitly what you mean by it?"

"I mean—" he hesitated, pondering his definition—"the glow of a young man . . . (I'm afraid I shall have to use a portentous expression, but it isn't portentously meant) . . . I mean the glow of a young man who has just discovered some great work of literature. It isn't the book which he has discovered which is so important; it is his glow over it. There you have the sense of adventure, of newness, the old idea seen freshly in some new aspect. It is this which university instructors should be on the watch for, and should respect wherever it appears, instead of being a trifle irritated at overeager young men."

"Coming as I did from the Midwest, I had the feeling that in New England enthusiasm was bad form. Harvey Cushing, who came from out there, had noticed it and said that, for himself, the resistance of inert mind and matter to any innovation, surgical or other, was so heavy that a man who had (as he had) anything new and difficult to accomplish must have as great enthusiasm as a flywheel to carry the saw of his idea through knots in the log."

"Coming from England to New England, as we did," said Mrs. Whitehead, "we experienced not a drop in temperature, as you did coming from the Midwest, but a rise. After the social climate of England, that of New England seemed a blast from a furnace."

"New England's intellect," I said, "(a good many strangers have noticed it) often makes a better first impression than New England's heart."

"Had it occurred to you," asked Mrs. Whitehead, "that New Englanders may be timid?"

"No. It hadn't. But they often are, the best of them. And if I hadn't liked them, why did I stay? I admire the people, and the scenery, and the mellowed culture, and the libraries, and the orchestra, and I can hardly remember having heard good conversation among young men until I came here."

"There is a club in Cambridge," said Whitehead, "to which I had access as a young man. Tennyson and his friend Hallam, the one who died young, were among its founders. They called themselves 'the Apostles,' the members are undergraduates and when you are graduated you 'take wings' and become an 'Angel.' The new members are chosen entirely by undergraduates and on the ground that they are likely to prove interesting. At each meeting—they were on Saturday nights—some member presents a paper setting forth ideas for discussion. This takes about twenty minutes. The members have previously drawn lots for the order of their speaking after the initial presentation of ideas. Each one is expected, when his turn comes, to stand on the hearth and say whatever is in his mind. The understanding is that nothing of what is said here shall ever be repeated outside as having come from any member. In fact, no one is supposed to know who the members are, though, as a matter of fact, they are sometimes guessed. Quite a number of distinguished men have come through the 'Apostles,' and once a year they have a dinner in London which the 'Angels' attend. The chairman, who sits at the head of the table, is an 'Angel,' and the latest-chosen 'Apostle,' who sits at the other end of the table, is vice-chairman. Members of Cambridge colleges are not permitted to enter another college after ten o'clock, but we used to congregate just before ten o'clock, our number being restricted to twelve, and our conversations went on into the small hours. The quality of it held up surprisingly well—at least until the war."

Twilight had deepened into dusk and dusk to darkness. The room was so cool and pleasant with the night breeze coming in at windows that we had continued sitting in the darkness, which seemed, if anything, to promote conversation. We continued speaking from the restful shadows.

"Mr. Lowell's foundation of the Junior Fellows," said Mrs. Whitehead, "received mention by the newspapers of course, but not in anything like the proportion that its importance to the future deserved. What *is* 'news'? If Mrs. Lowell had run away with the chauffeur, or if Mr. Lowell had been carrying on an affair with the housemaid, the newspapers would not have so restricted their space as they did about the Junior Fellows."

"You are asking," said I, "who is to blame. It depends on whom you ask. If you ask me, I think the necessity of a newspaper's paying its way as an article of commerce is at the bottom of it. What is needed is a Hippocratic Oath for journalists. What would a university be like, if it had to live by its fees?"

"It wouldn't exist," said Whitehead.

"In southern England," Mrs. Whitehead took it up, "there used to be very little music. The people there were supposed to be congenitally unmusical. Of late, since the B.B.C. has been broadcasting only good music, they have grown very fond of music, have started groups of village musicians, and want only the best music themselves. In England each owner of a radio set has to pay a small tax: that supports the

B.B.C. and no advertisements are allowed on the air. The damnable heresy is that people don't want the best. On that plea they are given whatever debased matter may be expected to sell and the tendency of this is steadily downward."

"Having combated that damnable heresy inside a newspaper office for more than half a lifetime and proved that it *is* a heresy—not without, it is only fair to say, some collaboration from its management and its owners—I am still astonished when I see decent-looking people in the public vehicles reading small type under the most blatantly vulgar headlines. They don't look like people who would care for that kind of thing."

Mrs. Whitehead suggested, "They may finally succumb and learn to like the poison after they have been sufficiently tainted. . . ."

"On the credit side," said Whitehead, "I notice that a large part of what is written for the serious columns of your newspapers is to set before the readers their responsibility for maintaining the social system. The aspects of this are various, but that in the end is what it all comes to: the readers are being reminded that the preservation of a social system depends on them. Now responsibility for a social system is the groundwork of civilization. Without a society in which life and property are to some extent secure, existence can continue only at the lowest levels—you cannot have a good life for those you love, nor can you devote your energies to activity on the higher level. Consequently, a sense of responsibility for the continuance of a social system is basic to any morality. Now this form of responsibility is almost entirely absent from Christianity. Jesus hardly mentions it, except for one or two remarks."

"And one of these," said Mrs. Whitehead, " 'Render unto Caesar,' was evasive."

"There were historical reasons for this lack, I grant you," he continued. "The Hebrews had no independent state to govern, and a man cannot be blamed for failing to consider what there was in his period no occasion for considering. He said what an able thinker might be expected to say. His historical situation did not elicit a code of ethics concerned with responsibility for a social system; but the absence of such responsibility has been a characteristic of the Jews for centuries. That is one reason for their unpopularity. You may say that the way they have been treated in many of the countries of their sojourn has not permitted such participation, and I quite agree. But that absence has involved Christianity in an almost perpetual self-contradiction. It held that the externals of life are not worth caring about and at the same time insisted on types of moral conduct which cannot be observed

—without perishing—unless the externals of life are sufficiently well organized. A society run on strictly Christian principles could not survive at all."

"That kept appearing," I remarked, "in the social criticism of the nineteenth century, especially among the Russians, like Tolstoy and Kropotkin; Christian anarchist, and philosophical anarchist. But in the other European (and American) nineteenth-century social critics, one keeps encountering this sense of puzzled exasperation: 'You call yourselves Christians and your society Christendom; then why don't you . . . ?' What has appeared now, which hadn't then, is that the comparative social stability of the century from 1815 to 1914 had deluded even many of the ablest thinkers into regarding a stable social system as an assured thing."

"It was not until the unification of the modern world by scientific techniques," he replied, "that people realized that social stability would have to be one of the prerequisites of ethical behavior. This has been forced on us by the types of men in control of the state machinery in certain countries, who have obliged us to fight them in order to be able to maintain any of the social decencies."

"Yet the moment we have admitted that," I raised the question, "what sort of morality do we want a stable social system to maintain? A few evenings ago I was startled by hearing an author, a man I very much respect, refer to someone, in a book or a public speech, as 'extolling all the bourgeois virtues.' Now I have heard the bourgeois criticized sharply enough and know some of the grounds for that criticism. But couldn't our world do with a few bourgeois virtues?"

"One of their virtues," said Whitehead, "is paying their debts. And a robust virtue it is. You can't have a stable society without it."

The clock in Memorial Hall had struck ten. Knowing that I had a train to catch, Mrs. Whitehead considerately rose and switched on a light. We had been sitting in the darkness for nearly an hour past.

Mr. Whitehead went out with me to the elevator. "I always feel," said he, "that I have two duties to perform with a parting guest: one, to see that he doesn't forget anything that is his; the other, to see that he doesn't take anything that is mine."

d. h. lawrence

---

why the novel matters

D. H. Lawrence (1885-1930) has been called the "last genius" in English letters. Whatever one may think of this statement, it is a fact that although his books have been ridiculed and some of them even suppressed, he has remained a commanding influence on many readers who, even when they don't agree with his message, are affected by the moral intensity and lyrical beauty of his writing. As the most casual reading of "Why The Novel Matters" will show, Lawrence writes on even an "esthetic" subject like the novel with the passion of the ancient prophets. It is not only the novel that matters (if indeed it is the *novel* as a literary form that really matters so much to him); it is the holiness of life itself, life unencumbered by absolutes, life which—as Lawrence thinks—can be expressed in its freedom and fullness only by the novel.

Yet Lawrence's enthusiasm for the novel needs a little historical background. It is a fact that the novel is the most modern of all the great literary forms; and not only is it the most widely read form, but "telling a story" in prose has for some time seemed to many great writers the only possible way of representing the great variety of modern experience—without pointing a moral at the reader. And it is true that such great artists in the novel as Dickens, Dostoevsky, Tolstoy, Balzac; twentieth-century novelists such as James Joyce, Marcel Proust (and D. H. Lawrence himself), have been able to convey the great power and depth of human experience without forcing any explicit meaning on the reader. In the eyes of many novelists, only the novel as a form can represent life-for-it's-own-sake, life in its perhaps chaotic fullness. The novel as a form has significantly been compared to a road or a river carrying life along.

This is Lawrence's thesis. But the real value of his essay is that it brings home to us, on the irresistible moral energy of Lawrence's style, a kind of writing that for sheer naturalness and spontaneity no one has equalled in our time. Lawrence's particular skill as a writer was this uncanny ability to capture in prose the *easy* and casual rhythms of a man talking. Lawrence writes as if he were talking only to you—and talking as the spirit moves him, talking brilliantly, sharply, with the particular emphasis of a man trying to convince *you*—and looking you straight in the face as he talks.

But equally important in Lawrence's essay is an imagery that is always affirmative, positive, electrically alive. Lawrence thinks naturally in terms of upsurge, greenness, growing, light. And it is because of this extraordinary charge of spiritual vitality in his work that his style pulses with the excitement of a man who finds good everything that is natural, and who makes us feel renewed value just in the fact that we are alive.

To identify this with the novel as a form may open up more questions than it answers. But there can be no question of the effectiveness of Lawrence's style. He phrases his sentences with the ease of a man taking full breath; the sentences ripple along as if he found writing as natural as breathing; as if it *were* a form of breathing:

"The novel is the one bright book of life. Books are not life. They are only tremulations on the ether. But the novel as a tremulation can make the whole man alive tremble. . . . only in the novel are *all* things given full play, or at least, they may be given full play, when we realize that life itself, and not inert safety, is the reason for living. For out of the full play of all things emerges the only thing that is anything, the wholeness of a man, the wholeness of a woman, man alive, and live woman."

Look at that last phrase again and ask yourself why, coming when it does after *man alive,* the next phrase avoids the expected parallelism of *woman alive* and reverses it. The greatest of Lawrence's many skills was his knowledge of how a phrase should *sound.*

We have curious ideas of ourselves. We think of ourselves as a body with a spirit in it, or a body with a soul in it, or a body with a mind in it. *Mens sana in corpore sano.* The years drink up the wine, and at last throw the bottle away, the body, of course, being the bottle.

It is a funny sort of superstition. Why should I look at my hand, as it so cleverly writes these words, and decide that it is a mere nothing compared to the mind that directs it? Is there really any huge difference between my hand and my brain? Or my mind? My hand is alive, it flickers with a life of its own. It meets all the strange universe in touch, and learns a vast number of things, and knows a vast number of things. My hand, as it writes these words, slips gaily along, jumps like a grass-hopper to dot an *i,* feels the table rather cold, gets a little bored if I write too long, has its own rudiments of thought, and is just as much *me* as is my brain, my mind, or my soul. Why should I imagine that there is a *me* which is more *me* than my hand is? Since my hand is absolutely alive, me alive.

Whereas, of course, as far as I am concerned, my pen isn't alive at all.

WHY THE NOVEL MATTERS: From *Phoenix* by D. H. Lawrence. Copyright 1936 by Frieda Lawrence. Reprinted by permission of The Viking Press, Inc.

My pen *isn't me* alive. Me alive ends at my finger-tips.

Whatever is me alive is me. Every tiny bit of my hands is alive, every little freckle and hair and fold of skin. And whatever is me alive is me. Only my finger-nails, those ten little weapons between me and an inanimate universe, they cross the mysterious Rubicon between me alive and things like my pen, which are not alive, in my own sense.

So, seeing my hand is all alive, and me alive, wherein is it just a bottle, or a jug, or a tin can, or a vessel of clay, or any of the rest of that nonsense? True, if I cut it it will bleed, like a can of cherries. But then the skin that is cut, and the veins that bleed, and the bones that should never be seen, they are all just as alive as the blood that flows. So the tin can business, or vessel of clay, is just bunk.

And that's what you learn, when you're a novelist. And that's what you are very liable *not* to know, if you're a parson, or a philosopher, or a scientist, or a stupid person. If you're a parson, you talk about souls in heaven. If you're a novelist, you know that paradise is in the palm of your hand, and on the end of your nose, because both are alive; and alive, and man alive, which is more than you can say, for certain, of paradise. Paradise is after life, and I for one am not keen on anything that is *after* life. If you are a philosopher, you talk about infinity, and the pure spirit which knows all things. But if you pick up a novel, you realize immediately that infinity is just a handle to this self-same jug of a body of mine; while as for knowing, if I find my finger in the fire, I know that fire burns, with a knowledge so emphatic and vital, it leaves Nirvana merely a conjecture. Oh, yes, my body, me alive, *knows,* and knows intensely. And as for the sum of all knowledge, it can't be anything more than an accumulation of all the things I know in the body, and you, dear reader, know in the body.

These damned philosophers, they talk as if they suddenly went off in steam, and were then much more important than they are when they're in their shirts. It is nonsense. Every man, philosopher included, ends in his own finger-tips. That's the end of his man alive. As for the words and thoughts and sighs and aspirations that fly from him, they are so many tremulations in the ether, and not alive at all. But if the tremulations reach another man alive, he may receive them into his life, and his life may take on a new color, like a chameleon creeping from a brown rock on to a green leaf. All very well and good. It still doesn't alter the fact that the so-called spirit, the message or teaching of the philosopher or the saint, isn't alive at all, but just a tremulation upon the ether, like a radio message. All this spirit stuff is just tremulations upon the ether. If you, as man alive, quiver from the tremulation of the ether into new life, that is because you are man alive, and you take sustenance and stimulation into your alive man in a myriad ways. But to say that the message, or the spirit which is communicated to you, is more important than your living body, is nonsense. You might as well say that the potato at dinner was more important.

Nothing is important but life. And for myself, I can absolutely see life nowhere but in the living. Life with a capital L is only man alive. Even a cabbage in the rain is cabbage alive. All things that are alive are amazing. And all things that are dead are subsidiary to the living. Better a live dog than a dead lion. But better a live lion than a live dog. *C'est la vie!*

It seems impossible to get a saint, or a philosopher, or a scientist, to stick to this simple truth. They are all, in a sense, renegades. The saint wishes to offer himself up as spiritual food for the multitude. Even Francis of Assisi turns himself into a sort of angel-cake, of which anyone may take a slice. But an angel-cake is rather less than man alive. And poor St. Francis might well apologize to his body, when he is dying: "Oh, pardon me, my body, the wrong I did you through the years!" It was no wafer, for others to eat.

The philosopher, on the other hand, because he can think, decides that nothing but thoughts matter. It is as if a rabbit, because he can make little pills, should decided that nothing but little pills matter. As for the scientist, he has absolutely no use for me so long as I am man alive. To the scientist, I am dead. He puts under the microscope a bit of dead me, and calls it me. He takes me to pieces, and says first one piece, and then another piece, is me. My heart, my liver, my stomach have all been scientifically me, according to the scientist; and nowadays I am either a brain, or nerves, or glands, or something more up-to-date in the tissue line.

Now I absolutely flatly deny that I am a soul, or a body, or a mind, or an intelligence, or a brain, or nervous system, or a bunch of glands, or any of the rest of these bits of me. The whole is greater than the part. And therefore, I, who am man alive, am greater than my soul, or spirit, or body, or mind, or consciousness, or anything else that is merely a part of me. I am a man, and alive. I am man alive, and as long as I can, I intend to go on being man alive.

For this reason I am a novelist. And being a novelist, I consider myself superior to the saint, the scientist, the philosopher, and the poet, who are all great masters of different bits of man alive, but never get the whole hog.

The novel is the one bright book of life. Books are not life. They are only tremulations on the ether. But the novel as a tremulation can make the whole man alive tremble. Which is more than poetry, philosophy, science, or any other book-tremulation can do.

The novel is the book of life. In this sense, the Bible is a great con-fused novel. You may say, it is about God. But it is really about man alive. Adam, Eve, Sarai, Abraham, Isaac, Jacob, Samuel, David, Bath-Sheba, Ruth, Esther, Solomon, Job, Isaiah, Jesus, Mark, Judas, Paul, Peter: what is it but man alive, from start to finish? Man alive, not mere bits. Even the Lord is another man alive, in a burning bush, throwing the tablets of stone at Moses's head.

I do hope you begin to get my idea, why the novel is supremely im-portant, as a tremulation on the ether. Plato makes the perfect ideal being tremble in me. But that's only a bit of me. Perfection is only a bit, in the strange make-up of man alive. The Sermon on the Mount makes the selfless spirit of me quiver. But that, too, is only a bit of me. The Ten Commandments set the old Adam shivering in me, warning me that I am a thief and a murderer, unless I watch it. But even the old Adam is only a bit of me.

I very much like all these bits of me to be set trembling with life and the wisdom of life. But I do ask that the whole of me shall tremble in its wholeness, some time or other.

And this, of course, must happen in me, living.

But as far as it can happen from a communication, it can only hap-pen when a whole novel communicates itself to me. The Bible—but *all* the Bible—and Homer, and Shakespeare: these are the supreme old novels. These are all things to all men. Which means that in their wholeness they affect the whole man alive, which is the man himself, beyond any part of him. They set the whole tree trembling with a new access of life, they do not just stimulate growth in one direction.

I don't want to grow in any one direction any more. And, if I can help it, I don't want to stimulate anybody else into some particular di-rection. A particular direction ends in a *cul-de-sac*. We're in a *cul-de-sac* at present.

I don't believe in any dazzling revelation, or in any supreme Word. "The grass withereth, the flower fadeth, but the Word of the Lord shall stand for ever." That's the kind of stuff we've drugged ourselves with. As a matter of fact, the grass withereth, but comes up all the greener for that reason, after the rains. The flower fadeth, and therefore the bud opens. But the Word of the Lord, being man-uttered and a mere vibration on the ether, becomes staler and staler, more and more bor-ing, till at last we turn a deaf ear and it ceases to exist, far more finally than any withered grass. It is grass that renews its youth like the eagle, not any Word.

We should ask for no absolutes, or absolute. Once and for all and for ever, let us have done with the ugly imperialism of any absolute. There is no absolute good, there is nothing absolutely right. All things flow and change, and even change is not absolute. The whole is a strange assembly of apparently incongruous parts, slipping past one another.

Me, man alive, I am a very curious assembly of incongruous parts. My yea! of to-day is oddly different from my yea! of yesterday. My tears of to-morrow will have nothing to do with my tears of a year ago. If the one I love remains unchanged and unchanging, I shall cease to love her. It is only because she changes and startles me into change and defies my inertia, and is herself staggered in her inertia by my changing, that I can continue to love her. If she stayed put, I might as well love the pepper-pot.

In all this change, I maintain a certain integrity. But woe betide me if I try to put my finger on it. If I say of myself, I am this, I am that!— then, if I stick to it, I turn into a stupid fixed thing like a lamp-post. I shall never know wherein lies my integrity, my individuality, my me. I *can* never know it. It is useless to talk about my ego. That only means that I have made up an *idea* of myself, and that I am trying to cut myself out to pattern. Which is no good. You can cut your cloth to fit your coat, but you can't clip bits off your living body, to trim it down to your idea. True, you can put yourself into ideal corsets. But even in ideal corsets, fashions change.

Let us learn from the novel. In the novel, the characters can do nothing but *live*. If they keep on being good, according to pattern, or bad, according to pattern, or even volatile, according to pattern, they cease to live, and the novel falls dead. A character in a novel has got to live, or it is nothing.

We, likewise, in life have got to live, or we are nothing.

What we mean by living is, of course, just as indescribable as what we mean by *being*. Men get ideas into their heads, of what they mean by Life, and they proceed to cut life out to pattern. Sometimes they go into the desert to seek God, sometimes they go into the desert to seek cash, sometimes it is wine, woman, and song, and again it is water, political reform, and votes. You never know what it will be next: from killing your neighbour with hideous bombs and gas that tears the lungs, to supporting a Foundlings' Home and preaching infinite Love, and being co-respondent in a divorce.

In all this wild welter, we need some sort of guide. It's no good inventing Thou Shalt Nots!

What then? Turn truly, honorably to the novel, and see wherein you are man alive, and wherein you are dead man in life. You may love a woman as man alive, and you may be making love to a woman as sheer dead man in life. You may eat your dinner as man alive, or as a mere masticating corpse. As man alive you may have a shot at your enemy. But as a ghastly simulacrum of life you may be firing bombs into men who are neither your enemies nor your friends, but just things you are dead to. Which is criminal, when the things happen to be alive.

To be alive, to be man alive, to be whole man alive: that is the point. And at its best, the novel, and the novel supremely, can help you. It can help you not to be dead man in life. So much of a man walks about dead and a carcass in the street and house, to-day: so much of women is merely dead. Like a pianoforte with half the notes mute.

But in the novel you can see, plainly, when the man goes dead, the woman goes inert. You can develop an instinct for life, if you will, instead of a theory of right and wrong, good and bad.

In life, there is right and wrong, good and bad, all the time. But what is right in one case is wrong in another. And in the novel you see one man becoming a corpse, because of his so-called goodness, another going dead because of his so-called wickedness. Right and wrong is an instinct: but an instinct of the whole consciousness in a man, bodily, mental, spiritual at once. And only in the novel are *all* things given full play, or at least, they may be given full play, when we realize that life itself, and not inert safety, is the reason for living. For out of the full play of all things emerges the only thing that is anything, the wholeness of a man, the wholeness of a woman, man alive, and live woman.

randall jarrell

walt whitman: he had his nerve

Randall Jarrell, born in Nashville, Tennessee in 1914, is a Southern poet and critic who has a particular gift for writing with wit and passion about poets he likes. The present essay, taken from Jarrell's fine book of essays, *Poetry and The Age,* has done more to make Whitman seem alive to our generation than anything else written about him in years. The reason for this previous neglect of Whitman is that the poet's essential poetic originality and idiosyncrasy have been lost in the official figure of the "poet of democracy" and "the good gray poet." Although Whitman is acclaimed in textbooks and in literary histories as a great democratic rebel and iconoclast, his poems too often tend to bore the reader who cares for poetry—the reader who has learned from contemporary poetry to look for more sharpness and concentration—and brevity!—in poems. What Jarrell has done here is to concentrate on *lines* from Whitman, and to show us, through an examination of Whitman's best lines, that Whitman is not the plaster saint of poetry that he said he was, but a poet who is often delightfully off-beat, spare, original and strange. This Whitman can be read for pleasure, not edification.

It is not only Jarrell's selection of texts that gets him to provide so witty a frame for his critical remarks. Jarrell's own style is always freshly personal. It cultivates directness, sauciness, original humor. Yet Jarrell, like Robert Lowell (see p. 229), writes so well because he writes prose with that ease and wit which so many Southern poets have absorbed from the deeply cultivated tradition of their class. There is something unmistakably patrician about Jarrell's style, as there is about his point of view, even when the intensity of his feelings as a critic brings him to the edge of conscious buffoonery. He says of some of Whitman's "howlers"—"We are right to resent his having made up his own horrors, instead of sticking to the ones that we ourselves employ." This is witty writing, and as you can see from other examples in this book, penetrating criticism is usually writing that is well written.

Whitman, Dickinson, and Melville seem to me the best poets of the 19th Century here in America. Melville's poetry has been grotesquely underestimated, but of course it is only in the last four or five years that it has been much read; in the long run, in spite of the awkwardness and amateurishness of so much of it, it will surely be thought well of. (In the short run it will probably be thought entirely too well of. Melville is a great poet only in the prose of *Moby Dick*.) Dickinson's poetry has been thoroughly read, and well though undifferentiatingly loved—after a few decades or centuries almost everybody will be able to see through Dickinson to her poems. But something odd has happened to the living changing part of Whitman's reputation: nowadays it is people who are not particularly interested in poetry, people who say that they read a poem for what it says, not for how it says it, who admire Whitman most. Whitman is often written about, either approvingly or disapprovingly, as if he were the Thomas Wolfe of 19th Century democracy, the hero of a de Mille movie about Walt Whitman. (People even talk about a war in which Walt Whitman and Henry

WALT WHITMAN: HE HAD HIS NERVE: Reprinted from *Poetry and The Age* by Randall Jarrell, by permission of Alfred A. Knopf, Inc. Copyright 1953 by Randall Jarrell.

James chose up sides, to begin with, and in which you and I will go on fighting till the day we die.) All this sort of thing, and all the bad poetry that there of course is in Whitman—for any poet has written enough bad poetry to scare away anybody—has helped to scare away from Whitman most "serious readers of modern poetry." They do not talk of his poems, as a rule, with any real liking or knowledge. Serious readers, people who are ashamed of not knowing all Hopkins by heart, are not all ashamed to say, "I don't really know Whitman very well." This may harm Whitman in your eyes, they know, but that is a chance that poets have to take. Yet "their" Hopkins, that good critic and great poet, wrote about Whitman, after seeing five or six of his poems in a newspaper review: "I may as well say what I should not otherwise have said, that I always knew in my heart Walt Whitman's mind to be more like my own than any other man's living. As he is a very great scoundrel this is not a very pleasant confession." And Henry James, the leader of "their" side in that awful imaginary war of which I spoke, once read Whitman to Edith Wharton (much as Mozart used to imitate, on the piano, the organ) with such power and solemnity that both sat shaken and silent; it was after this reading that James expressed his regret at Whitman's "too extensive acquaintance with the foreign languages." Almost all the most "original and advanced" poets and critics and readers of the last part of the 19th Century thought Whitman as original and advanced as themselves, in manner as well as in matter. Can Whitman really be a sort of Thomas Wolfe or Carl Sandburg or Robinson Jeffers or Henry Miller—or a sort of Balzac of poetry, whose every part is crude but whose whole is somehow great? He is not, nor could he be; a poem, like Pope's spider, "lives along the line," and all the dead lines in the world will not make one live poem. As Blake says, "all sublimity is founded on minute discrimination," and it is in these "minute particulars" of Blake's that any poem has its primary existence.

To show Whitman for what he is one does not need to praise or explain or argue, one needs simply to quote. He himself said, "I and mine do not convince by arguments, similes, rhymes,/We convince by our presence." Even a few of his phrases are enough to show us that Whitman was no sweeping rhetorician, but a poet of the greatest and oddest delicacy and originality and sensitivity, so far as words are concerned. This is, after all, the poet who said, "Blind loving wrestling touch, sheath'd hooded sharp-tooth'd touch"; who said, "Smartly attired, countenance smiling, form upright, death under the breast-bones, hell under the skull-bones"; who said, "Agonies are one of my changes of garments"; who saw grass as the "flag of my disposition," saw "the sharp-peak'd farmhouse, with its scallop'd scum and slender shoots from the gutters," heard a plane's "wild ascending lisp," and saw and heard how at the amputation "what is removed drops horribly in a pail." This is the poet for whom the sea was "howler and scooper of storms," reaching out to us with "crooked inviting fingers"; who went "leaping chasms with a pike-pointed staff, clinging to topples of brittle and blue"; who, a runaway slave, saw how "my gore dribs, thinn'd with the ooze of my skin"; who went "lithographing Kronos . . . buying drafts of Osiris"; who stared out at the "little plentiful mannikins skipping around in collars and tail'd coats,/ I am aware who they are, (they are positively not worms or fleas)." For he is, at his best, beautifully witty: he says gravely, "I find I incorporate gneiss, coals, long-threaded moss, fruits, grain, esculent roots,/ And am stucco'd with quadrupeds and birds all over"; and of these quadrupeds and birds "not one is respectable or unhappy over the whole earth." He calls advice: "Unscrew the locks from the doors! Unscrew the doors from their jambs!" He publishes the results of research: "Having pried through the strata, analyz'd to a hair, counsel'd with doctors and calculated close,/ I find no sweeter fat than sticks to my own bones." Everybody remembers how he told the Muse to "cross out please those immensely overpaid accounts,/ That matter of Troy and Achilles' wrath, and Aeneas', Odysseus' wanderings," but his account of the arrival of the "illustrious emigré" here in the New World is even better: "Bluff'd not a bit by drainpipe, gasometer, artificial fertilizers,/ Smiling and pleas'd with palpable intent to stay,/ She's here, install'd amid the kitchenware." Or he sees, like another Breughel, "the mechanic's wife with the babe at her nipple interceding for every person born,/ Three scythes at harvest whizzing in a row from three lusty angels with shirts bagg'd out at their waists,/ The snag-toothed hostler with red hair redeeming sins past and to come"—the passage has enough wit not only (in Johnson's phrase) to keep it sweet, but enough to make it believable. He says:

> *I project my hat, sit shame-faced, and beg.*
>
> *Enough! Enough! Enough!*
> *Somehow I have been stunn'd. Stand back!*
> *Give me a little time beyond my cuff'd head, slumbers,*
> *   dreams, gaping,*
> *I discover myself on the verge of a usual mistake.*

There is in such changes of tone as these the essence of wit. And Whitman is even more far-fetched than he is witty; he can say about Doubters, in the most improbable and explosive of juxtapositions: "I know every one of you, I know the sea of torment, doubt, despair and unbelief./ How the flukes splash! How they contort rapid as lightning, with splashes and spouts of blood!" Who else would have said about God: "As the hugging and loving bed-fellow sleeps at my side through the night, and withdraws at the break of day with stealthy tread,/ Leaving me baskets cover'd with white towels, swelling the house with their plenty"?—the Psalmist himself, his cup running over, would have looked at Whitman with dazzled eyes. (Whitman was persuaded by friends to hide the fact that it was God he was talking about.) He says, "Flaunt of the sunshine I need not your bask—lie over!" This unusual employment of verbs is usual enough in participle-loving Whitman, who also asks you to "look in my face while I snuff the sidle of evening," or tells you, "I effuse my flesh in eddies, and drift it in lacy jags." Here are some typical beginnings of poems: "City of orgies, walks, and joys. . . . Not heaving from my ribb'd breast only. . . . O take my hand Walt Whitman! Such gliding wonders! Such sights and sounds! Such join'd unended links. . . ." He says to the objects of the world, "You have waited, you always wait, you dumb, beautiful ministers"; sees "the sun and stars that float in the open air,/ The apple-shaped earth"; says, "O suns— O grass of graves— O perpetual transfers and promotions,/ If you do not say anything how can I say anything?" Not many poets have written better, in queerer and more convincing and more individual language, about the world's *gliding wonders:* the phrase seems particularly right for Whitman. He speaks of those "circling rivers the breath," of the "savage old mother incessantly crying,/ To the boy's soul's questions sullenly timing, some drown'd secret hissing"— ends a poem, once, "We have voided all but freedom and our own joy." How can one quote enough? If the reader thinks that all this is like Thomas Wolfe he *is* Thomas Wolfe; nothing else could explain it. Poetry like this is as far as possible from the work of any ordinary rehetorician, whose phrases cascade over us like suds of the oldest and most-advertised detergent.

The interesting thing about Whitman's worst language (for, just as few poets have ever written better, few poets have ever written worse) is how unusually absurd, how really ingeniously bad, such language is. I will quote none of the most famous examples; but even a line like *O culpable! I acknowledge. I exposé!* is not anything that you and I could do—only a man with the most extraordinary feel for language, or none whatsoever, could have cooked up Whitman's worst messes. For instance: what other man in all the history of this planet would have said, "I am a habitan of Vienna"? (One has an immediate vision of him as a sort of French-Canadian halfbreed to whom the Viennese are offering, with trepidation, through the bars of a zoological garden, little mounds of whipped cream.) And *enclaircise*—why, it's as bad as *explicate!* We are right to resent his having made up his own horrors, instead of sticking to the ones that we ourselves employ. But when Whitman says, "I dote on myself, there is that lot of me and all so luscious," we should realize that we are not the only ones who are amused. And the queerly bad and merely queer and queerly good will often change into one another without warning: "Hefts of the moving world, at innocent gambols silently rising, freshly exuding,/ Scooting obliquely high and low"—not good, but *queer!*—suddenly becomes, "Something I cannot see puts up libidinous prongs,/ Seas of bright juice suffuse heaven," and it is sunrise.

But it is not in individual lines and phrases, but in passages of some length, that Whitman is at his best. In the following quotation Whitman has something difficult to express, something that there are many formulas, all bad, for expressing; he expresses it with complete success, in language of the most dazzling originality:

> *The orchestra whirls me wider than Uranus flies,*
> *It wrenches such ardors from me I did not know I possess'd them,*
> *It sails me, I dab with bare feet, they are lick'd by the indolent waves,*
> *I am cut by bitter and angry hail, I lose my breath,*
> *Steep'd amid honey'd morphine, my windpipe throttled in fakes*
>   *of death,*
> *At length let up again to feel the puzzle of puzzles,*
> *And that we call Being.*

One hardly knows what to point at—everything works. But *wrenches* and *did not know I possess'd them;* the incredible *it sails me, I dab with bare feet; lick'd by the indolent; steep'd amid honey'd morphine; my windpipe throttled in fakes of death*—no wonder Crane admired Whitman! This originality, as absolute in its way as that of Berlioz' orchestration, is often at Whitman's command:

> *I am a dance—play up there! the fit is whirling me fast!*
>
> *I am the ever-laughing—it is new moon and twilight,*
> *I see the hiding of douceurs, I see nimble ghosts whichever way*
>   *I look,*
> *Cache and cache again deep in the ground and sea, and where it is*
>   *neither ground nor sea.*
> *Well do they do their jobs those journeymen divine,*
> *Only from me can they hide nothing, and would not if they could,*
> *I reckon I am their boss and they make me a pet besides,*
> *And surround me and lead me and run ahead when I walk,*

To lift their sunning covers to signify me with stretch'd arms,
    and resume the way;
Onward we move, a gay gang of blackguards! with mirth-
    shouting music and wild-flapping pennants of joy!

If you did not believe Hopkins' remark about Whitman, that *gay gang of blackguards* ought to shake you. Whitman shares Hopkins' passion for "dappled" effects, but he slides in and out of them with ambiguous swiftness. And he has at his command a language of the calmest and most prosaic reality, one that seems to do no more than present:

The little one sleeps in its cradle.
I lift the gauze and look a long time, and silently brush away flies
    with my hand.
The youngsters and the red-faced girl turn aside up the bushy hill,
I peeringly view them from the top.

The suicide sprawls on the bloody floor of the bedroom.
I witness the corpse with its dabbled hair, I note where the pistol
    has fallen.

It is like magic: that is, something has been done to us without our knowing how it was done; but if we look at the lines again we see the *gauze, silently, youngster, red-faced, bushy, peeringly, dabbled*—not that this is all we see. "Present! present!" said James; these are presented, put down side by side to form a little "view of life," from the cradle to the last bloody floor of the bedroom. Very often the things presented form nothing but a list:

The pure contralto sings in the organ loft,
The carpenter dresses his plank, the tongue of his foreplane whistles
    its wild ascending lisp,
The married and unmarried children ride home to their
    Thanksgiving dinner,
The pilot seizes the king-pin, he heaves down with a strong arm,
The mate stands braced in the whale-boat, lance and harpoon are
    ready,
The duck-shooter walks by silent and cautious stretches,
The deacons are ordain'd with cross'd hands at the altar,
The spinning-girl retreats and advances to the hum of the big wheel,
The farmer stops by the bars as he walks on a First-day loafe and
    looks at the oats and rye,
The lunatic is carried at last to the asylum a confirm'd case,
(He will never sleep any more as he did in the cot in his mother's
    bed-room;)
The jour printer with gray head and gaunt jaws works at his case,

> *He turns his quid of tobacco while his eyes blur with the*
> * manuscript,*
> *The malform'd limbs are tied to the surgeon's table,*
> *What is removed drops horribly in a pail; . . .*

It is only a list—but what a list! And how delicately, in what different ways—likeness and opposition and continuation and climax and anti-climax—the transitions are managed, whenever Whitman wants to manage them. Notice them in the next quotation, another "mere list":

> *The bride unrumples her white dress, the minute-hand of the clock*
> * moves slowly,*
> *The opium-eater reclines with rigid head and just-open'd lips,*
> *The prostitute draggles her shawl, her bonnet bobs on her tipsy*
> * and pimpled neck. . . .*

The first line is joined to the third by *unrumples* and *draggles, white dress* and *shawl;* the second to the third by *rigid head, bobs, tipsy, neck;* the first to the second by *slowly, just-open'd,* and the slowing-down of time in both states. And occasionally one of these lists is metamorphosed into something we have no name for; the man who would call the next quotation a mere list—anybody will feel this—would boil his babies up for soap:

> *Ever the hard unsunk ground,*
> *Ever the eaters and drinkers, ever the upward and downward sun,*
> *Ever myself and my neighbors, refreshing, wicked, real,*
> *Ever the old inexplicable query, ever that thorned thumb, that breath*
> * of itches and thirsts,*
> *Ever the vexer's hoot! hoot! till we find where the sly one hides*
> * and bring him forth,*
> *Ever the sobbing liquid of life,*
> *Ever the bondage under the chin, ever the trestles of death.*

Sometimes Whitman will take what would generally be considered an unpromising subject (in this case, a woman peeping at men in bathing naked) and treat it with such tenderness and subtlety and understanding that we are ashamed of ourselves for having thought it unpromising, and murmur that Chekhov himself couldn't have treated it better:

> *Twenty-eight young men bathe by the shore,*
> *Twenty-eight young men and all so friendly,*
> *Twenty-eight years of womanly life and all so lonesome.*
>
> *She owns the fine house by the rise of the bank,*
> *She hides handsome and richly drest aft the blinds of the window.*

Which of the young men does she like the best?
Ah the homeliest of them is beautiful to her.

Where are you off to, lady? for I see you,
You splash in the water there, yet stay stock still in your room.
Dancing and laughing along the beach came the twenty-ninth bather,
The rest did not see her, but she saw them and loved them.

The beards of the young men glistened with wet, it ran from their
     long hair,
Little streams pass'd all over their bodies.

An unseen hand also pass'd over their bodies,
It descended tremblingly from their temples and ribs.

The young men float on their backs, their white bellies bulge to the sun,
     they do not ask who seizes fast to them,
They do not know who puffs and declines with pendant and
     bending arch,
They do not know whom they souse with spray.

And in the same poem (that "Song of Myself" in which one finds
half his best work) the writer can say of a sea-fight:

Stretched and still lies the midnight,
Two great hulls motionless on the breast of the darkness,
Our vessel riddled and slowly sinking, preparations to pass to the
     one we have conquer'd,
The captain on the quarter-deck coldly giving his orders through
     a countenance white as a sheet,
Near by the corpse of the child that serv'd in the cabin,
The dead face of an old salt with long white hair and carefully curl'd
     whiskers,
The flames spite of all that can be done flickering aloft and below,
The husky voices of the two or three officers yet fit for duty,
Formless stacks of bodies and bodies by themselves, dabs of flesh
     upon the masts and spars,
Cut of cordage, dangle of rigging, slight shock of the soothe of waves,
Black and impassive guns, litter of powder-parcels, strong scent,
A few large stars overhead, silent and mournful shining,
Delicate snuffs of sea-breeze, smells of sedgy grass and fields by the
     shore, death-messages given in charge to survivors,
The hiss of the surgeon's knife, the gnawing teeth of his saw,
Wheeze, cluck, swash of falling blood, short wild scream, and long,
     dull, tapering groan,
These so, these irretrievable.

There are faults in this passage, and they *do not matter:* the serious
truth, the complete realization of these last lines make us remember

that few poets have shown more of the tears of things, and the joy of things, and of the reality beneath either tears or joy. Even Whitman's most general or political statements sometimes are good: everybody knows his "When liberty goes out of a place it is not the first to go, nor the second or third to go,/ It waits for all the rest to go, it is the last"; these sentences about the United States just before the Civil War may be less familiar:

> *Are those really Congressmen? are those the great Judges?*
>   *is that the President?*
> *Then I will sleep awhile yet, for I see that these States sleep,*
>   *for reasons;*
> *(With gathering murk, with muttering thunder and lambent shoots*
>   *we all duly awake,*
> *South, North, East, West, inland and seaboard, we will surely awake.)*

How well, with what firmness and dignity and command, Whitman does such passages! And Whitman's doubts that he has done them or anything else well—ah, there is nothing he does better:

> *The best I had done seemed to me blank and suspicious,*
> *My great thoughts as I supposed them, were they not in reality meagre?*
> *I am he who knew what it was to be evil,*
> *I too knitted the old knot of contrariety . . .*
> *Saw many I loved in the street or ferry-boat or public assembly,*
>   *yet never told them a word,*
> *Lived the same life with the rest, the same old laughing, gnawing,*
>   *sleeping,*
> *Played the part that still looks back on the actor and actress,*
> *The same old role, the role that is what we make it . . .*

Whitman says once that the "look of the bay mare shames silliness out of me." This is true—sometimes it is true; but more often the silliness and affection and cant and exaggeration are there shamelessly, the Old Adam that was in Whitman from the beginning and the awful new one that he created to keep it company. But as he says, "I know perfectly well my own egotism,/ Know my omnivorous lines and must not write any less." He says over and over that there are in him good and bad, wise and foolish, anything at all and its antonym, and he is telling the truth; there is in him almost everything in the world, so that one responds to him, willingly or unwillingly, almost as one does to the world, that world which makes the hairs of one's flesh stand up, which seems both evil beyond any rejection and wonderful beyond any acceptance. We cannot help seeing that there is something absurd about any judgment we make of its whole—for there is no "point of view" at which we can stand to make the judgment, and the moral categories that mean most to us seem no more to apply to its whole than our spatial or temporal or causal categories seem to apply to its beginning or its end. (But we need no arguments to make our judgments seem absurd—we feel their absurdity without argument.) In some like sense Whitman is a world, a waste with, here and there, systems blazing at random out of the darkness. Only an innocent and rigidly methodical mind will reject it for this disorganization, particularly since there are in it, here and there, little systems as beautifully and astonishingly organized as the rings and satellites of Saturn:

> I understand the large hearts of heroes,
> The courage of present times and all times,
> How the skipper saw the crowded and rudderless wreck of the
>   steam-ship, and Death chasing it up and down the storm,
> How he knuckled tight and gave not back an inch, and was faithful
>   of days and faithful of nights,
> And chalked in large letters on a board, Be of good cheer, we will
>   not desert you;
> How he follow'd with them and tack'd with them three days and
>   would not give it up,
> How he saved the drifting company at last,
> How the lank loose-gown'd women looked when boated from the side
>   of their prepared graves,
> How the silent old-faced infants and the lifted sick, and the
>   sharp-lipp'd unshaved men;
> All this I swallow, it tastes good, I like it well, it becomes mine,
> I am the man, I suffered, I was there.

In the last lines of this quotation Whitman has reached—as great writers always reach—a point at which criticism seems not only unnecessary but absurd: these lines are so good that even admiration feels like insolence, and one is ashamed of anything that one can find to say about them. How anyone can dismiss or accept patronizingly the man who wrote them, I do not understand.

The enormous and apparent advantages of form, of omission and selection, of the highest degree of organization, are accompanied by important disadvantages—and there are far greater works than *Leaves of Grass* to make us realize this. But if we compare Whitman with that very beautiful poet Alfred Tennyson, the most skillful of all Whitman's contemporaries, we are at once aware of how limiting Tennyson's forms have been, of how much Tennyson has had to leave out, even in those discursive poems where he is trying to put everything in. Whitman's poems *represent* his world and himself much more satis-

factorily than Tennyson's do his. In the past a few poets have both
formed and represented, each in the highest degree; but in modern
times what controlling, organizing, selecting poet has created a world
with as much in it as Whitman's, a world that so plainly *is* the world?
Of all modern poets he has, quantitatively speaking, "the most comprehensive soul"—and, qualitatively, a most comprehensive and compre-
hending one, with charities and concessions and qualifications that are
rare in any time.

"Do I contradict myself? Very well then I contradict myself," wrote
Whitman, as everybody remembers, and this is not naive, or something he got from Emerson, or a complacent pose. When you organize
one of the contradictory elements out of your work of art, you are
getting rid not just of it, but of the contradiction of which it was a
part; and it is the contradictions in works of art which make them able
to represent to us—as logical and methodical generalizations cannot—
our world and our selves, which are also full of contradictions. In
Whitman we do not get the controlled, compressed, seemingly con-
cordant contradictions of the great lyric poets, of a poem like, say,
Hardy's "During Wind and Rain"; Whitman's contradictions are sometimes announced openly, but are more often scattered at random
throughout the poems. For instance: Whitman specializes in ways of
saying that there is in some sense (a very Hegelian one, generally) no
evil—he says a hundred times that evil is not Real; but he also specializes in making lists of the evil of the world, lists of an unarguable
reality. After his minister has recounted "the rounded catalogue divine
complete," Whitman comes home and puts down what has been left
out: "the countless (nineteen-twentieths) low and evil, crude and
savage . . . the barren soil, the evil men, the slag and hideous rot." He
ends another such catalogue with the plain unexcusing "All these—all
meanness and agony without end I sitting look out upon,/ See, hear,
and am silent." Whitman offered himself to everybody, and said brilliantly and at length what a good thing he was offering:

> *Sure as the most certain sure, pumb in the uprights, well entretied,*
> *braced in the beams,*
> *Stout as a horse, affectionate, haughty, electrical,*
> *I and this mystery here we stand.*

Just for oddness, characteristicalness, differentness, what more could
you ask in a letter of recommendation? (Whitman sounds as if he were
recommending a house—haunted, but what foundations!) But after a
few pages he is oddly different:

Apart from the pulling and hauling stands what I am,
Stands amused, complacent, compassionating, idle, unitary,
Looks down, is erect, or bends an arm on an impalpable certain rest
Looking with side curved head curious what will come next,
Both in and out of the game and watching and wondering at it.

Tamburlaine is already beginning to sound like Hamlet: the employer feels uneasily, "Why, I might as well hire myself. . . ." And, a few pages later, Whitman puts down in ordinary-sized type, in the middle of the page, this warning to any *new person drawn toward me:*

Do you think I am trusty and faithful?
Do you see no further than this façade, this smooth and tolerant
   manner of me?
Do you suppose yourself advancing on real ground toward a real
   heroic man?
Have you no thought O dreamer that it may be all maya, illusion?

Having wonderful dreams, telling wonderful lies, was a temptation Whitman could never resist; but telling the truth was a temptation he could never resist, either. When you buy him you know what you are buying. And only an innocent and solemn and systematic mind will condemn him for his contradictions: Whitman's catalogues of evils represent realities, and his denials of their reality represent other realities, of feeling and intuition and desire. If he is faithless to logic, to Reality As It Is—whatever that is—he is faithful to the feel of things, to reality as it seems; this is all that a poet has to be faithful to, and philosophers have been known to leave logic and Reality for it.

Whitman is more coordinate and parallel than anybody, is *the* poet of parallel present participles, of twenty verbs joined by a single subject: all this helps to give his work its feeling of raw hypnotic reality, of being that world which also streams over us joined only by *ands,* until we supply the subordinating conjunctions; and since as children we see the *ands* and not the *becauses,* this method helps to give Whitman some of the freshness of childhood. How inexhaustibly interesting the world is in Whitman! Arnold all his life kept wishing that he could see the world "with a plainness as near, as flashing" as that with which Moses and Rebekah and the Argonauts saw it. He asked with elegiac nostalgia, "Who can see the green earth any more/ As she was by the sources of Time?"—and all the time there was somebody alive who saw it so, as plain and near and flashing, and with a kind of calm, pastoral, Biblical dignity and elegance as well, sometimes. The *thereness* and *suchness* of the world are incarnate in Whitman as they are in few other writers.

They might have put on his tombstone WALT WHITMAN: HE HAD HIS NERVE. He is the rashest, the most inexplicable and unlikely—the most impossible, one wants to say—of poets. He somehow *is* in a class by himself, so that one compares him with other poets about as readily as one compares *Alice* with other books. (Even his free verse has a completely different effect from anybody else's.) Who would think of comparing him with Tennyson or Browning or Arnold or Baudelaire?—it is Homer, or the sagas, or something far away and long ago, that comes to one's mind only to be dismissed; for sometimes Whitman *is* epic, just as *Moby Dick* is, and it surprises us to be able to use truthfully this word that we have misused so many times. Whitman *is* grand, and elevated, and comprehensive, and real with an astonishing reality, and many other things—the critic points at his qualities in despair and wonder, all method failing, and simply calls them by their names. And the range of these qualities is the most extraordinary thing of all. We can surely say about him, "He was a man, take him for all in all. I shall not look upon his like again"—and wish that people had seen this and not tried to be his like: one Whitman is miracle enough, and when he comes again it will be the end of the world.

I have said so little about Whitman's faults because they are so plain: baby critics who have barely learned to complain of the lack of ambiguity in *Peter Rabbit* can tell you all that is wrong with *Leaves of Grass*. But a good many of my readers must have felt that it is ridiculous to write an essay about the obvious fact that Whitman is a great poet. It is ridiculous—just as, in 1851, it would have been ridiculous for anyone to write an essay about the obvious fact that Pope was no "classic of our prose" but a great poet. Critics have to spend half their time reiterating whatever ridiculously obvious things their age or the critics of their age have found it necessary to forget: they say despairingly, at parties, that Wordsworth is a great poet, and *won't* bore you, and tell Mr. Leavis that Milton is a great poet whose deposition *hasn't* been accomplished with astonishing ease by a few words from Eliot. . . . There is something essentially ridiculous about critics, anyway: what is good is good without our saying so, and beneath all our majesty we know this.

Let me finish by mentioning another quality of Whitman's—a quality, delightful to me, that I have said nothing of. If some day a tourist notices, among the ruins of New York City, a copy of *Leaves of Grass*, and stops and picks it up and reads some lines in it, she will be able to say to herself: "How very American! If he and his country had not existed, it would have been impossible to imagine them."

lionel trilling

huckleberry finn

Lionel Trilling was born in New York in 1905 and received his bachelor's and doctor's degrees from Columbia University, where he has for a number of years been professor of English. His first book, *Matthew Arnold* (1939), established his reputation as a critic, and through other books, notably *The Liberal Imagination* (1950), and his influence as a teacher, Trilling has become one of the key figures in American literary thought of our day.

The present essay was written as an introduction to an edition of *Huckleberry Finn* designed for college students, and it displays in equal measure both the persuasiveness of thought and the easiness of style that have made Trilling so influential. The mark of a first-rate critic can be seen in the directness of his relation to the work he is discussing; he consults his own mind, not "authorities" on the subject, and he analyzes even the most celebrated virtues of a book as if no one had seen things in quite this light before, or had been able to say them in so authoritative a voice.

Trilling is writing here about the most universally admired of all American works of literary imagination—a book which is peculiarly the symbol of a distinctly "American" literature. Yet without attempting any radically new and arbitrary interpretation of *Huckleberry Finn,* Trilling is able to make us see this great book in a new light by associating the greatness of the book with a boy's feeling for the truth. Many people have written about Mark Twain as an artist of the real; not many critics have been able to locate the creative value of the novel so much in a *boy's* instinctive commitment to truth itself. Trilling asks of the book—"Wherein does its greatness lie? Primarily in its power of telling the truth. . . . Truth is the whole of a boy's conscious demand upon the world of adults. He is likely to believe that the adult world is in a conspiracy to lie to him, and it is this belief, by no means unfounded, that arouses Tom and Huck . . . to . . . their everlasting concern with justice, which they call fairness."

Similarly, in describing the dominating and "god-like" effect of the Mississippi in *Huckleberry Finn,* Trilling is able in a sentence of singular grace to contrast the earlier America celebrated in the novel with the America after the Civil War in which the book was written— "Against the money-god stands the river-god, whose comments are silent

—sunlight, space, uncrowded time, stillness, and danger." And Trilling draws his analysis to a close by relying, as a first-rate critic will, on the kind of writing that in its own passion and clarity and point will bring home to the student the greatness of the book he is describing. "He is the master of the style that escapes the fixity of the printed page, that sounds in our ears with the immediacy of the heard voice, the very voice of unpretentious truth."

In 1876 Mark Twain published *The Adventures of Tom Sawyer* and in the same year began what he called "another boys' book." He set little store by the new venture and said that he had undertaken it "more to be at work than anything else." His heart was not in it—"I like it only tolerably well as far as I have got," he said, "and may possibly pigeonhole or burn the MS when it is done." He pigeonholed it long before it was done and for as much as four years. In 1880 he took it out and carried it forward a little, only to abandon it again. He had a theory of unconscious composition and believed that a book must write itself; the book which he referred to as "Huck Finn's Auto-biography" refused to do the job of its own creation and he would not coerce it.

But then in the summer of 1887 Mark Twain was possessed by a charge of literary energy which, as he wrote to Howells, was more intense than any he had experienced for many years. He worked all day and every day, and periodically he so fatigued himself that he had to recruit his strength by a day or two of smoking and reading in bed. It is impossible not to suppose that this great creative drive was con-nected with—was perhaps the direct result of—the visit to the Missis-sippi he had made earlier in the year, the trip which forms the matter of the second part of *Life on the Mississippi*. His boyhood and youth on the river he so profoundly loved had been at once the happiest and most significant part of Mark Twain's life; his return to it in middle age stirred memories which revived and refreshed the idea of *Huckle-berry Finn*. Now at last the book was not only ready but eager to write itself. But it was not to receive much conscious help from its author. He was always full of second-rate literary schemes and now, in the early weeks of the summer, with *Huckleberry Finn* waiting to complete itself, he turned his hot energy upon several of these sorry projects, the completion of which gave him as much sense of satisfying produc-tivity as did his eventual absorption in *Huckleberry Finn*.

HUCKLEBERRY FINN: From Lionel Trilling's Introduction to *The Adventures of Huckleberry Finn*, Rinehart Editions. Copyright 1948, by Lionel Trilling. Re-printed by permission of the publishers, Holt Rinehart and Winston, Inc.

When at last *Huckleberry Finn* was completed and published and widely loved, Mark Twain became somewhat aware of what he had accomplished with the book that had been begun as journeywork and depreciated, postponed, threatened with destruction. It is his masterpiece, and perhaps he learned to know that. But he could scarcely have estimated it for what it is, one of the world's great books and one of the central documents of American culture.

Wherein does its greatness lie? Primarily in its power of telling the truth. An awareness of this quality as it exists in *Tom Sawyer* once led Mark Twain to say of the earlier work that "it is *not* a boys' book at all. It will be read only by adults. It is written only for adults." But this was only a manner of speaking, Mark Twain's way of asserting, with a discernible touch of irritation, the degree of truth he had achieved. It does not represent his usual view either of boys' books or of boys. No one, as he well knew, sets a higher value on truth than a boy. Truth is the whole of a boy's conscious demand upon the world of adults. He is likely to believe that the adult world is in a conspiracy to lie to him, and it is this belief, by no means unfounded, that arouses Tom and Huck and all boys to their moral sensitivity, their everlasting concern with justice, which they call fairness. At the same time it often makes them skillful and profound liars in their own defense, yet they do not tell the ultimate lie of adults: they do not lie to themselves. That is why Mark Twain felt that it was impossible to carry Tom Sawyer beyond boyhood—in maturity "he would lie just like all the other one-horse men of literature and the reader would conceive a hearty contempt for him."

Certainly one element in the greatness of *Huckleberry Finn*, as also in the lesser greatness of *Tom Sawyer*, is that it succeeds first as a boys' book. One can read it at ten and then annually ever after, and each year find that it is as fresh as the year before, that it has changed only in becoming somewhat larger. To read it young is like planting a tree young—each year adds a new growth ring of meaning, and the book is as little likely as the tree to become dull. So, we may imagine, an Athenian boy grew up together with the *Odyssey*. There are few other books which we can know so young and love so long.

The truth of *Huckleberry Finn* is of a different kind from that of *Tom Sawyer*. It is more intense truth, fiercer and more complex. *Tom Sawyer* has the truth of honesty—what it says about things and feelings is never false and always both adequate and beautiful. *Huckleberry Finn* deals directly with the virtue and depravity of man's heart.

Perhaps the best clue to the greatness of *Huckleberry Finn* has been given to us by a writer who is as different from Mark Twain as it is possible for one Missourian to be from another. T. S. Eliot's poem, "The Dry Salvages," the third of his *Four Quartets,* begins with a meditation on the Mississippi, which Mr. Eliot knew in his St. Louis boyhood:

> *I do not know much about gods; but I think that the river*
> *Is a strong brown god . . .*

And the meditation goes on to speak of the god as

> almost forgotten
> *By the dwellers in cities—ever, however, implacable,*
> *Keeping his seasons and rages, destroyer, reminder of*
> *What men choose to forget. Unhonoured, unpropitiated*
> *By worshippers of the machine, but waiting, watching and waiting.*[1]

Huckleberry Finn is a great book because it is about a god—about, that is, a power which seems to have a mind and will of its own, and which to men of moral imagination appears to embody a great moral idea.

Huck himself is the servant of the river-god, and he comes very close to being aware of the divine nature of the being he serves. The world he inhabits is perfectly equipped to accommodate a deity, for it is full of presences and meanings which it conveys by natural signs and also by prenatural omens and taboos: to look at the moon over the left shoulder, to shake the tablecloth after sundown, to handle a snakeskin, are ways of offending the obscure and prevalent spirits. Huck is at odds, on moral and aesthetic grounds, with the only form of established religion he knows, and his very intense moral life may be said to derive almost wholly from his love of the river. He lives in a perpetual adoration of the Mississippi's power and charm. Huck, of course, always expresses himself better than he can know, but nothing draws upon his gift of speech like his response to his deity. After every sally into the social life of the shore, he returns to the river with relief and thanksgiving; and at each return, regular and explicit as a chorus in a Greek tragedy, there is a hymn of praise to the god's beauty, mystery, and strength, and to his noble grandeur in contrast with the pettiness of men.

Generally the god is benign, a being of long sunny days and spacious nights. But, like any god, he is also dangerous and deceptive. He generates fogs which bewilder, and contrives echoes and false distances which confuse. His sand bars can ground and his hidden snags can mortally wound a great steamboat. He can cut away the solid earth from under a man's feet and take his house with it. The sense of the

---

[1] Copyright, 1943, by T. S. Eliot, reprinted by permission of Harcourt, Brace and Company.

danger of the river is what saves the book from any touch of the sentimentality and moral ineptitude of most works which contrast the life of nature with the life of society.

The river itself is only divine; it is not ethical and good. But its nature seems to foster the goodness of those who love it and try to fit themselves to its ways. And we must observe that we cannot make—that Mark Twain does not make—an absolute opposition between the river and human society. To Huck much of the charm of the river life is human: it is the raft and the wigwam and Jim. He has not run away from Miss Watson and the Widow Douglas and his brutal father to a completely individualistic liberty, for in Jim he finds his true father, very much as Stephen Dedalus in James Joyce's *Ulysses* finds his true father in Leopold Bloom.[2] The boy and the Negro slave form a family, a primitive community—and it is a community of saints.

Huck's intense and even complex moral quality may possibly not appear on a first reading, for one may be caught and convinced by his own estimate of himself, by his brags about his lazy hedonism, his avowed preference for being alone, his dislike of civilization. The fact is, of course, that he is involved in civilization up to his ears. His escape from society is but his way of reaching what society ideally dreams of for itself. Responsibility is the very essence of his character, and it is perhaps to the point that the original of Huck, a boyhood companion of Mark Twain's named Tom Blenkenship, did, like Huck, "light out for the Territory," only to become a justice of the peace in Montana, "a good citizen and greatly respected."

Huck does indeed have all the capacities for simple happiness he says he has, but circumstances and his own moral nature make him the least carefree of boys—he is always "in a sweat" over the predicament of someone else. He has a great sense of the sadness of human life, and although he likes to be alone, the words "lonely" and "loneliness" are frequent with him. The note of his special sensibility is struck early in the story: "Well, when Tom and me got to the edge of the hilltop we looked away down into the village and could see three or four lights twinkling where there were sick folks, maybe; and the stars over us was sparkling ever so fine; and down by the village was the river, a whole mile broad, and awful still and grand." The identification of the lights as the lamps of sick-watches defines Huck's character.

His sympathy is quick and immediate. When the circus audience

2 In Joyce's *Finnegans Wake* both Mark Twain and Huckleberry Finn appear frequently. The theme of rivers is, of course, dominant in the book; and Huck's name suits Joyce's purpose, for Finn is one of the many names of his hero. Mark Twain's love of and gift for the spoken language make another reason for Joyce's interest in him.

laughs at the supposedly drunken man who tries to ride the horse, Huck is only miserable: "It wasn't funny to me . . . ; I was all of a tremble to see his danger." When he imprisons the intending murderers on the wrecked steamboat, his first thought is of how to get someone to rescue them, for he considers "how dreadful it was, even for murderers, to be in such a fix. I says to myself, there ain't no telling but I might come to be a murderer myself yet, and then how would I like it." But his sympathy is never sentimental. When at last he knows that the murderers are beyond help, he has no inclination to false pathos. "I felt a little bit heavy-hearted about the gang, but not much, for I reckoned that if they could stand it I could." His will is genuinely good and he has no need to torture himself with guilty second thoughts.

Not the least remarkable thing about Huck's feeling for people is that his tenderness goes along with the assumption that his fellow men are likely to be dangerous and wicked. He travels incognito, never telling the truth about himself and never twice telling the same lie, for he trusts no one and the lie comforts him even when it is not necessary. He instinctively knows that the best way to keep a party of men away from Jim on the raft is to beg them to come aboard to help his family stricken with small pox. And if he had not already had the knowledge of human weakness and stupidity and cowardice, he would soon have acquired it, for all his encounters forcibly teach it to him—the insensate feud of the Graingerfords and Shepherdsons, the invasion of the raft by the Duke and the King, the murder of Boggs, the lynching party, and the speech of Colonel Sherburn. Yet his profound and bitter knowledge of human depravity never prevents him from being a friend to man.

No personal pride interferes with his well-doing. He knows what status is and on the whole he respects it—he is really a very *respectable* person and inclines to like "quality folks"—but he himself is unaffected by it. He himself has never had status, he has always been the lowest of the low, and the considerable fortune he had acquired in *The Adventures of Tom Sawyer* is never real to him. When the Duke suggests that Huck and Jim render him the personal service that accords with his rank, Huck's only comment, "Well, that was easy so we done it." He is injured in every possible way by the Duke and the King, used and exploited and manipulated, yet when he hears that they are in danger from a mob, his natural impulse is to warn them. And when he fails of his purpose and the two men are tarred and feathered and ridden on a rail, his only thought is, "Well, it made me sick to see it; and I was sorry for them poor pitiful rascals, it seemed like I couldn't ever feel any hardness against them any more in the world."

And if Huck and Jim on the raft do indeed make a community of saints, it is because they do not have an ounce of pride between them. Yet this is not perfectly true, for the one disagreement they ever have is over a matter of pride. It is on the occasion when Jim and Huck have been separated by the fog. Jim has mourned Huck as dead, and then, exhausted, has fallen asleep. When he awakes and finds that Huck has returned, he is overjoyed; but Huck convinces him that he has only dreamed the incident, that there has been no fog, no separation, no chase, no reunion, and then allows him to make an elaborate "interpretation" of the dream he now believes he has had. Then the joke is sprung, and in the growing light of the dawn Huck points to the debris of leaves on the raft and the broken oar.

> Jim looked at the trash, and then looked at me, and back at the trash again. He had got the dream fixed so strong in his head that he couldn't seem to shake it loose and get the facts back into its place again right away. But when he did get the thing straightened around he looked at me steady without ever smiling, and says:
>
> "What do dey stan' for? I'se gwyne to tell you. When I got all wore out wid work, en wid de callin' for you, en went to sleep, my heart wuz mos' broke bekase you wuz los', en I didn' k'yer no mo' what became er me en de raf'. En when I wake up en fine you back agin, all safe en soun', de tears come, en I could a got down on my knees en kiss yo' foot, I's so thankful. En all you wuz thinkin' 'bout wuz how you could make a fool uv ole Jim wid a lie. Dat truck dah is *trash;* en trash is what people is dat puts dirt on de head er dey fren's en makes 'em ashamed."
>
> Then he got up slow and walked to the wigwam, and went in there without saying anything but that.

The pride of human affection has been touched, one of the few prides that has any true dignity. And at its utterance, Huck's one last dim vestige of pride of status, his sense of position as a white man, wholly vanishes: "It was fifteen minutes before I could work myself up to go and humble myself to a nigger; but I done it, and I warn't sorry for it afterwards either."

This incident is the beginning of the moral testing and development which a character so morally sensitive as Huck's must inevitably undergo. And it becomes an heroic character when, on the urging of affection, Huck discards the moral code he has always taken for granted and resolves to help Jim in his escape from slavery. The intensity of his struggle over the act suggests how deeply he is involved in the society which he rejects. The satiric brilliance of the episode lies, of course, in Huck's solving his problem not by doing "right" but by doing "wrong." He has only to consult his conscience, the conscience of a Southern boy in the middle of the last century, to know that he ought to return Jim to slavery. And as soon as he makes the decision according to conscience and decides to inform on Jim, he has all the warmly gratifying emotions of conscious virtue. "Why, it was astonishing, the way I felt as light as feather right straight off, and my troubles all gone. . . . I felt good and all washed clean of sin for the first time I had ever felt so in my life, and I knowed I could pray now." And when at last he finds that he cannot endure his decision but must sacrifice the comforts of the pure heart and help Jim in his escape, it is not because he has acquired any new ideas about slavery—he believes that he detests Abolitionists; he himself answers when he is asked if the explosion of a steamboat boiler had hurt anyone, "No'm, killed a nigger," and of course finds nothing wrong in the responsive comment, "Well, it's lucky because sometimes people do get hurt." Ideas and ideals can be of no help to him in his moral crisis. He no more condemns slavery than Tristram and Lancelot condemn marriage; he is as consciously *wicked* as any illicit lover of romance and he consents to be damned for a personal devotion, never questioning the justice of the punishment he has incurred.

Huckleberry Finn was once barred from certain libraries and schools for its alleged subversion of morality. The authorities had in mind the book's endemic lying, the petty thefts, the denigrations of respectability and religion, the bad language, and the bad grammar. We smile at that excessive care, yet in point of fact *Huckleberry Finn* is a subversive book—no one who reads thoughtfully the dialectic of Huck's great moral crisis will ever again be wholly able to accept without some question and some irony the assumptions of the respectable morality by which he lives, nor will ever again be certain that what he considers the clear dictates of moral reason are not merely the engrained customary beliefs of time and place.

We are not likely to miss in *Huckleberry Finn* the subtle, implicit moral meaning of the great river. But we are likely to understand these moral implications as having to do only with personal and individual conduct. And since the sum of individual pettiness is on the whole pretty constant, we are likely to think of the book as applicable to mankind in general and at all times and in all places, and we praise it by calling it "universal." And so it is; but like many books to which that large adjective applies, it is also local and particular. It has a particular moral reference to the United States in the period after the Civil War. It was then when, in Mr. Eliot's phrase, the river was forgotten, and precisely by the "dwellers in cities," by the "worshippers of the machine."

The Civil War and the development of the railroads ended the great days when the river was the central artery of the nation. No contrast could be more moving than that between the hot, turbulent energy of the river life of the first part of *Life on the Mississippi* and the melancholy reminiscence of the second part. And the war that brought the end of the rich Mississippi days also marked a change in the quality of life in America which, to many men, consisted of a deterioration of American moral values. It is of course a human habit to look back on the past and to find it a better and more innocent time than the present. Yet in this instance there seems to be an objective basis for the judgment. We cannot disregard the testimony of men so diverse as Henry Adams, Walt Whitman, William Dean Howells, and Mark Twain himself, to mention but a few of the many who were in agreement on this point. All spoke of something that had gone out of American life after the war, some simplicity, some innocence, some peace. None of them was under any illusion about the amount of ordinary human wickedness that existed in the old days, and Mark Twain certainly was not. The difference was in the public attitude, in the things that were now accepted and made respectable in the national ideal. It was, they all felt, connected with new emotions about money. As Mark Twain said, where formerly "the people had desired money," now they "fall down and worship it." The new gospel was, "Get money. Get it quickly. Get it in abundance. Get it in prodigious abundance. Get it dishonestly if you can, honestly if you must."[3]

With the end of the Civil War capitalism had established itself. The relaxing influence of the frontier was coming to an end. Americans increasingly became "dwellers in cities" and "worshippers of the machine." Mark Twain himself became a notable part of this new dispensation. No one worshiped the machine more than he did, or thought he did—he ruined himself by his devotion to the Paige typesetting machine, by which he hoped to make a fortune even greater than he had made by his writing, and he sang the praises of the machine age in *A Connecticut Yankee in King Arthur's Court*. He associated intimately with the dominant figures of American business enterprise. Yet at the same time he hated the new way of life and kept bitter memoranda of his scorn, commenting on the low morality or the bad taste of the men who were shaping the ideal and directing the destiny of the nation.

[3] *Mark Twain in Eruption,* edited by Bernard De Voto, p. 77.

Mark Twain said of *Tom Sawyer* that it "is simply a hymn, put into prose form to give it worldly air." He might have said the same, and with even more reason, of *Huckleberry Finn,* which is a hymn to an older America forever gone, an America which had its great national faults, which was full of violence and even of cruelty, but which still maintained its sense of reality, for it was not yet enthralled by money, the father of ultimate illusion and lies. Against the money-god stands the river-god, whose comments are silent—sunlight, space, uncrowded time, stillness, and danger. It was quickly forgotten once its practical usefulness had passed, but, as Mr. Eliot's poem says, "The river is within us. . . ."

In form and style *Huckleberry Finn* is an almost perfect work. Only one mistake has ever been charged against it, that it concludes with Tom Sawyer's elaborate, too elaborate, game of Jim's escape. Certainly this episode is too long—in the original draft it was much longer—and certainly it is a falling off, as almost anything would have to be, from the incidents of the river. Yet it has a certain formal aptness—like, say, that of the Turkish initiation which brings Molière's *Le Bourgeois Gentilhomme* to its close. It is a rather mechanical development of an idea, and yet some device is needed to permit Huck to return to his anonymity, to give up the role of hero, to fall into the background which he prefers, for he is modest in all things and could not well endure the attention and glamour which attend a hero at a book's end. For this purpose nothing could serve better than the mind of Tom Sawyer with its literary furnishings, its conscious romantic desire for experience and the hero's part, and its ingenious schematization of life to achieve that aim.

The form of the book is based on the simplest of all novelforms, the so-called picaresque novel, or novel of the road, which strings its incidents on the line of the hero's travels. But, as Pascal says, "rivers are roads that move," and the movement of the road in its own mysterious life transmutes the primitive simplicity of the form: the road itself is the greatest character in this novel of the road, and the hero's departures from the river and his returns to it compose a subtle and significant pattern. The linear simplicity of the picaresque novel is further modified by the story's having a clear dramatic organization: it has a beginning, a middle, and an end, and a mounting suspense of interest.

As for the style of the book, it is not less than definitive in American literature. The prose of *Huckleberry Finn* established for written prose the virtues of American colloquial speech. This has nothing to do with pronunciation or grammar. It has something to do with ease and freedom in the use of language. Most of all it has to do with the structure of the sentence, which is simple, direct, and fluent, maintaining the rhythm of the word-groups of speech and the intonation of the speaking voice.

In the matter of language, American literature had a special problem. The young nation was inclined to think that the mark of the truly literary product was a grandiosity and elegance not to be found in the common speech. It therefore encouraged a greater breach between its vernacular and its literary language than, say, English literature of the same period ever allowed. This accounts for the hollow ring one now and then hears even in the work of our best writers in the first half of the last century. English writers of equal stature would never have made the lapses into rhetorical excess that are common in Cooper and Poe and that are to be found even in Melville and Hawthorne.

Yet at the same time that the language of ambitious literature was high and thus always in danger of falseness, the American reader was keenly interested in the actualities of daily speech. No literature, indeed, was ever so taken up with matters of speech as ours was. "Dialect," which attracted even our serious writers, was the accepted common ground of our popular humorous writing. Nothing in social life seemed so remarkable as the different forms which speech could take—the brogue of the immigrant Irish or the mispronunciation of the German, the "affectation" of the English, the reputed precision of the Bostonian, the legendary twang of the Yankee farmer, and the drawl of the Pike County man. Mark Twain, of course, was in the tradition of humor that exploited this interest, and no one could play with it nearly so well. Although today the carefully spelled-out dialects of nineteenth-century American humor are likely to seem dull enough, the subtle variations of speech in *Huckleberry Finn,* of which Mark Twain was justly proud, are still part of the liveliness and flavor of the book.

Out of his knowledge of the actual speech of America Mark Twain forged a classic prose. The adjective may seem a strange one, yet it is apt. Forget the misspellings and the faults of grammar, and the prose will be seen to move with the greatest simplicity, directness, lucidity, and grace. These qualities are by no means accidental. Mark Twain, who read widely, was passionately interested in the problems of style; the mark of the strictest literary sensibility is everywhere to be found in the prose of *Huckleberry Finn.*

It is this prose that Ernest Hemingway had chiefly in mind when he said that "all modern American literature comes from one book by Mark Twain called *Huckleberry Finn.*" Hemingway's own prose stems from it directly and consciously; so does the prose of the two modern writers who most influenced Hemingway's early style, Gertrude Stein and Sherwood Anderson (although neither of them could maintain the robust purity of their model); so too, does the best of William Faulkner's prose, which, like Mark Twain's own, reinforces the colloquial tradition with the literary tradition. Indeed, it may be said that almost every contemporary American writer who deals conscientiously with the problems and possibility of prose must feel, directly or indirectly, the influence of Mark Twain. He is the master of the style that escapes the fixity of the printed page, that sounds in our ears with the immediacy of the heard voice, the very voice of unpretentious truth.

alfred kazin

moby-dick

Alfred Kazin was born in New York City in 1915; his books include a critical history of modern American literature, *On Native Grounds;* an autobiography, *A Walker In The City;* and a selection from his critical essays, *The Inmost Leaf.*

The following essay was written as the introduction to the Riverside edition of Herman Melville's *Moby-Dick* (1956). It is meant, as is perhaps much of this author's literary criticism, to come to grips with the central element, the creative essence, of the book being discussed; for this reason phrases like "What Melville did through Ishmael," or "This is Ahab's quest," point up the critic's intention to reveal the *focus* of Melville's creative energy in his masterpiece.

This essential and organizing element would seem to consist in the fact that *Moby-Dick* is *not* a realistic novel, which is too often the only kind of novel we are familiar with today. *Moby-Dick* appears to this critic as a "new kind of book. . . . It is a book which is neither a saga, though it deals in large natural forces, nor a *classical* epic, for we feel too strongly the individual who wrote it. It is a book that is at once primitive, fatalistic, and merciless, like the very oldest books, and yet peculiarly personal, like so many twentieth-century novels, in its significant emphasis on the subjective individual consciousness. The book grows out of a single word, 'I,' and expands until the soul's voyage of this 'I' comes to include a great many things that are unseen and unsuspected by most of us."

Moby-Dick is not only a very big book; it is also a peculiarly full and rich one, and from the very opening it conveys a sense of abundance, of high creative power, that exhilarates and enlarges the imagination. This quality is felt immediately in the style, which is remarkably easy, natural and "American," yet always literary, and which swells in power until it takes on some of the roaring and uncontainable rhythms with which Melville audibly describes the sea. The best description of this style is Melville's own, when he speaks of the "bold and nervous lofty language" that Nantucket whaling captains learn straight from nature. We feel this abundance in heroic types like the Nantucketers themselves, many of whom are significantly named after Old Testament prophets and kings, for these, too, are mighty men, and the mightiest of them all, Captain Ahab, will challenge the very order of the creation itself. This is the very heart of the book—so much so that we come to feel that there is some shattering magnitude of theme before Melville as he writes, that as a writer he had been called to an heroic new destiny.

It is this constant sense of power that constitutes the book's appeal to us, that explains its hold on our attention. *Moby-Dick* is one of those books that try to bring in as much of life as a writer can get both hands on. Melville even tries to create an image of life itself as a ceaseless creation. The book is written with a personal force of style, a passionate learning, a steady insight into our forgotten connections with the primitive. It sweeps everything before it; it gives us the happiness that only great vigor inspires.

If we start by opening ourselves to this abundance and force, by welcoming not merely the story itself, but the manner in which it speaks to us, we shall recognize in this restlessness, this richness, this persistent atmosphere of magnitude, the essential image on which the book is founded. For *Moby-Dick* is not so much a book *about* Captain Ahab's quest for the whale as it is an experience *of* that quest. This is only to say, what we say of any true poem, that we cannot reduce its essential substance to a subject, that we should not intellectualize and summarize it, but that we should recognize that its very force and beauty lie in the way it is conceived and written, in the qualities that flow from its being a unique entity.

In these terms, *Moby-Dick* seems to be far more of a poem than it is

MOBY-DICK: From the introduction to the Riverside Edition of *Moby-Dick* by Alfred Kazin. Copyright 1956 by Houghton Mifflin Company. Reprinted by permission of the publisher.

a novel, and since it is a narrative, to be an epic, a long poem on an heroic theme, rather than the kind of realistic fiction that we know today. Of course Melville did not deliberately set out to write a formal epic; but half-consciously, he drew upon many of the traditional characteristics of epic in order to realize the utterly original kind of novel *he* needed to write in his time—the spaciousness of theme and subject, the martial atmosphere, the association of these homely and savage materials with universal myths, the symbolic wanderings of the hero, the indispensable strength of such a hero in Captain Ahab. Yet beyond all this, what distinguishes *Moby-Dick* from modern prose fiction, what ties it up with the older, more formal kind of narrative that was once written in verse, is the fact that Melville is not interested in the meanness, the literal truthfulness, the representative slice of life, that we think of as the essence of modern realism. His book has the true poetic emphasis in that the whole story is constantly being meditated and unravelled through a single mind.

"Call me Ishmael," the book begins. This Ishmael is not only a character in the book; he is also the single voice, or rather the single mind, from whose endlessly turning spool of thought the whole story is unwound. It is Ishmael's contemplativeness, his *dreaming,* that articulates the wonder of the seas and the fabulousness of the whale and the terrors of the deep. All that can be meditated and summed up and hinted at, as the reflective essence of the story itself, is given us by Ishmael, who possesses nothing but man's specifically human gift, which is language. It is Ishmael who tries to sum up the whole creation in a single book and yet keeps at the center of it one American whaling voyage. It is Ishmael's gift for speculation that explains the terror we come to feel before the whiteness of the whale; Ishmael's mind that ranges with mad exuberance through a description of all the seas; Ishmael who piles up image after image of "the mightiest animated mass that has survived the flood." It is Ishmael who, in the wonderful chapter on the masthead, embodies for us man as a thinker, whose reveries transcend space and time as he stands watch high above the seas. And of course it is Ishmael, both actually and as the symbol of man, who is the one survivor of the voyage. Yet utterly alone as he is at the end of the book, floating on the Pacific Ocean, he manages, buoyed up on a coffin that magically serves as his life-buoy, to give us the impression that life itself can be honestly confronted only in the loneliness of each human heart. Always it is this emphasis on Ishmael's personal vision, on the richness and ambiguity of all events as the sceptical, fervent, experience-scarred mind of Ishmael feels and thinks them, that gives us, from the beginning, the new kind of book that *Moby-Dick* is. It is a book which is neither a saga, though it deals in large natural forces, nor a *classical* epic, for we feel too strongly the individual who wrote it. It is a book that is at once primitive, fatalistic, and merciless, like the very oldest books, and yet peculiarly personal, like so many twentieth-century novels, in its significant emphasis on the subjective individual consciousness. The book grows out of a single word, "I," and expands until the soul's voyage of this "I" comes to include a great many things that are unseen and unsuspected by most of us. And this material is always tied to Ishmael, who is not merely a witness to the story—someone who happens to be on board the *Pequod* —but the living and germinating mind who grasps the world in the tentacles of his thought.

The power behind this "I" is poetical in the sense that everything comes to us through a constant intervention of language instead of being presented flatly. Melville does not wish, as so many contemporary writers do, to reproduce ordinary life and conventional speech. He seeks the marvellous and the fabulous aspects that life wears in secret. He exuberantly sees the world through language—things exist as his words for them—and **much** of the exceptional beauty of the book lies in the unusual incidence of passages that, in the most surprising contexts, are so piercing in their poetic intensity. But the most remarkable feat of language in the book is Melville's ability to make us see that man is not a blank slate passively open to events, but a mind that constantly seeks meaning in everything it encounters. In Melville the Protestant habit of moralizing and the transcendental passion for symbolizing all things as examples of "higher laws" combined to make a mind that instinctively brought an inner significance to each episode. Everything in *Moby-Dick* is saturated in a mental atmosphere. Nothing happens for its own sake in this book, and in the midst of the chase, Ishmael can be seen meditating it, pulling things apart, drawing out its significant point.

But Ishmael is not just an intellectual observer; he is also very much in the story. He suffers; he is there. As his name indicates, he is an estranged and solitary man; his only friend is Queequeg, a despised heathen from the South Seas. Queequeg, a fellow "isolato" in the smug world of white middle-class Christians, is the ony man who offers Ishmael friendship; thanks to Queequeg, "no longer my splintered heart and maddened hand were turned against the wolfish world. This soothing savage had redeemed it." Why does Ishmael feel so alone? There are background reasons, Melville's own: his father went bankrupt and then died in debt when Melville was still a boy. Melville-Ishmael went to sea—"And at first," he tells us, "this sort of thing is unpleasant enough. It touches one's sense of honor, particularly if you come of an old established family in the land." But there is a deeper, a more universal reason for Ishmael's apartness, and it is one that will strangely make him kin to his daemonic captain, Ahab. For the burden of his thought, the essential cause of his estrangement, is that he cannot come to any conclusion about anything. He feels at home with ships and sailors because for him, too, one journey ends only to begin another; "and a second ended, only begins a third and so on, for ever and for aye. Such is the endlessness, yea, the intolerableness of all earthly effort."

Ishmael is not merely an orphan; he is an exile, searching alone in the wilderness, with a black man for his only friend. He suffers from doubt and uncertainty far more than he does from homelessness. Indeed, this agony of disbelief *is* his homelessness. For him nothing is ever finally settled and decided; he is man, or as we like to think, modern man, cut off from the certainty that was once his inner world. Ishmael no longer has any sure formal belief. All is in doubt, all is in eternal flux, like the sea. And so condemned, like "all his race from Adam down," to wander the seas of thought, far from Paradise, he now searches endlessly to put the whole broken story together, to find a meaning, to ascertain—where but in the ceaselessness of human thought?—"the hidden cause we seek." Ishmael does not perform any great actions, as Ahab does; he is the most insignificant member of the fo'c'sle and will get the smallest share of the take. But his inner world of thought is almost unbearably symbolic, for he must think, and think, and think, in order to prove to himself that there is a necessary connection between man and the world. He pictures his dilemma in everything he does on board the ship, but never so clearly as when he is shown looking at the sea, searching a meaning to existence from the inscrutable waters.

What Melville did through Ishmael, then, was to put man's distinctly modern feeling of "exile," of abandonment, directly at the center of his stage. For Ishmael there are no satisfactory conclusions to anything; no final philosophy is ever possible. All that man owns in this world, Ishmael would say, is his insatiable mind. This is why the book opens on a picture of the dreaming contemplativeness of mind itself: men tearing themselves loose from their jobs to stand "like silent sentinels all around the town . . . thousands of mortal men fixed in ocean reveries." Narcissus was bemused by that image which "we ourselves see in all rivers and oceans," and this, says Ishmael when he is most desperate, is all that man ever finds when he searches the waters —a reflection of himself. All is inconclusive, restless, and endless flow.

And Melville's own style rises to its highest level not in the neo-Shake-spearean speeches of Ahab, which are sometimes bombastic, but in those amazing prose flights on the whiteness of the whale and on the Pacific where Ishmael reproduces, in the rhythms of the prose itself, man's brooding interrogation of nature.

II

But Ishmael is a witness not only to his own thoughts, but also a witness to the actions of Captain Ahab. The book is not only a great skin of language stretched to fit the world of man's philosophic wandering; it is also a world of moral tyranny and violent action, in which the principal actor is Ahab. With the entry of Ahab a harsh new rhythm enters the book, and from now on two rhythms—one reflective, the other forceful—alternate to show us the world in which man's thinking and man's doing each follows its own law. Ishmael's thought consciously extends itself to get behind the world of appearances; he wants to see and to understand everything. Ahab's drive is to *prove,* not to discover; the world that tortures Ishmael by its horrid vacancy has tempted Ahab into thinking that he can make it over. He seeks to dominate nature, to impose and to inflict his will on the outside world—whether it be the crew that must jump to his orders or the great white whale that is essentially indifferent to him. As Ishmael is all rumination, so Ahab is all will. Both are thinkers, the difference being that Ishmael thinks as a bystander, has identified his own state with man's utter unimportance in nature. Ahab, by contrast, actively seeks the whale in order to assert man's supremacy over what swims before him as "the monomaniac incarnation" of a superior power:

> If man will strike, strike through the mask! How can the prisoner reach outside except by thrusting through the wall? To me, the white whale is that wall, shoved near to me. Sometimes I think there's naught beyond. But 'tis enough. He tasks me; he heaps me; I see in him outrageous strength, with an inscrutable malice sinewing it. That inscrutable thing is chiefly what I hate; and be the white whale agent, or be the white whale principal, I will wreak that hate upon him. Talk not to me of blasphemy, man; I'd strike the sun if it insulted me. For could the sun do that, then could I do the other; since there is ever a sort of fair play herein, jealousy presiding over all creations. But not my master, man, is even that fair play. Who's over me? Truth hath no confines.

This is Ahab's quest—and Ahab's magnificence. For in this speech Ahab expresses more forcibly than Ishmael ever could, something of the impenitent anger against the universe that all of us can feel. Ahab may be a mad sea captain, a tyrant of the quarter deck who disturbs the crew's sleep as he stomps along on his ivory leg. But this Ahab does indeed speak for all men who, as Ishmael confesses in the frightening meditation on the whiteness of the whale, suspect that "though in many of its aspects this visible world seems formed in love, the invisible spheres were formed in fright." So man, watching the sea heaving around him, sees it as a mad steed that has lost its rider, and looking at his own image in the water, is tortured by the thought that man himself may be an accident, of no more importance in this vast oceanic emptiness than one of Ahab's rare tears dropped into the Pacific.

To the degree that we feel this futility in the face of a blind impersonal nature that "heeds us not," and storm madly, like Ahab, against the dread that there's "naught beyond"—to this extent all men may recognize Ahab's bitterness, his unrelentingness, his inability to rest in that uncertainty which, Freud has told us, modern man must learn to endure. Ahab figures in a symbolic fable; he is acting out thoughts which we all share. But Ahab, even more, is a hero; we cannot insist enough on that. Melville believed in the heroic and he specifically wanted to cast his hero on American lines—someone noble by nature, not by birth, who would have "not the dignity of kings and robes, but that abounding dignity which has no robed investiture." Ahab sinned against man and God, and like his namesake in the Old Testament, becomes a "wicked king." But Ahab is not just a fanatic who leads the whole crew to their destruction; he is a hero of thought who is trying, by terrible force, to reassert man's place in nature. And it is the struggle that Ahab incarnates that makes him so magnificent a *voice,* thundering in Shakespearean rhetoric, storming at the gates of the inhuman, silent world. Ahab is trying to give man, in one awful, final assertion that his will *does* mean something, a feeling of relatedness with his world.

Ahab's effort, then, is to reclaim something that man knows he has lost. Significantly, Ahab proves by the bitter struggle he has to wage that man is fighting in an unequal contest; by the end of the book Ahab abandons all his human ties and becomes a complete fanatic. But Melville has no doubt—nor should we!—that Ahab's quest is *humanly* understandable. And the quest itself supplies the book with its technical *raison d'être.* For it leads us through all the seas and around the whole world; it brings us past ships of every nation. Always it is Ahab's drive that makes up the *passion* of *Moby-Dick,* a passion that is revealed in the descriptive chapters on the whale, whale-fighting, whale-burning, on the whole gory and fascinating industrial process aboard ship that reduces the once proud whale to oil-brimming barrels in the hold. And this passion may be defined as a passion of longing, of hope, of striving: a passion that starts from the deepest loneliness that man can know. It is the great cry of man who feels himself exiled from his "birthright, the merry May-day gods of old," who looks for a new god "to enthrone . . . again in the now egotistical sky; in the now unhaunted hill." The cry is Ahab's—"Who's to doom, when the judge himself is dragged to the bar?"

Behind Ahab's cry is the fear that man's covenant with God has been broken, that there is no purpose to our existence. The *Pequod* is condemned by Ahab to sail up and down the world in search of— a symbol. But this search, mad as it seems to Starbuck the first mate, who is a Christian, nevertheless represents Ahab's real humanity. For the ancient covenant is never quite broken so long as man still thirsts for it. And because Ahab, as Melville intended him to, represents the aristocracy of intellect in our democracy, because he seeks to transcend the limitations that good conventional men like Starbuck, philistine materialists like Stubb, and unthinking fools like Flask want to impose on everybody else, Ahab speaks for the humanity that belongs to man's imaginative vision of himself.

Yet with all this, we must not forget that Ahab's quest takes place, unceasingly, in a very practical world of whaling, as part of the barbaric and yet highly necessary struggle by man to support himself physically in nature. It is this that gives the book its primitive vitality, its burning authenticity. For *Moby-Dick,* it must be emphasized, is not simply a symbolic fable; nor, as we have already seen, can it possibly be construed as simply a "sea story." It is the story of agonizing thought in the midst of brutal action, of thought that questions every action, that annuls it from within, as it were—but that cannot, in this harsh world, relieve man of the fighting, skinning, burning, the backbreaking row to the whale, the flying harpoons, the rope that can take you off "voicelessly as Turkish mutes bowstring their victims." *Moby-Dick* is a representation of the passionate mind speaking, for its metaphysical concerns, out of the very midst of life. So, after the first lowering, Queequeg is shown sitting all night in a submerged boat, holding up a lantern like an "imbecile candle in the heart of that almighty forlornness . . . the sign and symbol of a man without hope, hopelessly holding up hope in the midst of despair." Melville insists that our thinking is *not* swallowed up by practical concerns, that man constantly searches for a reality equal to his inner life of thought—and it is his ability to show this in the midst of a brutal, dirty whaling voyage that makes *Moby-Dick* such an astonishing book. Just as Ahab is a hero, so *Moby-Dick* itself is a heroic book. What concerns Melville is not merely the heroism that gets expressed in physical action, but the heroism of thought itself as it rises above its seeming insignificance and proclaims, in the very teeth of a seemingly hostile and malevolent creation, that man's voice *is* heard for something against the watery waste and the deep, that man's thought has an echo in the universe.

III

This is the quest. But what makes *Moby-Dick* so fascinating, and in a sense even uncanny, is that the issue is always in doubt, and remains so to the end. Melville was right when he wrote to Hawthorne: "I have written a wicked book, and feel as spotless as the lamb." And people who want to construe *Moby-Dick* into a condemnation of mad, bad Ahab will always miss what Melville meant when he wrote of his book: "It is not a piece of fine feminine Spitalfields silk—but it is of the horrible texture of a fabric that should be woven of ships' cables & hawsers. A Polar wind blows through it, & birds of prey hover over it." For in the struggle between man's effort to find meaning in nature, and the indifference of nature itself, which simply eludes him (nature here signifies the whole external show and force of animate life in a world suddenly emptied of God, one where an "intangible malignity" has reigned from the beginning), Melville often portrays the struggle from the side of nature itself. He sees the whale's view of things far more than he does Ahab's: and Moby-Dick's milk-white head, the tail feathers of the sea birds streaming from his back like pennons, are described with a rapture that is like the adoration of a god. Even in the most terrible scenes of the shark massacre, where the sharks bend around like bows to bite at their own entrails, or in the ceaseless motion of "my dear Pacific," the "Potters' fields of all four continents," one feels that Melville is transported by the naked reality of things, the great unending flow of the creation itself, where the great shroud of the sea rolls over the doomed ship "as it rolled five thousand years ago." Indeed, one feels in the end that it is only the necessity to keep one person alive as a witness to the story that saves Ishmael from the general ruin and wreck. In Melville's final vision of the whole, it is not fair but it is entirely *just* that the whale should destroy the ship, that man should be caught up on the beast. It is just in a cosmic sense, not in the sense that the prophet (Father Mapple) predicts the punishment of man's disobedience in the telling of Jonah's story from the beginning, where the point made is the classic reprimand of God to man when He speaks out of the whirlwind. What Melville does is to speak for the whirlwind, for the watery waste, for the sharks.

It **is** this that gives *Moby-Dick* its awful and crushing power. It is a unique gift. Goethe said that he wanted, as a writer, to know what it is like to be a woman. But Melville sometimes makes you feel that he knows, as a writer, what it is like to be the eyes of the rock, the magnitude of the whale, the scalding sea, the dreams that lie buried in the Pacific. It is all, of course, seen through human eyes—yet there is in Melville a cold, final, ferocious hopelessness, a kind of ecstatic masochism, that delights in punishing man, in heaping coals on his head, in drowning him. You see it in the scene of the whale running through the herd with a cutting spade in his body, cutting down his own; in the sharks eating at their own entrails and voiding from them in the same convulsion; in the terrible picture of Pip the cabin boy jumping out of the boat in fright and left on the Pacific to go crazy; in Tashtego falling into the "honey head" of the whale; in the ropes that suddenly whir up from the spindles and carry you off; in the final awesome picture of the whale butting its head against the *Pequod*. In all these scenes there is an ecstasy in horror, the horror of nature in itself, nature "pure," without God or man: the void. It is symbolized by the whiteness of the whale, the whiteness that is not so much a color as the absence of color. "Is it that by its indefiniteness it shadows forth the heartless voids and immensities of the universe, and thus stabs us from behind with the thought of annihilation, when beholding the white depths of the milky way?" And it is this picture of existence as one where man has only a peep-hole on the mystery itself, that constitutes the most remarkable achievement of Melville's genius. For as in the meditation on the whiteness of the whale, it becomes an uncanny attempt to come to grips with nature as it might be conceived with man entirely left out; or, what amounts to the same thing, with man losing his humanity and being exclusively responsive to primitive and racial memories, to the trackless fathomless nothing that has been from the beginning, to the very essence of a beginning that, in contradiction to all man's scriptures, had no divine history, no definite locus, but just *was*—with man slipped into the picture much later.

This view of reality, this ability to side with nature rather than with man, means an ability to love what has no animation, what is inhumanly still, what is not in search, as man himself is—a hero running against time and fighting against "reality." Here Melville puts, as it were, his ear to reality itself: to the rock rather than to the hero trying to get his sword out of the rock. He does it by constantly, and bitterly, and savagely, in fact, comparing man with the great thing he is trying to understand. Ahab may be a hero by trying to force himself on what is too much for him, but Melville has no doubt that man is puny and presumptuous and easily overwhelmed—in short, drowned—in the great storm of reality he tries to encompass.

This sense of scale lies behind the chapters on the natural history of the whale, and behind the constant impressing on our minds of the contrast between man and the whale—man getting into a small boat, man being overwhelmed by his own weapons. The greatest single metaphor in the book is that of bigness, and even when Melville laughs at himself for trying to hook this Leviathan with a pen—"Bring me a condor's quill! Bring me Vesuvius' crater for an inkstand!"—we know that he not merely feels exhilaration at attempting this mighty subject, but that he is also abashed, he feels grave; mighty waters are rolling around him. This compelling sense of magnitude, however, gets him to organize the book brilliantly, in a great flood of chapters—some of them very small, one or two only a paragraph long, in the descriptive method which is the great homage that he pays to his subject, and which so provides him with an inexhaustible delight in devoting himself to every conceivable detail about the whale. And, to go back to a theme mentioned earlier, it is this sense of a limitless subject that gives the style its peculiarly loping quality, as if it were constantly looking for connectives, since on the subject of the whale no single word or statement is enough. But these details tend, too, to heap up in such a staggering array as to combine into the awesomeness of a power against which Ahab's challenge is utterly vain, and against which his struggle to show his superiority over the ordinary processes of nature becomes blasphemous. The only thing left to man, Melville seems to tell us, is to take the span of this magnitude—to feel and to record the power of this mighty torrent, this burning fire.

And it is this, this poetic power, rather than any specifically human one, this power of transcription rather than of any alteration of life that will admit human beings into its tremendous scale, that makes up the greatness of the book—by giving us the measure of Melville's own relation to the nature that his hero so futilely attempts to master or defy. For though Melville often takes a grim and almost cruel pleasure in showing man tumbling over before the magnitude of the universe, and though much of the book is concerned, as in the sections on fighting and "cooking" the whale, with man's effort to get a grip on external nature, first through physical assault and then by scientific and industrial cunning, man finds his final relatedness to nature neither as a hero (Ahab) nor by heeding Father Mapple's old prophetic warning of man's proper subservience to God. Though all his attempted gains from nature fail him, and all goes down with the *Pequod*—all man's hopes of profit, of adjustment to orthodoxy (Starbuck), even of the wisdom that is in madness (Pip)—man, though forever alien to the world, an Ishmael, is somehow in tune with it, with its torrential rhythms, by dint of his art, by the directness with which his words grasp the world, by the splendor of his perceptions, by the lantern which he holds up "like a candle in the midst of the almighty forlornness." Man is not merely a waif in the world; he is an ear listening to the sea that almost drowns him; an imagination, a mind, that hears the sea in the shell, and darts behind all appearance to the beginning of things, and runs riot with the frightful force of the sea itself. There, in man's incredible and unresting mind, is the fantastic gift with which we enter into what is not our own, what is even against us—and for this, so amazingly, we can speak.

III

edmund wilson

the old stone house

Edmund Wilson was born in Red Bank, New Jersey, in 1895, and is a graduate of Princeton. He was overseas with the American Army in the First World War, later served on the editorial staffs of *Vanity Fair* and *The New Republic,* and through a series of extraordinarily well-written books, the best known of which are *Axel's Castle, The Wound and The Bow, The Triple Thinkers, To The Finland Station, The Shores of Light,* has become the most celebrated of American literary critics.

Wilson's particular gifts as a literary and intellectual analyst are a permanent resource of American criticism. The present selection, "The Old Stone House," shows Wilson as an equally gifted and evocative writer of autobiography. Wilson wrote this essay in 1933, in the depths of the depression; the journey he describes to his ancestral home in Talcottville, in upper New York State, is meant to offer a vision of an American past—before the country hardened fully, under the influence of industrial capitalism, into the character that it has today. The essay seeks deliberately to call up an American past more austere and more dedicated than the contemporary America in which Wilson was struggling to find his bearings. Yet in his luminous inquiry back into the past, Wilson recreates, from the foundation of the old stone house, an America which could *not* come back—and which, by sensitive intelligences like himself, could not be forgotten.

As he comes back to his home in New York, Wilson recognizes that the journey he has been describing, a journey that takes place simultaneously in space and in his own mind, did not bring him what he sought. He feels himself caught between the world of his ancestors, which in depression America he cannot reclaim, and the contemporary world in which he *has* to live—but which he cannot respect. The journey back into the past, the journey that he describes as if he were reliving all the hopes and experiences of his ancestors, ends in the great city world in which he has to live. "It is this . . . which has been rankling and causing my gloom: to have left that early world behind yet never to have really succeeded in what was till yesterday the new."

As I go north for the first time in years, in the slow, the constantly stopping, milk train—which carries passengers only in the back part of the hind car and has an old stove to heat it in winter—I look out through the dirt-yellowed double pane and remember how once, as a child, I used to feel thwarted in summer till I had got the windows open and there was nothing between me and the widening pastures, the great boulders, the black and white cattle, the rivers, stony and thin, the lone elms like feather-dusters, the high air which sharpens all outlines, makes all colors so breathtakingly vivid, in the clear light of late afternoon.

The little stations again: Barnevald, Stittville, Steuben—a tribute to the Prussian general who helped drill our troops for the Revolution. The woman behind me in the train talks to the conductor with a German accent. They came over here for land and freedom.

Boonville, the pale boxlike building, smooth gray, with three floors of slots that look in on darkness and a roof like a flat overlapping lid—cold dark clear air, fresh water. Like nothing else but upstate New York. Rivers that run quick among stones, or, deeper, stained dark with dead leaves. I used to love to follow them—should still. A fresh breath of water off the Black River, where the blue closed gentians grow. Those forests, those boulder-strewn pastures, those fabulous distant falls!

There was never any train to Talcottville. Our house was the center of the town. It is strange to get back to this now: it seems not quite like anything else that I have ever known. But is this merely the apparent uniqueness of places associated with childhood?

The settlers of this part of New York were a first westward migration from New England. At the end of the eighteenth century, they drove ox-teams from Connecticut and Massachusetts over into the wild northern country below Lake Ontario and the St. Lawrence River, and they established here an extension of New England.

Yet an extension that was already something new. I happened last week to be in Ipswich, Mass., the town from which one branch of my family came; and, for all the New England pride of white houses and green blinds, I was oppressed by the ancient crampedness. Even the House of the Seven Gables, which stimulated the imagination of Hawthorne, though it is grim perhaps, is not romantic. It, too, has the

THE OLD STONE HOUSE: From *The American Earthquake*. Published by Doubleday & Company, Inc. Copyright © 1958 by Edmund Wilson. Reprinted by permission of the author.

tightness and the self-sufficiency of that little provincial merchant society, which at its best produced an intense little culture, quite English in its concreteness and practicality—as the block letters of the signs along the docks made Boston look like Liverpool. But life must have hit its head on those close and low-ceilinged coops. That narrowness, that meagerness, that stinginess, still grips New England today: the drab summer cottages along the shore seem almost as slit-windowed and pinched as the gray twin-houses of a mill town like Lawrence or Fall River. I can feel the relief myself of coming away from Boston to these first uplands of the Adirondacks, where, discarding the New England religion but still speaking the language of New England, the settlers found limitless space. They were a part of the new America, now forever for a century on the move; and they were to move on themselves before they would be able to build here anything comparable to the New England civilization. The country, magnificent and vast, has never really been humanized as New England has: the landscape still overwhelms the people. But this house, one of the few of its kind among later wooden houses and towns, was an attempt to found a civilization. It blends in a peculiar fashion the amenities of the eastern seaboard with the rudeness and toughness of the new frontier.

It was built at the end of the eighteenth century: the first event recorded in connection with it is a memorial service for General Washington. It took four or five years in the building. The stone had to be quarried and brought out of the river. The walls are a foot and a half thick, and the plaster was applied to the stone without any intervening lattice. The beams were secured by enormous nails, made by hand and some of them eighteen inches long. Solid and simple as a fortress, the place has also the charm of something which has been made to order. There is a front porch with white wooden columns which support a white wooden balcony that runs along the second floor. The roof comes down close over the balcony, and the balcony and the porch are draped with vines. Large ferns grow along the porch, and there are stone hitching-posts and curious stone ornaments, cut out of the quarry like the house: on one side, a round-bottomed bowl in which red geraniums bloom, and on the other, an unnamable object, crudely sculptured and vaguely pagoda-like. The front door is especially handsome: the door itself is dark green and equipped with a brass knocker, and the woodwork which frames it is white; it is crowned with a wide fanlight and flanked by two narrow panes of glass, in which a white filigree of ironwork makes a webbing like ice over winter ponds. On one of the broad sides of the building, where the mortar has come off the stone, there is a dappling of dark gray under pale gray like the dappling of light in shallow water, and the feathers of the elms make dapplings of sun among their shadows of large lace on the grass.

The lawn is ungraded and uneven like the pastures, and it merges eventually with the fields. Behind, these are great clotted masses of myrtle-beds, lilac-bushes, clumps of pink phlox and other things I cannot identify; pink and white hollyhocks, some of them leaning, fine blue and purple dye of larkspur; a considerable vegetable garden, with long rows of ripe gooseberries and currants, a patch of yellow pumpkin flowers, and bushes of raspberries, both white and red—among which are sprinkled like confetti the little flimsy California poppies, pink, orange, white and red. In an old dark red barn behind, where the hayloft is almost collapsing, I find spinning-wheels, a carder, candle-molds, a patent boot-jack, obsolete implements of carpentry, little clusters of baskets for berry-picking and a gigantic pair of scales such as is nowadays only seen in the hands of allegorical figures.

The house was built by the Talcotts, after whom the town was named. They owned the large farm in front of the house, which stretches down to the river and beyond. They also had a profitable grist mill, but—I learn from the county history—were thought to have "adopted a policy adverse to the building up of the village at the point where natural advantages greatly favored," since they "refused to sell village lots to mechanics, and retained the water power on Sugar River, although parties offered to invest liberally in manufactures." In time, there were only two Talcotts left, an old maid and her widowed sister. My great-grandfather, Thomas Baker, who lived across the street and had been left by the death of his wife with a son and eight daughters, paid court to Miss Talcott and married her. She was kind to the children, and they remembered her with affection. My great-grandfather acquired in this way the house, the farm and the quarry.

All but two of my great-grandfather's daughters, of whom my grand-mother was one—"six of them beauties," I understand—got married and went away. Only one of them was left in the house at the time when I first remember Talcottville: my great-aunt Rosalind, a more or less professional invalid and a figure of romantic melancholy, whose fiancé had been lost at sea. When I knew her, she was very old. It was impressive and rather frightening to call on her—you did it only by special arrangement, since she had to prepare herself to be seen. She would be beautifully dressed in a lace cap, a lavender dress and a white crocheted shawl, but she had become so bloodless and shrunken as dreadfully to resemble a mummy and reminded one uncomfortably of Miss Havisham in Dickens's *Great Expectations*. She had a certain high and formal coquetry and was the only person I ever knew who really talked like the characters in old novels. When she had been able to get about, she had habitually treated the townspeople with a condescension almost baronial. According to the family legend, the great-grandmother of great-grandmother Baker had been a daughter of one of the Earls of Essex, who had eloped with a gardener to America.

Another of my Baker great-aunts, who was one of my favorite relatives, had married and lived in the town and had suffered tragic disappointments. Only her strong intellectual interests and a mind capable of philosophic pessimism had maintained her through the wreck of her domestic life. She used to tell me how, a young married woman, she had taught herself French by the dictionary and grammar, sitting up at night alone by the stove through one of their cold and dark winters. She had read a great deal of French, subscribed to French magazines, without ever having learned to pronounce it. She had rejected revealed religion and did not believe in immortality; and when she felt that she had been relieved of the last of her family obligations—though her hair was now turning gray—she came on to New York City and lived there alone for years, occupying herself with the theater, reading, visits to her nephews and nieces—with whom she was extremely popular—and all the spectacle and news of the larger world which she had always loved so much but from which she had spent most of her life removed.

When she died, only the youngest of the family was left, the sole brother, my great-uncle Tom. His mother must have been worn out with childbearing—she died after the birth of this ninth child—and he had not turned out so well as the others. He had been born with no roof to his mouth and was obliged to wear a false gold palate, and it was difficult to understand him. He was not really simple-minded—he had held a small political job under Cleveland, and he usually beat me at checkers—but he was childlike and ill-equipped to deal with life in any very effective way. He sold the farm to a German and the quarry to the town. Then he died, and the house was empty, except when my mother and father would come here to open it up for two or three months in the summer.

I have not been back here in years, and I have never before examined the place carefully. It has become for me something like a remembered dream—unearthly with the powerful impressions of childhood. Even now that I am here again, I find I have to shake off the dream. I keep walking from room to room, inside and outside, upstairs and down, with uneasy sensations of complacency that are always falling through to depression.

These rooms are very well proportioned; the white mantelpieces are elegant and chaste, and the carving on each one is different. The larger of the two living rooms now seems a little bare because the various members of the family have claimed and taken away so many things; and there are some disagreeable curtains and carpets, for which the wife of my great-uncle Tom is to blame. But here are all the things, I take note, that are nowadays sold in antique stores: red Bohemian-glass decanters; a rusty silver snuff-box; a mirror with the American eagle painted at the top of the glass. Little mahogany tables with slim legs; a set of curly-maple furniture, deep seasoned yellow like satin; a yellow comb-backed rocker, with a design of green conch-shells that look like snails. A small bust of Dante with the nose chipped, left behind as defective by one of my cousins when its companion piece, Beethoven, was taken away; a little mahogany melodeon on which my Aunt "Lin" once played. Large engravings of the family of Washington and of the "Reformers Presenting Their Famous Protest before the Diet of Spires"; a later engraving of Dickens. Old tongs and poker, impossibly heavy. A brown mahogany desk inlaid with yellow birdwood, which contains a pair of steel-rimmed spectacles and a thing for shaking sand on wet ink. Daguerreotypes in fancy cases: they seem to last much better than photographs—my grandmother looks fresh and cunning—I remember that I used to hear that the first time my grandfather saw her, she was riding on a load of hay—he came back up here to marry her as soon as he had got out of medical school. An old wooden flute—originally brought over from New England, I remember my great-uncle's telling me, at the time when they traveled by ox-team—he used to get a lonely piping out of it—I try it but cannot make a sound. Two big oval paintings, in tarnished gilt frames, of landscapes romantic and mountainous: they came from the Utica house of my great-grandfather Baker's brother—he married a rich wife and invented excelsior—made out of the northern lumber—and was presented with a solid-silver table service by the grateful city of Utica.

Wallpaper molded by the damp from the stone; uninviting old black haircloth furniture. A bowl of those enormous upcountry sweet peas, incredibly fragrant and bright—they used to awe and trouble me—why?

In the dining room, a mahogany china closet, which originally—in the days when letters were few and great-grandfather Baker was postmaster—was the whole of the village post office. My grandmother's pewter tea-service, with its design of oak-leaves and acorns, which I remember from her house in New Jersey. Black iron cranes, pipkins and kettles for cooking in the fireplace; a kind of flat iron pitchfork for lifting the bread in and out, when they baked at the back of the hearth. On the sideboard, a glass decanter with a gilt black-letter label: "J. Rum." If there were only some rum in the decanter!—if the life of the house were not now all past!—the kitchens that trail out behind are almost too old-smelling, too long deserted, to make them agreeable to visit—in spite of the delightful brown crocks with long-tailed blue birds painted on them, a different kind of bird on each crock.

In the ample hall with its staircase, two large colored pictures of trout, one rising to bait, one leaping. Upstairs, a wooden pestle and mortar; a perforated tin box for hot coals to keep the feet warm in church or on sleigh-rides; a stuffed heron; a horrible bust of my cousin Dorothy Read in her girlhood, which her mother had done of her in in Germany. The hair-ribbon and the ruffles are faithfully reproduced in marble, and the eyes have engraved pupils. It stands on a high pedestal, and it used to be possible, by pressing a button, to make it turn around. My Cousin Grace, Dorothy's mother, used to show it off and invite comparison with the original, especially calling attention to the nose; but what her mother had never known was that Dorothy had injured her nose in some rather disgraceful row with her sister. One day when the family were making an excursion, Dorothy pleaded indisposition and bribed a man with a truck to take the bust away and drop it into a pond. But Uncle Tom got this out of the man, dredged the statue up and replaced it on its pedestal. An ugly chair with a round rag back; an ugly bed with the head of Columbus sticking out above the pillows like a figurehead. Charming old bedquilts, with patterns of rhomboids in softened browns, greens and pinks, or of blue polka-dotted hearts that ray out on stiff phallic stalks. A footstool covered in white, which, however, when you step on a tab at the side, opens up into a cuspidor—some relic, no doubt, of the times when the house was used for local meetings. (There used to be a musical chair, also brought back from Germany, but it seems to have disappeared.) A jar of hardly odorous dried rose-leaves, and a jar of little pebbles and shells that keep their bright colors in alcohol.

The original old panes up here have wavy lines in the glass. There are cobweb-filthy books, which I try to examine: many religious works, the annals of the state legislature, a book called *The Young Wife, or Duties of Women in the Marriage Relation,* published in Boston in 1838 and containing a warning against tea and coffee, which "loosen the tongue, fire the eye, produce mirth and wit, excite the animal passions, and lead to remarks about ourselves and others, that we should not have made in other circumstances, and which it were better for us and the world, never to have made." But there is also, I noticed downstairs, Grant Allan's *The Woman Who Did* from 1893.

I come upon the *History of Lewis County* and read it with a certain pride. I am glad to say to myself that it is a creditable piece of work—admirably full in its information on geology, flora and fauna, on history and local politics; diversified with anecdotes and biographies never overflattering and often pungent; and written in a sound English style. Could anyone in the county today, I wonder, command such a sound English style? I note with gratification that the bone of a prehistoric cuttlefish, discovered in one of the limestone caves, is the largest of its kind on record, and that a flock of wild swans was seen in 1821. In the eighties, there were still wolves and panthers. There are still bears and deer today.

I also look into the proceedings of the New York State Assembly. My great-grandfather Thomas Baker was primarily a politician and at that time a member of the Assembly. I have heard that he was a Jacksonian Democrat, and that he made a furious scene when my grandmother came back from New Jersey and announced that she had become a Republican: it "spoiled her whole visit." There is a photograph of great-grandfather Baker in an oval gilt frame, with his hair sticking out in three spikes and a wide and declamatory mouth. I look through the Assembly record to see what sort of role he played. It is the forties; the Democrats are still angry over the Bank of United States. But when I look up Thomas Baker in the index, it turns out that he figures solely as either not being present or as requesting leave of absence. They tell me he used to go West to buy cattle.

That sealed-up space on the second floor which my father had knocked out—who did they tell me was hidden in it? I have just learned from one of the new road-signs which explain historical associations that there are caves somewhere here in which slaves were hidden. Could this have been a part of the underground route for smuggling Negroes over the border into Canada? Is the attic, the "kitchen chamber," which is always so suffocating in summer, still full of those carpet-bags and crinolines and bonnets and beaver-hats that we used to get out of the old cowhide trunks and use to dress up for charades?

It was the custom for the married Baker daughters to bring their children back in the summer; and their children in time brought their children. In those days, how I loved coming up here! It was a reunion with cousins from Boston and New York, Ohio and Wisconsin, as well as with the Talcottville and Utica ones: we fished and swam in the rivers, had all sorts of excursions and games. Later on, I got to dislike it: the older generation died, the younger did not much come. I wanted to be elsewhere, too. The very fullness with life of the past, the memory of those many families of cousins and uncles and aunts, made the emptiness of the present more oppressive. Isn't it still?—didn't my gloom come from that, the night of my first arrival? Wasn't it the dread of that that kept me away? I am aware, as I walk through the rooms, of the amplitude and completeness of the place—the home of a big old-fashioned family that had to be a city in itself. And not merely did it house a clan: the whole life of the community passed through it. And now for five sixths of the year it is nothing but an unheated shell, a storehouse of unused antiques, with no intimate relation to the county.

The community itself today is somewhat smaller than the community of those days, and its condition has very much changed. It must seem to the summer traveler merely one of the clusters of houses that he shoots through along the state highway; and there may presently be little left save our house confronting, across the road, the hot-dog stand and the gasoline station.*

For years I have had a recurrent dream. I take a road that runs toward the west. It is summer; I pass by a strange summer forest, in which there are mysterious beings, though I know that, on the whole, they are shy and benign. If I am fortunate and find the way, I arrive at a wonderful river, which runs among boulders, with rapids, between alders and high-spread trees, through a countryside fresh, green and wide. We go in swimming; it is miles away from anywhere. We plunge in the smooth flowing pools. We make our way to the middle of the stream and climb up on the pale round gray stones and sit naked in the sun and the air, while the river glides away below us. And I know that it is the place for which I have always longed, the place of wildness and freedom, to find which is the height of what one may hope for—the place of unalloyed delight.

As I walk about Talcottville now, I discover that the being-haunted forest is a big grove which even in daytime used to be lonely and dark and where great white Canadian violets used to grow out of the deep black leaf-mold. Today it is no longer dark, because half the trees have been cut down. The river of my dream, I see, is simply an idealized version of the farther and less frequented and more adventurous bank of Sugar River, which had to be reached by wading. Both river and forest

---

* This description may seem inconsistent with my account of our Talcottville location in another book, *A Piece of My Mind,* but the main highway was later shifted, put through along another road, and my mother had succeeded, in the meantime, in getting rid of the hot-dog stand by buying back the lot across the street.

are west of the road that runs through the village, which accounts for my always taking that direction in my dream. I remember how Sugar River—out of the stone of which our house is built—used, in my boyhood, so to fascinate me that I had an enlargement made of one of the photographs I had taken of it—a view of "the Big Falls"—and kept it in my room all winter. Today the nearer bank has been largely blasted away to get stone for the new state highway, and what we used to call "the Little Falls" is gone.

I visit the house of my favorite great-aunt, and my gloom returns and overwhelms me. The huge root of an elm has split the thick slabs of the pavement so that you have to walk over a hump; and one of the big square stone fence-posts is toppling. Her flowers, with no one to tend them, go on raggedly blooming in their seasons. There has been nobody in her house since she died. It is all too appropriate to her pessimism—that dead end she always foresaw. As I walk around the house, I remember how, once on the black porch there, she sang me old English ballads, including that gruesome one, "Oh, where have you been, Randall, my son?"—about the man who had gone to Pretty Peggy's house and been given snakes to eat:

> *"What had you for supper, Randall, my son?"*
> *"Fresh fish fried in butter. Oh, make my bed soon!*
> *For I'm sick at my heart and I fain would lie down!"*

She was old then—round-shouldered and dumpy—after the years when she had looked so handsome, straight-backed and with the fashionable aigrette in her hair. And the song she sang seemed to have been drawn out of such barbarous reaches of the past, out of something so surprisingly different from the college-women's hotels in New York in which I had always known her as living: that England to which, far though she had come from it, she was yet so much nearer than I—that queer troubling world of legend which I knew from Percy's *Reliques* but with which she had maintained a real contact through centuries of women's voices—for she sang it without a smile, completely possessed by its spirit—that it made my flesh creep, disconcerted me.

My great-aunt is dead, and all her generation are dead—and the new generations of the family have long ago left Talcottville behind and have turned into something quite different. They were already headed for the cities by the middle of the last century, as can be seen by the rapid dispersal of great-grandfather Baker's daughters. Yet there were still, in my childhood, a few who stayed on in this country as farmers. They were very impressive people, the survivors of a sovereign race who had owned their own pastures and fields and governed their own community. Today the descendants of these are performing mainly minor functions in a machine which they do not control. They have most of them become thoroughly urbanized, and they are farther from great-grandfather Baker than my grandmother, his daughter, was when she came back from New Jersey a Republican. One of her children, a retired importer in New York, was complaining to me the other day that the outrageous demands of the farmers were making business recovery impossible, and protesting that if the advocates of the income tax had their way, the best people would no longer be able to live up to their social positions. A cousin, who bears the name of one of his Ipswich ancestors, a mining engineer on the Coast and a classmate and admirer of Hoover, invested and has lost heavily in Mexican real estate and the industrial speculations of the boom. Another, with another of the old local names, is now at the head of an organization whose frankly avowed purpose is to rescue the New York manufacturers from taxation and social legislation. He has seen his native city of Utica decline as a textile center through the removal of its mills to the South, where taxes are lighter and labor is cheaper; and he is honestly convinced that his efforts are directed toward civic betterment.

Thus the family has come imperceptibly to identify its interests with those of what my great-grandfather Baker would have called the "money power." They work for it and acquiesce in it—they are no longer the sovereign race of the first settlers of Lewis County, and in the cities they have achieved no sovereignty. They are much too scrupulous and decent, and their tastes are too comparatively simple for them ever to have rolled up great fortunes during the years of expansion and plunder. They have still the frank accent and the friendly eye of the older American world, and they seem rather taken aback by the turn that things have been taking.

And what about me? As I come back in the train, I find that—other causes contributing—my depression of Talcottville deepens. I did not find the river and the forest of my dream—I did not find the magic of the past. I have been too close to the past: there is that house, in that remote little town which has never known industrial progress since the Talcotts first obstructed the development of the water power of Sugar River, you can see exactly how rural Americans were living a century and a half ago. And who would go back to it? Not I. Let people who have never known country life complain that the farmer has been spoiled by his radio and his Ford. Along with the memory of exaltation at the immensity and freedom of that countryside, I have memories of horror at its loneliness: houses burning down at night, sometimes with people in them, where there was no fire department to save them, and husbands or wives left alone by death—the dark nights and the prisoning winters. I do not grudge the sacrifice of the Sugar River falls for the building of the new state highway, and I do not resent the hot-dog stand. I am at first a little shocked at the sight of a transformer on the road between Talcottville and Boonville, but when I get to the Talcottville house, I am obliged to be thankful for it—no more oil-lamps in the evenings! And I would not go back to that old life if I could: that civilization of northern New York—why should I idealize it?—was too lonely, too poor, too provincial.

I look out across the Hudson and see Newburgh: with the neat-windowed cubes of its dwellings and docks, distinct as if cut by a burin, built so densely up the slope of the bank and pierced by an occasional steeple, undwarfed by tall modern buildings and with only the little old-fashioned ferry to connect it with the opposite bank, it might still be an eighteenth-century city. My father's mother came from there. She was the granddaughter of a carpet-importer from Rotterdam. From him came the thick Spanish coins which the children of my father's family were supposed to cut their teeth on. The business, which had been a considerable one, declined as the sea trade of the Hudson became concentrated in New York. My father and mother went once—a good many years ago—to visit the old store by the docks, and were amazed to find a solitary old clerk still scratching up orders and sales on a slate that hung behind the counter.

And the slate and the Spanish coins, though they symbolize a kind of life somewhat different from that evoked by Talcottville, associate themselves in my mind with such things as the old post office turned china closet. And as I happen to be reading Herndon's *Life of Lincoln,* that, too, goes to flood out the vision with its extension still further west, still further from the civilized seaboard, of the life of the early frontier. Through Herndon's extraordinary memoir, one of the few really great American books of its kind, which America has never accepted, preferring to it the sentimentalities of Sandburg and the ladies who write Christmas stories—the past confronts me even more plainly than through the bootjacks and daguerreotypes of Talcottville, and makes me even more uneasy. Here you are back again amid the crudeness and the poverty of the American frontier, and here is a man of genius coming out of it and perfecting himself. The story is not merely moving, it becomes almost agonizing. The ungainly boorish boy from the settler's clearing, with nobody and nothing behind him, hoping that his grandfather had been a planter as my great-aunt Rosalind hoped that she was a descendant of the Earls of Essex, the morbid young man looking passionately toward the refinement and the training of the East but unable to bring himself to marry the women who represented it for him—rejoining across days in country stores, nights in godforsaken hotels, rejoining by heroic self-discipline the creative intelligence of the race, to find himself the conscious focus of its terrible unconscious parturition—his miseries burden his grandeur. At least they do for me at this moment.

> *Old Abe Lincoln came out of the wilderness,*
> *Out of the wilderness, out of the wilderness—*

The echo of the song in my mind inspires me with a kind of awe—I can hardly bear the thought of Lincoln.

Great-grandfather Baker's politics and the Talcottville general store, in which people sat around and talked before the new chain store took its place—Lincoln's school was not so very much different. And I would not go back to that.

Yet as I walk up the steps of my house in New York, I am forced to recognize, with a sinking, that I have never been able to leave it. This old wooden booth I have taken between First and Second Avenues— what is it but the same old provincial America? And as I open the door with its loose knob and breathe in the musty smell of the stair-carpet, it seems to me that I have not merely stuck in the world where my fathers lived but have actually, in some ways, lost ground in it. This gray paintless clapboarded front, these lumpy and rubbed yellow walls—they were probably once respectable, but they must always have been commonplace. They have never had even the dignity of the house in Lewis County. But I have rented them because, in my youth, I had been used to living in houses and have grown to loathe city apartments.

So here, it seems, is where I must live: in an old cramped and sour frame-house—having failed even worse than my relatives at getting out of the American big-business era the luxuries and the prestige that I unquestionably should very much have enjoyed. Here is where I end by living—among the worst instead of the best of this city that took the trade away from Newburgh—the sordid and unhealthy children of my sordid and unhealthy neighbors, who howl outside my windows night and day. It is this, in the last analysis—there is no doubt about it now! —which has been rankling and causing my gloom: to have left that early world behind yet never to have really succeeded in what was till yesterday the new.

d. w. brogan

a fresh appraisal of the civil war

D(enis) W(illiam) Brogan was born in Glasgow in 1900, and was educated at Glasgow University, Oxford and Harvard. He has for a number of years been professor of political science at Cambridge University.

Brogan is famous for writing as well about the political system of the United States as he does about Britain itself; he is in a great tradition of British and European writers on America who have often been able to explain American institutions to Americans themselves. But unlike many foreign commentators in our day, Brogan writes about America with enthusiasm as well as with intelligence. He has never lost the conviction that marked many liberal intellectuals of the nineteenth century—that the development of the United States was the greatest epic of modern times. It is characteristic of Brogan's intellectual passion and his extraordinarily informed knowledge of American history that, in this new and brilliant interpretation of the Civil War, he is able to bring so much positive excitement to a subject that, to judge from the unending production of books on the Civil War, has been documented to the point of satiation.

Brogan's essay is superb because he is concerned with bringing back the significance of the Civil War to our generation. He dramatizes the irreconcilable loyalties that made the war inevitable. Unlike so many recent American historians, who have bogged down in purely economic and deterministic interpretations of the war, Brogan communicates the excitement—and the tragedy—of a cause, of two great causes. And because Brogan has not only a passion for the national American cause but also the ability, as a Scotsman, to communicate the national feeling of a small country doomed to a lost cause (like that of once-independent Scotland), his essay is both decisive in its interpretation and yet moving with admiration for both sides.

In Brogan's pages we see history live again, history as the struggle to realize human hopes and aims—the kind of history that kindles the historian to learn everything he can and to marshal his facts with clarity as well as with fervor. Brogan's feeling for historical fact, his marvelous curiosity for the little-known detail, make this essay one of the most useful and *inspiring* contributions to the history of the Civil War. In the pages of this British historian, American history lives again as the great cause that, properly regarded, it has always been seen to be.

And the reason why the essay is so stirring is that Brogan works with concrete historical facts as a painter does with colors, a novelist with scenes. A particular example of this is the long passage on how the war came between families, and his listing of several tragic examples where the war saw father fighting against son, and brother with brother.

"Happy the country that has no history."

This famous expression of a sardonic view of human destiny may be no more than a generalized version of the old Chinese curse: "May you live in interesting times." But I think it is more than that. For the country that has a "history," dramatic, moving, tragic, has to live with it— with the problems it raised but did not solve, with the emotions that it leaves as a damaging legacy, with the defective vision that preoccupation with the heroic, with the disastrous, with the expensive past fosters.

But there is more to be said than this; the inheritance of a past rich in suffering, in vicissitudes, in heroism adds something to the national assets, even though the price is always high and often grossly excessive. It would be too much to say that the nations that have known no such catastrophes *envy* their less fortunate but more interesting neighbors, but they do feel something lacking. Like the man or woman who has never been in love, they feel that they *have* missed something, including, no doubt, a great deal of trouble and expense.

And perhaps the first thing to say about the American Civil War is that it put the American people, decisively, once and for all, among the peoples who have lived in interesting times and who have paid an extravagantly high price for this experience. It may well be a sign of savagery, but the world picture of America, the American picture of America is deeply different, more impressive, more *attractive* than if it had been just one long success story. I do not for a moment suggest that the American Civil War was a good thing—merely that it was and is felt by the unregenerate (a majority of the Western races now and for as long as we can inspect the past) to be the most moving, interesting, dignified thing that has ever occurred in America.*

What is most important in the American preoccupation with their Civil War is not to be exhausted by a politico-economic balance sheet. What is important is the preoccupation, the living memory, the curi-

---

* Matthew Arnold, in his high aesthetic fashion, thought that the War, and especially the assassination of Lincoln to the tune of a Latin moto, *Sic semper tyrannis,* made American history quite respectable.

A FRESH APPRAISAL OF THE CIVIL WAR: From *Harper's Magazine,* April, 1960. Copyright © 1960 Harper & Brothers. Reprinted by permission of the author.

osity, the nostalgia. The Civil War is not only refought in an incessant flow of books, articles, and speeches; it is refought hypothetically. If Paris had not run away with Helen, how different the history of the Greeks and Trojans would have been! To want to remake history is to show how much that history means.

But is my emphasis on the American preoccupation with their Civil War justified? Suppose there is going to be a flood of books about the Civil War in the next few years, so what? The publishers know when they are in on a good thing. I am sure they do, but it is naïve to suggest that they have simply invented the good thing. The flood—though varying in volume—has never ceased since the War itself ended. I will go so far as to assert that quite soon the flag that was lowered and raised over Fort Sumter will mean more than the flag that was raised over Iwo Jima. Appomattox will soon mean more, again, than Rheims or the USS *Missouri* in Tokyo Bay. What songs of other wars (with the exception of "The Star-Spangled Banner") compare with "John Brown's Body" and "Dixie" to name only two? Perhaps it was because of the shots fired on Sumter, as much as because of the shots fired on Fort McHenry, that the United States chose its anthem. And if it is only in the South that people still talk simply of "The War," all over the restored Union I believe that it is still *the* war.

There are, it seems to me, in the experience of nations, ordeals so novel, so disastrous, physically or morally, so dramatic a destruction of hope, the prelude to some long period of humiliation or despair, that they are watersheds in the nation's history. It may be the case of a single disastrous battle, Mohács for the Hungarians, Kossovo for the Serbs, Flodden for the Scots. The history of a nation may be so rich in disasters that it is difficult to make a choice. Thus Ireland has an *embarras de richesses* in this type of experience. It is, however, my conviction that the great famine of 1846-47 was the shock from which Ireland has not yet recovered (and may not be recovering). For the French until very recent years and perhaps still (I hope not) it was that great *déception d'amour,* "The Revolution." For the Germans it was, until this century, the first Thirty Years War; now it may be (nobody knows, least of all the Germans) the Second Thirty Years War. For Britain it was (I believe) not the loss of Empire in the Second World War but the bloodletting and faithletting of the First. For the Americans it was the Civil War.

This will be readily admitted by most people if we confine the notion to the South. "I was born a child of Appomattox," said Lyndon Johnson, revealingly and rightly. The whole South is a child of Appomattox and of the years just before and the decades after. It is so in fact; it is more deeply so in folk legend and folk memory. Appomattox is the Southern Flodden Field; the Reconstruction is the Southern folk legend and memory equivalent to the Irish memory summed up in: "The curse of Cromwell on ye."

That would be enough to account for the careful cultivation of Confederate memories. (I once half-formed the impression that the only books sold in some Southern towns were religious, Confederate, or sexy.) But what of the North? The North won, didn't it? The Northern monuments are not tributes to "the Lost Cause" but to the saving of "the last, best hope of earth." Even the monuments to Lincoln are monuments to one "who hath outsoared the shadow of our night," to one who now "belongs to the ages"—as Stanton, for once rivaling Shelley, put it. I think that is too simple a description and analysis of the "myths after Lincoln," but it can be let stand for the moment.

WHY WAS IT NECESSARY?

But we have to ask ourselves why was "the last, best hope of earth" endangered? We have to ask what led to the first great political crime in American history—a President assassinated like a tyrant in corrupt and king-ridden Europe? We have to ask why it was necessary for so many hundreds of thousand of men to "give the last full measure of devotion"? We have to ask the question of what happened to the American dream of manifest destiny, of easy immunity at home, of easy moral, political, and social superiority abroad? For that dream was deeply cherished. True, from 1850 on it was an uneasy dream. Now many, perhaps most, had heard Jefferson's "firebell in the night." But it is evident that up till the moment that Beauregard's guns opened on Sumter, the majority of Americans, North and South, did not believe that it would come to ordeal by battle.

The breed of John Brown and Édmund Ruffin was a minority in every state and section, even in Massachusetts, even in South Carolina. Without saying that there was a general pacific temper (Mexicans and Indians might have demurred), there was a horror of *fraternal* war. There was naturally, also, the simple refusal of the average man and woman to believe that things can really be about to get as bad as they are going to be. In most times and countries, the mass of the people don't believe the man who cries "wolf" even the first time.

So it was in 1860-61. That is the psychological weight behind Lincoln's words in the Second Inaugural, "and the war came." True, Seward had talked of an "irrepressible conflict" but when the crisis was really upon the country, no one was more fertile in plans and dodges to avert the conflict. Lincoln had talked of a "house divided," but it is evident from his actions that he did not believe that the division would have to be ended by the sword. (Again the Second Inaugural which puts the burden of explanation and justification on the inscrutable God of Lincoln's political Calvinism is revealing.) Despite the fiery words and the outrages that we now see as the preliminaries to the dread and dreaded conflict, despite Bleeding Kansas and John Brown and the assault on Senator Sumner, people didn't see the war as coming, inevitably, with only the date uncertain, as most saw it by 1939 in Europe and many saw it in 1914. What if all the evidence pointed one way? It was too bad to be true. I doubt if Jefferson Davis wanted war, or even wanted secession. It is certain that many Southern leaders, who held out to the end, including the greatest of all, Lee, wanted neither.

"And the war came." The American people, the rightly favored children of God, were suddenly reminded of their humanity and mortality. (They were reminded again at Pearl Harbor and didn't like it then either.) "You can't do this to me" is a slightly irreverent shorthand account of an attitude that was human and general. If the French Revolution was a *déception d'amour,* this was a *déception d'espoir.*

THE ROOTS OF A LEGEND

One thing all foreign visitors to the U.S. before the Civil War noted was the nearly universal self-approbation and the desire to have that self-approbation not so much confirmed, as applauded. The American asked the visitor—Tocqueville, Dickens, who have you—"Don't you think we are wonderful?" but it was a question put in the form of the Latin "nonne" which expects the answer, "Yes—and how." In the Land of the Free few troubling questions were asked—or, if asked, listened to or even tolerated, as Tocqueville noted.

Especially the one black question mark of slavery was not allowed to be put after the rodomontade of the daily Fourth of July oration. Even in the darkening years of the 'fifties, the paean of self-praise was heard round the world. The South was beginning to say "yes, but." But my business, at the moment, is with the North that "won" and yet found the fruits of victory bitter and, in some cases, actually poisonous.

Maybe the traumatic shock would not have been so great or lasted so long if the optimists on either side had been right, if the war, when it came had been *"courte, fraiche, et joyeuse."* But the war lasted four years and was the most deadly war between Waterloo and the Marne. The most deadly, not the most bloody, because of more than half a million deaths, most took place not on the battlefields but in the hospitals. (It has been calculated that more Union soldiers died of diarrhea than died in combat.) But that made the loss less, not more, endurable. *"Dulce et decorum est pro patria mori"* is possibly comforting when the loved son or husband or father dies in actual battle. But it is less becoming to die of the camp-bred diseases, of the aftermath of measles, of typhoid, of pneumonia, of barbarous surgery or witch-doctor medicine. And hundreds of thousands died that way. If the first shock to American complacency was the manifest failure of the sacred Constitution to prevent the conflict, the second shock and, we may be certain, even more wounding, was the human misery caused not only to the sufferers in the fields, ditches, trains, wagons, ambulances, hospitals, but to their kin and friends. John Bright had condemned the recent Crimean War in a famous image:

"The Angel of Death has been abroad throughout the land."

A far more terrible angel of death was abroad between 1861 and 1865. It chilled the hopes of millions. How many hearts it broke we shall never know. I can remember how the news of the landing on Gallipoli and then of Loos and the Somme came to my small home town in Scotland. So must it have been with the news of Shiloh and Cold Harbor.

So I would suggest as the first reason for the hold of "the War" on the American memory and the American heart, is just this human tragedy on a scale never equaled in American history before or since. (Even *absolutely* the United States lost more lives in the Civil War than in the Second World War and proportionately far more. It lost more proportionately than Britain did in the First World War.)

But, it will be objected, the American people today still devote as much time, thought, and money to the legend of "The Winning of the West" as to the saving of the Union. They do, but they devote even more time and money to tobacco. There is a great difference between a legend that diverts and a legend that touches and can cause distress as well as joy. I would be the last to denigrate the *"matière d'Amérique,"* or to forget that the United States is the only country since the Middle Ages that has created a legend to set beside the story of Achilles, Robin Hood, Roland, and Arthur. But even the most devoted TV fan is aware that "the West" is a remote ideal world, not differing very much from science-fiction worlds. Even the sophisticated westerns, with their neurotic heroes and floozies with hearts of stone, are in the Never Never World of fiction. There are many good books on the West, but the representative Western work of art, book, play, TV script, comic strip is fiction; the representative Civil War book is or professes to be fact.

Then there is the mass of devoted amateurs, the Civil War buffs. Is it not significant that the most distinguished living military historian

of the War, Kenneth P. Williams, is a Professor of Mathematics? That
Carl Sandburg should have devoted so much time and effort to Lincoln? We have *John Brown's Body;* why didn't Benét write on the War
of the Revolution? At all levels, here is the great purging experience of
the American people, their shame and their pride.

Scale is one reason for the domination of the American historical
memory by the War. Americans like things big and this one was big, all
right. Compared with it, the War of the Revolution, the War of 1812,
the Mexican War were petty affairs. And as for the Spanish-American
War, a good Labor Day weekend kills nearly as many people on the
roads. The First and Second World Wars and the Korean War are
more impressive affairs, but not only did they not kill as many men
relatively or absolutely (unless you count the influenza casualties of
1918), they were fought outside the United States. And that is deeply
important.

It is not only that the battlefields of the Civil War are more acces-
sible than the Argonne or the Ardennes—not to speak of Iwo Jima or
Inchon—but being fought on American soil, they are especially sacred.
There is no *less* American sentiment than the one expressed by Rupert
Brooke, "that there's some corner of a foreign field that is forever England." American boys, if they have to die in war, should die on American soil. (One of the oddest aspects of the Civil War to Europeans was
the traveling undertakers who followed the armies and sent the bodies
back home.) This was *the* American War, since the soldiers on each
side were Americans; and both sides, today at any rate, can take pride
in the heroism of the other side. Robert E. Lee is one of the top heroes
of the national pantheon, honored by a memorial in Washington as
well as in Richmond. At West Point he is regarded as the *beau idéal*
as cadet, officer, and Superintendent. There are millions of synthetic
Southerners who, as O. Henry put it, have never been south of Hobo-
ken, and we have recently seen a Congress, controlled by the South,
honoring the one hundred and fiftieth anniversary of the birth of
Lincoln.

We can be sure that for the overwhelming majority of Americans,
the flood of centennial celebrations will bring little bitterness. (That
doesn't mean that there was no irony or humor in the recent Virginian
suggestion that there ought to be a re-enactment of the First Battle of
Bull Run, in uniform, to start the ball rolling.) But we should remember that this "era of good feeling" dates from this century, that the
War left plenty of bitterness at the time, that many things that Americans now share in common pride were then grounds of fierce difference. Then the captured Confederate flags were trophies (that great

but not magnanimous soldier, Sheridan, used to ride with a team of orderlies carrying them behind him). When Sumner in one of the few magnanimous actions of his life proposed that they should be given back, he was not listened to and when President Grover Cleveland actually decided to give them back, he had to retreat before the wrath of the Grand Army of the Republic.

It was a long time before Lee became a national hero for everyone, for we must remember that many in the North resented more hostilely the "treason" of the regular officers who "went with their states" than they did the treason of the politicians. The West Point officers were a privileged and unpopular class, fed, clothed, and paid from their youth by the Union, the only servants of the Union (apart from Federal judges and of course Navy officers) who had secure tenure. The officers who went South were biting the hand that had fed them. On the other hand, some West Pointers who had left the Army rushed to rejoin it because they felt a special duty to serve a government that had trained them for the service in arms that they could now give. Among them was ex-Captain Grant.

THE WAR OF THE BROTHERS-IN-LAW

But was it a civil war? There has been more than one protest against the title. The "War of the Rebellion" and the "War Between the States" are terms of art, each expressing the political and legal view of the conflict that the sides held or professed to hold. It has become common, in this generation, to talk of the "War for Southern Independence" and that is a just title as far as it goes. But it doesn't go far enough, for this really was a war between citizens of a hitherto united body politic designed, on each side, to establish one view of the character of that body politic. The Confederate States did not merely set up a new government for a new "country" (I avoid the word nation). They claimed to be the legitimate heirs of the old government in the area they sought to control.

The War was a civil war because it set brother against brother, father against son. Thousands of Northerners (like George Cary Eggleston) served in the ranks of the Confederate Army. Thousands of Southerners served in the ranks of the Union Army. It is hardly necessary to mention the more famous cases, of Thomas, Farragut, Scott serving the Union; Cooper, Pemberton, Gorgas serving the Confederacy. Mrs. Lincoln's brothers fought for the South and two Crittenden brothers became generals in opposing armies. The son of the commander of the Confederate Navy served in the Union Navy. Then, as now, West Pointers tended to marry each other's sisters and the War might be called the war of the brothers-in-law. (After Appomattox, even the unsentimental Sheridan went off at once to see his friends from "the old Army.")

And it was not only a matter of soldiers. Slidell, one of the few competent diplomatic agents the Confederacy had, was a New Yorker by origin. Wayne of Georgia stayed on the bench of the Supreme Court and there may be some reason to believe that Campbell of Georgia regretted having to leave it. It is these ambiguous loyalties and confused duties that mark a civil war. Lee is probably the only soldier who has ever been offered the command of both armies in a war—and when he made his choice, he entered the conflict in a far more ambivalent frame of mind than that of Robert the Bruce or Patrick Sarsfield or Charles de Gaulle.

I have always thought that this side of the War is best illustrated by a story about a personally quite unimportant boy who yet being the son of Governor Wise of Virginia was in the thick of things. As a cadet of the Virginia Military Institute, he fought at New Market and as General Wise's son he was sent on bold and risky rides across country as the Confederacy collapsed. So he saw Lee on the eve of Appomattox and Jefferson Davis at Danville just before Davis's last flight. When the collapse did come, young Wise was sent North to Philadelphia, but despite his experiences he was deemed too young to attend a dinner party given by his uncle and had to eat in the nursery with the other children. His uncle was George Gordon Meade, Commander of the Army of the Potomac.

Then in the border states, there was civil war of the classical kind. There were many thousands of men from Kentucky, Maryland, Missouri in each army. Regiments in the opposing armies bore the same names and in one disastrous instance wore nearly the same uniform. Men from the same village met in battle. And in Missouri (and Kansas) the Civil War was truly civil—that is savage, with murder and rapine rampant. Quantrill, the Confederate partisan, might have served with the Black and Tans or the Nazi SS and it was in this semi-private war that the James Boys learned their trade. And when we read that Mr. Truman's grandmother would not let him enter her house in United States uniform, we should remember what crimes that uniform had covered in Missouri.

Even the geographical distribution of the combatants was not as simple as it often is made to seem. There were bitter Union partisans in nearly every Confederate state. Even if the legend of a county "seceding" from the Confederacy *is* legend, it is revealing legend and there was an attempt to vote for Lincoln in North Carolina in 1864.

There is an Illinois legend that it was only the influence of Stephen Douglas that kept "Black Jack" Logan from joining the Confederate Army and sent him off to the Union Army instead. There were Confederate partisans and passionate defenders of slavery as far north as Vermont, and the Chief Justice of the United States, Roger Taney, had no sympathy with the cause of the government of which he was the judicial head.

THE GUILT OF CAIN

In any civil war, the question of war guilt is of the deepest importance. The origins of the English Civil War were debated heatedly for two centuries. How great was the guilt (so the Popular party thought) of P. Scipio Nasica who slew Tiberius Gracchus and opened the century of Roman civil wars! In the Second Inaugural Lincoln was to rise above this battle: "Let us judge not that we be not judged." But he was outside the usual range of human possibility.

So the American concern with the origins of the War differed greatly from that of a European nation obsessed with the success or failure of its government's policy. There was, to return to a basic theme, the sense that there must be some great guilt somewhere, to account for the ending of the Union (it *was* ended for a time). Each side, in a deeply Christian country, was anxious to throw the guilt of Cain on the other. The leaders of the South were anxious, after the War was over, to explain that they had been right but unfortunate, to refute the charge of treason leveled against them and their religion.

The North and its leaders were equally anxious to pin the guilt on the other side, for this was one way—perhaps the only way—to secure the triumph of the Republican party and the great mass of economic interests now clustered round the quondam "party of moral ideas." And both sides were composed of Americans, one of the most legally-minded peoples the world has seen.

THE CASE FOR THE SOUTH

Nowhere is the American passion for legality better displayed than in Jefferson Davis's long, often tedious apologia, *The Rise and Fall of the Confederate Government*. Davis had much to tell and a case to plead. By the time he wrote his book, he had moved from being the scapegoat of 1865 to being a hero (if not a warmly loved one) in the South and a highly respectable old gentleman in the eyes of nearly everybody in the North who had not a political or financial interest in "waving the bloody shirt." The inside story of the Confederate government, of the President's relations with his Cabinet, with the

Confederate Congress, with the generals, with the people, would have been fascinating. The great debates over his policies, over his relationship with Benjamin, his unintelligible devotion to Braxton Bragg, his difficulties with Beauregard, his removal of Joe Johnston, his choice of Hood—themes bitterly debated even before the Confederacy fell—do get some treatment, but there is no revelation of what made Davis tick (and some of the accounts of military disasters are comic in their inadequacy). But there is one theme on which Davis is tireless, the constitutionality of secession and the illegality of the conduct of Abraham Lincoln. The French courtiers who listened to the exiled James II explaining the wickedness of the traitors who had driven him into exile had no need to go further to discover why James II was bound to have been driven into exile. And one feels that the failure of the Confederacy is at least partly explained by this legalistic obsession of Davis.

The real answer to Davis was given by Daniel Webster in 1850 when he asserted that to talk of peaceable and constitutional secession was nonsense, but that for the South talk and practice of revolution was not necessarily nonsense. Yet the South was committed by its leaders (not only by Davis; Alexander Stephens was worse if possible) to a revolution on legal grounds; and even when the Confederacy was doomed, Davis reports how he was shocked at the impudence of Lincoln talking of his loyalty to the Federal Constitution when he notoriously refused to enforce the Fugitive Slave clauses of that document. The same legalistic nonsense afflicted his foreign policy. Palmerston and Napoleon III were given lectures on the nature of the old Constitution which they obviously misunderstood. There was, of course, some political advantage in trying to deprive the government of the United States of the prestige of legitimacy, of refuting the charge of rebellion, but the South was prohibited by its legalistic obsession from issuing an effective declaration of independence.

This is not to say that the South had no case. It did, but many a litigant who has a good case is ill advised to go to law about it. No one knows what the intentions of the framers of the Constitution were in the matter of secession.

Just as even very loving American couples who get married can't quite ignore the fact that divorce is easy and common, the "People" and the leaders who made up "We the People of the United States" who entered the "more perfect union" were willing to give it a try. If they had been told they could never repent of their bargain, they might not have made it.

But this is very different from having a built-in right of secession to be used at any moment one of the high contracting parties thought fit. No government could run for long under this perpetual threat of peaceful dissolution. Nor is this all. Apart from Texas (the only state with a really plausible theory of secession) what right of secession had the new states? They were mostly formed from territory bought by the United States from France or Spain. What sovereignty was Louisiana "resuming"—Louisiana, a fragment of a territory sold just like a prime field hand? Why should the United States—*i.e.,* the states that didn't repent of their bargain—give up their rights in this great common asset? I think on examination that the case for secession was in practice a case for *dissolution* of the Union. On strict State Rights theory, each state "resumed" its sovereignty, but why should that have dissolved the United States even if the government of the United States permitted or recognized the secession? What claim on the Indian Territory (Oklahoma to you) had the states that left the United States? What the South was claiming was that when enough states decided to leave the partnership (or agency, for that was a way they liked to refer to the government of the United States), all the assets were to be divided among the partners.*

Of course, the South was right in resisting and resenting the imputation of special moral turpitude, in seceding. Talk of secession or of resistance to Federal tyranny had been common form. It was right to recall to supercilious New Englanders their attitude to "Mr. Madison's War," to recall the Hartford Convention. Since the Republicans claimed to be the true heirs of Thomas Jefferson, it was good tactics to recall the Kentucky Resolutions. It was effective debate to stress the disloyalty of the Abolitionists and their allies. But it was no more than that. States hadn't seceded over the Alien and Sedition Acts, over the War of 1812, over the Tariff of Abominations, over the Mexican War. They seceded over one thing and fought over one thing, slavery.

DID SLAVERY REALLY START IT?

That this was so, nobody, I suspect, doubted when the War was on. That pathological constitutionalist Alexander Stephens, who was against secession before it happened and not enthusiastic about it even when he was Vice President of the Confederacy, let the cat out of the

* A curious and otherwise unimportant obiter dictum of Davis is yet revealing. He suggests that instead of taking their ships into Union ports, Southern officers in the Navy of the United States should have taken them into Southern ports so that when the division of assets took place, the South would have its hands on them. But this is not a political doctrine of secession. Apart from involving Southern officers and gentlemen in despicable conduct, this course of action recalls a nervous and not too scrupulous director or partner who wants to get his hands on some of the firm's property before the liquidator does.

bag when he said: "Our new government is founded on the exactly opposite idea [to the equality of races]; its cornerstone rests upon the great truth that the Negro is not equal to the white man." This natural and incurable inequality had as its most suitable and—in Southern circumstances—essential embodiment, the "peculiar institution" of slavery. These were the new "Laws of Nature and of Nature's God."

It was about this conception and its institutional embodiment and the passions, fears, interests linked with the Institution, that the war was fought. As Lincoln put it in the Second Inaugural, the "slaves consituted a peculiar and powerful interest. All knew that this interest was somehow the cause of the war."

This judgment, which I think few doubted in 1865, has been often challenged since—not only by legalists, but also by naïve realists like Charles Beard. (His limitations as historian and thinker were seldom more manifestly revealed than in his attempt to find an explanation for the War that could be reduced to his naïve doctrine of self-interest.) There has only been one institution in American history that had the necessary emotional as well as (and more important than) the necessary material weight to make so great a war possible. I do not say that the abolition of slavery was the cause of the War, or that the simple defense of slavery was the cause. But the War was about slavery. True, the North fought to save the Union; but the Union was menaced only by the slavery question. The South fought for the Southern way of life, using State Rights as a weapon; but the mark, as Catholic theologicians put it, of the Southern way of life was slavery—or so the South thought.

In doing this it raised an issue that would not die. If the South could only exist on the basis of slavery, did it have a right to exist at all? It has long been fashionable to play down the moral content of the slavery issue. But the moral content was there. It did make a lot of difference whether, like Lincoln, you thought it mattered whether slavery was voted up or down or like Douglas professed not to care. (It made a difference to their styles.) The most famous of all American novels is and was *Uncle Tom's Cabin* and Lincoln had some justice on his side when he greeted Mrs. Stowe with, "So you're the little woman who made this big war." No doubt *Uncle Tom's Cabin* is a fantastic picture of the normal working of slavery. But it is not an impossible picture. (The one impossible character is not Simon Legree but Uncle Tom.) Slavery did insult human nature and make possible horrible crimes (one especially horrible occurred in Jefferson's family). And the issue was put in the greatest of American novels when Huck

Finn, the American version of Antigone, decides to commit the crime of helping Nigger Jim to steal himself.

It has become customary to argue that only agitators kept the issue alive, that wise men had more urgent things to talk about—tariffs and land sales and railroads and the like. This was the argument of a more serious historian than Charles Beard, J. G. Randall. But to tell the past what it *should* have talked about is not the work of the historian. To write off, as Randall does, the men who insisted on talking about slavery as mere mischief-makers is to ignore the role of morals and moralists, ideas and ideologues in history. What we should notice is that every effort to keep slavery out of politics failed—compromises, deals, agreements among sensible men, all failed. Again and again, the American people were summoned to a harmony banquet and each time the Banquo's ghost of slavery insisted on turning up. (I am here reducing to a crude simplification the acute argument of my friend, Professor Pieter Geyl of Utrecht, in the *New England Quarterly,* June 1951.)

Slavery was a ghost that walked and could not be laid by silence or by a national policy of "togetherness." This was perhaps a pity but it was also a fact. Because I believe this to be so, I cannot take much interest in the careful, ingenious, almost convincing explanations of how the War could have been avoided. Suppose Dr. Otto Eisenschiml is right in his ingenious guess that it was an accident that Fort Sumter was not evacuated, what of it? The clash would have come somewhere else. True, it might have come in circumstances less disadvantageous to the South, and that has led to ingenious speculation that Lincoln provoked Jefferson Davis, that Major Anderson was left, like the lamb tethered under the tree, to excite the tiger. (The same theory has been used to impute high treason to Roosevelt for provoking Pearl Harbor.) Unless Lincoln had been willing to abondon his conception of his duties as legally elected President of the United States, the war would have come. As far as Lincoln is guilty it is because, as Professor David Potter has shown, he refused in the period between his election and inauguration to surrender any of his fundamental principles (or dogmas) to reassure the South. Seward might believe that all could be settled by what the Italians call a *combinazione* but Lincoln did not. He did not foresee what kind of war was beginning or, if you like, he was beginning. Maybe if he had, he would have held his hand; I doubt it. He was the toughest of war leaders, inflexible about few things but inflexible about them.

What does it mean to contrast the torpor (or panic) of the last months of the Buchanan Administration or the first month of the

Lincoln Administration with the explosion that followed the firing on Sumter? The gunpowder was there; Beauregard applied the match. If Lincoln grievously underestimated the strength of sectional feeling in the South, the South did not understand the forces that moved the North. There was the Union, the flag, the great past, and the great promise of what the vast majority north of the Mason-Dixon line thought of as their country and thought of as a nation. They agreed with Captain Philip Sheridan, USA, "This government is too great and good to be destroyed."

There is no need to believe in the legend of an "aggressive slavocracy" to see in slavery the cause of the War. Whether the North was painting the South into a corner or the South was doing it to her own doom does not really matter. The crisis was there. The South was demanding of the North what it was less and less willing to give— theoretical and, as far as possible, practical equality for the "peculiar institution." To get that the South was willing to break up the last unifying force, the Democratic party. If you want the date when the war became inevitable, it was when the Charleston Convention broke up over the nomination of Stephen Douglas. The South wanted more than any possible Northern candidate could now give. As Senator Pugh said:

"Gentlemen of the South, you mistake us—we will not do it."

That, not the firing on Sumter, was the signal for war.

THE LAST CHANCE FOR THE SOUTH

What drove the South to this extremity? Was it the nature of the slave system that it had to expand or die? That is very doubtful. Was slavery economically doomed unless fresh soil could be secured for it to exploit and exhaust? This too is very doubtful. No doubt many in the South wanted to expand, wanted to revive the slave trade (openly not covertly). But the real cause of the increasing desperation of the South was the pressure of the modern world on an archaic economic and social system. Slavery was both more profitable and more threatened than it had been in the days when Washington and Jefferson thought it an evil doomed—and rightly doomed—to disappear.

But more was involved than that. The South felt the hostility of the world and resented it. It wanted to be approved as well as tolerated (and it wondered how long its social system would be tolerated). There was natural resentment of the moral smugness of New England (and of Old England). Their virtue, it was rightly felt, was due more to geography than to sanctity. The North, if it increasingly tolerated Abolitionist attacks on slavery, showed no signs of offering to share

the burden and risks of emancipation. (It would have made no practical difference if the North had offered, but the moral case would have
been clearer.) The risks seemed real, especially after the Nat Turner
rebellion in Virginia. True, the Abolitionists did not preach servile
war. They wanted to convert the masters, not rouse the slaves; but to
cast doubt on the rightness of slavery was to threaten the whole Southern system. For the echoes of the controversy were heard in the slave
quarters.

Then there was John Brown. It was not so much the attempt of this
crazy and murderous fanatic to raise servile war as the way his execution was received in the North that rightly alarmed the South. "Gallows glorious" indeed! The complacent comments of sedentary literary
gentlemen in Concord were ground enough, if not for secession, at any
rate for a strong dose of counter-righteousness. If the new Republican
party dug itself in, if the Federal administration was to pass into hostile
hands, how could the system survive? The new President thought
slavery wrong; he would tolerate it as his oath bound him to, but that
was all. And the North, in each decade, was getting stronger and more
hostile. It was now or never. And indeed if the South had to fight for
its life, 1860 was perhaps the last time she could do it with any chance
of success. So "the war came."

CONFEDERATE ILLUSIONS

In the Southern decision there was a strong and deadly element of
self-deception. Less and less had the South permitted reflection on or
objective assessment of its position. It had constructed an iron lung
outside which it could not breathe. Inside it lived on illusions. It
underestimated the political handicap of slavery. So it sent as diplomatic agent to England, to be the Franklin of the new revolution,
James M. Mason—known, if he was known at all, as the chief defender
of the Fugitive Slave Act. And everybody Mason met in England, including his friends and the friends of the South, had read *Uncle
Tom's Cabin* and was on the side of Eliza, not of her hunters. Not until
the Confederacy was doomed and slavery visibly perishing, did the
leaders of the South think of throwing slavery overboard and even
then the egregious Mason in his last and necessarily fruitless interview
with Palmerston could not bring himself to utter the fatal words!

There were other illusions. (The North had them too but could
afford them.) There was the illusion of "King Cotton," the revival of
the old Jeffersonian agrarian illusion that you could coerce Europe by
cutting off supplies. The Federal blockade and the Confederate em-
bargo caused immense distress in Britain and France, but they did not

drive Palmerston into intervention and Napoleon III would not move alone. What the South did do was lose the advantage of her greatest asset and cut off her nose to spite herself.

Less commonly remembered is another Southern illusion and a most revealing one. If the North was amazed that the South should fight so hard for State Rights (or slavery), the South was astonished that the notoriously mean-spirited Yankees would fight for anything. The South saw itself as "The Chivalry." It was Ivanhoe—and the North was at best Isaac of York, at worst Shylock. Since the North could only be fighting to make money, the War was a plundering expedition. Since obviously it couldn't pay as that, you had only to show this arithmetical fact to the Yankees and they would give up. Alternatively you could promise them a favorable commercial treaty and they could have no object in fighting. This theme is repeated again and again and you can find echoes of it in the last proclamation Jefferson Davis issued to his people. Davis had been answered, four years before, by a retired army officer, U. S. Grant, who wrote to his Southern father-in-law, "It is all a mistake about the Northern pocket being so sensitive." It was the old illusion about the "nation of shopkeepers"; it was dearly paid for.

After the war was over, the pugnacious journalist and contemporary historian of the Confederacy, Edward A. Pollard, in computing the assets left to the South, more than once emphasized their old superiority in the art of politics. Yet all of Pollard's journalism and historical writing was imbued by a contempt for Jefferson Davis which was only exceeded by his contempt for the Confederate Congress. It was as much as anything the political incompetence of the South that ruined her cause. If Fort Sumter was a trap, Jefferson Davis fell into it. If "cotton was King," the royal weapon was most incompetently used. If British intervention was necessary for Southern success, how badly the South played its cards! Benjamin was as clever a man as Seward but he was a very inferior Secretary of State. Chase was an Alexander Hamilton compared with Memminger. Welles and Stanton, St. Vincent and Carnot compared with the Confederate Secretaries of the Navy and of War (though something can be said for Mallory). What were those Confederate Governors who were not actually Federal assets like Joe Brown and Zeb Vance compared with Andrew and Curtin and the ruthless and unscrupulous and highly useful Oliver Morton? Who cared then, and who cares now, about the eloquence of Senator Wigfall or knows what the Confederate Congress did or left undone? And the comparison between Lincoln and Davis is almost comically unequal. Yet Davis, for all his faults, was probably the best President the

Confederacy could have got. How long would it have lasted under a self-satisfied pedant like Alexander Stephens?

THE SOUTH'S STRENGTH

The Confederacy labored under the fatal disadvantage of its origins. "In my end is my beginning"—the motto of Mary, Queen of Scots—serves the Confederacy well. Faced with the fact that the War could not be won on the theory of State Rights that justified secession, people like Stephens acted as if they preferred to lose the War rather than their theory (as Jefferson Davis was provoked to remark long after Appomattox). Governors tried to run private wars for Georgia and North Carolina, and the correspondence of Governor Vance with the Confederate authorities is a lesson in political folly. The weak and shrinking authority of the Confederate government was continually threatened by the activities of politicians and lawyers who rightly saw that Jefferson Davis was, in many ways, like the tyrant Lincoln, but refused to see that this tyranny was necessary for the salvation of the South. Congress refused to set up a Supreme Court (as the Confederate Constitution demanded) partly because it might be too "national" and the immense difficulties of mobilizing men and resources in a backward economy were made almost insuperable by constitutional jurists.

Yet within these limits, the South did raise armies, make a fleet, and, more remarkable, create a war industry and keep it going until the last doomed months. True, this was done wastefully. The fiscal policy of the South *was* bad, both federally and in the states. (Only South Carolina had a good record.) It could have been better but possibly not much better, once the cotton crop was not shipped out. The South was immensely handicapped by its rural character, which in 1861 was innocently seen as an advantage. It was handicapped by its "colonial" economic position, by its poor transportation system, by its miserably inadequate industrial equipment.

Yet if its handicaps are allowed for, it worked wonders. The South showed, all things considered, more Yankee ingenuity than the North. That it was able to keep armies and a fleet in being should be remembered. And it was in a dilemma. Nothing did Southern morale more harm than the so-called "twenty nigger" law, which exempted overseers of twenty slaves or more from the Army. Yet it was perhaps the best way of organizing the turnover from cotton production to food production that was absolutely essential. But it fed the feeling that this was "a rich man's war and a poor man's fight" that finally broke down Southern morale and justified the desertions that destroyed Lee's last hopes.

Were those hopes ever justified? It was the opinion of many sensible people like General Joe Johnston that the South had a good chance of winning that was thrown away. There were two ways in which the War might have been won; by military triumphs so complete that Britain and France would have felt it safe—and so right—to recognize the Confederacy even at the risk of war with the United States. That chance went at Antietam not at Gettysburg. By July 1863, with Vicksburg doomed, no possible victory in the East would have altered the policy of the British government—which was to wait and be quite sure that Jefferson Davis had, as Gladstone had rashly put it a year before, "made a nation."*

A victory at Antietam might have brought British recognition and might have led to the victory of the Democrats in the Congressional elections of 1862. (They were after all won by Lincoln only after a great deal of very sharp practice.) But even after Vicksburg and Gettysburg, the South, cut in two, steadily shrinking in the West, could have won by playing on the war weariness of the North. They almost brought it off (we have Lincoln's testimony for that). But the removal of Joe Johnston and Davis's still more fatal decision to replace him by Hood doomed the South.

Many Southerners must have read Macaulay on Frederick the Great and noted the parallel. Frederick was saved by the death of his enemy, the Tsarina Elizabeth. The equivalent opportunity for the South was the Presidential election of 1864. Had the South still held Atlanta in November 1864, the Northern will to war might have snapped, the summary of the Democratic platform, "The War is a failure," might have been accepted. The demonstration by Sherman that the Confederate government could no longer protect the heart of the Confederacy began the process of demoralization which made Appomattox merely the QED of the proposition.

Then all the grievances—inflation, semi-starvation in the towns, the inequalities of conscription, the ill-gotten gains of the Snopes family rapidly climbing in the dying planter society—these had added to

---

* It has not, as far as I know, been noted that this was the one thing that, on Confederate theory, Jefferson Davis could *not* do. The Confederate States were no more a nation than, in their theory, the United States had been. Yet all Southerners kept on talking of "the country," "my country." What did they mean? It is possible that a Virginian or a South Carolinian exhausted all the meaning of the word when he contemplated his own state. But a citizen of Arkansas or Florida? There was a nation struggling to birth, the "South." It did not survive and it could not have passed adolescence if it had lived up to the baptismal promises made for it in 1861.

them the loss of faith in the future of the Confederacy. There were more deserters than men under arms and the eloquence of Davis nerved only the cilivians of Richmond. It was touch and go but Lincoln, who supported the long ordeal of Grant's bloody failures, saved the Union as the neurotic Davis lost the Confederacy its last and only chance.

GRANT AND LEE

Grant's failures? I know how much I am running against the tide of current historical opinion when I use such terms. Yet what other name can we give to the campaign of 1864? Where Grant was, was at worst humiliating defeat, at best a bloody stalemate. It was Sherman and Sheridan who kept alive the Northern faith in victory. That Grant was the best Union Commander who had directed the Army of the Potomac is true. That he was a good organizer is true; that he had resolution and clarity of mind is true; that he had an admirable literary style is true and important. He was no Haig or Nivelle or Cardorna. But he was not the equal of Robert E. Lee. Mathematicians, I am told, distinguish between solutions that are adequate and solutions that are elegant. Except possibly at Chattanooga, Grant's solutions were never elegant. Lee's often were.

They may even have been too elegant at times. He demanded and did not get from his raw troops in the early summer of 1862 a perfection of march and battle discipline that Napoleon got from the Grande Armée in 1805 and 1806, Marlborough from his troops in 1704, Frederick from his at Rossbach and Leuthen. But there is the boldness (so unusual in an engineer) before Second Manassas, at Chancellorsville, in the Wilderness, worthy of the greatest captains. And where he failed (as he did fail at Gettysburg) he failed in a curious parallel with Napoleon. Just as Stuart was absent when most needed, so D'Erlon fought neither at Quatre Bras nor Ligny. Just as Lee left too much to the too cautious Longstreet, Napoleon left too much to the foolish aggressive Ney.

Of course, Grant deserves credit for the overall strategy of the Union Armies in 1864-65, for backing Sherman and choosing Sheridan. Had he taken Sherman's advice and remained in the West, his reputation might have gained. It was Grant's opinion that the best of the Union generals (himself presumably excepted) was Sheridan. He was, at any rate, the most modern in his attitude to war. The contrast between Stuart and Sheridan illustrates much in the history of the War. Jeb Stuart was the flower of chivalry. He was consciously the heir of Murat. But he was dead a week after Sheridan took the field as commander of the cavalry corps of the Army of the Potomac. Sheridan was no Murat; he was the ancestor of Patton and Rommel. The brilliant cavalry officer, Charles Lowell, who served under him in the Valley, paid him the highest compliment he could think of: "He works like a mill owner or an ironmaster, not like a soldier." Sheridan, who had been a bookkeeper, inspected his army like a businessman taking over a bankrupt firm, and his ruthlessness, while less flamboyant than Sherman's, was more deliberate.

In our modern savage age with memories of Belsen and Hiroshima, Lidice and Oradour-sur-Glane, it is hard to take seriously the repeated Southern comparisons of Sherman and Sheridan to Attila or the march through Georgia to the worst horrors of the Thirty Years War. But there was plundering and outrage (though few murders and few rapes). "You can't expect all the cardinal virtues for thirteen dollars a month," as the soldier said to Sherman. And by his trail of destruction, Sherman not only made the South "howl," he broke its will to resist. As he said, "War is hell"; wherever he went, he made it so. If in the degree of destruction caused, the War was only in a minor degree "hell" by modern standards, it was nevertheless the prefiguration of modern war. "Unconditional surrender" is another inheritance (if a misunderstood one) of the War.

But it is from the technical point of view that the War is the first modern war. It was modern in the use of railroads, of the telegraph, of field works. (Some of the photographs of Confederate trenches round Atlanta or Petersburg could, with a little touching up, be passed off for photographs of the First World War.) Both sides showed astonishing technical enterprise and ingenuity and gave the world the first examples of that American genius for beating plowshares into weapons that has twice altered the history of this century. (And that would not have done it if the Union had been defeated and dissolved.) The South, as has been suggested, was even more ingenious than the North; it had land mines and sea mines (Farragut's "torpedoes"); it had submarines; and we forget too easily that the *Merrimac* was only the most famous of the ironclads that the South created out of its meager resources. The North, with far greater resources, was almost equally fertile in invention, and infant American industry was immensely expanded by the War and met all the demands on it. Or almost all. For the ideas were often in advance of the technical resources to execute them, as the vicissitudes of Federal naval architecture showed.

BLUNDERS OF THE NORTH

And there were curious failures to utilize the technical superiority of the North. The Federal cavalry was equipped toward the end of the War with repeating carbines which worked havoc among the Confederates. But there was no general attempt to equip the Union Army with breechloaders. Maybe there was no weapon then available as effective as the Remingtons with which the Turks were to mow down the Russians at Plevna in 1877, but even an inferior breechloader, a *chassepot* or a "needle gun," would have given the North an immense advantage.

It is less surprising that the Union did not produce a breechloading field gun. The problem was really one of metallurgy and there was no Krupp steel in America. (Many of the failures of the new Federal warships were due to poor metallurgy.) But it is odder that so much smoothbore artillery was continued in use since the French had already demonstrated, in the Italian War of 1859, the great superiority of rifled artillery. There was a lack of enterprise here. It is true that Sheridan, in 1870, professed not to think much of the Krupp guns, but Sheridan was not a gunner.

In another way, too, the War was modern. Many of the complaints made against McClellan, Meade, Grant, and even against Lee, for not fully exploiting their victories reflected the belief that all battles should be and could be like Jena and Waterloo, what the Germans called "battles without a morrow." But modern war has not been rich in Waterloos or Jenas. It took the unlimited imbecility of Bazaine and MacMahon to give Moltke his deceptively easy triumphs in 1870. (The two French generals were as incompetent as Pope or Hood, nay, as that unending ass, Ambrose E. Burnside.) The Russo-Japanese War and World War I were to be wars like the Civil War in which the complete, quick, and final victory was rare. Old General Scott complained that only Sheridan had what he called "finish," but Sheridan was lucky.

The War was modern in another way. It marked the end of cavalry in the old sense. There were few or no cavalry charges, foolish and heroic like the Charge of the Light Brigade or the charge of the French Cuirassiers at Reichshofen—or even desperate but not foolish like Von Bredow's "death ride" at Mars-la-Tour. Jeb Stuart was the last knight, but perhaps the great Southern cavalry chief was the less romantic Forrest. As for Sheridan, he used horses to get his men to the battle, not as missiles in themselves. Few swords and not many bayonets were effectively used in the War and no European army in 1914 had assimilated these lessons of the "armed mobs," as Moltke called them, who learned so much more of real war between 1861 and 1865 than the Prussians did in their too easy campaigns in 1870. Europe had to learn the hard way in 1914 many lessons learned in Virginia and Tennessee two generations before.

And the War showed the overwhelming importance of industrial power. It was not merely a matter of weapons but of locomotives and wagons, of clothing and tinned food, of hospital trains—and of that ancestor of the world-girdling "PX," the Sanitary Commission. It may be that the War did actually increase Northern wealth; certainly the North increased its capital equipment all during the War. It may have been only a catalyst but the War precipitated the entry of the United States into the modern industrial world, made "the takeoff" (to use Professor W. W. Rostow's brilliant metaphor) come sooner. And by providing such emotional talking points as the crimes of Andersonville, the War made the political job of inducing the American farmer to pay, through the tariff, for the forced-draft development of American industry much easier than it might otherwise have been. The ex-Confederates who began to come back to Washington by 1870 were in a new world, one from which the South was still excluded, except as a colonial tributary.

Before the War, during the War, and after, the North was baffled by the readiness of the non-slaveholding population of the South—that is the great majority of the free Southern population—to fight for "Southern independence" which, in fact, meant fighting for a slavery system that, many outsiders thought with plausibility, was the curse of most whites as well as blacks.

That there was something in the Northern attitude is suggested by the rage provoked by Helper's *Impending Crisis of the South* in 1857, the only book that got under Southern skins as successfully as *Uncle Tom's Cabin* had done. No abolitionist tract, no bale of *Liberators* was as dangerous as Helper, for the slaves were unlikely to see or read the tracts; but the poor whites might read *The Impending Crisis*. Its message was simple. Helper was no "nigger lover." He was basically against slavery because of the harm it did to his own people, the non-slaveholding whites.

Helper and his admirers (who were numerous in the North where his book was a best seller) could point to the indisputable fact that most Southerners had no direct profit from slavery. In 1860, there were "385,000 owners of slaves distributed among 1,516,000 free families. Nearly three-fourths of all free Southerners had no connection with slavery through either family ties or direct ownership."* And if we take as the rulers and leaders of slave society the owners of more than one hundred slaves (and the owners of less than one hundred slaves were hardly the "planters" of Southern tradition or the whiskey advertisements) there were only three thousand of them.

This, the really privileged class, was less numerous, relatively and absolutely, than the privileged orders in France in 1789. Why was there no rising against a system based on such an inverted pyramid of power and wealth? Why was the contrast between the economic and political status of the free farmers in the North and his brethren in the South not politically more effective? Why without accepting Helper's exact bill to be sent to the "introducers, aiders, and abettors of slavery" (it was exactly $7,544,148,825) did not the majority of the free population of the South let the slavocracy fight for the system?

THE MYSTERY OF THE SOUTHERN MIND

For one thing, the kind of political arithmetic that Helper and more serious economists practiced exaggerated the rational, calculating elements in the political reactions of *any* people at *any* time. Wars are not made on either side by totally rational peoples. As the Germans used to say, a reasonable army would run away. But the Northern illusion was made illusory by more than the power of human folly. It was easier to say that the non-slaveholding whites were the true victims of the slavery system than to get the whites themselves to understand that. If emancipation of the slaves was the only way to the true freedom of whites, the whites—especially the poor whites—did not know it.

For one thing, the only rag of dignity that a poor white had was his status as a white man. As long as he was above all niggers, even prosperous free niggers, the poor white had a way of laying the flattering unction of superiority to his soul. The numerous class of free farmers who were not in the derogatory sense "poor whites" (though they were not rich) had even more reason to welcome the boost to their ago that the slave system gave every white from Wade Hampton down to the most miserable "cracker." It is possible too that the whites who did think slavery an obstacle to the rise of themselves and their families (like the presumably smaller group who thought it intrinsically wrong) did emigrate from the slave states. For if it is difficult to think of Tom Lincoln moving from Kentucky into Indiana under the pressure of conscience or ambition, his son Abraham might have done so had he come to his majority in a slave state. Perhaps there

---

* Kenneth M. Stampp, *The Peculiar Institution*, New York, Knopf, 1956.

was a steady sifting of the white population; perhaps the majority of skeptics and trouble-makers simply got out. (The history of the border counties of Illinois, Indiana, and Ohio suggests that a good many migrated North with a fine stock of Southern principles and prejudices.)

There is no doubt still a mystery for us in this attitude. The rank-and-file of the Confederate Armies did not write books, did not keep diaries, did not write newspapers, were seldom represented by their own kind in the high command, political or military. So we have to guess why they disappointed their well-wishers in the North. No doubt, if the Southern politician had advocated on the hustings the aristocratic doctrines that justified slavery on grounds that would apply to the poor white as well as to the Negro, there might have been a glimmering of doubt in even the thickest skulls. But the politicians, as apart from the ideologues, were too wise for that. They flattered the Southern masses and not so much imposed on them as "sold" them the romantic idea of Southern superiority—not only over all Negroes but over all Yankees. "Farmer and cracker admired and shared more than vicariously in this ideal—shall we call it?—created by the impact of the aristocratic idea on the romantic pattern."*

And when all is said and done, how was the non-slaveholding white—already jealous of the competition not only of free Negroes but of Negro craftsmen hired out by their masters—to know that the emancipated Negro would not be a more formidable competitor? How was he to see that the common interests of the poor ought to unite him with those whom he despised and feared? How was he to see a common class interest, when some labor unions still restrict their membership to "Caucasians" a century later?

The War, of course, educated a good many. First of all, the natural leaders led and lost. The hostility to Jefferson Davis that was gleefully reported to the North after the end of the War may have been widespread and deep. The exemptions given to slaveholders, to jobholders, to the people who got into "the bombproofs" as safe jobs were called, bred natural resentment. The suffering inflicted on the families of soldiers by inflation and by the breakdown of Confederate organization shook the faith of others. Yet the South (and the North), if they had only known it, shamed their Revolutionary ancestors and showed more tenacity and courage in the face of Grant and Sherman (or Lee and Johnston) than had been shown in face of Cornwallis.

---

* W. J. Cash, *The Mind of the South*, New York, Knopf, 1941. I am aware that Cash was not a scientific historian or sociologist but he was what is in this context better, a poet who saw through the poetry of the Southern vision but felt its power.

And this devotion was of long-term political importance. For it meant that the North could not separate the classes of the South so as to win a political as well as a military victory. There was not even possible a Southern version of the Weimar Republic. Even had there been no Reconstruction, the memories of the South would have been "disloyal."

WHAT THE SOUTH LOST

If the North was disillusioned by the Southern loyalty of the poor whites, the South was disillusioned by the limited loyalty of the slaves. Lucius Quintus Cincinnatus Lamar told Henry Adams that he ceased to believe in slavery when he realized that it could not stand a war. It didn't. Everywhere that the Union Armies came, the system collapsed. The Christian slaves had no scruples about stealing themselves by the hundreds of thousands. The many authentic stories of fidelity to the Master refer, for the most part, to the house slaves. The field hands had no such feudal spirit. Even the house servants were not totally reliable. The intelligent Mrs. Chesnut keeps on speculating about what was really going on behind the smooth, smiling, servile faces. Sometimes the secret came out. Both Jefferson Davis and Governor Wise suffered the shock of the desertion of trusted servants and, by the last year of the War, the not very intelligent J. B. Jones, the "Rebel War Clerk," began to suspect the loyalty of the slaves. And the revelation of the fragility of the slave system, of the true sentiments of its four million "beneficiaries," was an added drop of gall in the full cup of the defeated South.

The ambiguity of the Southern attitude was reflected in calculations of war losses. The "loss" of the slaves was estimated at from two billion to five billion dollars. But of course this was a loss only for the owners, not for the South; the vast majority of the former slaves were in the South still and were the basis of the Southern economy. They and the soil remained.

What had the South lost? Here we must distinguish carefully and kindly between fact and legend. Just as France is full of families who lost "their all" in the Revolution (including families that in fact did well out of it), the South has its share of mythical heirs of great plantations wrecked by Sherman's raiders. Whether Sherman did or did not set fire to Columbia or Atlanta, they did burn. (Charleston suffered as much from the accidental fire of 1861 as by Federal gunfire, and central Richmond was fired by Ewell's retreating garrison, again perhaps by accident.) More serious was the destruction of the South's already inadequate transport system. And the meager industrial equipment, mostly turned over to the war effort, was mainly wrecked by one side or the other.

Yet at first hearing or at second, it is irritating to find present Southern weaknesses explained in terms of the crimes of Sherman or Sheridan. Was Columbia in 1865 any worse off than Berlin in 1945 or for that matter than London? Is not the cultivation of such memories an obstacle to clear thinking about what the South needs? It is nearly a century since these crimes were committed. Isn't it time they were forgotten?

THE DEFEATED

Third thoughts suggest a difference. If Berlin and London and Rotterdam have largely recovered and perhaps have largely forgotten their dreadful recent history, this is in part due to the generosity of the victorious United States. The United States was not so generous in 1865. What the South needed was Marshall Plan aid. Just as the North refused, before the War, to accept its share in the sin or burden of slavery, it refused (apart from the issue of rations and a little aid given to the Freedman's Bureau) to make any sacrifices to get the stricken South onto its feet. No doubt, it would have been asking a great deal to ask the North to pay more taxes to "help the Rebels." "Reconstruction," however it was organized politically, was bound to be a bitter ordeal for the South since the bills were coming in and the South had to pay them out of her meager and diminished resources. She needed capital, but what businessman with the immense possibilities of the North and West open to him was going to risk his dollars in the former Confederacy?

It is not a creditable story; yet it is hard to see what, given the conditions of the age, could have been done better. There was first of all the disaster of the assassination of Lincoln. Even he could not have wrought miracles, but his prestige, his resolution, his preternatural political sagacity were such that some of the worst mistakes or neglects might have been avoided. (As Mrs. Brodie has pointed out in her recent admirable life of Thaddeus Stevens, the common belief that President Johnson simply applied Lincoln's policies ignores important differences between Lincoln and his successor.) But even if that honest, stubborn, violent, limited man, Andrew Johnson, had been a wiser man and a better politician, the problem might have been insoluble for that generation.

For Southern illusions did not die at Appomattox. It is an illusion of the conquered that they can determine the use made by the victors of their power. It was useless to demand of the North in 1865 the Constitution or the temper of 1861. Yet the South tried to minimize the Northern victory, notably by making the emancipation of the slaves as nearly meaningless as possible. The "black codes" are enough to explain if not to justify the worst errors of Radical reconstruction. As Mr. Ralph McGill has recently reminded us (and as we should have expected *a priori*), it was Mississippi that led the South down this path of folly. To expect the North to accept this nullification of victory was a vain thing.

We must not exaggerate the extent of the disaster. Is there much reason to believe that South Carolina was more corruptly governed than New York or Philadelphia? It could afford the graft less, that is all. There was nowhere in the United States the kind of governmental organization, the kind of civil service, the kind of sociological knowledge (if I may risk using that dirty word) that was needed. But as Reconstruction made the "Solid South" even more solid, so Southern intransigence made "waving the bloody shirt" profitable and this poisoned the political life of the United States for more than a generation. And as far as the memory of Reconstruction was successfully used (long after Reconstruction was over) to justify such parodies of democracy and world scandals as the present political state of Mississippi, it was one of the most disastrous results of the War.

Perhaps we exaggerate the impact of the War. Perhaps the "Gilded Age" would have been as base, perhaps a President as incompetent as Grant would have reached the White House anyway. Perhaps in no other way could the American experiment have been purged of the poisonous infection of slavery in the country "dedicated to the proposition that all men are created equal." For we must not forget that slavery *was* abolished, the Union *was* saved, "the last best hope of earth" not debased and destroyed. The price was high and is still being paid. Like the chief captain, the American people can say that "with a great sum obtained I this freedom." That is why the War lies so close to the American heart.

To think that on the whole and on nearly all the great issues the North was right is possibly an unfashionable doctrine; it is at any rate an unromantic doctrine. But it is mine. I agree with Augustine Birrell that for once "the great twin brethren, Might and Right" fought on the same side.

MY OWN SIDE

As a boy, like all boys I hope, I was for the South as I was a Jacobite. Boys are all for Hector against Achilles (and still more against Agamemnon), for Hannibal against Scipio (and still more against

Fabius Cunctator). That is right and proper. But "when I was a child, I spake as a child, I understood as a child, I thought as a child; but when I became a man, I put away childish things." The issue of the War was fortunate in the sense that it was the least unfortunate issue that was possible. Of this civil war one is inclined to say with Andrew Marvell, "The cause *was* too good to have been fought for." But it was fought for and the right side won.

But there is another side to the War and one that it would be wrong to ignore or minimize—the side of glory. There was glory enough for each side. The North has its legends (true legends) as well as the South. There is the desperate and fruitless courage of Fredericksburg; there is the rush by Missionary Ridge; there are the heroic stories of units like the 20th Maine at Gettysburg; there is Sheridan riding on to the field at Cedar Creek and turning the tide of battle like Desaix at Marengo. There is most impressive of all, the disciplined and despairing advance at Cold Harbor. Here is glory. But whether the South has more glory than the North or not (I think it has), it needs it more and, as is right, cherishes it more. It cherishes the fame of the most Plutarchian (and greatest) American soldier, "Marse Robert." It cherishes the memory of Jackson "standing like a stone wall" at Bull Run and striking Hooker's flank at Chancellorsville. It cherishes or should cherish, with Pickett's attack, the memory of Hood's men advancing to their doom at Franklin. And for the individual heroic actions, their name is legion. It should remember with pride, not that there were so few under arms to surrender with Lee or Johnston, but that there were still so many.

It was the bad luck of the South that the only great poet who commemorated the "strange sad war" was Walt Whitman of Manhattan. But Timrod's lines on the Confederate dead in Magnolia Cemetery at Charleston may serve as a final text:

> *In seeds of laurel in the earth*
> *The blossom of your fame is blown,*
> *And somewhere, waiting for its birth,*
> *The shaft is in the stone.*

The laurels have grown; the shafts are all around us. They cannot be too numerous or too high.

c. vann woodward

the irony of southern history

C. Vann Woodward was born in Arkansas in 1908, received his Ph.D. from the University of North Carolina, and has taught at several Southern universities. He is now professor of American history at The Johns Hopkins University.

As one might expect from this background, Woodward's books have been concerned largely with issues in Southern history; they are extraordinarily good books in their field, notable for the detachment and sanity with which Woodward has explored subjects that usually are occasions for self-centered passion. He is one of the most satisfying and reliable of all contemporary historians, and probably no scholar in our generation has written with more point on the Southern question than Woodward has in his notable book *Tom Watson: Agrarian Rebel* (1938), in *Origins of The New South* (1951), and in his demonstration— *The Strange Career of Jim Crow* (1955)—of just how unexpectedly recent, not traditional, that bitter "tradition" is.

As an historical analyst of his own region, Woodward has not been blinded by sectional loyalties. Yet equally important, he has been unfailingly sensitive to the historical travail of the South—the only part of the United States that has known what it is to be defeated in a great war, and on its own soil; the only region that has known, in the European sense, that history is a tragic affair and that sooner or later no people is immune from suffering.

It is this sympathy of a native son for the South's historical experience that has led him to the significant point he makes in "The Irony of Southern History." As Woodward recognizes, the South before the Civil War obstinately and sometimes unnaturally defended itself in behalf of its peculiar institution, slavery; so today the United States as a whole, conceivably identifying itself too much with its economic system alone, constantly thinks of itself as innocent and aggrieved in its relations with the rest of the world, and cannot admit that in the dynamism of events, it may be we who are now isolated by the rapid social acceleration of others. So the South, which thought of itself as isolated and aggrieved, could not understand the rest of the world or confront itself.

Yet interestingly enough, the South today, precisely because it is no longer able to think of itself as innocent or untouched by history, has an intellectual advantage over the rest of the country, an advantage of a riper and more human perspective on history in general. This is the final "irony" of Southern history—the fact that the region that so often seemed as peculiar as its peculiar institution has in fact so much to teach the rest of us about the real nature of history, a nature which excepts no one and involves all in the same human condition. And though Woodward begins his essay with the admission that ". . . the regional historian is likely to be oppressed by a sense of his unimportance. . . . the South is thought to be hedged about with peculiarities that set it apart as unique," it is, of course, exactly the fact that he is a regional historian that has enabled him to find so rich a perspective on the troubled relations of America today with the rest of the world.

On the whole, professional historians in America are not usually this thoughtful. One reason is that they take American history too much for granted, and though it is a wholly modern and therefore limited subject, they do not bring enough ideas to it to avoid telling the familiar story over and over with the same set of classically liberal ideas. Woodward, by contrast, *thinks* about American history; he does not just tell the story, he gets under the surface. Like so many Southern novelists and poets in our day, he has had the good luck to feel himself somewhat out of the normal scheme of things.

Consequently, the essential mark of Woodward's style is a certain grave abstractness. Southerners tend to be somewhat more courtly and stately in their style than other Americans—they have a tradition of rhetoric all their own. And American professional historians, as Woodward's style sufficiently indicates, tend to assume something of the public deliberateness that our statesmen, once upon a time, used to exhibit. Woodward's style is the product of all these influences. But above all, as the reader will notice from a certain effort required to keep Woodward's points in mind, Woodward writes from a connected and firmly logical point of view, and it is this essential reasoning that makes his essay so valuable in its content and so grave in its music.

Ⅰn a time when nationalism sweeps everything else before it, as it does at present, the regional historian is likely to be oppressed by a sense of his unimportance. America is the all-important subject, and national ideas, national institutions, and national policies are the themes that compel attention. Foreign peoples, eager to know what this New-World colossus means to them and their immediate future, are impatient with details of regional variations, and Americans, intent on the need for

THE IRONY OF SOUTHERN HISTORY: From *The Burden of Southern History* by C. Vann Woodward. © 1960 by the Louisiana State University Press. Reprinted by permission of the author and publisher.

national unity, tend to minimize their importance. New England, the West, and other regions are occasionally permitted to speak for the nation. But the South is thought to be hedged about with peculiarities that set it apart as unique. As a standpoint from which to write American history it is regarded as eccentric and, as a background for an historian, something of a handicap to be overcome.

Of the eccentric position of the South in the nation there are admittedly many remaining indications. I do not think, however, that this eccentricity need be regarded as entirely a handicap. In fact, I think that it could possibly be turned to advantage by the Southern historian, both in understanding American history and in interpreting it to non-Americans. For from a broader point of view it is not the South but America that is unique among the peoples of the world. This peculiarity arises out of the American legend of success and victory, a legend that is not shared by any other people of the civilized world. The collective will of this country has simply never known what it means to be confronted by complete frustration. Whether by luck, by abundant resources, by ingenuity, by technology, by organizing cleverness, or by sheer force of arms America has been able to overcome every major historic crisis—economic, political, or foreign—with which it has had to cope. This remarkable record has naturally left a deep imprint upon the American mind. It explains in large part the national faith in unlimited progress, in the efficacy of material means, in the importance of mass and speed, the worship of success, and the belief in the invincibility of American arms.

The legend has been supported by an unbroken succession of victorious wars. Battles have been lost, and whole campaigns—but not wars. In the course of their national history Americans, who have been called a bellicose though unmartial people, have fought eight wars, and so far without so much as one South African fiasco such as England encountered in the heyday of her power. This unique good fortune has isolated America, I think rather dangerously, from the common experience of the rest of mankind, all the great peoples of which have without exception known the bitter taste of defeat and humiliation. It has fostered the tacit conviction that American ideals, values, and principles inevitably prevail in the end. That conviction has never received a name, nor even so much explicit formulation as the old concept of Manifest Destiny. It is assumed, not discussed. And the assumption exposes us to the temptation of believing that we are somehow immune from the forces of history.

The country that has come nearest to approximating the American legend of success and victory is England. The nearness of continental rivals and the precariousness of the balance of power, however, bred in the English an historical sophistication that prevented the legend from flourishing as luxuriantly as it has in the American climate. Only briefly toward the end of the Victorian period did the legend threaten to get out of hand in England. Arnold J. Toynbee has recalled those piping days in a reminiscent passage. "I remember watching the Diamond Jubilee procession myself as a small boy," he writes. "I remember the atmosphere. It was: well, here we are on the top of the world, and we have arrived at this peak to stay there—forever! There is, of course, a thing called history, but history is something unpleasant that happens to other people. We are comfortably outside all that. I am sure, if I had been a small boy in New York in 1897 I should have felt the same. Of course, if I had been a small boy in 1897 in the Southern part of the United States, I should not have felt the same; I should then have known from my parents that history had happened to my people in my part of the world."

The South has had its full share of illusions, fantasies, and pretensions, and it has continued to cling to some of them with an astonishing tenacity that defies explanation. But the illusion that "history is something unpleasant that happens to other people" is certainly not one of them—not in the face of accumulated evidence and memory to the contrary. It is true that there have been many Southern converts to the gospel of progress and success, and there was even a period following Reconstruction when it seemed possible that these converts might carry a reluctant region with them. But the conversion was never anywhere near complete. Full participation in the legend of irresistible progress, success, and victory could, after all, only be vicarious at best. For the inescapable facts of history were that the South had repeatedly met with frustration and failure. It had learned what it was to be faced with economic, social, and political problems that refused to yield to all the ingenuity, patience, and intelligence that a people could bring to bear upon them. It had learned to accommodate itself to conditions that it swore it would never accept, and it had learned the taste left in the mouth by the swallowing of one's own words. It had learned to live for long decades in quite un-American poverty, and it had learned the equally un-American lesson of submission. For the South had undergone an experience that it could share with no other part of America—though it is shared by nearly all the peoples of Europe and Asia—the experience of military defeat, occupation, and reconstruction. Nothing about this history was conducive to the theory that the South was the darling of divine providence.

2

In his book, *The Irony of American History*, Reinhold Niebuhr conducts an astute analysis of national character and destiny that emphasizes another set of American pretensions, which he calls the illusions of innocence and virtue. These illusions have their origins in both North and South, though at a period before there was any distinct regional consciousness. They were fostered by the two great moral traditions of early national life, New England Calvinism and Virginia deism of the Jeffersonian school. While they differed upon theology, theocrats and deists were agreed that their country was "God's American Israel," called out of a wicked and corrupt Old World and set apart by Providence to create a new humanity and restore man's lost innocence. I believe that Niebuhr would agree that what I have described as the American legend of success and victory has assisted in fostering and perpetuating these illusions of innocence and virtue. At any rate he demonstrates that these illusions have been preserved past infancy and into national adulthood. Arriving at man's estate, we have suddenly found ourselves in possession of immense and undreamed of power and compelled to use this power in ways that are not innocent and that cover us with guilt. In clinging to our infant illusions of innocence along with our new power, writes the theologian, we are "involved in ironic perils which compound the experiences of Babylon and Israel"—the perils of overweening power and overweening virtue.

Our opposite numbers in the world crisis, the Russian Communists, are bred on illusions of innocence and virtue that parallel our own with ironic fidelity, even though they are of very different origin and have been used to disguise (perhaps even from themselves) what seems to us much greater guilt of oppression and cruelty. They combine these illusions with Messianic passions that find a paler reflection in one layer of American conscience. Looking upon their own nation as the embodiment of innocence and justice, the Russians take it for granted that America is the symbol of the worst form of capitalistic injustice. Both America and Russia find it almost impossible to believe that anyone would think ill of them and are persuaded that only malice could prompt suspicions of motives so obviously virtuous. Each tends to regard the other as the only force wilfully thwarting its dream of bringing happiness to all mankind.

There are many perils, both for our nation and for the world, inherent in this situation—and they do not all come from abroad. We are exasperated by the ironic incongruities of our position. Having more power than ever before, America ironically enjoys less security than in the days of her weakness. Convinced of her virtue, she finds that even her allies accuse her of domestic vices invented by her enemies. The liberated prove ungrateful for their liberation, the reconstructed for their reconstruction, and the late colonial peoples vent their resentment upon our nation—the most innocent, we believe, of the imperial powers. Driven by these provocations and frustrations, there is the danger that America may be tempted to exert all the terrible power she possesses to compel history to conform to her own illusions. The extreme, but by no means the only expression, would be the so-called preventive war. This would be to commit the worst heresy of the Marxists, with whom it is dogma that they can compel history to conform to the pattern of their dreams by the ruthless use of force.

To save ourselves from these moral perils, Dr. Niebuhr adjures us to disavow the pretensions and illusions of innocence derived from our national childhood, along with all self-righteousness, complacency, and humorless idealism. If we would understand our plight and prepare for the role we must play, we must grasp the ironic implications of our history. I realize that Niebuhr's view of human strivings is based on theology, a subject definitely beyond my province. Whatever its theological implications—and I have frankly never explored them—the view has a validity apart from them that appeals to the historian. Yet the ironic interpretation of history is rare and difficult. In the nature of things the participants in an ironic situation are rarely conscious of the irony, else they would not become its victims. Awareness must ordinarily be contributed by an observer, a nonparticipant, and the observer must have an unusual combination of detachment and sympathy. He must be able to appreciate both elements in the incongruity that go to make up the ironic situation, both the virtue and the vice to which pretensions of virtue lead. He must not be so hostile as to deny the element of virtue or strength on the one side, nor so sympathetic as to ignore the vanity and weakness to which the virtue and strength have contributed. Obviously, the qualifications of the ironic historian are pretty hard to come by.

3

Now the South is deeply involved at present in the ironic plight of our country as a full-fledged participant. In fact, the headlong precipitancy with which the South has responded to the slogans of nationalism in recent world crises has often exceeded that of other sections of the country. Mass response sometimes suggests the zeal of recent converts. Yet there are aspects of its history and experience that make the South an observer as well as a participant, which set it apart in certain

ways from the experience of the rest of the country, and which constitute a somewhat detached point of view. From that vantage point I
believe it is possible for the Southern historian, and indeed all those
absorbed in the study of Southern history, to make a special contribution to the understanding of the irony of American history, as well as
that of the South's history.

Ironic implications of Southern history are not concealed by any
legend of success and victory nor by the romantic legend of the Lost
Cause. To savor the full irony of the confident and towering ante-
bellum dream of a Greek Democracy for the New World one has only
to recall the words of a speech that Robert Barnwell Rhett made when
South Carolina seceded. The orator was picturing the historian of
2000 A.D. writing this passage: "And extending their empire across this
continent to the Pacific, and down through Mexico to the other side
of the great gulf, and over the isles of the sea, they established an empire and wrought out a civilization which has never been equalled or
surpassed—a civilization teeming with orators, poets, philosophers,
statesmen, and historians equal to those of Greece and Rome—and
presented to the world the glorious spectacle of a free, prosperous and
illustrious people." As a matter of fact, in the eyes of the true believer
the coming of the Golden Age did not have to await the year 2000. It
had already arrived, full blown, here and now. For as Charles Sydnor
has observed, "the affirmation of Southern perfection" meant just that.
Blind to evils and imperfections all around them, Southerners described
what they saw as the ultimate in social perfection. "Fighting to defend
their way of life," says Sydnor, "they had taken refuge in a dream
world, and they insisted that others accept their castle in the sky as an
accurate description of conditions in the South."

The shattering of this dream and the harsh education that followed
has not made the South the home of a race of philosophers. Nor does
it seem to have made Southerners any wiser than their fellow countrymen. But it has provided them with a different point of view from
which they might, if they will, judge and understand their own history
and American history, and from which to view the ironic plight of
modern America.

The meaning of the contrast between the 1930's and the 1940's is a
case in point. This transformation took place too recently for anyone
to have forgotten, though many seem to have forgotten it entirely. In
the thirties and well into the following decade there occurred the most
thoroughgoing inquest of self-criticism that our national economy has
ever undergone—not even excepting that of the muckraking and progressive era. No corner nor aspect nor relationship of American capi-

talism was overlooked, and no shibboleth of free enterprise went un-challenged. The prying and probing went on at every level from the share croppers to holding companies and international cartels. Sub-poenas brought mighty bankers and public utility empire-builders to the witness stand. Nor was this activity merely the work of the wild-eyed and the woolly-haired, nor the exclusive concern of one of the major parties. It was a popular theme of the radio, the press, the screen, the theater, and even the pulpit. Some churches took up the theme and incorporated it into their programs. Universities hummed and throbbed with it. And in 1940 the former president of a public utility holding company, then candidate for President of the United States on the Republican ticket, made the theme a part of his campaign. Some of the outpouring of criticism in the thirties and forties was mis-directed, some was perhaps a bit silly. But the electorate repeatedly endorsed with large majorities the party that was the more closely iden-tified with the movement. On the whole, the people regarded it as pro-ductive of good. It was at least indicative of a healthy and self-confident society, uninhibited by fear.

Then in the mid-forties something happened. It happened rather suddenly. The floodstream of criticism dwindled to a trickle and very nearly ceased altogether. It was as if some giant sluice gate had been firmly shut. The silence that followed was soon filled with the clamor of voices lifted in accusation, denial, or recantation. No reputation was now secure from the charges of the heresy hunters, the loyalty investi-gators, and the various committees on public orthodoxy and conformity. Choruses were lifted in rapturous praise of the very institutions that had been so recently the objects of attack—and the choruses were joined by many of the former critics.

Surveying this remarkable transformation, the historian of the South can hardly escape the feeling that all this has happened before—or something strongly suggestive of it: that what happened in the 1940's had its counterpart in the 1830's. The earlier development was on a smaller scale, to be sure, and there were certain other obvious discrep-ancies to be taken into account. The dangers inherent in any such com-parison between historical epochs are numerous and forbidding, for certainly no analogy is perfect since no two eras, movements, nor events are entirely alike. To suggest that modern capitalism is comparable with slavery as a system of labor would be to indulge in the loose and irresponsible language of polemics and propaganda. With due precau-tion and full awareness of the risks, however, one may venture a com-parison, not between the two institutions, but between the public attitudes toward them and the transformations that took place in those attitudes.

What happened in the South during the 1830's is too familiar a story to require elaboration here. Before it happened, however, we know that the Jeffersonian tradition protected and fostered a vigorous school of antislavery thought in the South. The great Virginians of the Revolutionary generation, nearly all of whom were on record for emancipation, lent their prestige to the movement. Critics of slavery spared no aspect of the peculiar institution. They spoke out against the effect on the master as well as on the slave; they exposed the harm done the manners and morals of the South as well as its economy and society. Nor were critics mere misfits and radicals. They included men of influence and standing—politicians, editors, professors, and clergymen. Antislavery thought appeared in respectable newspapers and infiltrated evangelical sects of the Upper South particularly. In the 1820's the slave states contained a great many more antislavery societies than the free states and furnished leadership for the movement in the country. It would be false to suggest that slavery was on the way out, or, in spite of some amelioration, that the reformers made any very substantial alterations. But it is not too much to say that this was a society unafraid of facing its own evils. The movement reached a brilliant climax in the free and full debates over emancipation in the Virginia legislature during the session of 1831-1832. The effort to abolish slavery failed there as elsewhere. But as Joseph Roberts writes, "The institution was denounced as never before; it was condemned wholesale fashion by legal representatives of a slave-holding people. The vigor and breadth of the assault provided the debate with its most obvious distinction."

In spite of the vigor of the movement and the depth of its root in Southern tradition, it withered away to almost nothing in a very brief period during the middle thirties. By 1837 there was not one antislavery society remaining in the whole South. Of the thousands of voices that had been raised in outspoken protest a short while before there were to be heard only a few whispers. Opponents changed their opinions or held their tongues. Loyalty to the South came to be defined in terms of conformity of thought regarding one of its institutions. Past records and associates were scrutinized closely, and the recency with which one had denounced Northern abolitionism became a matter of public concern. The South concentrated its energies upon the repression of heresy and raised intellectual barricades against the ideas of a critical and unfriendly world. The institution that had so recently been blamed for a multitude of the region's ills was now pictured as the secret of its superiority and the reason for its fancied perfection.

4

Causes behind the transformation of attitudes in the South were numerous and complex. So are the reasons behind the transformation that has taken place in the attitudes of contemporary America. Broadly speaking, however, both of these revolutions in public attitudes were reactions to contests for power in which the two societies found themselves involved. These great struggles included many clashes of interest and issues quite apart from those concerning morals and contrasting labor systems. Even in the absence of ideological differences the strains of conflict would have been severe in each case. In the 1850's as in the 1950's, however, the crisis tended to be increasingly dramatized as a clash between different systems of labor—as slave labor versus free labor. In both the nineteenth-century war of words and the twentieth-century cold war each party to the conflict, of course, contended that the other practiced the more immoral, wicked, and shameless type of exploitation and that its own system was benevolent, idealistic, and sound. Our own opinions as to which of the parties in each crisis was the more deluded or disingenuous in its contentions are likely to be pretty firmly fixed already, and the problem is such that it need not detain us.

The point is that there exists, in spite of obvious differences, a disquieting suggestion of similarity between the two crises and the pattern of their development. The mistakes of the South, some of which have already been suggested, are readily apparent and their meaning open to all who would read and understand. In the first place the South permitted the opposition to define the issue, and naturally the issue was not defined to the South's advantage. In the second place the South assumed the moral burden of proof. Because the attack centered upon slavery, the defense rallied around that point. As the clamor increased and the emotional pitch of the dispute intensified, the South heedlessly allowed its whole cause, its way of life, its traditional values, and its valid claims in numerous nonmoral disputes with the North to be identified with one institution—and that an institution of which the South itself had furnished some of the most intelligent critics. It was a system known to have reached the natural limits of its expansion in this country already and one which was far gone on its way to abandonment abroad. Yet, in its quest for friends and allies, the South made the mistake of competing with the North for the favor of the West by insisting upon the acceptance of a system totally unadapted to the conditions and needs of the territories and often offensive to their moral sensibilities. And in looking to Europe for support from England and France, powers that might reasonably have been expected to be drawn to its cause for reasons of self-interest, the South encountered difficulties from the start. Some, though certainly not all, of these difficulties were due to the fact that those countries had already repudiated the system upon which the South had elected to stand or fall.

The knowledge that it was rapidly being isolated in the world community as the last champion of an outmoded system under concerted moral attack contributed to the South's feeling of insecurity and its conviction that it was being encircled and menaced from all sides. In place of its old eagerness for new ideas and its out-going communicativeness the South developed a suspicious inhospitality toward the new and the foreign, a tendency to withdraw from what it felt to be a critical world. Because it identified the internal security of the whole society with the security of its labor system, it refused to permit criticism of that system. To guarantee conformity of thought it abandoned its tradition of tolerance and resorted to repression of dissent within its borders and to forceful exclusion of criticism from outside. And finally it set about to celebrate, glorify, and render all but sacrosanct with praise the very institution that was under attack and that was responsible for the isolation and insecurity of the South.

Modern America is more fortunate than the ante-bellum South in having an economic system which, though threatened with abondonment by other countries, has shown few of the serious weaknesses and is covered with little of the moral obloquy from which slavery suffered. And in spite of verbal orthodoxy regarding the doctrine of capitalistic free enterprise, the American political genius has shown willingness to experiment extensively with heterodox cures for ills of the orthodox system. This experimentation has, of course, been accompanied by loud protests of loyalty to the true faith. Again, modern America is not inherently nor necessarily handicapped in the struggle against its powerful antagonist by all the weaknesses that helped to doom the South to defeat.

There is, however, no cause for complacency in this good fortune. Nor does it rule out entirely the analogy that is here suggested. We should not deceive ourselves about the opinions of other peoples. While we see ourselves as morally sound and regard our good fortune as the natural and just reward of our soundness, these views are not shared by large numbers of people in many parts of the world. They look on our great wealth not as the reward of our virtue but as proof of our wickedness, as evidence of the ruthless exploitation, not only of our own working people but of themselves. For great masses of people who live in abject poverty and know nothing firsthand of our system or of industrialism of any kind are easily persuaded that their misery is due to capitalist exploitation rather than to the shortcomings of their own economies. Hundreds of millions of these people are taught to believe that we are as arrogant, brutal, immoral, ruthless, and wicked as ever the South was pictured in an earlier war of words. Among their leaders are extremists ready with the conclusion that people so wicked do not deserve to live and that any means whatever used to destroy their system is justified by the end. One of these means is the subversive indoctrination of our labor force for insurrection. The malevolent caricature of our society contrasts so glaringly with what we believe to be the demonstrable facts—not to mention the contrast with our traditional illusions of virtue and innocence—that we are driven to indignation. And when we hear faint echoes of the same propaganda from our own allies, who no longer share our dedication to capitalism, our indignation turns into a sense of outrage.

Fortunately modern America has not yet followed the course of the South between 1830 and 1860, but the pattern of response evoked by these exasperations is not a wholly unfamiliar one. There are some unhappy similarities. Threatened with isolation as the last important defender of an economic system that has been abandoned or rejected without a trial by most of the world and that is under constant moral attack from several quarters, we have rallied to the point of attack. We have showed a tendency to allow our whole cause, our traditional values, and our way of life to be identified with one economic institution. Some of us have also tended to identify the security of the country with the security of that institution. We have swiftly turned from a mood of criticism to one of glorifying the institution as the secret of our superiority. We have showed a strong disposition to suppress criticism and repel outside ideas. We have been tempted to define loyalty as conformity of thought, and to run grave risk of moral and intellectual stultification.

Opposing each of these dangerous tendencies there is still healthy and wholesome resistance struggling to reassert our ancient tradition of tolerance and free criticism, to maintain balance and a sense of humor, to repel the temptation of self-righteousness and complacency, and to reject the fallacy that the whole American cause and tradition must stand or fall with one economic dogma. But it is too early to say that on any one of these points the healthy resistance is certain of triumph. In fact the fight is uphill, and in many instances the issue is doubtful. I am not contending that successful resistance to all the tendencies I have deplored will guarantee peace and solve the problems that plagued the 1950's, any more than I am sure that the same course would have resulted as happily in the 1850's. But I believe I am safe in contending that, in view of the South's experience, each of these tendencies should be the subject of gravest concern.

5

In the field of diplomacy and foreign relations modern America suffers from a divided mind, torn between one policy that is reminiscent of the way of the South and another more suggestive of the way of the North in the Civil War crisis. On the one hand are those who would meet the foreign challenge by withdrawing from a critical community of nations teeming with heresies and, by erecting an impregnable barricade, forcibly keep out all alien ways, influences, and ideas. Another modern group that has a counterpart in at least one school of Southerners in the 1850's are those who in the 1960's, heedless of world opinion, would brook no opposition, would not co-operate with, nor consult, other people's views, but insist that America must be strong enough to carry her way by economic coercion or by force. Suggestive also of the Southern way are those who, in competing with our opponents for the favor of uncommitted peoples, would urge upon them institutions and abstract ideas of our own that have little or no relevance to their real needs and circumstances. There are those who resent as evidence of disloyalty any defection on the part of our allies from the particular economic faith upon which we have decided to take our stand.

More reminiscent of the way of the North, on the other hand, are those who hold that this is an irrepressible conflict, that a world divided against itself cannot stand, that the issue is essentially a moral one, that we are morally obliged to liberate the enslaved peoples of the earth, punish the wicked oppressors, and convert the liberated peoples to our way of thought. The true American mission, according to those who support this view, is a moral crusade on a world-wide scale. Such people are likely to concede no validity whatever and grant no hearing to the opposing point of view, and to appeal to a higher law to justify bloody and revolting means in the name of a noble end. For what end could be nobler, they ask, than the liberation of man? Fortunately wiser counsel has generally prevailed, counsel which has charted a course of foreign policy between the perilous extremes of isolationism and world crusade. But each of the extreme courses still has powerful advocates, and neither can yet be regarded as a dead issue.

We have been admonished lately to heed the ironic consequences of the characteristic American approach to international affairs since the beginning of the present century. The main deficiencies of our policy of the last fifty years, we are told, are our legalistic and moralistic approaches to foreign relations. It is possible and even desirable, I believe, to accept the validity of this critical insight without embracing the strictly amoral, pragmatic, power-conscious policy of national self-interest that has been proposed as an alternative by those who criticize the moralistic approach. It is all too apparent that the association of the legalistic with the moralistic concept results in a torrent of indignation and bitterness against the lawbreaker and a blinding conviction of moral superiority to the enemy. Expressed in military policy and war aims these passions overwhelm reason and find no bounds short of complete submission, unconditional surrender, and total domination of the defeated people. The irony of the moralistic approach, when exploited by nationalism, is that the high motive to end injustice and immorality actually results in making war more amoral and horrible than ever and in shattering the foundations of the political and moral order upon which peace has to be built.

There would appear to be valid grounds for seeking the origins of our moralistic aberrations in the period of the Civil War. While both sides to that dispute indulged in legalistic as well as moralistic pretensions, it was the South that was predominantly legalistic and the North that was overwhelmingly moralistic in its approach. Although Southern historians have made important contributions to the understanding of that crisis, it is doubtful whether anyone has stated more aptly the ironic consequence of the moralistic approach than a Northern historian. "Yankees went to war," writes Kenneth Stampp, "animated by the highest ideals of the nineteenth-century middle classes. . . . But what the Yankees achieved—for their generation at least—was a triumph not of middle-class ideals but of middle-class vices. The most striking products of their crusades were the shoddy aristocracy of the North and the ragged children of the South. Among the masses of Americans there were no victors, only the vanquished."

Ironic contrasts between noble purposes and sordid results, between idealistic aims and pragmatic consequences, are characteristic of reconstruction periods as well as war crises. This is nowhere more readily apparent than in the postwar period through which we have recently lived and with the problems of which we are still struggling. It is especially in such times that moralistic approaches and high-minded war aims come home to roost. As usual, it is only after the zeal of wartime idealism has spent itself that the opportunity is gained for realizing the ideals for which the war has been fought. When the idealistic aims are then found to be in conflict with selfish and pragmatic ends, it is the ideals that are likely to be sacrificed. The probability of moral confusion in reconstruction policy is increased when a nation finds itself called on to gird for a new world moral crusade before the reconstruction consequent upon the last is fairly launched. Opportunities for moral confusion are still further multiplied when the new crusade promises to be fought in alliance with the public enemies of the previous moral crusade and when the new enemy happens to have been an ally in the previous crusade.

Americans have in common the memories of an earlier experiment with reconstruction and are generally conscious of some of the shortcomings of that effort. But again, the South experienced that same historic episode from a somewhat different point of view. Once Southern historians have purged their minds of rancor and awakened out of a narrow parochialism they should be in a singularly strategic position to teach their fellow countrymen something of the pitfalls of radical reconstruction: of the disfranchisement of old ruling classes and the indoctrination of liberated peoples, of the occupation of conquered territory and the eradication of racial dogma, of the problems of reunion and the hazards of reaction. They should at least have a special awareness of the ironic incongruities between moral purpose and pragmatic result, of the way in which laudable aims of idealists can be perverted to sordid purposes, and of the readiness with which high-minded ideals can be forgotten.

With all her terrible power and new responsibilities, combined with her illusions of innocence and her legends of immunity from frustration and defeat, America stands in greater need than she ever did of understanding her own history. Our European friends, appalled by the impetuosity and naïveté of some of our deeds and assumptions, have attributed our lack of historical sophistication to our lack of a history —in their sense of the word. America's apparent immunity to the tragic and ironic aspects of man's fate—that charmed and fabled immunity that once made America the Utopia of both the common men and the philosophers of Europe—has come to be pictured as Europe's curse. For the fear that haunts Europeans is the fear that America's lack of a common basis of experience and suffering will blind her to the true nature of their dilemmas and end by plunging them into catastrophe. But the Europeans are not entirely right. America has a history. It is only that the tragic aspects and the ironic implications of that history have been obscured by the national legend of success and victory and by the perpetuation of infant illusions of innocence and virtue.

America has had cynical disparagement of her ideals from foreign, unfriendly, or hostile critics. But she desperately needs criticism from historians of her own who can penetrate the legend without destroying the ideal, who can dispel the illusion of pretended virtue without denying the genuine virtues. Such historians must have learned that virtue has never been defined by national or regional boundaries, and that morality and rectitude are not the monopolies of factions or parties. They must reveal the fallacy of a diplomacy based on moral bigotry, as well as the fallacy of one that relies on economic coercion through the fancied indispensability of favored products. Their studies would show the futility of erecting intellectual barricades against unpopular ideas, of employing censorship and repression against social criticism, and of imposing the ideas of the conqueror upon defeated peoples by force of arms. Such historians would teach that economic systems, whatever their age, their respectability, or their apparent stability, are transitory and that any nation which elects to stand or fall upon one ephemeral institution has already determined its fate. The history they write would also constitute a warning that an overwhelming conviction in the righteousness of a cause is no guarantee of its ultimate triumph, and that the policy which takes into account the possibility of defeat is more realistic than one that assumes the inevitability of victory.

Such historians must have a rare combination of detachment and sympathy, and they must have established some measure of immunity from the fevers and prejudices of their own times, particularly those bred of nationalism, with all its myths and pretensions, and those born of hysteria that closes the mind to new ideas of all kinds. America might find such historians anywhere within her borders, North as well as South. But surely some of them might reasonably be expected to arise from that region where it is a matter of common knowledge that history has happened to their people in their part of the world.

winston churchill

---

dunkirk

Winston Churchill (1874-   ) has been described as the greatest of all British prime ministers. He has certainly been the most effective, the most dramatic and the most universally admired leader of Britain in modern times, and without his staunch determination never to let his country fall to Hitler, the 1939-1945 war might have ended very differently.

Churchill has been a leader in the *grand* style, as an impassioned and brilliant orator summoning his people to fulfill their destiny. He has been not just a statesman who happens to write and to speak well, but a national leader whose gift for words has been the very basis of his leadership. And nowhere has this historic quality, of great captains and kings, been seen to greater advantage than in the famous speech he made to the House of Commons after the British Army had been forced, in the summer of 1940, back across the channel from Dunkirk.

On this occasion Churchill had to present news of a military defeat that had just narrowly escaped being a total disaster for the British army, and he had to summon up the entire British people against the invasion that was momentarily expected from France. Churchill did not merely *report* that the British army had been evacuated from the beaches of Dunkirk—he began, typically enough, by picturing for the Commons what *might* have happened. "The whole root and core and brain of the British Army, on which and around which we were to build, and are to build . . . seemed about to perish upon the field or to be led into an ignominious and starving captivity." Nor did he end up by saying that the British would fight—with the true writer's passion for the concrete detail, he went on to build up his defiance, stroke by stroke, by picturing every possible place where the British would make their stand—"We shall go on to the end, we shall fight in France, we shall fight on the seas and oceans . . . we shall fight on the beaches, we shall fight on the landing grounds, we shall fight in the fields and in the streets, we shall fight in the hills; we shall never surrender . . ."

No one who was old enough on June 4, 1940 to hear or to read these words will ever forget the thrill of admiration, of positive exultation, that this speech awoke in everyone who in those days lived for the victory of democracy over Hitlerism. It is reported, however, that after crying out that the British would fight with their hands, Churchill whispered to a friend that the British had better, since they had nothing else to fight with!

The true writer can always kindle hope from the imagination and make real what he has only dreamed of. For this speech certainly helped to inspire a belief in victory—and eventually victory came.

The House of Commons
June 4, 1940

From the moment that the French defenses at Sedan and on the Meuse were broken at the end of the second week of May, only a rapid retreat to Amiens and the south could have saved the British and French Armies who had entered Belgium at the appeal of the Belgian King; but this strategic fact was not immediately realized. The French

High Command hoped they would be able to close the gap, and the Armies of the north were under their orders. Moreover, a retirement of this kind would have involved almost certainly the destruction of the fine Belgian Army of over 20 divisions and the abandonment of the whole of Belgium. Therefore, when the force and scope of the German penetration were realized and when a new French General-issimo, General Weygand, assumed command in place of General Gamelin, an effort was made by the French and British Armies in Belgium to keep on holding the right hand of the Belgians and to give their own right hand to a newly created French Army which was to have advanced across the Somme in great strength to grasp it.

However, the German eruption swept like a sharp scythe around the right and rear of the Armies of the north. Eight or nine armored divisions, each of about four hundred armored vehicles of different kinds, but carefully assorted to be complementary and divisible into small self-contained units, cut off all communications between us and the main French Armies. It severed our own communications for food and ammunition, which ran first to Amiens and afterwards through Abbeville, and it shore its way up the coast to Boulogne and Calais, and almost to Dunkirk. Behind this armored and mechanized on-slaught came a number of German divisions in lorries, and behind them again there plodded comparatively slowly the dull brute mass of the ordinary German Army and German people, always so ready to be led to the trampling down in other lands of liberties and comforts which they have never known in their own.

I have said this armored scythe-stroke almost reached Dunkirk—almost but not quite. Boulogne and Calais were the scenes of desperate fighting. The Guards defended Boulogne for a while and were then withdrawn by orders from this country. The Rifle Brigade, the 60th Rifles, and the Queen Victoria's Rifles, with a battalion of British tanks and 1,000 Frenchmen, in all about four thousand strong, de-fended Calais to the last. The British Brigadier was given an hour to surrender. He spurned the offer, and four days of intense street fight-ing passed before silence reigned over Calais, which marked the end of a memorable resistance. Only 30 unwounded survivors were brought off by the Navy, and we do not know the fate of their comrades. Their sacrifice, however, was not in vain. At least two armored divisions, which otherwise would have been turned against the British Expedi-tionary Force, had to be sent to overcome them. They have added an-other page to the glories of the light divisions, and the time gained en-abled the Graveline water lines to be flooded and to be held by the French troops.

Thus it was that the port of Dunkirk was kept open. When it was found impossible for the Armies of the north to reopen their communications to Amiens with the main French Armies, only one choice remained. It seemed, indeed, forlorn. The Belgian, British and French Armies were almost surrounded. Their sole line of retreat was to a single port and to its neighboring beaches. They were pressed on every side by heavy attacks and far outnumbered in the air.

When, a week ago today, I asked the House to fix this afternoon as the occasion for a statement, I feared it would be my hard lot to announce the greatest military disaster in our long history. I thought— and some good judges agreed with me—that perhaps 20,000 or 30,000 men might be re-embarked. But it certainly seemed that the whole of the French First Army and the whole of the British Expeditionary Force north of the Amiens-Abbeville gap would be broken up in the open field or else would have to capitulate for lack of food and ammunition. These were the hard and heavy tidings for which I called upon the House and the nation to prepare themselves a week ago. The whole root and core and brain of the British Army, on which and around which we were to build, and are to build, the great British Armies in the later years of the war, seemed about to perish upon the field or to be led into an ignominious and starving captivity.

That was the prospect a week ago. But another blow which might well have proved final was yet to fall upon us. The King of the Belgians had called upon us to come to his aid. Had not this Ruler and his Government severed themselves from the Allies, who rescued their country from extinction in the late war, and had they not sought refuge in what has proved to be a fatal neutrality, the French and British Armies might well at the outset have saved not only Belgium but perhaps even Poland. Yet at the last moment, when Belgium was already invaded, King Leopold called upon us to come to his aid, and even at the last moment we came. He and his brave, efficient Army, nearly half a million strong, guarded our left flank and thus kept open our only line of retreat to the sea. Suddenly, without prior consultation, with the least possible notice, without the advice of his Ministers and upon his own personal act, he sent a plenipotentiary to the German Command, surrendered his Army, and exposed our whole flank and means of retreat.

I asked the House a week ago to suspend its judgment because the facts were not clear, but I do not feel that any reason now exists why we should not form our own opinions upon this pitiful episode. The surrender of the Belgian Army compelled the British at the shortest notice to cover a flank to the sea more than 30 miles in length. Otherwise all would have been cut off, and all would have shared the fate to which King Leopold had condemned the finest Army his country had ever formed. So in doing this and in exposing this flank, as anyone who followed the operations on the map will see, contact was lost between the British and two out of the three corps forming the First French Army, who were still farther from the coast than we were, and it seemed impossible that any large number of Allied troops could reach the coast.

The enemy attacked on all sides with great strength and fierceness, and their main power, the power of their far more numerous Air Force, was thrown into the battle or else concentrated upon Dunkirk and the beaches. Pressing in upon the narrow exit, both from the east and from the west, the enemy began to fire with cannon upon the beaches by which alone the shipping could approach or depart. They sowed magnetic mines in the channels and seas; they sent repeated waves of hostile aircraft, sometimes more than a hundred strong in one formation, to cast their bombs upon the single pier that remained, and upon the sand dunes upon which the troops had their eyes for shelter. Their U-boats, one of which was sunk, and their motor launches took their toll of the vast traffic which now began. For four or five days an intense struggle reigned. All their armored divisions—or what was left of them—together with great masses of infantry and artillery, hurled themselves in vain upon the ever-narrowing, ever-contracting appendix within which the British and French Armies fought.

Meanwhile, the Royal Navy, with the willing help of countless merchant seamen, strained every nerve to embark the British and Allied troops; 220 light warships and 650 other vessels were engaged. They had to operate upon the difficult coast, often in adverse weather, under an almost ceaseless hail of bombs and an increasing concentration of artillery fire. Nor were the seas, as I have said, themselves free from mines and torpedoes. It was in conditions such as these that our men carried on, with little or no rest, for days and nights on end, making trip after trip across the dangerous waters, bringing with them always men whom they had rescued. The numbers they have brought back are the measure of their devotion and their courage. The hospital ships, which brought off many thousands of British and French wounded, being so plainly marked were a special target for Nazi bombs; but the men and women on board them never faltered in their duty.

Meanwhile, the Royal Air Force, which had already been intervening in the battle, so far as its range would allow, from home bases, now used part of its main metropolitan fighter strength, and struck at the German bombers and at the fighters which in large numbers protected them. This struggle was protracted and fierce. Suddenly the scene has cleared, the crash and thunder has for the moment—but only for the moment—died away. A miracle of deliverance, achieved by valor, by perseverance, by perfect discipline, by faultless service, by resource, by skill, by unconquerable fidelity, is manifest to us all. The enemy was hurled back by the retreating British and French troops. He was so roughly handled that he did not hurry their departure seriously. The Royal Air Force engaged the main strength of the German Air Force, and inflicted upon them losses of at least four to one; and the Navy, using nearly 1,000 ships of all kinds, carried over 335,000 men, French and British, out of the jaws of death and shame, to their native land and to the tasks which lie immediately ahead. We must be very careful not to assign to this deliverance the attributes of a victory. Wars are not won by evacuations. But there was a victory inside this deliverance, which should be noted. It was gained by the Air Force. Many of our soldiers coming back have not seen the Air Force at work; they saw only the bombers which escaped its protective attack. They underrate its achievements. I have heard much talk of this; that is why I go out of my way to say this. I will tell you about it.

This was a great trial of strength between the British and German Air Forces. Can you conceive a greater objective for the Germans in the air than to make evacuation from these beaches impossible, and to sink all these ships which were displayed, almost to the extent of thousands? Could there have been an objective of greater military importance and significance for the whole purpose of the war than this? They tried hard, and they were beaten back; they were frustrated in their task. We got the Army away; and they have paid fourfold for any losses which they have inflicted. Very large formations of German aeroplanes—and we know that they are a very brave race—have turned on several occasions from the attack of one-quarter of their number of the Royal Air Force, and have dispersed in different directions. Twelve aeroplanes have been hunted by two. One aeroplane was driven into the water and cast away by the mere charge of a British aeroplane, which had no more ammunition. All of our types—the Hurricane, the Spitfire and the new Defiant—and all our pilots have been vindicated as superior to what they have at present to face.

When we consider how much greater would be our advantage in defending the air above this Island against an overseas attack, I must say that I find in these facts a sure basis upon which practical and reassuring thoughts may rest. I will pay my tribute to these young airmen. The great French Army was very largely, for the time being, cast back and disturbed by the onrush of a few thousands of armored vehicles. May it not also be that the cause of civilization itself will be defended by the skill and devotion of a few thousand airmen? There never has been, I suppose, in all the world, in all the history of war, such an opportunity for youth. The Knights of the Round Table, the Crusaders, all fall back into the past—not only distant but prosaic; these young men, going forth every morn to guard their native land and all that we stand for, holding in their hands these instruments of colossal and shattering power, of whom it may be said that

> *Every morn brought forth a noble chance*
> *And every chance brought forth a noble knight,*

deserve our gratitude, as do all of the brave men who, in so many ways and on so many occasions, are ready, and continue ready, to give life and all for their native land.

I return to the Army. In the long series of very fierce battles, now on this front, now on that, fighting on three fronts at once, battles fought by two or three divisions against an equal or somewhat larger number of the enemy, and fought fiercely on some of the old grounds that so many of us knew so well—in these battles our losses in men have exceeded 30,000 killed, wounded and missing. I take occasion to express the sympathy of the House to all who have suffered bereavement or who are still anxious. The President of the Board of Trade[1] is not here today. His son has been killed, and many in the House have felt the pangs of affliction in the sharpest form. But I will say this about the missing: We have had a large number of wounded come home safely to this country, but I would say about the missing that there may be very many reported missing who will come back home, some day, in one way or another. In the confusion of this fight it is inevitable that many have been left in positions where honor required no further resistance from them.

Against this loss of over 30,000 men, we can set a far heavier loss certainly inflicted upon the enemy. But our losses in material are enormous. We have perhaps lost one-third of the men we lost in the opening days of the battle of 21st March, 1918, but we have lost nearly as many guns—nearly one thousand—and all our transport, all the armored vehicles that were with the Army in the north. This loss will impose a further delay on the expansion of our military strength. That expansion had not been proceeding as fast as we had hoped. The best of all we had to give had gone to the British Expeditionary

[1] Sir Andrew Duncan, now Minister of Supply.

Force, and although they had not the numbers of tanks and some articles of equipment which were desirable, they were a very well and finely equipped Army. They had the first-fruits of all that our industry had to give, and that is gone. And now here is this further delay. How long it will be, how long it will last, depends upon the exertions which we make in this Island. An effort the like of which has never been seen in our records is now being made. Work is proceeding every-where, night and day, Sundays and week days. Capital and Labor have cast aside their interests, rights, and customs and put them into the common stock. Already the flow of munitions has leaped forward. There is no reason why we should not in a few months overtake the sudden and serious loss that has come upon us, without retarding the development of our general program.

Nevertheless, our thankfulness at the escape of our Army and so many men, whose loved ones have passed through an agonizing week, must not blind us to the fact that what has happened in France and Belgium is a colossal military disaster. The French Army has been weakened, the Belgian Army has been lost, a large part of those fortified lines upon which so much faith had been reposed is gone, many valuable mining districts and factories have passed into the enemy's possession, the whole of the Channel ports are in his hands, with all the tragic consequences that follow from that, and we must expect another blow to be struck almost immediately at us or at France. We are told that Herr Hitler has a plan for invading the British Isles. This has often been thought of before. When Napoleon lay at Bou-logne for a year with his flat-bottomed boats and his Grand Army, he was told by someone, "There are bitter weeds in England." There are certainly a great many more of them since the British Expeditionary Force returned.

The whole question of home defense against invasion is, of course, powerfully affected by the fact that we have for the time being in this Island incomparably more powerful military forces than we have ever had at any moment in this war or the last. But this will not continue. We shall not be content with a defensive war. We have our duty to our Ally. We have to reconstitute and build up the British Expeditionary Force once again, under its gallant Commander-in-Chief, Lord Gort. All this is in train; but in the interval we must put our defenses in this Island into such a high state of organization that the fewest possible numbers will be required to give effective security and that the largest possible potential of offensive effort may be realized. On this we are now engaged. It will be very convenient, if it be the desire of the House, to enter upon this subject in a secret Session. Not that the

Government would necessarily be able to reveal in very great detail military secrets, but we like to have our discussions free, without the restraint imposed by the fact that they will be read the next day by the enemy; and the Government would benefit by views freely expressed in all parts of the House by Members with their knowledge of so many different parts of the country. I understand that some request is to be made upon this subject, which will be readily acceded to by His Majesty's Government.

We have found it necessary to take measures of increasing stringency, not only against enemy aliens and suspicious characters of other nationalities, but also against British subjects who may become a danger or a nuisance should the war be transported to the United Kingdom. I know there are a great many people affected by the orders which we have made who are the passionate enemies of Nazi Germany. I am very sorry for them, but we cannot, at the present time and under the present stress, draw all the distinctions which we should like to do. If parachute landings were attempted and fierce fighting attendant upon them followed, these unfortunate people would be far better out of the way, for their own sakes as well as for ours. There is, however, another class, for which I feel not the slightest sympathy. Parliament has given us the powers to put down Fifth Column activities with a strong hand, and we shall use those powers, subject to the supervision and correction of the House, without the slightest hesitation until we are satisfied, and more than satisfied, that this malignancy in our midst has been effectively stamped out.

Turning once again, and this time more generally, to the question of invasion, I would observe that there has never been a period in all these long centuries of which we boast when an absolute guarantee against invasion, still less against serious raids, could have been given to our people. In the days of Napoleon the same wind which would have carried his transports across the Channel might have driven away the blockading fleet. There was always the chance, and it is that chance which has excited and befooled the imaginations of many Continental tyrants. Many are the tales that are told. We are assured that novel methods will be adopted, and when we see the originality of malice, the ingenuity of aggression, which our enemy displays, we may certainly prepare ourselves for every kind of novel stratagem and every kind of brutal and treacherous maneuver. I think that no idea is so outlandish that it should not be considered and viewed with a searching, but at the same time, I hope, with a steady eye. We must never forget the solid assurances of sea power and those which belong to air power if it can be locally exercised.

I have, myself, full confidence that if all do their duty, if nothing is neglected, and if the best arrangements are made, as they are being made, we shall prove ourselves once again able to defend our Island home, to ride out the storm of war, and to outlive the menace of tyranny, if necessary for years, if necessary alone. At any rate, that is what we are going to try to do. That is the resolve of His Majesty's Government—every man of them. That is the will of Parliament and the nation. The British Empire and the French Republic, linked together in their cause and in their need, will defend to the death their native soil, aiding each other like good comrades to the utmost of their strength. Even though large tracts of Europe and many old and famous States have fallen or may fall into the grip of the Gestapo and all the odious apparatus of Nazi rule, we shall not flag or fail. We shall go on to the end, we shall fight in France, we shall fight on the seas and oceans, we shall fight with growing confidence and growing strength in the air, we shall defend our Island, whatever the cost may be, we shall fight on the beaches, we shall fight on the landing grounds, we shall fight in the fields and in the streets, we shall fight in the hills; we shall never surrender, and even if, which I do not for a moment believe, this Island or a large part of it were subjugated and starving, then our Empire beyond the seas, armed and guarded by the British Fleet, would carry on the struggle, until, in God's good time, the New World, with all its power and might, steps forth to the rescue and the liberation of the old.

h. r. trevor-roper

the death of hitler

H. R. Trevor-Roper was born in 1914 and is now Regius Professor of Modern History at Oxford. During the Second World War, he was a member of British Intelligence. Because the widespread uncertainty as to whether Hitler was actually dead might have revived Nazi hopes in Germany, Trevor-Roper was assigned by the British Government to make an official investigation of Hitler's end.

Trevor-Roper's report, *The Last Days of Hitler* (1947) is one of the most exciting works of contemporary history. As Arthur Schlesinger, Jr., said in his review of the book, "Trevor-Roper's triumph is all the more astonishing because it is achieved, not at the comparatively easy game of writing about the past, but at the tougher and more complex discipline of contemporary history." His triumph was reaffirmed in the third edition (London, 1956) when returned prisoners from Russia added nothing but corroborative detail to the firm record published in 1947. Trevor-Roper marshals his evidence with the precision of a scholar, and yet with the passion of a writer describing the most destructive tyrant of all time.

It is this fusion of scholarly exactness and the unexpressed passion of the subject itself that makes Trevor-Roper's book history in the grand manner, history that will live as literature. The writing in it could not be more sober, objective, factual. Witness after witness is called up to present his evidence. But the vital chapter on Hitler's actual end makes its impact through a series of visual details—the burning rag, Hitler's black trousers sticking out of the blanket in which the S.S. men are carrying him to the pyre. And in associating Hitler's death with that of Alaric, the Visigoth "barbarian" who stormed and sacked Rome in 410 A.D., Trevor-Roper, with the keen literary instinct for analogy that marks the historian as artist, has suggested the note of secrecy and mystery with which Hitler's death will, despite all the facts, always be identified. For it is said that Alaric was buried with his treasures near Cosenza in the bed of the Busento River, which was temporarily diverted from its course. "That the secret might be kept, the slaves employed in the labor were killed."

When von Below left the Bunker, Hitler was already preparing for the end. During the day the last news from the outside world had been brought in. Mussolini was dead. Hitler's partner in crime, the herald of Fascism, who had first shown to Hitler the possibilities of dictatorship in modern Europe, and had preceded him in the stages of disillusion and defeat, had now illustrated in a signal manner the fate which fallen tyrants must expect. Captured by partisans during the general uprising of northern Italy, Mussolini and his mistress Clara Petacci had been executed, and their bodies suspended by the feet in the market-place of Milan to be beaten and pelted by the vindictive crowd. If the full details were ever known to them, Hitler and Eva Braun could only have repeated the orders they had already given: their bodies were to be destroyed "so that nothing remains"; "I will not fall into the hands of an enemy who requires a new spectacle to divert his hysterical masses." In fact it is improbable that these details were reported, or could have strengthened an already firm decision. The fate of defeated despots has generally been the same; and Hitler, who had himself exhibited the body of a field-marshal on a meat-hook, had no need of remote historical examples or of a new and dramatic instance, to know the probable fate of his own corpse, if it should be found.[1]

In the afternoon, Hitler had had his favorite Alsatian dog, Blondi, destroyed. Professor Haase, his former surgeon, who was now tending the wounded in his clinic in Berlin, had come round to the Bunker and killed it with poison. The two other dogs belonging to the household had been shot by the sergeant who looked after them. After this, Hitler had given poison-capsules to his two secretaries, for use in extremity. He was sorry, he said, to give them no better parting gift; and praising them for their courage, he had added, characteristically, that he wished his generals were as reliable as they.[2]

In the evening, while the inhabitants of the two outer bunkers were dining in the general dining-passage of the Fuehrerbunker, they were visited by one of the S.S. guard, who informed them that the Fuehrer wished to say good-bye to the ladies and that no one was to go to bed till orders had been received. At about half-past two in the morning the orders came. They were summoned by telephone to the Bunker, and gathered again in the same general dining-passage, officers and women, about twenty persons in all. When they were assembled, Hitler came in from the private part of the Bunker, accompanied by Bormann. His look was abstracted, his eyes glazed over with that film of moisture which Hanna Reitsch had noticed. Some of those who saw him even suggested that he had been drugged; but no such explanation is needed of a condition upon which more familiar observers had often commented. He walked in silence down the passage and shook hands with all the women in turn. Some spoke to him, but he said nothing, or mumbled inaudibly. Ceremonies of silent hand-shaking had become quite customary in the course of that day.[3]

[1] It has often been stated, by those whose imagination is stronger than their memory, that Hitler's decision was affected by the fate of Mussolini. An account of the table-talk of the prisoners at Nuremberg, ascribed to the chief psychiatrist at the Trial and printed in the *Sunday Express*, 25th August 1946, even quotes Goering as saying, "You remember the Mussolini incident? We had pictures of Mussolini dead in the gutter with his mistress, and hanging in the air upside-down. They were awful! Hitler went into a frenzy, shouting: 'This will never happen to me!'" A glance at the dates disposes of this romance. Goering saw Hitler for the last time eight days before Mussolini's death. Goering may have seen pictures of Mussolini's body in captivity; Hitler never. Such is the value of unchecked human testimony, on which, however, much of written history is based.

[2] Frau Junge.

[3] Von Varo.

When he had left, the participants in this strange scene remained for a while to discuss its significance. They agreed that it could have one meaning only. The suicide of the Fuehrer was about to take place. Thereupon an unexpected thing happened. A great and heavy cloud seemed to roll away from the spirits of the Bunker-dwellers. The terrible sorcerer, the tyrant who had charged their days with intolerable melodramatic tension, would soon be gone, and for a brief twilight moment they could play. In the canteen of the Chancellery, where the soldiers and orderlies took their meals, there was a dance. The news was brought; but no one allowed that to interfere with the business of pleasure. A message from the Fuehrerbunker told them to be quieter; but the dance went on. A tailor[4] who had been employed in the Fuehrer's headquarters, and who was now immured with the rest in the Chancellery, was surprised when Brigadefuehrer Rattenhuber, the head of the police guard and a general in the S.S., slapped him cordially on the back and greeted him with democratic familiarity. In the strict hierarchy of the Bunker the tailor felt bewildered. It was as if he had been a high officer. "It was the first time I had ever heard a high officer say 'good evening'," he said; "so I noticed that the mood had completely changed." Then, from one of his equals, he learned the reason of this sudden and irregular affability. Hitler had said goodbye, and was going to commit suicide. There are few forces so solvent of class distinctions as common danger, and common relief.

Though Hitler might already be preparing for death, there was still one man at least in the Bunker who was thinking of life: Martin Bormann. If Bormann could not persuade the German armies to come and rescue Hitler and himself, at least he would insist on revenge. Shortly after the farewell ceremony, at a quarter-past three in the morning of 30th April, he sent another of these telegrams in which the neurosis of the Bunker is so vividly preserved. It was addressed to Doenitz at Ploen; but Bormann no longer trusted the ordinary communications, and sent it through the Gauleiter of Mecklenburg. It ran:

> DOENITZ!—Our impression grows daily stronger that the divisions in the Berlin theater have been standing idle for several days. All the reports we receive are controlled, suppressed, or distorted by Keitel. The Fuehrer orders you to proceed at once, and mercilessly, against all traitors.—BORMANN.[5]

A postscript contained the words: "The Fuehrer is alive, and is conducting the defense of Berlin". These words, containing no hint of the

---

[4] W. O. Mueller.

[5] In the German text the name of Keitel is represented by his code-name 'Teilhaus'.

approaching end,—indeed seeming to deny its imminence,—suggest that Bormann was reluctant even now to admit that his power would soon be over, or must be renewed from another, less calculable source.

Later in the same morning, when the new day's work had begun, the generals came as usual to the Bunker with their military reports. Brigadefuehrer Mohnke, the commandant of the Chancellery, announced a slight improvement: the Schlesischer railway station had been recaptured from the Russians; but in other respects the military situation was unchanged. By noon the news was worse again. The underground railway tunnel in the Friedrichstrasse was reported in Russian hands; the tunnel in the Vossstrasse, close to the Chancellery, was partly occupied; the whole area of the Tiergarten had been taken; and Russian forces had reached the Potsdamer Platz and the Weidendammer Bridge over the river Spree. Hitler received these reports without emotion. At about two o'clock he took lunch. Eva Braun was not there; evidently she did not feel hungry, or ate alone in her room; and Hitler shared his meal, as usually in her absence, with his two secretaries and the cook. The conversation indicated nothing unusual. Hitler remained quiet, and did not speak of his intentions. Nevertheless, preparations were already being made for the approaching ceremony.

In the morning, the guards had been ordered to collect all their rations for the day, since they would not be allowed to pass through the corridor of the Bunker again; and about lunch-time Hitler's S.S. adjutant, Sturmbannfuehrer Guensche, sent an order to the transport officer and chauffeur, Sturmbannfuehrer Erich Kempka, to send 200 litres of petrol to the Chancellery garden. Kempka protested that it would be difficult to find so large a quantity at once, but he was told that it must be found. Ultimately he found about 180 litres and sent it round to the garden. Four men carried it in jerricans[6] and placed it at the emergency exit of the Bunker. There they met one of the police guards, who demanded an explanation. They told him that it was for the ventilating plant. The guard told them not to be silly, for the plant was oil-driven. At this moment Hitler's personal servant, Heinz Linge, appeared. He reassured the guard, terminated the argument, and dismissed the men. Soon afterwards all the guards except those on duty were ordered to leave the Chancellery, and to stay away. It was not intended that any casual observer should witness the final scene.

Meanwhile Hitler had finished lunch, and his guests had been dismissed. For a time he remained behind; then he emerged from his suite, accompanied by Eva Braun, and another farewell ceremony took place. Bormann and Goebbels were there, with Burgdorf, Krebs,

6 A jerrican is a German petrol-can containing 4½ gallons.

Hewel, Naumann, Voss, Rattenhuber, Hoegl, Guensche, Linge, and the four women, Frau Christian, Frau Junge, Fraeulein Krueger, and Fraeulein Manzialy. Frau Goebbels was not present; unnerved by the approaching death of her children, she remained all day in her own room. Hitler and Eva Braun shook hands with them all, and then returned to their suite. The others were dimissed, all but the high-priests and those few others whose services would be necessary. These waited in the passage. A single shot was heard. After an interval they entered the suite. Hitler was lying on the sofa, which was soaked with blood. He had shot himself through the mouth. Eva Braun was also on the sofa, also dead. A revolver was by her side, but she had not used it; she had swallowed poison. The time was half-past three.[7]

Shortly afterwards, Artur Axmann, head of the Hitler Youth, arrived at the Bunker. He was too late for the farewell ceremony, but he was admitted to the private suite to see the dead bodies. He examined them, and stayed in the room for some minutes, talking with Goebbels. Then Goebbels left, and Axmann remained for a short while alone with the dead bodies. Outside, in the Bunker, another ceremony was being prepared: the Viking funeral.

After sending the petrol to the garden, Kempka had walked across to the Bunker by the subterranean passage which connected his office in the Hermann Goering Strasse with the Chancellery buildings. He was greeted by Guensche with the words, "The Chief is dead".[8] At that moment the door of Hitler's suite was opened, and Kempka too became a participant in the funeral scene.

While Axmann was meditating among the corpses, two S.S. men, one of them Hitler's servant Linge, entered the room. They wrapped Hitler's body in a blanket, concealing the bloodstained and shattered head, and carried it out into the passage, where the other observers easily recognised it by the familiar black trousers. Then two other S.S. officers carried the body up the four flights of stairs to the emergency exit, and so out into the garden. After this, Bormann entered the room and took up the body of Eva Braun. Her death had been tidier, and no blanket was needed to conceal the evidence of it. Bormann carried the body into the passage, and then handed it to Kempka, who took it to the foot of the stairs. There it was taken from him by Guensche; and Guensche in turn gave it to a third S.S. officer, who carried it too up-

[7] The method of death chosen by Hitler and Eva Braun has been reported identically by Fraeulein Krueger and Frau Junge (who had it from Guensche) and Frau Christian (from Linge), and by others who heard it from the same sources. It is also described by Axmann, who personally inspected the bodies. Kempka, who carried out the body of Eva Braun, unblanketed, observed no signs of blood.

[8] 'Der Chef ist tot'. Hitler's personal servants referred to him as 'der Chef'.

stairs to the garden. As an additional precaution, the other door of the Bunker, which led into the Chancellery, and some of the doors leading from the Chancellery to the garden, had been hastily locked against possible intruders.

Unfortunately, the most careful precautions are sometimes unavailing; and it was a direct result of this precaution that two unauthorized persons in fact witnessed the scene from which it was intended to exclude them. One of the police guards, one Erich Mansfeld, happened to be on duty in the concrete observation tower at the corner of the Bunker, and noticing through the opaque, sulphurous air a sudden, suspicious scurrying of men and shutting of doors, he felt it his duty to investigate. He climbed down from his tower into the garden and walked round to the emergency exit to see what was afoot. In the porch he collided with the emerging funeral procession. First there were two S.S. officers carrying a body wrapped in a blanket, with black-trousered legs protruding from it. Then there was another S.S. officer carrying the unmistakeable corpse of Eva Braun. Behind them were the mourners —Bormann, Burgdorf, Goebbels, Guensche, Linge, and Kempka. Guensche shouted at Mansfeld to get out of the way quickly; and Mansfeld, having seen the forbidden but interesting spectacle, returned to his tower.[9]

After this interruption, the ritual was continued. The two corpses were placed side by side, a few feet from the porch, and petrol from the cans was poured over them. A Russian bombardment added to the strangeness and danger of the ceremony, and the mourners withdrew for some protection under the shelter of the porch. There Guensche dipped a rag in petrol, set it alight, and flung it out upon the corpses. They were at once enveloped in a sheet of flame. The mourners stood to attention, gave the Hitler salute, and withdrew again into the Bunker, where they dispersed. Guensche afterwards described the spectacle to those who had missed it. The burning of Hitler's body, he said, was the most terrible experience in his life.[10]

Meanwhile yet another witness had observed the spectacle. He was another of the police guards, and he too came accidentally upon the scene in consequence of the precautions which should have excluded him. His name was Hermann Karnau. Karnau, like others of the guard who were not on duty, had been ordered away from the bunker by an officer of the S.S. Escort, and had gone to the Chancellery canteen; but

[9] This account is given independently by Kempka and Mansfeld, who agree. Kempka mentions the incident when a guard (*i.e.* Mansfeld) collided with the procession in the porch and was dismissed by Guensche. Some of the details were accidently noticed by Schwaegermann.

[10] Fraeulein Krueger, Frau Junge.

after a while, in spite of his orders, he had decided to return to the Bunker. On arrival at the door of the Bunker, he had found it locked. He had therefore made his way out into the garden, in order to enter the Bunker by the emergency exit. As he turned the corner by the tower where Mansfeld was on duty, he was surprised to see two bodies lying side by side, close to the door of the Bunker. Almost at the same instant they burst, spontaneously it seemed, into flame. Karnau could not explain this sudden combustion. He saw no one, and yet it could not be the result of enemy fire, for he was only three feet away. "Possibly someone threw a match from the doorway," he suggested; and his suggestion is essentially correct.

Karnau watched the burning corpses for a moment. They were easily recognizable, though Hitler's head was smashed. The sight, he says, was "repulsive in the extreme". Then he went down into the Bunker by the emergency exit. In the Bunker he met Sturmbannfuehrer Franz Schedle, the officer commanding the S.S. Escort. Schedle had recently been injured in the foot by a bomb. He was distracted with grief. "The Fuehrer is dead," he said; "he is burning outside"; and Karnau helped him to limp away.

Mansfeld, on duty in the tower, also watched the burning of the bodies. As he had climbed the tower, after Guensche had ordered him away, he had seen through a loophole a great column of black smoke rising from the garden. As the smoke diminished, he saw the same two bodies which he had seen being brought up the stairs. They were burning. After the mourners had withdrawn, he continued to watch. At intervals he saw S.S. men come out of the Bunker and pour more petrol on the bodies to keep them alight. Some time afterwards he was relieved by Karnau, and when Karnau had helped him to climb out of the tower, the two went together to look at the bodies again. By now the lower parts of both bodies had been burned away and the shinbones of Hitler's legs were visible. An hour later, Mansfeld visited the bodies again. They were still burning, but the flame was low.

In the course of the afternoon a third member of the police guard sought to watch the spectacle of the burning bodies. His name was Hans Hofbeck. He went up the stairs from the Bunker and stood in the porch; but he did not stay there. The stench of burning flesh was intolerable and drove him away.

Late that night Brigadefuehrer Rattenhuber, the head of the police guard, entered the Dog-bunker where the guards were spending their leisure, and spoke to a sergeant of the S.S. Escort. He told him to report to his commanding officer, Schedle, and to pick three trustworthy men to bury the corpses. Soon afterwards Rattenhuber returned to the Dog-bunker and addressed the men there. He made them promise to keep the events of the day a holy secret. Anyone talking about them would be shot. Shortly before midnight Mansfeld returned to duty in the tower. Russian shells were still falling, and the sky was illuminated by flares. He noticed that a bomb crater in front of the emergency exit had been newly worked upon, and that the bodies had disappeared. He did not doubt that the crater had been converted into a grave for them; for no shell could have piled the earth around it in so neat a rectangle. About the same time, Karnau was on parade with the other guards in the Vossstrasse, and one of his comrades said to him: "It is sad that none of the officers seems to worry about the Fuehrer's body. I am proud that I alone know where he is."[11]

That is all that is known about the disposal of the remnants of Hitler's and Eva Braun's bodies. Linge afterwards told one of the secretaries that they had been burned as Hitler had ordered, "till nothing remained"; but it is doubtful whether such total combustion could have taken place. 180 litres of petrol, burning slowly on a sandy bed, would char the flesh and dissipate the moisture of the bodies, leaving only an unrecognizable and fragile remainder; but the bones would withstand the heat. These bones have never been found. Perhaps they were broken up and mixed with the other bodies, the bodies of soldiers killed in the defence of the Chancellery, and the body of Fegelein, which were also buried in the garden. The Russians have occasionally dug in that garden, and many such bodies have been unearthed there. Perhaps, as Guensche is said to have stated, the ashes were collected in a box and conveyed out of the Chancellery. Or perhaps no elaborate explanation is necessary. Perhaps such investigations as have been made have been somewhat perfunctory. Investigators who left Hitler's engagement diary unobserved in his chair for five months may easily have overlooked other relics which were more deliberately concealed. Whatever the explanation, Hitler achieved his last ambition. Like Alaric, buried secretly under the river-bed of Busento, the modern destroyer of mankind is now immune from discovery.[12]

[11] In their narratives of the burning of the bodies, Karnau and Mansfeld agree on facts, but differ on dates and times. Both mistake the date. Mansfeld's times are correct where they can be checked, while Karnau's are hopelessly erratic. If Mansfeld is reliable throughout, the bodies were set alight at about 4 P.M. (this is almost certainly correct), and were still burning at 6:30; Rattenhuber's orders for burial were given "late at night"; and the bodies had been buried by 11 P.M.

[12] In the introduction to the third edition of his book (London, 1956) Trevor-Roper gives the history of his project. It is indispensable on many counts but on none more than for his discussion of the complex and contradictory history of the official Russian attitude toward the record of Hitler's last ten days. The Russians had captured the Chancellery and Hitler's Bunker. The charred bodies of Hitler

bruno bettelheim

the real lesson of
the concentration camps

Bruno Bettelheim was born in Vienna in 1903 and studied psycho-analysis there—the native city of Dr. Sigmund Freud. Like thousands upon thousands of other Austrian and German Jews, Dr. Bettelheim was sent by the Nazis to the infamous concentration camps at Dachau and Buchenwald—names which will never be eradicated from the memory of civilized men, for in these camps and in many more like them all over Europe, hundreds of thousands of human beings, among them mere children, were starved, beaten, humiliated, shot, gassed.

After coming to the United States in 1939, Dr. Bettelheim wrote a now-famous psychological study based upon his experiences in the Nazi camps—"Individual and Mass Behavior in Extreme Situations." As commander-in-chief of the Allied forces, General Eisenhower made this remarkable paper required reading for all military government officers in Europe. Dr. Bettelheim is now head of the University of Chicago's Sonia Shankman Orthogenic School, which under his wise leadership has done notable work in preventive psychology and psychiatry and has succeeded in rehabilitating many children who were completely unable to get along at home or at school.

The present selection from Dr. Bettelheim's most recent book, *The Informed Heart: Autonomy in a Mass Age,* should surprise and even shock people who have tended merely to bewail the innocent victims of the Nazis. Understandably, many people have been moved by Anne Frank's memorable diary of how she and her family lived in hiding from the Nazis. Many more have seen the touching motion picture based on the successful stage play. It is natural to be moved by Anne Frank's nobility, and by that of her family, in staunchly keeping together under the most desperate conditions of secrecy.

But Dr. Bettelheim makes a brave and unusual point. It is that the

---

and Eva Braun were taken to Russia by the Red Army. Precisely what happened to them remains unknown. The effort of the Russians, once they identified Hitler's corpse, Trevor-Roper says was "to hide it from the Germans, lest they should revere it." "Though further knowledge," he goes on, "has altered their circumstantial background, my original remark remains accidently true: 'Like Alaric, buried secretly under the river-bed of Busento, the modern destroyer of mankind is now immune from discovery.' " [Ed.]

Franks, like many other middle-class German Jews who wanted to keep up a "normal" life under excruciating conditions that made normality impossible, made a moral mistake and a political mistake. They perished precisely because of their failure to recognize how "extreme" the "situation" had indeed become for them—and for everyone else. If the Franks had responded in time to the Nazi danger by taking realistic measures of their own, they might have survived, or at least have taken some toll of those whose cruelty and sadism are unexampled in modern history. Of the six million Jews who perished at the hands of the Nazis, fully a million, it has been calculated, were children. Since the Nazis had announced their murderous intentions from the beginning and were absolutely pitiless in driving to their goal, Dr. Bettelheim asks why the Franks barricaded themselves inside an attic in Amsterdam like rats in a trap. His explanation is that the Franks wanted to keep up the fiction that in the most desperate circumstances, they, at least, could remain a family. But, as Dr. Bettelheim shows, this showed a concern for family life at the expense of political reality. The times were wholly "extreme," and were not likely to become less so.

Of course Dr. Bettelheim is not concerned only with Anne Frank and her family. He *is* disturbed, however, that perhaps the most celebrated book that has come out of the millions of martyrs and victims should be a record of domesticity kept up at any price. He is writing here about all those prisoners in the camps, doctors and intellectuals, professors and how many other law-abiding and respectful individuals, who really behaved as if, by being "good" enough, they might yet be saved. Dr. Bettelheim's point is precisely that it was this attempt to be "good," to be respectful and submissive, that proved fatal to these Jews—for their anxiety to toe the line was taken as a sign of weakness. As the author says, ". . . the story of the extermination camps shows that even in such an overpowering environment, certain defenses do offer some protection. . . . With enough understanding, the individual does not fool himself into believing that with every adjustment he makes he is protecting himself. He is able to recognize that much that on the surface seems protective, is actually self destructive."

A few words about the world's reaction to the concentration camps: BUSINESS AS USUAL the terrors committed in them were experienced as uncanny by most civilized persons. It came as a shock to their pride that supposedly civilized nations could stoop to such inhuman acts. The implication that modern man has such inadequate control over his cruelty was felt as a threat. Three different psychological mechanisms were most frequently

THE REAL LESSON OF THE CONCENTRATION CAMPS: From *The Informed Heart: Autonomy in a Mass Age* by Bruno Bettelheim. Copyright © 1960 by The Free Press, A Corporation. Reprinted by permission of the publisher.

used for dealing with the phenomenon of the concentration camp: (a) its applicability to man in general was denied by asserting (contrary to available evidence) that the acts of torture were committed by a small group of insane or perverted persons; (b) the truth of the reports was denied by ascribing them to deliberate propaganda. This method was favored by the German government which called all reports on terror in the camps horror propaganda (*Greuelpropaganda*); (c) the reports were believed, but the knowledge of the terror was repressed as soon as possible.

All three mechanisms could be seen at work after liberation. At first, after the "discovery" of the camps, a wave of extreme outrage swept the Allied nations. It was soon followed by a general repression of the discovery. It may be that this reaction of the general public was due to something more than the shock dealt their narcissism by the fact that cruelty is still rampant among men. It may also be that the memory of the tortures was repressed out of some dim realization that the modern state now has available the means for changing personality. To have to accept that one's personality may be changed against one's will is the greatest threat to one's self respect. It must therefore be dealt with by action, or by repression.

The universal success of the *Diary of Anne Frank* suggests how much the tendency to deny is still with us, while her story itself demonstrates how such denial can hasten our own destruction. It is an onerous task to take apart such a humane and moving story, arousing so much compassion for gentle Anne Frank. But I believe that its world-wide acclaim cannot be explained unless we recognize our wish to forget the gas chambers and to glorify attitudes of extreme privatization, of continuing to hold on to attitudes as usual even in a holocaust. Exactly because their going on with private life as usual brought destruction did it have to be glorified; in that way we could overlook the essential fact of how destructive it can be under extreme social circumstances.

While the Franks were making their preparations for going passively into hiding, thousands of other Jews in Holland and elsewhere in Europe were trying to escape to the free world, the better to survive or to be able to fight their executioners. Others who could not do so went underground—not simply to hide from the SS, waiting passively, without preparation for fight, for the day when they would be caught—but to fight the Germans, and with it for humanity. All the Franks wanted was to go on with life as nearly as possible in the usual fashion.

Little Anne, too, wanted only to go on with life as usual, and nobody can blame her. But hers was certainly not a necessary fate, much less a heroic one; it was a senseless fate. The Franks could have faced the facts and survived, as did many Jews living in Holland. Anne could have had a good chance to survive, as did many Jewish children in Holland. But for that she would have had to be separated from her parents and gone to live with a Dutch family as their own child.

Everybody who recognized the obvious knew that the hardest way to go underground was to do it as a family; that to hide as a family made detection by the SS most likely. The Franks, with their excellent connections among gentile Dutch families, should have had an easy time hiding out singly, each with a different family. But instead of planning for this, the main principle of their planning was to continue as much as possible with the kind of family life they were accustomed to. Any other course would have meant not merely giving up the beloved family life, but also accepting as reality man's inhumanity to man. Most of all it would have forced them to accept that going on with life as usual was not an absolute value, but can sometimes be the most destructive of all attitudes.

There is little doubt that the Franks, who were able to provide themselves with so much, could have provided themselves with a gun or two had they wished. They could have shot down at least one or two of the "green police" who came for them. There was no surplus of such police. The loss of an SS with every Jew arrested would have noticeably hindered the functioning of the police state. The fate of the Franks wouldn't have been any different, because they all died anyway except for Anne's father, though he hardly meant to pay for his survival with the extermination of his whole family. But they could have sold their lives dearly instead of walking to their death.

There is good reason why the so successful play ends with Anne stating her belief in the good in all men. What is denied is the importance of accepting the gas chambers as real so that never again will they exist. If all men are basically good, if going on with intimate family living no matter what else is what is to be most admired, then indeed we can all go on with life as usual and forget about Auschwitz. Except that Anne Frank died because her parents could not get themselves to believe in Auschwitz. And her story found wide acclaim because for us too, it denies implicitly that Auschwitz ever existed. If all men are good, there was never an Auschwitz.

HIGH TIME

At various places in this book I have mentioned how submitting to the total state leads to a disintegration of what once seemed a well integrated personality, plus a return to many infantile attitudes. At this point perhaps a theoretical speculation may be helpful. Years ago Freud postulated two opposite tendencies: the life instincts, which he called eros or sex, and the destructive tendencies, which he named the death instinct. The more mature the person becomes, the more he should be able to "fuse" these two opposing tendencies, making the resultant "ego" energy available for the task of meeting and shaping reality.

The more immature the person, the more these tendencies are apt to push the total personality, at one moment in one direction, at the next moment in the other. Thus the so-called childlike friendliness of some primitive people, followed in the next moment by extreme "thoughtless" cruelty. But the disintegration, or perhaps one should better say the "defusion" of ego energy under extreme stress—at one moment into pure destructive tendencies ("Let it be over, no matter how"), at the next moment into irrational life tendencies (Let's get something to eat now, even if it means death in short order")[1]—was only one aspect of man's primitivization in the total state. Another was engaging in infantile thought processes such as wishful thinking in place of a more mature evaluation of reality, and an infantile disregard for the possibility of death. These led many to think that they of all others would be spared and survive, and many more to simply disbelieve in the possibility of their own death. Not believing in its possibility, they did not prepare for it, including no preparation for how to defend their lives even when death became inescapable. Defending their lives before such time might have hastened their death. So up to a point, this "rolling with the punches" that the enemy dealt out was protective of life. But beyond that point it was destructive of both one's own life and that of others whose survival might be more certain too if one risked one's own life. The trouble is that the longer one "rolls" with the punches, the more likely it becomes that one will no longer have the strength to resist when death becomes imminent, particularly if this yielding to the enemy is accompanied not by an inner strengthening of the personality (which it would require) but an inner disintegration.[2]

Those who did not deny validity to death, who neither denied nor repressed its possibility, who embraced no childish belief in their in-

[1] For example, those prisoners who ate the whole day's ration the moment they got it had nothing left for their faltering energies toward the end of the working day. Those who divided the little food they had and saved some for the moment when exhaustion threatened them most, fared much better in the long run.

[2] This, too, could be observed in the story of the Franks who bickered with each other over trifles, instead of supporting each other's desire to resist the demoralizing impact of their living conditions.

destructibility, were those who prepared for it in time as a real possibility. It meant risking one's life for a self chosen purpose and in doing so, saving one's own life or that of others, or both. When Jews in Germany were restricted to their homes, those who did not allow inertia to take over used the imposing of such restrictions as a warning that it was high time to go underground, join the resistance movement, provide themselves with forged papers, etc., if they had not done so long ago. Most of them survived.

An example out of the lives of some distant relatives of mine may further illustrate. Early in the war, a young man living in a small Hungarian town banded together with a number of other Jews and they prepared themselves for what to do when the Germans invaded. As soon as the Nazis imposed curfews on the Jews, his group left for Budapest since the bigger the city, the better the chances for escaping detection. There, similar groups from other towns converged and joined those of Budapest. From among them they selected typically "Aryan" looking men who, equipped with false papers, immediately joined the Hungarian SS so as to be able to warn of impending actions, to report in advance when a particular district would be searched, etc.

This worked so well that most of the groups survived intact. But they had also equipped themselves with small arms, so that when detected they could put up enough of a fight for the majority to escape while a few would die fighting to gain time for the escape.[3] A few of the Jews who had joined the SS were discovered and immediately shot, probably a death preferable to one in the gas chambers. But even among their special group the majority survived, hiding within the SS up to the last moment.

My young relative was unable to convince some members of his family to go with him when he left. Three times, at tremendous risk to himself he returned, pointing out first the growing persecution of the Jews, later the fact that their transport to the gas chambers had already begun. He could not convince them to move out of their homes, to leave their possessions. On each visit he pleaded more desperately, on each visit he found them less willing or able to listen to him, much less able to take action. It was as if each time they were more on their way to the crematoria where they all in fact died.

---

[3] Compare this to the Franks' selection of a hiding place that was basically a trap without an outlet, and that in all their months there no emergency escape route was constructed through which some of their group could at least have tried to escape while one or two of the men blocked and defended one of the small entrances with a homemade barricade. Compare also, Mr. Frank's teaching typically academic high school subjects to the youngsters, rather than how to make a getaway: a token of the same inability to face the possibility of death.

On each visit his family clung more desperately to the old living arrangements, the possessions they had accumulated over a lifetime. It was like a parallel process in which their life energies were drained away while their possessions seemed to give them a pseudosecurity to replace the real assurance that no longer came from planning for their lives. Again like children, they preferred to cling desperately to some objects in which they had invested all the meaning they could no longer find in their lives. As they withdrew from the fight for survival, their lives began to reside more and more in these dead objects and the persons in them died piece by piece, little object by little object.

In Buchenwald, I talked to hundreds of German Jewish prisoners who were brought there in the fall of 1938. I asked them why they had not left Germany because of the utterly degrading conditions they were subjected to. Their answer was: How could we leave? It would have meant giving up our homes, our places of business. Their earthly possessions had so taken possession of them that they could not move; instead of using them, they were run by them.[4]

How the investing of possessions with one's life energy made people die piece by piece is also evident in the course of the Nazi attitude toward Jews. At the time of the first boycott of Jewish stores the whole external goal of the Nazis was the possessions of the Jews. They even let Jews take some of them out of the country if they would just go, leaving the bulk of their possessions behind. For a long time the intention of the Nazis, and of their first discriminatory laws, was to force undesirable minorities, including Jews, into emigration. Only when this did not work was the extermination policy instituted, though it also followed the inner logic of the Nazi racial ideology. But one wonders if the notion that millions of Jews (and later foreign nationals) would submit to extermination did not also result from seeing how much degradation they would accept without fighting back. The persecution of the Jews worsened, slow step by slow step, when no violent resistance occurred. It may have been Jewish acceptance, without fight, of ever harsher discrimination and degradation that first gave the SS the idea that they could be gotten to the point where they would walk to the gas chambers on their own.

Most Jews in Poland who did not believe in business as usual survived the second World War. As the Germans approached, they left everything behind and fled to Russia, much as many of them distrusted the Soviet system. But there, while perhaps citizens of a second order,

---

[4] The Franks, too, postponed going into hiding because they wished first to transfer more of their possessions to their hideout. They postponed it so long that it was nearly too late for Anne's sister, who was called to the SS.

they were at least accepted as human beings. Those who stayed on to continue business as usual moved toward their own destruction and perished. Thus in the deepest sense the walk to the gas chamber was only the last consequence of a philosophy of business as usual; a last step in no longer defying the death instinct, which might also be called the principle of inertia. Because the first step was taken long before one entered the death camp.

True, the same suicidal behavior has another meaning. It means that man can be pushed so far and no further; that beyond a certain point he chooses death to an inhuman existence. But the initial step toward this terrible choice was inertia.

Those who give in to it, who have withdrawn all vital energy from the world, can no longer act with initiative, and are threatened by it in others. They can no longer accept reality for what it is; having grown infantile, they see it only in the infantile perspective of a wishful denial of what is too unpleasant, of a wishful belief in their personal immortality. All this is dramatically illustrated in an experience of Lengyel's.[5] She reports that although she and her fellow prisoners lived just a few hundred yards from the crematoria and the gas chambers and knew what they were all about, yet after months most prisoners denied knowledge of them.[6] Realization of their true situation might have helped them to save either the life they were going to lose anyway, or the lives of others. But that realization they could not afford. When Lengyel and many other prisoners were selected to be sent to the gas chambers, they did not try to break away, as she successfully did. Worse, the first time she tried it, some of the fellow prisoners selected with her for the gas chambers called the supervisors, telling them she was trying to get away. Lengyel desperately asks the question: How was it possible that people denied the existence of the gas chambers when all day long they saw the crematoria burning and smelled the odor of burning flesh? How come they preferred not to believe in the extermination just to prevent themselves from fighting for their very own lives? She offers no explanation except that they begrudged anyone who might save himself from the common fate, because they lacked enough courage to risk action themselves. I believe they did it because they had given up their will to live, had permitted their death tendencies to flood them. As a result they now identified more closely with the SS who were devoting themselves to destruction, than to those

---

[5] Lengyel, O., *Five Chimneys, The Story of Auschwitz*, Chicago: Ziff Davis, 1947, pp. 54-55.

[6] German gentile civilians denied the gas chambers, too, but the same denial in them did not have the same meaning. By that time, civilians who faced facts and rebelled, invited death. Prisoners at Auschwitz were already doomed.

fellow prisoners who still had a grip on life and hence managed to escape death.

HUMAN COMPETENCE FOR WHAT?

When prisoners began to serve their executioners, to help them speed the death of their own kind, things had gone beyond simple inertia. By then, death instinct running rampant had been added to inertia. Those who tried to serve their executioners in what were once their civilian capacities were merely continuing if not business, then life as usual. Whereby they opened the door to their death.

Lengyel speaks of a Dr. Mengele, SS physician at Auschwitz, in a typical example of the "business as usual" attitude that enabled some prisoners, and certainly the SS, to retain whatever inner balance they could despite what they were doing. She describes how Dr. Mengele took all correct medical precautions during childbirth, rigorously observing all aseptic principles, cutting the umbilical cord with greatest care, etc. But only half an hour later he sent mother and infant to be burned in the crematorium.[7]

Still, having made his choice, Dr. Mengele and others like him had, after all, to delude themselves at times to be able to live with themselves and their experience. Only one personal document on the subject has come to my attention, that of Dr. Nyiszli, a prisoner serving as "research physician" at Auschwitz.[8] How Dr. Nyiszli fooled himself can be seen, for example, in his repeatedly referring to himself as a doctor, though he worked as the assistant of a criminal. He speaks of the Institute for Race, Biological, and Anthropological Investigation as "one of the most qualified medical centers of the Third Reich" though it was devoted to proving falsehoods. That Nyiszli was a doctor didn't at all change the fact that he, like any of the prisoner officials who served the SS better than some SS were willing to serve it, was a participant, an accessory to the crimes of the SS. How then could he do it and survive?

The answer was: by taking pride in his professional skills, irrespective of what purpose they were used for. Again and again this pride in his professional skill permeates his story of his own and other prisoners' sufferings. The important issue here is that Dr. Nyiszli, Dr. Mengele, and hundreds of other far more prominent physicians, men trained long before the advent of Hitler to power, were participants in these human experiments and in the pseudoscientific investigations that

---

[7] *Op. cit.,* p. 147.

[8] Nyiszli, Dr. Miklos, *Auschwitz: A Doctor's Eyewitness Account,* New York: Frederick Fell, Inc., 1960.

went with them.[9] It is this pride in professional skill and knowledge, irrespective of moral implications, that is so dangerous. As a feature of modern society oriented toward technological competence it is still with us, though the concentration camps and the crematoria are no longer here. Auschwitz is gone, but as long as this attitude remains with us we shall not be safe from the indifference to life at its core.

It is easy to see that achieving a subtle balance between extremes may be an ideal way of life. It is harder to accept that this holds true even in a holocaust. But even in extreme conditions, to give way only to the heart or only to the mind is neither a good way to live, nor the way to survive. Living only to keep his family intact, even all Mr. Frank's love did not keep them alive, as a better informed heart might have done. Dr. Nyiszli, carried away by his high level training as a pathologist, and against the prompting of the heart, lent himself to such debasement of his deepest pride, his medical science, that one wonders what can have survived except his body.

I have met many Jews, as well as gentile anti-Nazis, who survived in Germany and in the occupied countries, like the group in Hungary described earlier. But they were all people who realized that when a world goes to pieces, when inhumanity reigns supreme, man cannot go on with business as usual. One then has to radically re-evaluate all of what one has done, believed in, stood for. In short, one has to take a stand on the new reality, a firm stand, and not one of retirement into even greater privatization.

If today, Negroes in Africa march against the guns of a police that defends *apartheid*—even if hundreds of them will be shot down and tens of thousands rounded up in concentration camps—their march, their fight, will sooner or later assure them of a chance for liberty and equality. Millions of the Jews of Europe who did not or could not escape in time or go underground as many thousands did, could at least have marched as free men against the SS, rather than to first grovel, then wait to be rounded up for their own extermination, and finally walk themselves to the gas chambers.

Yet the story of the extermination camps shows that even in such an overpowering environment, certain defenses do offer some protection, most important of which is understanding what goes on in oneself, and why. With enough understanding, the individual does not

[9] Among the heads of clinics or chairmen of departments who participated knowingly in the experiments were Professors Sauerbruch of the University of Munich and Eppinger of the University of Vienna—teachers of whole generations of physicians before Hitler. Dr. Gebhardt, the president of the German Red Cross, was also among them. (Mitscherlich, A., and Miekle, F., *Doctors of Infamy*, New York: Henry Schuman, Inc., 1949.)

fool himself into believing that with every adjustment he makes he is protecting himself. He is able to recognize that much that on the surface seems protective, is actually self destructive. A most extreme example were those prisoners who volunteered to work in the gas chambers hoping it would somehow save their lives. All of them were killed after a short time. But many of them died sooner, and after weeks of a more horrible life, than might have been true if they had not volunteered.

FIGHTING BACK

Did no one of those destined to die fight back? Did none of them wish to die not by giving in but by asserting themselves in atacking the SS? A very few did. One of them was the twelfth *Sonderkommando,* prisoners working in the gas chambers.[10] Now all these *Kommandos* knew their fate since the first task of every *Sonderkommando* was to cremate the corpses of the preceding *Kommando,* exterminated just a few hours before.

In this single revolt of the twelfth *Sonderkommando,* seventy SS were killed, including one commissioned officer and seventeen noncommissioned officers; one of the crematoria was totally destroyed and another severely damaged. True, all eight hundred and fifty-three prisoners of the *Kommando* died. But this proves that a position in the *Sonderkommando* gave prisoners a chance of about ten to one to destroy the SS, a higher ratio than in the ordinary concentration camp.

The one *Sonderkommando* that revolted and took such heavy toll of the enemy did not die much differently than all other *Sonderkommandos.* Why, then—and this is the question that haunts all who study the extermination camps—why then did millions walk quietly, without resistance, to their death when right before them were examples such as this *Kommando* that managed to destroy and damage part of their own chambers of death and kill almost 10% of their number in SS? Why did so few of the millions of prisoners die like men, as did the men of only one of these *Kommandos?* Why did the rest of these *Kommandos* not revolt, but march themselves willingly to their death? Or what did it take for the exception to do so?

Perhaps another rare instance, an example of supreme self assertion, can shed light on the question. Once, a group of naked prisoners about to enter the gas chamber stood lined up in front of it. In some way the

---

10 Nyiszli, *op. cit.* Scattered revolts in the death camps (Treblinka, etc.) are mentioned elsewhere in the literature, though I have not myself seen witnessed reports. Civilian uprisings began to occur with the turn of the war tide against Germany, but as in the case of the Warsaw uprising, the hour was far too late for the millions already dead.

commanding SS officer learned that one of the women prisoners had been a dancer. So he ordered her to dance for him. She did, and as she danced, she approached him, seized his gun, and shot him down. She too was immediately shot to death.[11]

But isn't it probable that despite the grotesque setting in which she danced, dancing made her once again a person? Dancing, she was singled out as an individual, asked to perform in what had once been her chosen vocation. No longer was she a number, a nameless, depersonalized prisoner, but the dancer she used to be. Transformed, however momentarily, she responded like her old self, destroying the enemy bent on her destruction, even if she had to die in the process.

Despite the hundreds of thousands of living dead men who moved quietly to their graves, this one example, and there were several like her, shows that in an instant the old personality can be regained, its destruction undone, once we decide on our own that we wish to cease being units in a system. Exercising the last freedom that not even the concentration camp could take away—to decide how one wishes to think and feel about the conditions of one's life—this dancer threw off her real prison. This she could do because she was willing to risk her life to achieve autonomy once more. If we do that, then if we cannot live, at least we die as men.

truman capote

in leningrad

Truman Capote was born in New Orleans in 1924, and went to school in Greenwich, Connecticut. He describes himself as a "writer from early years," and a "painter on glass"; both this precocity and his remarkable sense of pictorial values were revealed in the first novel that made him famous, *Other Voices, Other Rooms* (1948).

Despite the slightly mischievous fame of this novel, Capote is one of the most skillful and accomplished writers of our day; at least two of his recent books are among the best things he has written—a novelette entitled *Breakfast At Tiffany's* (1958), and the brilliant little book of reportage, *The Muses Are Heard* (1956), from which the present selection is taken. *The Muses Are Heard* is the record of a trip to the Soviet Union made by the American company presenting *Porgy and Bess,* and Capote, who accompanied the troupe as a kind of "candid camera"

---

11 Kogon, *op. cit.,* p. 132.

reporter for *The New Yorker,* was able to set down with cool and amusing objectivity the often hilarious presence of so many temperamental American theater personalities in Russia.

The Muses Are Heard is not only an extremely clever and well-written book; it is also one of the shrewdest analyses we have of daily life in the Soviet Union. Capote has a gift for capturing the essence of whatever constitutes personal *style* in people—whether it is the way they talk, or look, or move. He captures with affectionate irony the contrast between our innocent pretensions, as human beings, at a certain kind of style—and the way we really look to his candid eye.

Because of this feeling for style, Capote has a lush, almost romantic feelings for the textures of things. And it is this charming gift for both admiration and irreverence that makes his writing both warm and shrewd, enthusiastic and sceptical. Take a passage like this, describing the beauty parlor (the "Institut De Beauté") in a Leningrad hotel: ". . . with its mottled whiteness, its painful appurtenances, [it] resembles a charity clinic supervised by not too sanitary nurses, and the coiffeur that Madame receives there is liable to leave her hair with a texture excellent for scouring pans." He does not merely *say* that Leningrad in winter was cold; he makes it clear that "the cold was like an anesthetic; gradually, I felt numb enough to undergo major surgery." Yet when he describes the grand, traditional and splendid beauty of Leningrad, he can apply words as if they were colors: ". . . Parisian blacks and greys predominate, but suddenly, here and there, the hot Italian palette intervenes: a palace of bitter green, of brilliant ochre, pale blue, orange."

The Leningrad premiere of *Porgy and Bess,* an event expected to reap international publicity, was planned for the evening of Monday, December 26 [1955], which gave the company five days to prepare and rehearse, a sufficient time considering that the show had been touring the world nearly four years. But Robert Breen, the production's director, was determined that the audience at the Leningrad premiere would see the finest possible rendering of the Negro opera. Breen, and his energetic partner-wife, Wilva, and their chief assistant, the gentle, yet highly strung Warner Watson, were confident that the Russians would be "stunned" by the musical folk tale, that they would "never have seen anything like it." Several observers, though sympathetic, were not as sure. However looked at, by the Americans or by their Russian sponsors, the opening night promised to be one of the most suspenseful in theatrical annals. But that event was, on the morning of arrival, over

a hundred hours away; and after the company had been driven in char-
tered buses from the Leningrad terminal to the Hotel Astoria, their
feelings of suspense were centered around room accommodations.

The Astoria, situated on the impressive expanse of St. Isaac's Square,
is an Intourist hotel, which means that it is run by the Soviet agency
in control of all hotels where foreigners are permitted to stay. The
Astoria justifiably claims to be the best hotel in Leningrad. Some think
it the Ritz of all Russia. But it contains few concessions to Western
ideas of a deluxe establishment. Of these, one is a room off the lobby
that advertises itself as an *Institut De Beauté,* where guests may obtain
Pedicure, Manicure, and *Coiffeur pour Madame.* The *Institut,* with
its mottled whiteness, its painful appurtenances, resembles a charity
clinic supervised by not too sanitary nurses, and the coiffeur that Madame receives there is liable to leave her hair with a texture excellent for
scouring pans. There is also on the lobby floor a trio of restaurants,
each leading into the other, cavernous affairs cheerful as airplane
hangars. The center one is Leningrad's smartest restaurant, and in the
evenings, from eight till midnight, an orchestra plays Russian jazz for
a local *haut monde* who seldom dance but sit morosely counting the
bubbles in syrupy glasses of Georgian champagne. The hotel's Intourist
office is located behind a low counter in the main lobby; its dozen
desks are so arranged that the employees have a broad view, which
simplifies their task of keeping tabs on the comings and goings of the
guests. It is a job they have made still simpler, or foolproof, by station-
ing dormitory matrons on each of the residential floors, vigilantes who
are on duty from dawn to dawn, never allowing anyone to leave his
room without giving him the key, and constantly, like human punch-
clocks, recording ins and outs in a bulky ledger. Perhaps Houdini
could've eluded them, but it is hard to see how, since they sit at desks
that face both the staircase and the elevator, an ancient bird cage that
creaks on its cables. Actually, there is a rear, unguarded staircase connecting the upper floors with a remote side-lobby; and for the clandes-
tine visitor, or the resident wishing to depart unnoticed, this would
make the ideal route. Would, except that it is barricaded top to bottom with wooden fences reinforced by old settees and armoires. It
might be that the management can find nowhere else to stash these
pieces of furniture. Certainly there is no more room in the rooms. For
the average Astoria abode is like the annex in a Victorian attic where
some poor relation lives buried among the family discards: a miasma of
romantic marble statuary, weak-bulbed lamps with tulle shades like
ballerina skirts, tables, several of them, covered with Oriental carpeting, chairs galore, plush settees, armoires that could store steamer

trunks, flower-papered walls kaleidoscopic with gilt-framed paintings of fruit and country idylls, beds concealed in cavelike alcoves behind dank velvet curtains: all this crammed into a tomb-dark, unventilated area (you can't open the windows in winter, and wouldn't want to if you could) quadruple the size of a train compartment. The hotel has grander quarters, of course, suites with five and six rooms, but the effect of the décor is the same, merely more abundantly so.

Nevertheless, the majority of the *Porgy and Bess* company were most approving of the Astoria, many because they had anticipated "something so much *worse*" and, instead, found their rooms "cozy," "kind of atmospheric" or, as the production's sophisticated publicist, Willem Van Loon, put it, "Full of art-nouveau charms. Really me!" But when the troupe first entered the lobby of the hotel, already milling with Chinese dignitaries and high-booted Cossacks, actual occupancy of these rooms was, in some instances, distant and debatable.

The Astoria's assigning of the rooms and, particularly, the suites seemed to be governed by a protocol, or lack of one, that embittered rather a few. Nancy Ryan volunteered a theory that the Russians had arrived at their system of room distribution by consulting Everyman Opera's payroll: "The less you get the more they give you." Whatever the reason, several of the leading players and prominent personalities, who were traveling as guests of the company, thought it "grotesque" and "crazy, man, crazy" that stagehands and wardrobe mistresses, carpenters and electricians were being led straight-away to the V.I.P. apartments, while they, the "real people," were supposed to content themselves with the hotel's backwater leftovers. "Are they kidding?" said Leonard Lyons. Another company guest, the New York financier, Herman Sartorius, had valid cause to complain; he'd been assigned no room at all. Nor had Mrs. Gershwin, who sat on her luggage in the lobby being soothed by Wilva Breen and Warner Watson.

"Don't you worry, baby," said Mrs. Breen, who had arrived the night before by plane and was ensconced with her husband in six rooms of Astorian splendor. "The Russians may be slow, they may get things a little mixed up, but everything comes out straight in the end. Look what happened when I went to Moscow," she added, referring to a visit she had made to Moscow the previous October in connection with the present tour. "It took me nine days to do two hours' work. But everything came out fine in the end."

"Sure, Lee," said Warner Watson, brushing down his greying crew-cut with an agitated hand. "Sure, honey, we'll get this room business fenced in."

"Darling, I'm perfectly happy, darling," Mrs. Gershwin assured them. "I just think it's so wonderful *being* here."

"To think we really made it," said Mrs. Breen, beaming round her. "And what sweet, kind, adorable people. Wasn't that adorable when the train arrived?"

"Adorable," said Mrs. Gershwin, glancing at the mass of wilting bouquets that had been given her at the station.

"And the hotel's simply beautiful, isn't it?"

"Yes, Wilva," said Mrs. Gershwin blankly, as though her friend's enthusiasm was beginning to tire her.

"You'll have a beautiful room, Lee," said Mrs. Breen, and Warner Watson added, "If you don't like it, you can change it. Anything you want, Lee, we'll get it fenced in."

"Darling, please. It's not important, not the tiniest bit. If they'll just put me *some*where, I wouldn't dream of moving," said Mrs. Gershwin, who was destined, in the course of the next few days, to insist on changing her accommodations three times.

The Ministry of Culture's delegation, headed by Nikolai Savchenko, the businesslike, formidable six-footer, were now in a whirl of pacifying, rectifying, promising everyone they would get the rooms they deserved. "Patience," pleaded one of them, the middle-aged Russian interpreter called Miss Lydia. "Do not contribute to the misery. We have plenty rooms. No one will stride the streets." Nancy Ryan said she wouldn't mind striding the streets, and suggested to me that we escape the confusion in the lobby by taking a walk.

St. Isaac's Square is hemmed on one side by a canal stemming from the Neva, a river that in winter threads through the city like a frozen Seine, and on the other by St. Isaac's Cathedral, which is now an antireligious museum. We walked toward the canal. The sky was sunless grey, and there was snow in the air, buoyant motes, playthings that seethed and floated like the toy flakes inside a crystal. It was noon, but there was no modern traffic on the square except for a car or two and a bus with its headlights burning. Now and then, though, horse-drawn sleds slithered across the snowy pavement. Along the embankments of the Neva, men on skis silently passed, and mothers aired their babies, dragging them in small sleds. Everywhere, like darting blackbirds, black-furred school children ice-skated on the sidewalks. Two of these children stopped to inspect us. They were twins, girls of nine or ten, and they wore grey rabbit coats and blue velvet bonnets. They had divided a pair of skates between them, but by holding hands and pushing together, they managed very well on one skate apiece. They looked at us with pretty brown puzzled eyes, as though wondering what made us different: Our clothes? Miss Ryan's lipstick? The soft waves in her loose blond hair? Most foreigners in Russia soon become accustomed to this: the slight frown of the passer-by who is disturbed by something about you that he can't at once put his finger on, and who stops, stares, keeps glancing back, even quite often feels compelled to follow you. The twins followed us onto a footbridge that crossed the Neva, and watched while we paused to look at the view.

The canal, no more than a snow ditch, was a sporting ground for children whose laughing shrillness combined with a ringing of bells, both sounds carrying on the strong, shivery winds that blow from the Bay of Finland. Skeleton trees, sheathed in ice, glittered against the austere fronts of palaces that lined the embankments and stretched to the distant Nevsky Prospekt. Leningrad, presently a city of four million, the Soviet Union's second largest and northernmost metropolis, was built to the taste of the Czars, and Czarist taste ran to French and Italian architecture, which accounts not only for the style but also for the coloring of the palaces along the Neva and in other old quarters. Parisian blacks and greys predominate, but suddenly, here and there, the hot Italian palette intervenes: a palace of bitter green, of brilliant ochre, pale blue, orange. A few of the palaces have been converted into apartments, most are used for offices. Peter the Great, who is given high marks by the current regime because he introduced the sciences to Russia, would probably approve the myriad television aerials that have settled like a swarm of metal insects on the roofs of his once Imperial city.

We crossed the bridge and wandered through opened iron gates into the deserted courtyard of a blue palace. It was the beginning of a labyrinth, an arctic Casbah where one courtyard led into another via arcades and tunnels and across narrow streets snow-hushed and silent except for sleigh horses stamping their hooves, a drifting sound of bells, an occasional giggle from the twins, still trailing behind us.

The cold was like an anesthetic; gradually, I felt numb enough to undergo major surgery. But Miss Ryan refused to turn back. She said, "This is St. Petersburg, for God's sake. We're not just walking anywhere. I want to see as much as I can. And I'd better. From now on, you know where *I'll* be? Locked in a room typing a lot of nonsense for the Breens." But I saw that she couldn't last much longer, her face was drunkard-red, a frostbite spot whitened the tip of her nose. Minutes later, feeling its first sting, she was ready to seek the Astoria.

The trouble was, we were lost. It amused the twins greatly to see us rotating round the same streets and courtyards. They screeched and hugged each other with laughter when we came on an old man chopping wood and begged him for directions by swinging our arms like compass needles and shouting, *Astoria! Astoria!* The woodchopper didn't understand; he put down his axe and accompanied us to a street corner, where we were required to repeat our pantomime for three swarthy friends of his, none of whom got the point, but nevertheless beckoned us up another street. On the way, out of curiosity, we were joined by a gangly boy carrying a violin case, and a woman who must have been a butcher, for over her coat she was wearing an apron splattered with blood. The Russians babbled and argued; we decided they were taking us to a police station, and neither of us cared, as long as it was heated. By now, the moisture in my nose had frozen, my eyes were unfocused with cold. Still, I could see well enough to know that abruptly we were back at the Neva Canal footbridge. I wanted to grab Miss Ryan's hand and run. But she felt our entourage had been so faithful they deserved to see the mystery solved. From woodchopper to violinist, the procession, led by the twins who skated ahead like pied pipers, convoyed us across the square and straight to the Astoria's entrance. While they surrounded one of the Intourist limousines that stay parked in front of the hotel, and began to question its chauffeur about us, we rushed inside, collapsed on a bench and sucked the warm air like divers who have been too long underwater.

Leonard Lyons walked by. "Looks like you've been out," he said. Miss Ryan nodded, and Lyons, lowering his voice, asked, "Anybody follow you?"

"Yes," said Miss Ryan, *"crowds."*

vladimir nabokov

a young entomologist
in old russia

Vladimir Nabokov was born in St. Petersburg, Russia, in 1899, of an aristocratic family famous for its cultivated and liberal traditions. His father was one of the leaders of the old Russian Liberal Party, and after the Revolution was assassinated in Paris by rabid Russian nationalists. After leaving Russia, Nabokov attended Cambridge University in England and in 1940 came to the United States. He is an American citizen and now writes in English. His most celebrated recent book, of course, is *Lolita*.

Nabokov is famous not only for his remarkable abilities as a novelist and poet, but also for his scholarly concern with the science of butterflies. He is an accredited expert in this field.

In this essay on his life-long passion for butterflies, taken from his memoir, *Speak, Memory,* Nabokov's own style is often as highly colorful as a butterfly, for the obvious intention of this remarkably evocative piece of writing is to identify his homesickness for old Russia with his pursuit of a butterfly. The shimmering colors that Nabokov finds in the past—the past that as an exile he feels that he can find again only in the imaginative tracery of autobiography—are identified with the beautiful and rare butterflies that he sought as a boy in Russia. The beauty of this writing consciously depends upon its nostalgia, its attempt to will back, in words, the world that the exile from Russia has lost.

It is this deliberate effort not merely to evoke the past, but almost literally to recreate it, that gives such vivid poignancy to Nabokov's style. The flashing rhetoric of this writing is, in part, certainly due to the desire of a highly gifted writer to take full possession of the language he came to in later life. But fundamentally, the quality of this language is due to Nabokov's constant identification of his passion for butterflies with the lost beauty of a Russia that he does not expect to see again. "I confess I do not believe in time. I like to fold my magic carpet . . . The highest enjoyment of timelessness—in a landscape selected at random—is when I stand among rare butterflies and their food plants. This is ecstasy, and behind the ecstasy is something else . . . a momentary vacuum into which rushes all that I love."

O
n a summer morning, in the legendary Russia of my boyhood, my first glance upon awakening was for the chink between the shutters. If it disclosed a watery pallor, one had better not open the shutters at all, and so be spared the sight of a sullen day sitting for its picture in a puddle. How resentfully one would deduce, from a line of dull light, the leaden sky, the sodden sand, the gruel-like mess of broken brown blossoms under the lilacs—and that flat, fallow leaf (the first casualty of the season) pasted upon a wet garden bench!

But if the chink was a long glint of dewy brilliancy, then I made haste to have the window yield its treasure. With one blow, the room would be cleft into light and shade. The foliage of birches moving in the sun had the translucent green tone of grapes, and in contrast to this there was the dark velvet of fir trees against a blue of extraordinary

A YOUNG ENTOMOLOGIST IN OLD RUSSIA: From *Conclusive Evidence,* Harper & Brothers, 1951 (reprinted as *Speak, Memory* by Grosset & Dunlap, Inc., 1960). Originally published in *The New Yorker,* June 12, 1948. Reprinted by permission of the author.

intensity, the like of which I rediscovered only many years later, in the montane zone of Colorado.

From the age of six, everything I felt in connection with a rectangle of framed sunlight was dominated by a single passion. If my first glance of the morning was for the sun, my first thought was for the butterflies it would engender. The original event had been banal enough. On some honeysuckle near the veranda, I had happened to see a Swallow-tail—a splendid, pale-yellow creature with black blotches and blue crenulations, and a cinnabar eyespot above each chrome-rimmed black tail. As it probed the inclined flower from which it hung, it kept rest-lessly jerking its great wings, and my desire for it was overwhelming. An agile footman caught it in my cap, after which it was transferred, cap and all, to a wardrobe, where the reek of naphthalene was fondly expected to kill it overnight. On the following morning, however, when my governess unlocked the wardrobe to take something out, the butter-fly, with a mighty rustle, flew into her face, then made for the open window, and presently was but a golden fleck dipping and dodging and soaring eastward, over timber and tundra, to Vologda, Viatka and Perm, and beyond the gaunt Ural range to Yakutsk and Verkhne Kolymsk, and from Verkhne Kolymsk, where it lost a tail, to the fair Island of St. Lawrence, and across Alaska to Dawson, and southward along the Rocky Mountains—to be finally overtaken and captured, after a forty-year race, on a bright-yellow dandelion in a bright-green glade above Boulder.

Soon after the wardrobe affair I found a spectacular moth, and my mother dispatched it with ether. In later years, I used many killing agents, but the least contact with the initial stuff would always cause the door of the past to fly open; once, as a grown man, I was under ether during an operation, and with the vividness of a decalcomania picture I saw my own self in a sailor suit mounting a freshly emerged Emperor moth under the guidance of my smiling mother. It was all there, brilliantly reproduced in my dream, while my own vitals were being exposed: the soaking, ice-cold absorbent cotton pressed to the lemurian head of the moth; the subsiding spasms of its body; the satis-fying crackle produced by the pin penetrating the hard crust of its thorax; the careful insertion of the point of the pin in the cork-bot-tomed groove of the spreading board; the symmetrical adjustment of the strong-veined, "windowed" wings under neatly affixed strips of semi-transparent paper.

I must have been eight or nine when, in a storeroom of our country house, among a medley of dusty objects, I discovered some wonderful books acquired in the days when my mother's mother had been interested in natural science and had had a famous university professor of zoology (Shimkevich) give private lessons to her daughter. Some of these books were mere curios, such as the four huge brown folios of Albertus Seba's work (*Locupletissimi Rerum Naturalium Thesauri Accurata Descriptio . . .*), printed in Amsterdam around 1750. On their coarse-grained pages I found woodcuts of serpents and butterflies and embryos. The fetus of an Ethiopian female child hanging by the neck in a glass jar, used to give me a nasty shock every time I came across it; nor did I much care for the stuffed hydra on plate CII, with its seven lion-toothed turtleheads on seven serpentine necks and its strange, bloated body which bore button-like tubercules along the sides and ended in a knotted tail.

Other books I found in that attic, among herbariums full of edelweiss flowers and crimson maple leaves, came closer to my subject. I took in my arms and carried downstairs glorious loads of fantastically attractive volumes: Maria Sibylla Merian's (1647-1717) lovely plates of Surinam insects, and Esper's noble *Die Schmetterlinge* (Erlangen, 1777), and Boisduval's *Icones Historiques de Lépidoptères Nouveaux ou Peu Connus* (Paris, begun in 1832). Still more exciting were the products of the latter half of the century—Newman's *Natural History of British Butterflies and Moths,* Hofmann's *Die Gross-Schmetterlinge Europas,* the Grand Duke Nikolai Mikhailovich's *Mémoires* on Asiatic lepidoptera (with incomparably beautiful figures painted by Kavrigin, Rybakov, Lang), Scudder's stupendous work on the *Butterflies of New England.*

By my early teens, I was voraciously reading entomological periodicals, especially English and Russian ones. Great upheavals were taking place in the development of systematics. Since the middle of the century, Continental lepidopterology had been, on the whole, a simple and stable affair, smoothly run by the Germans. Its high priest, Dr. Staudinger, was also the head of the largest firm of insect dealers. Even now, half a century after his death, German lepidopterists have not quite managed to shake off the hypnotic spell occasioned by his authority. He was still alive when his school began to lose ground as a scientific force in the world. While he and his followers stuck to specific and generic names sanctioned by long usage and were content to classify butterflies by characters visible to the naked eye, English-speaking authors were introducing nomenclatorial changes as a result of a strict application of the law of priority and taxonomic changes based on the microscopic study of organs. The Germans did their best to ignore the new trends and continued to cherish the philately-like side of entomology. Their solicitude for the "average collector who should not be made to dissect" is comparable to the way nervous publishers pamper the "average reader"—who should not be made to think.

There was another more general change, which coincided with my ardent adolescent interest in butterflies and moths. The Victorian and Staudingerian kind of species, hermetic and homogeneous, with sundry (alpine, polar, insular, etc.) "varieties" affixed to it from the outside, as it were, like incidental appendages, was replaced by a new, multiform and fluid kind of species, made up of geographical races or subspecies. The evolutional aspects of the case were thus brought out more clearly, by means of more flexible methods of classification, and further links between butterflies and the central problems of nature were provided by biological investigations.

The mysteries of mimicry had a special attraction for me. Its phenomena showed an artistic perfection usually associated with man-wrought things. Such was the imitation of oozing poison by bubble-like macules on a wing (complete with pseudo-refraction) or by glossy yellow knobs on a chrysalis ("Don't eat me—I have already been squashed, sampled and rejected"). When a certain moth resembled a certain wasp in shape and color, it also walked and moved its antennae in a waspish, un-mothlike manner. When a butterfly had to look like a leaf, not only were all the details of a leaf beautifully rendered but markings mimicking grub-bored holes were generously thrown in. "Natural selection," in the Darwinian sense, could not explain the miraculous coincidence of imitative aspect and imitative behavior nor could one appeal to the theory of "the struggle for life" when a protective device was carried to a point of mimetic subtlety, exuberance, and luxury far in excess of a predator's power of appreciation. I discovered in nature the nonutilitarian delights that I sought in art. Both were a form of magic, both were a game of intricate enchantment and deception.

3

Few things indeed have I known in the way of emotion or appetite, ambition or achievement, that could surpass in richness and strength the excitement of entomological exploration. From the very first it had a great many intertwinkling facets. One of them was the acute desire to be alone, since any companion, no matter how quiet, interfered with the concentrated enjoyment of my mania. Its gratification admitted of no compromise or exception. Already when I was ten, tutors and governesses knew that the morning was mine and cautiously kept away.

In this connection, I remember the visit of a schoolmate, a boy of whom I was very fond and with whom I had excellent fun. He arrived one summer night from a town some fifty miles away. His father had recently perished in an accident, the family was ruined and the stouthearted lad, not being able to afford the price of a railway ticket, had bicycled all those miles to spend a few days with me.

On the morning following his arrival, I did everything I could to get out of the house for my morning hike without his knowing where I had gone. Breakfastless, with hysterical haste, I gathered my net, pillboxes, sailor cap, and escaped through the window. Once in the forest, I was safe; but still I walked on, my calves quaking, my eyes full of scalding tears, the whole of me twitching with shame and self-disgust, as I visualized my poor friend, with his long pale face and black tie, moping in the hot garden—patting the panting dogs for want of something better to do, and trying hard to justify my absence to himself.

Let me look at my demon objectively. With the exception of my parents, no one really understood my obsession, and it was many years before I met a fellow-sufferer. One of the first things I learned was not to depend on others for the growth of my collection. Aunts, however, kept making me ridiculous presents—such as Denton mounts of resplendent but really quite ordinary insects. Our country doctor, with whom I had left the pupae of a rare moth when I went on a journey abroad, wrote me that everything had hatched finely; but in reality a mouse had got at the precious pupae, and upon my return the deceitful old man produced some common Tortoise-shell butterflies, which, I presume, he had hurriedly caught in his garden and popped into the breeding cage as plausible substitutes (so *he* thought). Better than he, was an enthusiastic kitchen boy who would sometimes borrow my equipment and come back two hours later in triumph with a bagful of seething invertebrate life and several additional items. Loosening the mouth of the net which he had tied up with a string, he would pour out his cornucopian spoil—a mass of grasshoppers, some sand, the two parts of a mushroom he had thriftily plucked on the way home, more grasshoppers, more sand, and one battered Cabbage butterfly.

I also found out very soon that an entomologist indulging in his quiet quest was apt to provoke strange reactions in other creatures. How often, when a picnic had been arranged, and I would be self-consciously trying to get my humble implements unnoticed into the tar-smelling charabanc (a tar preparation was used to keep flies away from the horses) or the tea-smelling Opel convertible (benzine forty years ago smelled that way), some cousin or aunt of mine would remark: "Must you *really* take that net with you? Can't you enjoy yourself like a normal boy? Don't you think you are spoiling everybody's pleasure?" Near a sign NACH BODENLAUBE, at Bad Kissingen, Bavaria, just as I was about to join for a long walk my father and majestic old Muromtsev (who, four years before, in 1906, had been President of the first Russian Parliament), the latter turned his marble head toward me, a vulnerable boy of eleven, and said with his famous solemnity: "Come with us by all means, but do not chase butterflies, child. It mars the rhythm of the walk." On a path above the Black Sea, in the Crimea, among shrubs in waxy bloom, in March, 1919, a bow-legged Bolshevik sentry attempted to arrest me for signaling (with my net, he said) to a British warship. In the summer of 1929, every time I walked through a village in the Eastern Pyrenees, which I was exploring lepidopterologically, and happened to look back, I would see in my wake the villagers frozen in the various attitudes my passage had caught them in, as if I were Sodom and they Lot's wife. A decade later, in the Maritime Alps, I once noticed the grass undulate in a serpentine way behind me because a fat rural policeman was wriggling after me on his belly to find out if I were not trapping song birds. America has shown even more of this morbid interest in my doings than other countries have—perhaps because I was in my forties when I came here to live, and the older the man, the queerer he looks with a butterfly net in his hand. Stern farmers have drawn my attention to NO FISHING signs; from cars passing me on the highway have come wild howls of derision; sleepy dogs, though unmindful of the worst bum, have perked up and come at me, snarling; tiny tots have pointed me out to their puzzled mammas; broadminded vacationists have asked me whether I was catching bugs for bait; and one morning on a wasteland, lit by tall yuccas in bloom, near Santa Fé, a big, black mare followed me for more than a mile.

4

When, having shaken off all pursuers, I took the rough, red road that ran from our house toward field and forest, the animation and luster of the day seemed like a tremor of sympathy around me. Black *Erebia* butterflies ("Ringlets" as the old English Aurelians used to call them), with a special gentle awkwardness peculiar to their kind, danced among the firs. From a flower head two male Coppers rose to a tremendous height, fighting all the way up—and then, after a while came the downward flash of one of them returning to his thistle. There were familiar insects, but at any moment something better might cause me to stop with a quick intake of breath. I remember one day when I warily brought my net closer and closer to a little *Thecla* that had daintily settled on a sprig. I could clearly see the White *W* on its chocolate-brown underside. Its wings were closed and the inferior ones were rubbing against each other in a curious circular motion—possibly producing some small, blithe crepitation pitched too high for a human ear to catch. I had long wanted that particular species, and, when near enough, I struck. You have heard champion tennis-players moan after muffing an easy shot. You have seen stunned golfers smile horrible, helpless smiles. But that day nobody saw me shake out a piece of twig from an otherwise empty net and stare at a hole in the tarlatan.

5

However, if the morning hunt had been a failure, one could still look forward to mothing. Colors would die a long death on June evenings. The lilac shrub in full bloom before which I stood, net in hand, displayed clusters of a fluffy grey in the dusk—the ghost of purple. A moist young moon hung above the mist of a neighboring meadow. In many a garden have I stood thus in later years—in Athens, Antibes, Atlanta—but never have I waited with such a keen desire as before those darkening lilacs. And suddenly it would come, the low buzz passing from flower to flower, the vibrational halo around the streamlined body of an olive and pink Hummingbird moth poised in the air above the corolla into which it had dipped its long tongue. Its handsome black larva (resembling a diminutive cobra when it puffed out its ocellated front segments) could be found on dank willow-herb two months later. Thus every hour and season had its delights. And, finally, on cold, or even frosty, autumn nights, one could sugar for moths by painting tree trunks with a mixture of molasses, beer, and rum. Through the gusty blackness, one's lantern would illumine the stickily glistening furrows of the bark and two or three large moths upon it imbibing the sweets, their nervous wings half open butterfly fashion, the lower ones exhibiting their incredible crimson silk from beneath the lichen-grey primaries. *"Catocala adultera!"* I would triumphantly shriek in the direction of the lighted windows of the house as I stumbled home to show my captures to my father.

6

The "English" park that separated our house from the hayfields was an extensive and elaborate affair with labyrinthine paths, Turgenevian benches, and imported oaks among the endemic firs and birches. The struggle that had gone on since my grandfather's time to keep the park from reverting to the wild state always fell short of complete success. No gardener could cope with the hillocks of frizzly black earth that the pink hands of moles kept heaping on the tidy sand of the main walk. Weeds and fungi, and ridgelike tree roots crossed and recrossed the sun-flecked trails. Bears had been eliminated in the eighties (two such stuffed giants stood on their hind legs in our entrance hall), but an occasional moose still visited the grounds. On a picturesque boulder, a little mountain ash and a still smaller aspen had climbed, holding hands, like two clumsy, shy children. Other, more elusive trespassers—lost picnickers or merry villagers—would drive our hoary gamekeeper Ivan crazy by scrawling ribald words on the benches and gates. The disintegrating process continues still, in a different sense, for when, nowadays, I attempt to follow in memory the winding paths from one given point to another, I notice with alarm that there are many gaps, due to oblivion or ignorance, akin to the terra-incognita blanks map-makers of old used to call "sleeping beauties."

Beyond the park, there were fields, with a continuous shimmer of butterfly wings over a shimmer of flowers—daisies, blue-bells, scabious, and others—which now rapidly pass by me in a kind of colored haze like those lovely, lush meadows, never to be explored, that one sees from the diner on a transcontinental journey. At the end of this grassy wonderland, the forest rose like a wall. There I roamed, scanning the three trunks (the enchanted, the silent part of a tree) for certain tiny moths, called Pugs in England—delicate little creatures that cling in the daytime to speckled surfaces, with which their flat wings and turned-up abdomens blend. There, at the bottom of that sea of sunshot greenery, I slowly spun round the great boles. Nothing in the world would have seemed sweeter to me than to be able to add, by a stroke of luck, some remarkable new species to the long list of Pugs already named by others. And my pied imagination, ostensibly, and almost grotesquely, groveling to my desire (but all the time, in ghostly conspiracies behind the scenes, coolly planning the most distant events of my destiny), kept providing me with hallucinatory samples of small print: ". . . the only specimen so far known . . ." ". . . the only specimen known of *Eupithecia petropolitanata* was taken by a Russian schoolboy . . ." ". . . by a young Russian collector . . ." ". . . by myself in the Government of St. Petersburg, Czarskoe Selo District, in 1912 . . . 1913 . . . 1914 . . ."

Then came a June day when I felt the urge to push on still farther and explore the vast marshland beyond the Oredezh. After skirting the river for three or four miles, I found a rickety footbridge. While crossing over, I could see the huts of a hamlet on my left, apple trees, rows of tawny pine logs lying on a green bank, and the bright patches made on the turf by the scattered clothes of peasant girls, who, stark naked in shallow water, romped and yelled, heeding me as little as if I were the discarnate carrier of my present reminiscences.

On the other side of the river, a dense crowd of small, bright-blue male butterflies that had been tippling on the rich, trampled mud and cow dung through which I had to trudge rose all together into the spangled air and settled again as soon as I had passed.

After making my way through some pine groves and alder scrub I came to the bog. No sooner had my ear caught the hum of diptera around me, the cry of a snipe overhead, the gulping sound of the morass under my foot, than I knew I would find here quite special arctic butterflies, whose pictures, or, still better, nonillustrated descriptions I had worshiped for several seasons. And the next moment I was among them. Over the bilberry shrubs, with fruit of a dim, dreamy blue, over the brown eye of stagnant water, over moss, over mire, over the intoxicating racemes of the lone and mysterious marsh-rocket, a dark little Fritillary, bearing the name of a Norse goddess, passed in a low, skimming flight. I pursued rose-margined Sulphurs, grey-marbled Satyrs. Unmindful of the mosquitoes that coated my forearms and neck, I stooped with a grunt of delight to snuff out the life of some silver-studded lepidopteron throbbing in the folds of my net. Through the smells of the bog, I caught the subtle perfume of butterfly wings on my fingers, a perfume which varies with the species—vanilla, or lemon, or musk, or a musty, sweetish odor difficult to define. Still unsated, I pressed forward. At last I saw I had come to the end of the marsh. The rising ground beyond was a paradise of lupines, columbines, and pentstemons. Mariposa lilies bloomed under Ponderosa pines. In the distance, fleeting cloud shadows dappled the dull green of slopes above timber line, and the grey and white of Longs Peak.

I confess I do not believe in time. I like to fold my magic carpet, after use, in such a way as to superimpose one part of the pattern upon another. Let visitors trip. And the highest enjoyment of timelessness—in a landscape selected at random—is when I stand among rare butterflies and their food plants. This is ecstasy, and behind the ecstasy is something else, which is hard to explain. It is like a momentary vacuum into which rushes all that I love. A sense of oneness with sun and stone. A thrill of gratitude to whom it may concern—to the contrapuntal genius of human fate or to tender ghosts humoring a lucky mortal.

robert lowell

91 revere street

Robert Lowell was born in 1917; he is one of the best of the new American poets who have come up since the Second World War. As a Lowell, he here describes his native and ancestral Boston with both irony and intimacy; these make an interesting contrast with the open attack on Boston (p. 238) by Elizabeth Hardwick (Mrs. Robert Lowell).

"91 Revere Street" is an autobiographical fragment in a fine book of poems, *Life Studies*. It is a remarkably subtle memoir of life among the Brahmins. The most important thing about it is that Lowell manages to suggest the most devastating criticism of his family's conventionality without ever identifying himself too much with this criticism. He never raises his voice or shows his hand. The style of this essay is polite and amused conversation. As a piece of writing, it is indeed as aristocratic as its subject—quiet to the point of being deceptive, faintly mischievous, yet so bold and unmistakably sharp-edged that you cannot help noticing that the details he picks of people are usually absurd. He writes that "In 1924 people still lived in cities," which is one way of distinguishing old families like the Lowells from those new families that now congregate in suburbs.

The very situation which saw the Lowells in 91 Revere Street is absurd, like something from Clarence Day's *Life With Father*. The Lowells bought the house ("looking out on an unbuttoned part of Beacon Hill . . .") because the poet's mother wanted to get her husband out of the navy, and she felt that a civilian address would do the trick, since the commander of the Boston Navy Yard disapproved of his officers living in town. "My mother felt a horrified giddiness about the adventure of our address. She once said, 'We are barely perched on the outer rim of the hub of decency.' "

This is funny as well as elegant—funny perhaps because it is all so elegant. But the attentive reader will not miss the contrast between the highly individual poet growing up under these shibboleths, and the comically self-righteous stuffiness that he describes. He says of his father, a naval engineer— "He was deep—not with profundity, but with the dumb depth of one who trusted in statistics and was dubious of personal experience." ". . . to judge from my father, men between the ages of six and sixty did nothing but meet new challenges, take on heavier responsibilities, and lose all freedom to explode."

In 1924 people still lived in cities. Late that summer, we bought the 91 Revere Street house, looking out on an unbuttoned part of Beacon Hill bounded by the North End slums, though reassuringly only four blocks away from my Grandfather Winslow's brown pillared house at 18 Chestnut Street. In the decades preceding and following the First World War, old Yankee families had upset expectation by regaining this section of the Hill from the vanguards of the lace-curtain Irish. This was bracing news for my parents in that topsy-turvy era when the Republican Party and what were called "people of the right spot" were no longer dominant in city elections. Still, even in the palmy, laissez-faire '20s, Revere Street refused to be a straightforward, immutable residential fact. From one end to the other, houses kept being sanded down, repainted, or abandoned to the flaking of decay. Houses, changing hands, changed their language and nationality. A few doors to our south the householders spoke "Beacon Hill British" or the flat *nay nay* of the Boston Brahmin. The parents of the children a few doors north spoke mostly in Italian.

My mother felt a horrified giddiness about the adventure of our address. She once said, "We are barely perched on the outer rim of the hub of decency." We were less than fifty yards from Louisburg Square, the cynosure of old historic Boston's plain-spoken, cold roast elite— the Hub of the Hub of the Universe. Fifty yards!

As a naval ensign, Father had done postgraduate work at Harvard. He had also done postgraduate work at M.I.T., preferred the purely scientific college, and condescended to both. In 1924, however, his tone began to change; he now began to speak warmly of Harvard as his second alma mater. We went to football games at the Harvard Stadium, and one had the feeling that our lives were now being lived in the brutal, fashionable expectancy of the stadium: we had so many downs, so many minutes, and so many yards to go for a winning touchdown. It was just such a winning financial and social advance that my parents promised themselves would follow Father's resignation from the Navy and his acceptance of a sensible job offered him at the Cambridge branch of Lever Brothers' Soap.

The advance was never to come. Father resigned from the service in 1927, but he never had a civilian *career;* he instead had merely twenty-two years of the civilian *life.* Almost immediately he bought a larger

91 REVERE STREET: From *Life Studies* by Robert Lowell. Copyright © 1956, 1959 by Robert Lowell. Used by permission of the publishers, Farrar, Straus and Cudahy, Inc.

and more stylish house; he sold his ascetic, stove-black Hudson and bought a plump brown Buick; later the Buick was exchanged for a high-toned, as-good-as-new Packard with a custom-designed royal blue and mahogany body. Without drama, his earnings more or less decreased from year to year.

But so long as we were on Revere Street, Father tried to come to terms with it and must have often wondered whether he on the whole liked or disliked the neighborhood's lack of side. He was still at this time rather truculently democratic in what might be described as an upper middle-class, naval, and Masonic fashion. He was a mumbler. His opinions were almost morbidly hesitant, but he considered himself a matter-of-fact man of science and had an unspoiled faith in the superior efficiency of northern nations. He modeled his allegiances and humor on the cockney imperialism of Rudyard Kipling's swearing Tommies, who did their job. Autochthonous Boston snobs, such as the Winslows or members of Mother's reading club, were alarmed by the brassy callousness of our naval visitors, who labeled the Italians they met on Revere Street as "grade-A" and "grade-B wops." The Revere Street "grade-B's" were Sicilian Catholics and peddled crummy second-hand furniture on Cambridge Street, not far from the site of Great-great-Grandfather Charles Lowell's disused West Church, praised in an old family folder as "a haven from the Sodom and Gomorrah of Trinitarian orthodoxy and the tyranny of the letter." Revere Street "grade-A's," good North Italians, sold fancy groceries and Colonial heirlooms in their shops near the Public Garden. Still other Italians were Father's familiars; they sold him bootleg Scotch and *vino rosso* in teacups.

The outside of our Revere Street house was a flat red brick surface unvaried by the slightest suggestion of purple panes, delicate bay, or triangular window-cornice—a sheer wall formed by the seamless conjunction of four inseparable façades, all of the same commercial and purgatorial design. Though placed in the heart of Old Boston, it was ageless and artless, an epitome of those "leveler" qualities Mother found most grueling about the naval service. 91 Revere Street was mass-produced, *regulation-issue,* and yet struck Boston society as stupidly out of the ordinary, like those white elephants—a mother-of-pearl scout knife or a tea-kettle barometer—which my father used to pick up on sale at an Army-Navy store.

The walls of Father's minute Revere Street den-parlor were bare and white. His bookshelves were bare and white. The den's one adornment was a ten-tube home-assembled battery radio set, whose loudspeaker had the shape and color of a Mexican sombrero. The radio's specialty was getting programs from Australia and New Zealand in the early hours of the morning.

My father's favorite piece of den furniture was his oak and "rhinoceros hide" armchair. It was ostentatiously a masculine, or rather a bachelor's, chair. It had a notched, adjustable back; it was black, cracked, hacked, scratched, splintered, gouged, initialed, gunpowder-charred and tumbler-ringed. It looked like pale tobacco leaves laid on dark tobacco leaves. I doubt if Father, a considerate man, was responsible for any of the marring. The chair dated from his plebe days at the Naval Academy, and had been bought from a shady, shadowy, roaring character, midshipman "Beauty" Burford. Father loved each disfigured inch.

My father had been born two months after his own father's death. At each stage of his life, he was to be forlornly fatherless. He was a deep boy brought up entirely by a mild widowed mother and an intense widowed grandmother. When he was fourteen and a half, he became a deep young midshipman. By the time he graduated from Annapolis, he had a high sense of abstract form, which he beclouded with his humor. He had reached, perhaps, his final mental possibilities. He was deep—not with profundity, but with the dumb depth of one who trusted in statistics and was dubious of personal experience. In his forties, Father's soul went underground: as a civilian he kept his high sense of form, his humor, his accuracy, but this accuracy was henceforth unimportant, recreational, *hors de combat*. His debunking grew myopic; his shyness grew evasive; he argued with a fumbling languor. In the twenty-two years Father lived after he resigned from the Navy, he never again deserted Boston and never became Bostonian. He survived to drift from job to job, to be displaced, to be grimly and literally that old cliché, a fish out of water. He gaped and wheezed with impotent optimism, took on new ideals with each new job, never ingeniously enjoyed his leisure, never even hid his head in the sand.

Mother hated the Navy, hated naval society, naval pay, and the trip-hammer rote of settling and unsettling a house every other year when Father was transferred to a new station or ship. She had been married nine or ten years and still suspected that her husband was savorless, unmasterful, merely considerate. Unmasterful—Father's specialized efficiency lacked utterly the flattering bossiness she so counted on from her father, my Grandfather Winslow. It was not Father's absence on sea-duty that mattered; it was the eroding necessity of moving *with* him, of keeping in step. When he was far away on the Pacific, she had her friends, her parents, a house to herself—Boston! Fully conscious of her uniqueness and normality she basked in the refreshing stimulation of dreams in which she imagined Father as suitably sublimed. She used to describe such a sublime man to me over tea and English muffins. He was Siegfried carried lifeless through the shining air by Brunnhilde to Valhalla, and accompanied by the throb of my Great Aunt Sarah playing his leitmotif in the released manner taught her by the Abbé Liszt. Or Mother's hero dove through the grottoes of the Rhine and slaughtered the homicidal and vulgar dragon coiled about the golden hoard. Mother seemed almost light-headed when she retold the romance of Sarah Bernhardt in *L'Aiglon* the Eaglet, the weakling! She would speak the word *weakling* with such amused vehemence that I formed a grandiose and false image of L'Aiglon's Father, the *big* Napoleon: he was a strong man who scratched under his paunchy little white vest a torso all hair, muscle, and manliness. Instead of the dreams, Mother now had the insipid fatigue of keeping house. Instead of the *Eagle,* she had a twentieth-century naval commander interested in steam, radio, and "the fellows." To avoid naval yards, steam, and "the fellows," Mother had impulsively bought the squalid, impractical Revere Street house. Her marriage daily forced her to squander her subconsciously hoarded energies.

"Weelawaugh, we-ee-eeelawaugh, weelawaugh," shrilled Mother's high voice. *"But-and, but-and, but-and!"* Father's low mumble would drone in answer. Though I couldn't be sure that I had caught the meaning of the word, I followed the sounds as though they were a movie. I felt drenched in my parents' passions.

91 Revere Street was the setting for those arthritic spiritual pains that troubled us for the two years my mother spent in trying to argue my father into resigning from the Navy. When the majestic, hollow boredom of the second year's autumn dwindled to the mean boredom of a second winter, I grew less willing to open my mouth. I bored my parents, they bored me.

"Weelawaugh, we-ee-eelawaugh, weelawaugh!" "But-and, but-and, but-and!"

During the week ends I was at home much of the time. All day I used to look forward to the nights when my bedroom walls would once again vibrate, when I would awake with rapture to the rhythm of my parents arguing, arguing one another to exhaustion. Sometimes, without bathrobe or slippers, I would wriggle out into the cold hall on my belly and ambuscade myself behind the banister. I could often hear actual words. "Yes, yes, yes," Father would mumble. He was "backsliding" and "living in the fool's paradise of habitual retarding and retarded do-nothing inertia." Mother had violently set her heart on the resignation. She was hysterical even in her calm, but like a patient and forbearing strategist, she tried to pretend her neutrality. One night she said with murderous coolness, "Bobby and I are leaving for Papá's." This was an ultimatum to force Father to sign a deed placing the Revere Street house in Mother's name.

I writhed with disappointment on the nights when Mother and Father only lowed harmoniously together like cows, as they criticized Helen Bailey or Admiral De Stahl. Once I heard my mother say, "A *man* must make up his *own* mind. Oh Bob, if you are going to resign, do it *now* so I can at least plan for your son's *survival* and education on a single continent."

About this time I was being sent for my *survival* to Dr. Dane, a Quaker chiropractor with an office on Marlborough Street. Dr. Dane wore an old-fashioned light tan druggist's smock; he smelled like a healthy old-fashioned drugstore. His laboratory was free of intimidating technical equipment, and had only the conservative lay roughness and toughness that was so familiar and disarming to us in my Grandfather Winslow's country study or bedroom. Dr. Dane's rosy hands wrenched my shoulders with tremendous éclat and made me feel a hero; I felt unspeakable joy whenever an awry muscle fell back into serenity. My mother, who had no curiosity or imagination for cranky occultism, trusted Dr. Dane's clean, undrugged manliness—so like home. She believed that chiropractic had cured me of my undiagnosed asthma, which had defeated the expensive specialists.

"A penny for your thoughts, Schopenhauer," my mother would say.
"I am thinking about pennies," I'd answer.
"When *I* was a child I used to love telling Mamá everything I had done," Mother would say.
"But you're not a child," I would answer.
I used to enjoy dawdling and humming "Anchors Aweigh" up Revere Street after a day at school. "Anchors Aweigh," the official Navy song, had originally been the song composed for my father's class. And yet my mind always blanked and seemed to fill with a clammy hollowness when Mother asked prying questions. Like other tongue-tied, difficult children, I dreamed I was a master of cool, stoical repartee. "What have you been doing, Bobby?" Mother would ask. "I haven't," I'd answer. At home I thus saved myself from emotional exhaustion.

At school, however, I was extreme only in my conventional mediocrity, my colorless, distracted manner, which came from restless dreams of being admired. My closest friend was Eric Burckhard, the son of a professor of architecture at Harvard. The Burckhards came from Zurich and were very German, not like Ludendorff, but in the kindly, comical, nineteenth-century manner of Jo's German husband in *Little Men,* or in the manner of the crusading *sturm und drang* liberal scholars in second year German novels. "Eric's mother and father are *both* called Dr. Burckhard," my mother once said, and indeed there was something endearingly repellent about Mrs. Burckhard with her doctor's degree, her long, unstylish skirts, and her dramatic, dulling blond braids. Strangely the Burckhards' sober continental bourgeois house was without golden mean—everything was either hilariously old Swiss or madly modern. The Frau Doctor Burckhard used to serve mid-morning hot chocolate with rosettes of whipped cream, and receive her friends in a long, uncarpeted hall-drawing room with lethal ferns and a yellow beeswaxed hardwood floor shining under a central skylight. On the wall there were large expert photographs of what at a distance appeared to be Mont Blanc—they were in reality views of Frank Lloyd Wright's Japanese hotel.

I admired the Burckhards and felt at home in their house, and these feelings were only intensified when I discovered that my mother was always ill at ease with them. The heartiness, the enlightenment, and the bright, ferny greenhouse atmosphere were too much for her.

Eric and I were too young to care for books or athletics. Neither of our houses had absorbing toys or an elevator to go up and down in. We were inseparable, but I cannot imagine what we talked about. I loved Eric because he was more popular than I and yet absolutely *sui generis* at the Brimmer School. He had a chalk-white face and limp, fine, white-blond hair. He was frail, elbowy, started talking with an enthusiastic Mont Blanc chirp and would flush with bewilderment if interrupted. All the other boys at Brimmer wore little tweed golf suits with knickerbockers, but Eric always arrived in a black suit coat, a Byronic collar, and cuffless, gray flannel trousers that almost hid his shoes. The long trousers were replaced on warm days by gray flannel shorts, such as were worn by children still in kindergarten. Eric's unenviable and freakish costumes were too old or too young. He accepted the whims of his parents with a buoyant tranquility that I found unnatural.

My first and terminating quarrel with Eric was my fault. Eventually almost our whole class at Brimmer had whooping cough, but Eric's seizure was like his long trousers—untimely: he was sick a month too early. For a whole month he was in quarantine and forced to play by

himself in a removed corner of the Public Garden. He was certainly
conspicuous as he skiproped with his Swiss nurse under the out-of-the-
way Ether Memorial Fountain far from the pond and the swan boats.
His parents had decided that this was an excellent opportunity for Eric
to brush up on his German, and so the absoluteness of his quarantine
was monstrously exaggerated by the fact that child and nurse spoke no
English but only a guttural, British-sounding, Swiss German. Round
and round and round the Fountain, he played intensely, frailly, obe-
diently, until I began to tease him. Though motioned away by him, I
came close. I had attracted some of the most popular Brimmer School
boys. For the first time I had gotten favorable attention from several
little girls. I came close. I shouted. Was Eric afraid of girls? I imitated
his German. *Ein, swei, drei, BEER.* I imitated Eric's coughing. "He is
afraid he will give you whooping cough if he talks or lets you come
nearer," the nurse said in her musical Swiss-English voice. I came
nearer. Eric flushed, grew white, bent double with coughing. He began
to cry, and had to be led away from the Public Garden. For a whole
week I routed Eric from the Garden daily, and for two or three days
I was a center of interest. "Come see the Lake Geneva spider monkey!"
I would shout. I don't know why I couldn't stop. Eric never told his
father, I think, but when he recovered we no longer spoke. The breach
was so unspoken and intense that our classmates were actually horrified. They even devised a solemn ritual for our reconciliation. We
crossed our hearts, mixed spit, mixed blood. The reconciliation was
hollow.

My parents' confidences and quarrels stopped each night at ten or
eleven o'clock, when my father would hang up his tuxedo, put on his
commander's uniform, and take a trolley back to the naval yard
at Charlestown. He had just broken in a new car. Like a chauffeur, he
watched this car, a Hudson, with an informed vigilance, always giving
its engine hair-trigger little tinkerings of adjustment or friendship,
always fearful lest the black body, unbeautiful as his boiled shirts,
should lose its outline and gloss. He drove with flawless, almost instru-
mental, monotony. Mother, nevertheless, was forever encouraging him
to walk or take taxis. She would tell him that his legs were growing vestigial from disuse and remind him of the time a jack had
slipped and he had broken his leg while shifting a tire. "Alone and
at night," she would say, "an amateur driver is unsafe in a car."
Father sighed and obeyed—only, putting on a martyred and penny-
saving face, he would keep his self-respect by taking the trolley rather
than a taxi. Each night he shifted back into his uniform, but his

departures from Revere Street were so furtive that several months passed before I realized what was happening—we had *two* houses! Our second house was the residence in the Naval Yard assigned to the third in command. It was large, had its own flagpole, and screen porches on three levels—yet it was something to be ashamed of. Whatever pomp or distinction its possession might have had for us was destroyed by an eccentric humiliation inflicted on Father by his superior, Admiral De Stahl, the commandant at Charlestown. De Stahl had not been consulted about our buying the 91 Revere Street house. He was outraged, stormed about "flaunting private fortunes in the face of naval tradition," and ordered my father to sleep on bounds at the Yard in the house provided for that purpose.

On our first Revere Street Christmas Eve, the telephone rang in the middle of dinner; it was Admiral De Stahl demanding Father's instant return to the Navy Yard. Soon Father was back in his uniform. In taking leave of my mother and grandparents he was, as was usual with him under pressure, a little evasive and magniloquent. "A woman works from sun to sun," he said, "but a sailor's watch is never done." He compared a naval officer's hours with a doctor's, hinted at surprise maneuvers, and explained away the uncommunicative arrogance of Admiral De Stahl: "The Old Man has to be hush-hush." Later that night, I lay in bed and tried to imagine that my father was leading his engineering force on a surprise maneuver through arctic wastes. A forlorn hope! "Hush-hush, hush-hush," whispered the snowflakes as big as street lamps as they broke on Father—broke and buried. Outside, I heard real people singing carols, shuffling snow off their shoes, opening and shutting doors. I worried at the meaning of a sentence I had heard quoted from the *Boston Evening Transcript:* "On this Christmas Eve, as usual, the whole of Beacon Hill can be expected to become a single old-fashioned open house—the names of mine host the Hill, and her guests will read like the contents of the Social Register." I imagined Beacon Hill changed to the snow queen's palace, as vast as the north pole. My father pressed a cold finger to his lip: "hush-hush," and led his surprise squad of sailors around an altar, but the altar was a tremendous cash register, whose roughened nickel surface was cheaply decorated with trowels, pyramids, and Arabic swirls. A great drawer helplessly chopped back and forth, unable to shut because choked with greenbacks. "Hush-hush!" My father's engineers wound about me with their eye-patches, orange sashes, and curtain-ring earrings, like the Gilbert and Sullivan pirates' chorus. . . . Outside on the streets of Beacon Hill, it was night, it was dismal, it was raining. Something disturbing had befallen the familiar and honorable Salvation Army band; its big drum and accordion were now accompanied by drunken voices howling: *The Old Gray Mare, she ain't what she used to be, when Mary went to milk the cow.* A sound of a bosun's whistle. Women laughing. Someone repeatedly rang our doorbell. I heard my mother talking on the telephone. "Your inebriated sailors have littered my doorstep with the dregs of Scollay Square." There was a gloating panic in her voice that showed she enjoyed the drama of talking to Admiral De Stahl. "Sir," she shrilled, "you have compelled my husband to leave me alone and defenseless on Christmas Eve!" She ran into my bedroom. She hugged me. She said, "Oh Bobby, it's such a comfort to have a man in the house." "I am not a man," I said, "I am a boy."

elizabeth hardwick

boston: the lost ideal

Elizabeth Hardwick is a novelist, born in Kentucky, who now lives in Boston. Whether as a woman, or as a novelist, or as a Southerner, she is not intimidated by Boston. Her essay, not calculated to please the natives, is nevertheless so brilliant in its language, in the very sharpness of its attack, that it is impossible to read it without admiration for its wit. She describes Boston as "wrinkled, spindly-legged," and says of famous old Boston worthies that theirs are "names that remain in one's mind, without producing an image or a fact, as the marks are left on the wall after the picture has been removed." She complains that "In Boston the night comes down with an incredibly heavy, small-town finality," and notes that in Boston even "French restaurants quickly become tea-roomy, as if some sort of rapid naturalization had taken place." She remarks of the descendants of old Boston families better known for family than for riches that "Their inevitable 'small income' is a sort of dynastic flaw, like hemophilia."

This is clever writing, but it is not contrived to get a laugh. Miss Hardwick is deadly serious, which is why she writes so well. She writes out of a disenchantment that many Americans are likely to feel just now. As she says, on the one hand "All the American regions are breaking up, ground down to a standard American corn meal," yet on the other, places that have kept their identity, like Boston, tend to capitalize on the past and to get ossified in it. These are faults that a

Southerner is familiar with, and the wit of this essay, its historical sense, the sympathy for the past and the despair over the confusions of the present, are very much in the Southern tradition.

With Boston and its mysteriously enduring reputation, "the reverberation is longer than the thunderclap," as Emerson observed about the tenacious fame of certain artists. Boston—wrinkled, spindly-legged, depleted of nearly all her spiritual and cutaneous oils, provincial, self-esteeming—has gone on spending and spending her inflated bills of pure reputation, decade after decade. Now, one supposes it is all over at last. The old jokes embarrass, the anecdotes are so many thrice-squeezed lemons, and no new fruit hangs on the boughs.

All the American regions are breaking up, ground down to a standard American corn meal. And why not Boston, which would have been the most difficult to maintain? There has never been anything quite like Boston as a creation of the American imagination, or perhaps one should say as a creation of the American scene. Some of the legend was once real, surely. Our utilitarian, fluid landscape has produced a handful of regional conceptions, popular images, brief and naked; the conservative Vermonter, the boastful Texan, the honeyed Southerner. "Graciousness is ours," brays a coarsened South; and the sheiks of Texas cruise around their desert.

The Boston image is more complex. The city is felt to have, in the end, a pure and special nature, absurd no doubt but sowehome valuable. An author can hardly fail to turn a penny or two on this magical subject. Everyone will consent to be informed on it, to be slyly entertained by it. The image lends itself to exaggerations, to dreams of social and ethnic purity, to notions of grand old families still existing as grand old families are supposed to exist. *Actual* Boston, the living city, is governed largely by people of Irish descent and more and more, recently, by men of Italian descent. Not long ago, the old Yankee, Senator Saltonstall, remarked wistfully that there were still a good many Anglo-Saxons in Massachusetts, his own family among them. Extinction is foreshadowed in the defense.

Plainness and pretension restlessly feuding and combining; wealth and respectability and firmness of character ending in the production of a number of diverting individual tics or, at the best, instances of high culture. Something of that sort is the legendary Boston soul or so one supposes without full confidence because the old citizens of Bos-

BOSTON: THE LOST IDEAL: From *Harper's Magazine*, December, 1959. Copyright ©
1959 Harper & Brothers. Reprinted by permission of the author.

ton vehemently hold to the notion that the city and their character are ineffable, unknowable. When asked for an opinion on the admirable novel, *Boston Adventure,* or even the light social history, *The Proper Bostonians,* the answer invariably comes, "Not Boston." The descriptive intelligence, the speculative mind, the fresh or even the merely open eye are felt to discover nothing but errors here, be they errors of praise or censure. Still, wrong-headedness flourishes, the subject fascinates, and the Athenaeum's list of written productions on this topic is nearly endless.

The best book on Boston is Henry James's novel, *The Bostonians.* By the bald and bold use of the place name, the unity of situation and person is dramatized. But poor James, of course, was roundly and importantly informed by everyone, including his brother William, that this too was "not Boston," and, stricken, he pushed aside a superb creation, and left the impregnable, unfathomable Boston to its mysteries. James's attitude toward the city's intellectual consequence and social charm is one of absolute impiety. A view of the Charles River reveals, ". . . an horizon indented at empty intervals with wooden spires, the masts of lonely boats, the chimneys of dirty 'works,' over a brackish expanse of anomalous character, which is too big for a river and too small for a bay" A certain house has "a peculiar look of being both new and faded—a kind of modern fatigue—like certain articles of commerce which are sold at a reduction as shopworn." However, there is little natural landscape in James's novel. The picture is, rather, of the psychological Boston of the 1870s, a confused scene, slightly mad with neurotic repressions, provincialism, and earnestness without intellectual seriousness.

James's view of Boston is not the usual one, although his irony and dissatisfaction are shared by Henry Adams, who says that "a simpler manner of life and thought could hardly exist, short of cave-dwelling," and by Santayana who spoke of Boston as a "moral and intellectual nursery, always busy applying first principles to trifles." The great majority of the writings on Boston are in another spirit altogether—frankly unctuous, for the town has always attracted men of quiet and timid and tasteful opinion, men interested in old families and things, in the charms of times recently past, collectors of anecdotes about those Boston worthies hardly anyone can still clearly identify, men who spoke and preached and whose style and fame deteriorated quickly. Rufus Choate, Dr. Channing, Edward Everett Hale, Phillips Brooks, and Theodore Parker: names that remain in one's mind, without producing an image or a fact, as the marks are left on the wall after the picture has been removed. William Dean Howells held a more usual view than Henry James or Adams or Santayana. Indeed Howell's original enthusiasm for garden and edifice, person and setting, is more than a little *exalté*. The first sight of the Chapel at Mount Auburn Cemetery moved him more than the "Acropolis, Westminster Abbey, and Santa Croce in one." The massive, gray stones of "the Public Library and the Athenaeum are hardly eclipsed by the Vatican and the Pitti." And so on.

The importance of Boston was intellectual and as its intellectual donations to the country have diminished, so it has declined from its lofty symbolic meaning, to become a more lowly image, a sort of farce of conservative exclusiveness and snobbish humor. Marquand's George Apley is a figure of the decline—fussy, sentimental, farcically mannered, archaic. He cannot be imagined as an Abolitionist, an author, a speaker; he is merely a "character," a very idiosyncratic and simpleminded one. The old Boston had something of the spirit of Bloomsbury: clannish, worldly, and intellectually serious. About the historian, Prescott, Van Wyck Brooks could say, ". . . for at least ten years, Prescott had been hard at work, harder, perhaps, than any Boston merchant."

History, indeed, with its long, leisurely, gentlemanly labors, the books arriving by post, the cards to be kept and filed, the sections to be copied, the documents to be checked, is the ideal pursuit for the New England mind. All the Adamses spent a good deal of their lives on one kind of history or another. The eccentricity, studiousness, and study-window slow pace of life of the historical gentleman lay everywhere about the Boston scene. For money, society, fashion, extravagance, one went to New York. But now, the descendants of the old, intellectual aristocracy live in the respectable suburbs and lead the healthy, restless, outdoor life that atrophies the sedentary nerves of culture. The blue-stocking, the eccentric, the intransigent bring a blush of uncertainty and embarrassment to the healthy young couple's cheek.

Boston today can still provide a fairly stimulating atmosphere for the banker, the broker, for doctors and lawyers. "Open end" investments prosper, the fish come in at the dock, the wool market continues, and workers are employed in the shoe factories in the nearby towns. For the engineer, the physicist, the industrial designer, for all the highly trained specialists of the electronic age, Boston and its area are of seemingly unlimited promise. Sleek, well-designed factories and research centers pop up everywhere; the companies plead, in the Sunday papers, for more chemists, more engineers, and humbly relate the executive benefits of salary and pension and advancement they are prepared to offer.

But otherwise, for the artist, the architect, the composer, the writer, the philosopher, the historian, for those humane pursuits for which the town was once noted and even for the delights of entertainment, for dancing, acting, cooking, Boston is a bewildering place. There is, first of all, the question of Boston or New York. (The question is not new; indeed it was answered in the last decades of the last century in favor of New York as the cultural center of America.) It is, in our day, only a private and personal question: where or which of the two Eastern cities should one try to live and work in? It is a one-sided problem. For the New Yorker, San Francisco or Florida, perhaps—Boston, never. In Boston, New York tantalizes; one of the advantages of Boston is said, wistfully, to be its nearness to New York. It is a bad sign when a man, who has come to Boston or Cambridge, Massachusetts, from another place begins to show an undivided acceptance of his new town. Smugness is the great vice of the two places. Between puffy self-satisfaction and the fatiguing wonder if one wouldn't be happier, more productive, more appreciated in New York a thoughtful man makes his choice.

Boston is not a small New York, as they say a child is not a small adult but is, rather, a specially organized small creature with its small-creature's temperature, balance, and distribution of fat. In Boston there is an utter absence of that wild electric beauty of New York, of the marvelous, excited rush of people in taxicabs at twilight, of the great Avenues and Streets, the restaurants, theatres, bars, hotels, delicatessens, shops. In Boston the night comes down with an incredibly heavy, small-town finality. The cows come home; the chickens go to roost; the meadow is dark. Nearly every Bostonian is in his own house or in someone else's house, dining at the home board, enjoying domestic and social privacy. The "nice, little dinner party"—for this the Bostonian would sell his soul. In the evenings, the old "accommodators" dart about the city, carrying their black uniforms and white aprons in a paper bag. They are on call to go, anywhere, to cook and serve dinners. Many of these women are former cooks and maids, now living on Social Security retirement pensions, supplemented by the fees for these evening "accommodations" to the community. Their style and the bland respectability of their cuisine keep up the social tone of the town. They are like those old slaves who stuck to their places and, even in the greatest deprivation, graciously went on toting things to the Massa.

There is a curious flimsiness and indifference in the commercial life

of Boston. The restaurants are, charitably, to be called mediocre. the
famous sea food is only palatable when raw. Otherwise it usually has
to endure the deep-fry method that makes everything taste like those
breaded pork chops of the Middle West, which in turn taste like the
fried sole of Boston. Here, French restaurants quickly become tea-
roomy, as if some sort of rapid naturalization had taken place. There
is not a single attractive eating place on the water front. An old
downtown restaurant of considerable celebrity, Locke-Ober's, has been
expanded, let out, and "costumed" by one of the American restaurant
decorators whose productions have a ready-made look, as if the designs
had been chosen from a catalogue. But for the purest eccentricity,
there is the "famous" restaurant, Durgin-Park, which is run like a
boarding house in a mining town. And so it goes.

Downtown Boston at night is a dreary jungle of honky-tonks for
sailors, dreary department-store windows, Loew's movie houses, hill-
billy bands, strippers, parking lots, undistinguished new buildings. Mid-
town Boston—small, expensive shops, the inevitable Elizabeth Arden
and Helena Rubinstein "salons," Brooks Brothers—is deserted at night,
except for people going in and out of the Ritz Carlton Hotel, the
only public place in Boston that could be called "smart." The mer-
chandise in the Newbury Street shops is designed in a high fashion,
elaborate, furred and sequined, but it is never seen anywhere. Perhaps it is for out-of-town use, like a traveling man's mistress.

Just as there is no smart life, so there is no Soho, no Greenwich
Village. Recently a man was murdered in a parking lot in the China-
town area. His address was given as the South End, a lower-class section,
and he was said to be a free-spender, making enough money as a summer bartender on Cape Cod to lead a free-wheeling life the rest of the
year. One paper referred to the unforunate man as a "member of the
Beacon Hill Bohemia set." This designation is of considerable interest
because there is no "Bohemia" in Boston, neither upper nor lower;
the detergent of bourgeois Boston cleans everything, effortlessly, completely. If there *were* a Bohemia, its members would indeed live on
Beacon Hill, the most beautiful part of Boston and, like the older
parts of most cities, fundamentally classless, providing space for the
rich in the noble mansions and for the people with little money in the
run-down alleys. For both of these groups the walled gardens of
Beacon Hill, the mews, the coach houses, the river views, the cobble-
stone streets are a necessity and the yellow-brick, sensible structures
of the Fenway—a plausible but unpoetical residential section near the
Art Museum—are poison. Espresso bars have sprung up, or rather dug
down in basements, but no summer of wild Bohemia is ushered into

town. This reluctance is due to the Boston legend and its endurance as a lost ideal, a romantic quest.

Something transcendental is always expected in Boston. There is, one imagines, behind the drapery on Mount Vernon Street a person of democratic curiosity and originality of expression, someone alas— and this is the tiresome Boston note—*well-born*. It is likely to be, even in imagination, a she, since women now and not the men provide the links with the old traditions. Of her, then, one expects a certain un-professionalism, but it is not expected that she will be superficial; she is profoundly conventional in manner of life but capable of radical insights. To live in Boston means to seek some connection with this famous local excellence, the regional type and special creation of the city. An angry disappointment attends the romantic soul bent upon this quest. When the archaeological diggings do turn up an authentic specimen it will be someone old, nearly gone, "whom you should have known when she was young"—and still could hear.

The younger Bostonians seem in revolt against the old excellence, with its indulgent, unfettered development of the self. Revolt, how-ever, is too active a word for a passive failure to perpetuate the ideal high-mindedness and intellectual effort. With the fashionable young women of Boston, one might just as well be on Long Island. Only in the nervous, shy, earnest women is there a lingering hint of the pecul-iar local development. Terrible *faux pas* are constantly being made by this reasonable, honorable person, followed by blushes and more false steps and explanations and the final blinking, retreating blush.

Among the men, the equivalent of the blushing, blurting, sensitive, and often "fine" woman, is a person who exists everywhere perhaps but nowhere else with such elaboration of type, such purity of ex-ample. This is the well-born failure, the amateur not by choice but from some fatal reticence of temperament. They are often descendants of intellectual Boston, odd-ball grandsons, charming and sensitive, puzzlingly complicated, living on a "small income." These unhappy men carry on their conscience the weight of unpublished novels, half-finished paintings, impossible historical projects, old-fashioned poems, unproduced plays. Their inevitable "small income" is a sort of dynastic flaw, like hemophilia. Much money seems often to impose obligations of energetic management; from great fortunes the living cells receive the hints of the possibilities of genuine power, enough to make some enormously rich Americans endure the humiliations and fatigues of political office. Only the most decadent and spoiled think of living in idleness on millions; but this notion does occur to the man afflicted with ten thousand a year. He will commit himself with a dreamy courage to whatever traces of talent he may have and live to see himself punished by the New England conscience which demands accomplishments, duties performed, responsibilities noted, and energies sensibly used. The dying will accuses and the result is a queer kind of Boston incoherence. It is literally impossible much of the time to tell what some of the most attractive men in Boston are talking about. Half-uttered witticisms, grave and fascinating obfuscations, points incredibly qualified, hesitations infinitely refined—one staggers about, charmed and confused, by the twilight.

But this person, with his longings, connects with the old possibilities and, in spite of his practical failure, keeps alive the memory of the best days. He may have a brother who has retained the mercantile robustness of nature and easy capacity for action and yet has lost all belief in anything except money and class, who may practice private charities, but entertain profoundly trivial national and world views. A Roosevelt, Harriman, or Stevenson is impossible to imagine as a member of the Boston aristocracy; in Boston the vein of self-satisfaction and conservatism cuts too deeply.

Harvard (across the river in Cambridge) and Boston are two ends of one mustache. Harvard is now so large and international it has altogether avoided the whimsical stagnation of Boston. But the two places need each other, as we knowingly say of a mismatched couple. Without the faculty, the visitors, the events that Harvard brings to the life here, Boston would be intolerable to anyone except genealogists, antique dealers, and those who find repletion in a closed local society. Unfortunately, Harvard, like Boston, has "tradition" and in America this always carries with it the risk of a special staleness of attitude, and of pride, incredibly and comically swollen like the traits of hypocrisy, selfishness, or lust in the old dramas. At Harvard some of the vices of "society" exist, of Boston society that is—arrogance and the blinding dazzle of being, *being at Harvard.*

The moral and social temptations of Harvard's unique position in American academic life are great and the pathos is seen in those young faculty members who are presently at Harvard but whose appointments are not permanent and so they may be thrown down, banished from the beatific condition. The young teacher in this position lives in a dazed state of love and hatred, pride and fear; their faces have a look of desperate yearning, for they would rather serve in heaven than reign in hell. For those who are not banished, for the American at least, since the many distinguished foreigners at Harvard need not endure these piercing and fascinating complications, something of Boston seems to seep into their characters. They may come from anywhere in America and yet to be at Harvard unites them with the transcendental, legendary Boston, with New England in flower. They begin to revere the old worthies, the houses, the paths trod by so many before, and they feel a throb of romantic sympathy for the directly-gazing portraits on the walls, for the old graves and old names in the Mount Auburn Cemetery. All of this has charm and may even have a degree of social and intellectual value—and then again it may not. Devious parochialisms, irrelevant snobberies, a bemused exaggeration of one's own productions, pimple the soul of a man upholding tradition in a forest of relaxation, such as most of America is thought to be. Henry James's observation in his book on Hawthorne bears on this:

> . . . it is only in a country where newness and change and brevity of tenure are the common substance of life, that the fact of one's ancestors having lived for a hundred and seventy years in a single spot would become an element of one's morality. It is only an imaginative American that would feel urged to keep reverting to this circumstance, to keep analyzing and cunningly considering it.

If the old things of Boston are too heavy and plushy, the new either hasn't been born or is appallingly shabby and poor. As early as Thanksgiving, Christmas decorations unequaled for cheap ugliness go up in the Public Garden and on the Boston Common. Year after year, the city fathers bring out crèches and camels and Mother and Child so badly made and of such tasteless colors they verge on blasphemy, or would seem to do so if it were not for the equally dismal, although secular, little men blowing horns and the canes of peppermint hanging on the lamps. The shock of the first sight is the most interesting; later the critical senses are stilled as year after year the same bits are brought forth and gradually one realizes that the whole thing is a permanent exhibition.

Recently the dying downtown shopping section of Boston was to be graced with flowers, an idea perhaps in imitation of the charming potted geraniums and tulips along Fifth Avenue in New York. Commercial Boston produced a really amazing display: old, gray square bins, in which were stuck a few bits of yellowing, dying evergreen. It had the look of exhausted greenery thrown out in the garbage and soon the dust-bins were full of other bits of junk and discard—people had not realized or recognized the decorative hope and saw only the rubbishy result.

The municipal, civic backwardness of Boston does not seem to bother its more fortunate residents. For them and for the observer, Boston's beauty is serene and private, an enclosed, intense personal life, rich with domestic variation, interesting stuffs and things, showing the hearthside vitality of a Dutch genre painting. Of an evening the spirits quicken, not to public entertainment, but instead to the sights behind the draperies, the glimpses of drawing-rooms on Louisburg Square, paneled walls, and French chandeliers on Commonwealth Avenue, bookshelves and flower-filled bays on Beacon Street. Boston is a winter city. Every apartment has a fireplace. In the town houses, old persons climb steps without complaint, four or five floors of them, cope with the maintenance of roof and gutter, and survive the impractical kitchen and resign themselves to the useless parlors. This is life: the house, the dinner party, the charming gardens, one's high ceilings, fine windows, lacy grillings, magnolia trees, inside shutters, glassed-in studios on the top of what were once stables, outlook on the "river side." Setting is serious.

When it is not serious, when a splendid old private house passes into less dedicated hands, an almost exuberant swiftness of deterioration can be noticed. A rooming house, although privately owned, is no longer in the purest sense a private house and soon it partakes of some of the feckless, ugly municipal neglect. The contrasts are startling. One of two houses of almost identical exterior design will have shining windows, a bright brass door-knocker, and its twin will show a "Rooms" sign peering out of dingy glass, curtained by those lengths of flowered plastic used in the shower bath. Garbage lies about in the alleys behind the rooming houses, discarded furniture blocks old garden gateways. The vulnerability of Boston's way of life, the meanness of most things that fall outside the needs of the upper classes are shown with a bleak and terrible fullness in the rooming houses on Beacon Street. And even some of the best houses show a spirit of mere "maintenance," which, while useful for the individual with money, leads to civic dullness, architectural torpor, and stagnation. In the Back Bay area, a voluntary, casual association of property owners exists for the purpose of trying to keep the alleys clean, the streets lighted beyond their present medieval darkness, and to pursue other worthy items of neighborhood value. And yet this same group will "protest" against the attractive Café Florian on Newbury Street (smell of coffee too strong!) and against the brilliantly exciting Boston Arts Festival held in the beautiful Public Garden for two weeks in June. The idea that Boston might be a vivacious, convenient place to live in is not uppermost in most residents' thoughts. Trying to buy groceries in the best sections of the Back Bay region is an interesting study in commercial apathy.

A great many of the young Bostonians leave town, often taking off with a sullen demand for a freer, more energetic air. And yet many of them return later, if not to the city itself, to the beautiful sea towns and old villages around it. For the city itself, who will live in it after the present human landmarks are gone? No doubt, some of the young people there at the moment will persevere, and as a reward for their fidelity and endurance will themselves later become monuments, old types interesting to students of what our colleges call American Civilization. Boston is defective, out-of-date, vain, and lazy, but if you're not in a hurry it has a deep, secret appeal. Or, more accurately, those who like it may make of its appeal a secret. The weight of the Boston legend, the tedium of its largely fraudulent posture of traditionalism, the disillusionment of the Boston present as a cultural force, make quick minds hesitate to embrace a region so deeply compromised. They are on their guard against falling for it, but meanwhile they can enjoy its very defects, its backwardness, its slowness, its position as one of the large, possible cities on the Eastern seacoast, its private, residential charm. They speak of going to New York and yet another season finds them holding back, positively enjoying the Boston life. . . .

. . . Outside it is winter, dark. The curtains are drawn, the wood is on the fire, the table has been checked, and in the stillness one waits for the guests who come stamping in out of the snow. There are lectures in Cambridge, excellent concerts in Symphony Hall, bad plays being tried out for the hungry sheep of Boston before going to the hungry sheep of New York. Arnold Toynbee or T. S. Eliot or Robert Frost or Robert Oppenheimer or Barbara Ward is in town again. The cars are double-parked so thickly along the narrow streets that a moving vehicle can scarcely maneuver; the pedestrians stumble over the cobbles; in the back alleys a cat cries and the rats, enormously fat, run in front of the car lights creeping into the parking spots. Inside it is cozy, Victorian, and gossipy. Someone else has *not* been kept on at Harvard. The old Irish "accommodator" puffs up stairs she had never seen before a few hours previously and announces that dinner is ready. A Swedish journalist is just getting off the train at the Back Bay Station. He has been exhausted by cocktails, reality, life, taxis, telephones, bad connections in New York and Chicago, pulverized by "a good time." Sighing, he alights, seeking old Boston, a culture that hasn't been alive for a long time . . . and rest.

IV

james baldwin

notes of a native son

The brilliant young Negro novelist, James Baldwin, born in 1924, has published two fine novels—*Go Tell It On The Mountain* and *Giovanni's Room*. But a book of autobiographical essays, *Notes Of A Native Son* (1955) is the most powerful work he has written on the unending stress of what it means to be an American with a black skin.

The present selection is the title essay from this book; it is a little masterpiece of candor, of desperate love and rage at the condition of the Negro in America; it presents in full the grim understanding that, as a Negro, one American has learned to endure. What makes this essay so peculiarly *strong* is the bluntness with which Baldwin seeks to portray an extreme situation. Three profound events took place in 1943 at the same time—Baldwin's father died, his mother gave birth to her last child, and a race riot erupted in Harlem. What makes the essay so remarkable is, first of all, Baldwin's ability to make us feel this trinity of death and birth and violence as the connected events they were in his own life. And secondly, an even more remarkable feature, the writing in the essay, though amazing in its candor, is never self-centered. The bitterness and pain which pervaded Baldwin's experience now remain with us as we read his account. Nor does Baldwin pretend that the writing of this essay has brought him peace; he wrote it to discharge a burden of emotion, and the emotion is still hot within him—and ourselves—as we read him.

On the 29th of July, in 1943, my father died. On the same day, a few hours later, his last child was born. Over a month before this, while all our energies were concentrated in waiting for these events, there had been, in Detroit, one of the bloodiest race riots of the century. A few hours after my father's funeral, while he lay in state in the undertaker's chapel, a race riot broke out in Harlem. On the morning of the 3rd of August, we drove my father to the graveyard through a wilderness of smashed plate glass.

The day of my father's funeral had also been my nineteenth birthday. As we drove him to the graveyard, the spoils of injustice, anarchy, discontent, and hatred were all around us. It seemed to me that God himself had devised, to mark my father's end, the most sustained and brutally dissonant of codas. And it seemed to me, too, that the violence which rose all about us as my father left the world had been devised as a corrective for the pride of his eldest son. I had declined to believe in that apocalypse which had been central to my father's vision; very well, life seemed to be saying, here is something that will certainly pass for an apocalypse until the real thing comes along. I had inclined to be contemptuous of my father for the conditions of his life, for the conditions of our lives. When his life had ended I began to wonder about that life and also, in a new way, to be apprehensive about my own.

I had not known my father very well. We had got on badly, partly because we shared, in our different fashions, the vice of stubborn pride. When he was dead I realized that I had hardly ever spoken to him. When he had been dead a long time I began to wish I had. It seems to be typical of life in America where opportunities, real and fancied, are thicker than anywhere else on the globe, that the second generation has no time to talk to the first. No one, including my father, seems to have known exactly how old he was, but his mother had been born during slavery. He was of the first generation of free men. He, along with thousands of other Negroes, came North after 1919 and I was part of that generation which had never seen the landscape of what Negroes sometimes call the Old Country.

He had been born in New Orleans and had been a quite young man there during the time that Louis Armstrong, a boy, was running errands for the dives and honky-tonks of what was always presented to me as one of the most wicked of cities—to this day, whenever I think of New Orleans, I also helplessly think of Sodom and Gomorrah. My father never mentioned Louis Armstrong, except to forbid us to play his records; but there was a picture of him on our wall for a long time. One of my father's strong-willed female relatives had placed it there and forbade my father to take it down. He never did, but he eventually maneuvered her out of the house and when, some years later, she was in trouble and near death, he refused to do anything to help her.

He was, I think, very handsome. I gather this from photographs and from my own memories of him, dressed in his Sunday best and on his way to preach a sermon somewhere, when I was little. Handsome, proud, and ingrown, "like a toe-nail," somebody said. But he looked to me, as I grew older, like pictures I had seen of African tribal chieftains: he really should have been naked, with war-paint on and barbaric mementos, standing among spears. He could be chilling in the pulpit and indescribably cruel in his personal life and he was certainly the most bitter man I have ever met; yet it must be said that there was something else in him, buried in him, which lent him his tremendous power and, even, a rather crushing charm. It had something to do with his blackness, I think—he was very black—with his blackness and his beauty, and with the fact that he knew that he was black but did not know that he was beautiful. He claimed to be proud of his blackness but it had also been the cause of much humiliation and it had fixed bleak boundaries to his life. He was not a young man when we were growing up and he had already suffered many kinds of ruin; in his outrageously demanding and protective way he loved his children, who were black like him and menaced, like him; and all these things sometimes showed in his face when he tried, never to my knowledge with any success, to establish contact with any of us. When he took one of his children on his knee to play, the child always became fretful and began to cry; when he tried to help one of us with our homework the absolutely unabating tension which emanated from him caused our minds and our tongues to become paralyzed, so that he, scarcely knowing why flew into a rage and the child, not knowing why, was punished. If it ever entered his head to bring a surprise home for his children, it was, almost unfailingly, the wrong surprise and even the big watermelons he often brought home on his back in the summertime led to the most appalling scenes. I do not remember in all those years, that one of his children was ever glad to see him come home. From what I was able to gather of his early life, it seemed that this inability to establish contact with other people had always marked him and had been one of the things which had driven him out of New Orleans. There was something in him therefore, groping and tentative, which was never expressed and which was buried with him. One saw it most clearly when he was facing new people and hoping to impress them. But he never did, not for long. We went from church to smaller and more improbable church, he found himself in less and less demand as a minister, and by the time he died none of his friends had come to see him for a long time. He had lived and died in an intolerable bitterness of spirit and it frightened me, as we drove him to the graveyard through those unquiet, ruined streets, to see how powerful and overflowing this bitterness could be and to realize that this bitterness now was mine.

When he died I had been away from home for a little over a year. In that year I had had time to become aware of the meaning of all my father's bitter warnings, had discovered the secret of his proudly pursed lips and rigid carriage: I had discovered the weight of white people in the world. I saw that this had been for my ancestors and now would be for me an awful thing to live with and that the bitterness which had helped to kill my father could also kill me.

He had been ill a long time—in the mind, as we now realized, reliving instances of his fantastic intransigence in the new light of his affliction and endeavoring to feel a sorrow for him which never, quite, came true. We had not known that he was being eaten up by paranoia, and the discovery that his cruelty, to our bodies and our minds, had been one of the symptoms of his illness was not, then, enough to enable us to forgive him. The younger children felt, quite simply, relief that he would not be coming home anymore. My mother's observation that it was he, after all, who had kept them alive all these years meant nothing because the problems of keeping children alive are not real for children. The older children felt, with my father gone, that they could invite their friends to the house without fear that their friends would be insulted or, as had sometimes happened with me, being told that their friends were in league with the devil and intended to rob our family of everything we owned. (I didn't fail to wonder, and it made me hate him, what on earth we owned that anybody else would want.)

His illness was beyond all hope of healing before anyone realized that he was ill. He had always been so strange and had lived, like a prophet, in such unimaginably close communion with the Lord that his long silences which were punctuated by moans and hallelujahs and snatches of old songs while he sat at the living-room window never seemed odd to us. It was not until he refused to eat because, he said, his family was trying to poison him that my mother was forced to accept as a fact what had, until then, been only an unwilling suspicion. When he was committed, it was discovered that he had tuberculosis and, as it turned out, the disease of his mind allowed the disease of his body to destroy him. For the doctors could not force him to eat, either, and, though he was fed intravenously, it was clear from the beginning that there was no hope for him.

In my mind's eye I could see him, sitting at the window, locked up in his terrors; hating and fearing every living soul including his children who had betrayed him, too, by reaching towards the world which had despised him. There were nine of us. I began to wonder what it could have felt like for such a man to have had nine children whom he could barely feed. He used to make little jokes about our poverty, which never, of course, seemed very funny to us; they could not have seemed very funny to him, either, or else our all too feeble response to them would never have caused such rages. He spent great energy and achieved, to our chagrin, no small amount of success in keeping us away from the people who surrounded us, people who had all-night rent parties to which we listened when we should have been sleeping, people who cursed and drank and flashed razor blades on Lenox Avenue. He could not understand why, if they had so much energy to spare, they could not use it to make their lives better. He treated almost everybody on our block with a most uncharitable asperity and neither they, nor, of course, their children were slow to reciprocate.

The only white people who came to our house were welfare workers and bill collectors. It was almost always my mother who dealt with them, for my father's temper, which was at the mercy of his pride, was never to be trusted. It was clear that he felt their very presence in his home to be a violation: this was conveyed by his carriage almost ludicrously stiff, and by his voice, harsh and vindictively polite. When I was around nine or ten I wrote a play which was directed by a young, white schoolteacher, a woman, who then took an interest in me, and gave me books to read and, in order to corroborate my theatrical bent, decided to take me to see what she somewhat tactlessly referred to as "real" plays. Theatergoing was forbidden in our house, but, with the really cruel intuitiveness of a child, I suspected that the color of this woman's skin would carry the day for me. When, at school, she suggested taking me to the theater, I did not, as I might have done if she had been a Negro, find a way of discouraging her, but agreed that she should pick me up at my house one evening. I then, very cleverly, left all the rest to my mother, who suggested to my father, as I knew she would, that it would not be very nice to let such a kind woman make the trip for nothing. Also, since it was a schoolteacher, I imagine that my mother countered the idea of sin with the idea of "education," which word, even with my father, carried a kind of bitter weight.

Before the teacher came my father took me aside to ask *why* she was coming, what *interest* she could possibly have in our house, in a boy like me. I said I didn't know but I, too, suggested that it had something to do with education. And I understood that my father was waiting for me to say something—I didn't quite know what; perhaps that I wanted his protection against this teacher and her "education." I said none of these things and the teacher came and we went out. It was clear, during the brief interview in our living room, that my father was agreeing very much against his will and that he would have refused permission if he had dared. The fact that he did not dare caused me to despise him: I had no way of knowing that he was facing in that living room a wholly unprecedented and frightening situation.

Later, when my father had been laid off from his job, this woman became very important to us. She was really a very sweet and generous woman and went to a great deal of trouble to be of help to us, particularly during one awful winter. My mother called her by the highest name she knew: she said she was a "christian." My father could scarcely disagree but during the four or five years of our relatively close association he never trusted her and was always trying to surprise in her open, Midwestern face the genuine, cunningly hidden, and hideous motivation. In later years, particularly when it began to be clear that this "education" of mine was going to lead me to perdition, he became more explicit and warned me that my white friends in high school were not really my friends and that I would see, when I was older, how white people would do anything to keep a Negro down. Some of them could be nice, he admitted, but none of them were to be trusted and most of them were not even nice. The best thing was to have as little to do with them as possible. I did not feel this way and I was certain, in my innocence, that I never would.

But the year which preceded my father's death had made a great change in my life. I had been living in New Jersey, working in defense plants, working and living among southerners, white and black. I knew about the south, of course, and about how southerners treated Negroes and how they expected them to behave, but it had never entered my mind that anyone would look at me and expect *me* to behave that way. I learned in New Jersey that to be a Negro meant, precisely, that one was never looked at but was simply at the mercy of the reflexes the color of one's skin caused in other people. I acted in New Jersey as I had always acted, that is as though I thought a great deal of myself—I had to *act* that way—with results that were, simply, unbelievable. I had scarcely arrived before I had earned the enmity, which was extraordinarily ingenious, of all my superiors and nearly all my co-workers. In the beginning, to make matters worse, I simply did not know what was happening. I did not know what I had done, and I shortly began to wonder what *anyone* could possibly do, to bring about such unanimous, active, and unbearably vocal hostility. I knew about jim-crow but I had never experienced it. I went to the same self-service restaurant three times and stood with all the Princeton boys before the counter, waiting for a hamburger and coffee; it was always an extraordinarily long time before anything was set before me; but it was not until the fourth visit that I learned that, in fact, nothing had ever been set before me: I had simply picked something up. Negroes were not served there, I was told, and they had been waiting for me to realize that I was always the only Negro present. Once I was told this, I determined to go there all the time. But now they were ready for me and, though some dreadful scenes were subsequently enacted in that restaurant, I never ate there again.

It was the same story all over New Jersey, in bars, bowling alleys, diners, places to live. I was always being forced to leave, silently, or with mutual imprecations. I very shortly became notorious and children giggled behind me when I passed and their elders whispered or shouted—they really believed that I was mad. And it did begin to work on my mind, of course; I began to be afraid to go anywhere and to compensate for this I went places to which I really should not have gone and where, God knows, I had no desire to be. My reputation in town naturally enhanced my reputation at work and my working day became one long series of acrobatics designed to keep me out of trouble. I cannot say that these acrobatics succeeded. It began to seem that the machinery of the organization I worked for was turning over, day and night, with but one aim: to eject me. I was fired once, and contrived, with the aid of a friend from New York, to get back on the payroll; was fired again, and bounced back again. It took a while to fire me for the third time, but the third time took. There were no loopholes anywhere. There was not even any way of getting back inside the gates.

That year in New Jersey lives in my mind as though it were the year during which, having an unsuspected predilection for it, I first contracted some dread, chronic disease, the unfailing symptom of which is a kind of blind fever, a pounding in the skull and fire in the bowels. Once this disease is contracted, one can never be really carefree again, for the fever, without an instant's warning, can recur at any moment. It can wreck more important things than race relations. There is not a Negro alive who does not have this rage in his blood— one has the choice, merely, of living with it consciously or surrendering to it. As for me, this fever has recurred in me, and does, and will until the day I die.

My last night in New Jersey, a white friend from New York took me to the nearest big town, Trenton, to go to the movies and have a few drinks. As it turned out, he also saved me from, at the very least, a violent whipping. Almost every detail of that night stands out very clearly in my memory. I even remember the name of the movie we saw because its title impressed me as being so patly ironical. It was a movie about the German occupation of France, starring Maureen O'Hara and Charles Laughton and called *This Land Is Mine*. I remember the name of the diner we walked into when the movie ended: it was the "American Diner." When we walked in the counterman asked what we wanted and I remember answering with the casual sharpness which had become my habit: "We want a hamburger and a cup of coffee, what do you think we want?" I do not know why, after a year of such rebuffs, I so completely failed to anticipate his answer, which was, of course, "We don't serve Negroes here." This reply failed to discompose me, at least for the moment. I made some sardonic comment about the name of the diner and we walked out into the streets.

This was the time of what was called the "brown-out," when the lights in all American cities were very dim. When we re-entered the streets something happened to me which had the force of an optical illusion, or a nightmare. The streets were very crowded and I was facing north. People were moving in every direction but it seemed to me, in that instant, that all of the people I could see, and many more than that, were moving toward me, against me, and that everyone was white. I remember how their faces gleamed. And I felt, like a physical sensation, a *click* at the nape of my neck as though some interior string connecting my head to my body had been cut. I began to walk. I heard my friend call after me, but I ignored him. Heaven only knows what was going on in his mind, but he had the good sense not to touch me—I don't know what would have happened if he had—and to keep me in sight. I don't know what was going on in my mind, either; I certainly had no conscious plan. I wanted to do something to crush these white faces, which were crushing me. I walked for perhaps a block or two until I came to an enormous, glittering, and fashionable restaurant in which I knew not even the intercession of the Virgin would cause me to be served. I pushed through the doors and took the first vacant seat I saw, at a table for two, and waited.

I do not know how long I waited and I rather wonder, until today, what I could possibly have looked like. Whatever I looked like, I frightened the waitress who shortly appeared, and the moment she appeared all of my fury flowed towards her. I hated her for her white face, and for her great, astounded, frightened eyes. I felt that if she found a black man so frightening I would make her fright worthwhile.

She did not ask me what I wanted, but repeated, as though she had learned it somewhere, "We don't serve Negroes here." She did not say it with the blunt, derisive hostility to which I had grown so accustomed, but, rather, with a note of apology in her voice, and fear. This made me colder and more murderous than ever. I felt I had to do something with my hands. I wanted her to come close enough for me to get her neck between my hands.

So I pretended not to have understood her, hoping to draw her closer. And she did step a very short step closer, with her pencil poised incongruously over her pad, and repeated the formula: ". . . don't serve Negroes here."

Somehow, with the repetition of that phrase, which was already ringing in my head like a thousand bells of a nightmare, I realized that she would never come any closer and that I would have to strike from a distance. There was nothing on the table but an ordinary watermug half full of water, and I picked this up and hurled it with all my strength at her. She ducked and it missed her and shattered against the mirror behind the bar. And, with that sound, my frozen blood abruptly thawed, I returned from wherever I had been, I *saw*, for the first time, the restaurant, the people with their mouths open, already, as it seemed to me, rising as one man, and I realized what I had done, and where I was, and I was frightened. I rose and began running for the door. A round, potbellied man grabbed me by the nape of the neck just as I reached the doors and began to beat me about the face. I kicked him and got loose and ran into the streets. My friend whispered, *"Run!"* and I ran.

My friend stayed outside the restaurant long enough to misdirect my pursuers and the police, who arrived, he told me, at once. I do not know what I said to him when he came to my room that night. I could not have said much. I felt, in the oddest, most awful way, that I had somehow betrayed him. I lived it over and over and over again, the way one relives an automobile accident after it has happened and one finds oneself alone and safe. I could not get over two facts, both equally difficult for the imagination to grasp, and one was that I could have been murdered. But the other was that I had been ready to commit murder. I saw nothing very clearly but I did see this: that my life, my *real* life, was in danger, and not from anything other people might do but from the hatred I carried in my own heart.

II

I had returned home around the second week in June—in great haste because it seemed that my father's death and my mother's confinement were both but a matter of hours. In the case of my mother, it soon became clear that she had simply made a miscalculation. This had always been her tendency and I don't believe that a single one of us arrived in the world, or has since arrived anywhere else, on time. But none of us dawdled so intolerably about the business of being born as did my baby sister. We sometimes amused ourselves, during those endless, stifling weeks, by picturing the baby sitting within in the safe, warm dark, bitterly regretting the necessity of becoming a part of our chaos and stubbornly putting it off as long as possible. I understood her perfectly and congratulated her on showing such good sense so soon. Death, however, sat as purposefully at my father's bedside as life stirred within my mother's womb and it was harder to understand why he so lingered in that long shadow. It seemed that he had bent, and for a long time, too, all of his energies towards dying. Now death was ready for him but my father held back.

All of Harlem, indeed, seemed to be infected by waiting. I had never before known it to be so violently still. Racial tensions throughout this country were exacerbated during the early years of the war, partly because the labor market brought together hundreds of thousands of ill-prepared people and partly because Negro soldiers, regardless of where they were born, received their military training in the south. What happened in defense plants and army camps had repercussions, naturally, in every Negro ghetto. The situation in Harlem had grown bad enough for clergymen, policemen, educators, politicians, and social workers to assert in one breath that there was no "crime wave" and to offer, in the very next breath, suggestions as to how to combat it. These suggestions always seemed to involve playgrounds, despite the fact that racial skirmishes were occurring in the playgrounds, too. Playground or not, crime wave or not, the Harlem police force had been augmented in March, and the unrest grew—perhaps, in fact, partly as a result of the ghetto's instinctive hatred of policemen. Perhaps the most revealing news item, out of the steady parade of reports of muggings, stabbings, shootings, assaults, gang wars, and accusations of police brutality, is the item concerning six Negro girls who set upon a white girl in the subway because, as they all too accurately put it, she was stepping on their toes. Indeed she was, all over the nation.

I had never before been so aware of policemen, on foot, on horseback, on corners, everywhere, always two by two. Nor had I ever been so aware of small knots of people. They were on stoops and on corners and in doorways, and what was striking about them, I think, was that they did not seem to be talking. Never, when I passed these groups, did the usual sound of a curse or a laugh ring out and neither did there seem to be any hum of gossip. There was certainly, on the other hand, occurring between them communication extraordinarily intense. Another thing that was striking was the unexpected diversity of the people who made up these groups. Usually, for example, one would see a group of sharpies standing on the street corner, jiving the passing chicks; or a group of older men, usually, for some reason, in the vicinity of a barber shop, discussing baseball scores, or the numbers, or making rather chilling observations about women they had known. Women, in a general way, tended to be seen less often together—unless they were church women, or very young girls, or prostitutes met together for an unprofessional instant. But that summer I saw the strangest combinations: large, respectable, churchly matrons standing on the stoops or the corners with their hair tied up, together with a girl in sleazy satin whose face bore the marks of gin and the razor, or heavy-set, abrupt, no-nonsense older men, in company with the most disreputable and fanatical "race" men, or these same "race" men with the sharpies, or these sharpies with the churchly women. Seventh Day Adventists and Methodists and Spiritualists seemed to be hobnobbing with Holyrollers and they were all, alike, entangled with the most flagrant disbelievers; something heavy in their stance seemed to indicate that they had all, incredibly, seen a common vision, and on each face there seemed to be the same strange, bitter shadow.

The churchly women and the matter-of-fact, no-nonsense men had children in the Army. The sleazy girls they talked to had lovers there, the sharpies and the "race" men had friends and brothers there. It would have demanded an unquestioning patriotism, happily as uncommon in this country as it is undesirable, for these people not to have been disturbed by the bitter letters they received, by the newspaper stories they read, not to have been enraged by the posters, then to be found all over New York, which described the Japanese as "yellow-bellied Japs." It was only the "race" men, to be sure, who spoke ceaselessly of being revenged—how this vengeance was to be exacted was not clear—for the indignities and dangers suffered by Negro boys in uniform; but everybody felt a directionless, hopeless bitterness, as well as that panic which can scarcely be suppressed when one knows that a human being one loves is beyond one's reach, and in danger. This helplessness and this gnawing uneasiness does something, at length, to even the toughest mind. Perhaps the best way to sum all this up is to say that the people I knew felt, mainly, a peculiar kind of relief when they knew that their boys were being shipped out of the south, to do battle overseas. It was, perhaps, like feeling that the most dangerous part of a dangerous journey had been passed and that now, even if death should come, it would come with honor and without the complicity of their countrymen. Such a death would be, in short, a fact with which one could hope to live.

It was on the 28th of July, which I believe was a Wednesday, that I visited my father for the first time during his illness and for the last time in his life. The moment I saw him I knew why I had put off this visit so long. I had told my mother that I did not want to see him because I hated him. But this was not true. It was only that I *had* hated him and I wanted to hold on to this hatred. I did not want to look on him as a ruin: it was not a ruin I had hated. I imagine that one of the reasons people cling to their hates so stubbornly is because they sense, once hate is gone, that they will be forced to deal with pain.

We traveled out to him, his older sister and myself, to what seemed to be the very end of a very Long Island. It was hot and dusty and we wrangled, my aunt and I, all the way out, over the fact that I had recently begun to smoke and, as she said, to give myself airs. But I knew that she wrangled with me because she could not bear to face the fact of her brother's dying. Neither could I endure the reality of her despair, her unstated bafflement as to what had happened to her brother's life, and her own. So we wrangled and I smoked and from time to time she fell into a heavy reverie. Covertly, I watched her face, which was the face of an old woman; it had fallen in, the eyes were sunken and lightless; soon she would be dying, too.

In my childhood—it had not been so long ago—I had thought her beautiful. She had been quick-witted and quick-moving and very generous with all the children and each of her visits had been an event. At one time one of my brothers and myself had thought of running away to live with her. Now she could no longer produce out of her handbag some unexpected and yet familiar delight. She made me feel pity and revulsion and fear. It was awful to realize that she no longer caused me to feel affection. The closer we came to the hospital the more querulous she became and at the same time, naturally, grew more dependent on me. Between pity and guilt and fear I began to feel that there was another me trapped in my skull like a jack-in-the-box who might escape my control at any moment and fill the air with screaming.

She began to cry the moment we entered the room and she saw him lying there, all shriveled and still, like a little black monkey. The great, gleaming apparatus which fed him and would have compelled him to be still even if he had been able to move brought to mind, not beneficence, but torture; the tubes entering his arm made me think of pictures I had seen when a child, of Gulliver, tied down by the pygmies on that island. My aunt wept and wept, there was a whistling sound in my father's throat; nothing was said; he could not speak. I wanted to take his hand, to say something. But I do not know what I could have said, even if he could have heard me. He was not really in that room with us, he had at last really embarked on his journey; and though my aunt told me that he said he was going to meet Jesus, I did not hear anything except that whistling in his throat. The doctor came back and we left, into that unbearable train again, and home. In the morning came the telegram saying that he was dead. Then the house was suddenly full of relatives, friends, hysteria, and confusion and I quickly left my mother and the children to the care of those impressive women, who, in Negro communities at least, automatically appear at times of bereavement armed with lotions, proverbs, and patience, and an ability to cook. I went downtown. By the time I returned, later the same day, my mother had been carried to the hospital and the baby had been born.

III

For my father's funeral I had nothing black to wear and this posed a nagging problem all day long. It was one of those problems, simple, or impossible of solution, to which the mind insanely clings in order to avoid the mind's real trouble. I spent most of that day at the downtown apartment of a girl I knew, celebrating my birthday with whiskey and wondering what to wear that night. When planning a birthday celebration one naturally does not expect that it will be up against competition from a funeral and this girl had anticipated taking me out that night, for a big dinner and a night club afterwards. Sometime during the course of that long day we decided that we would go out anyway, when my father's funeral service was over. I imagine *I* decided it, since, as the funeral hour approached, it became clearer and clearer to me that I would not know what to do with myself when it was over. The girl, stifling her very lively concern as to the possible effects of the whiskey on one of my father's chief mourners, concentrated on being conciliatory and practically helpful. She found a black shirt for me somewhere and ironed it and, dressed in the darkest pants and jacket I owned, and slightly drunk, I made my way to my father's funeral.

The chapel was full, but not packed, and very quiet. There were, mainly, my father's relatives, and his children, and here and there I saw faces I had not seen since childhood, the faces of my father's one-time friends. They were very dark and solemn now, seeming somehow to suggest that they had known all along that something like this would happen. Chief among the mourners was my aunt, who had quarreled with my father all his life; by which I do not mean to suggest that her mourning was insincere or that she had not loved him. I suppose that she was one of the few people in the world who had, and their incessant quarreling proved precisely the strength of the tie that bound them. The only other person in the world, as far as I knew, whose relationship to my father rivaled my aunt's in depth was my mother, who was not there.

It seemed to me, of course, that it was a very long funeral. But it was, if anything, a rather shorter funeral than most, nor, since there were no overwhelming, uncontrollable expressions of grief, could it be called

—if I dare to use the word—successful. The minister who preached my father's funeral sermon was one of the few my father had still been seeing as he neared his end. He presented to us in his sermon a man whom none of us had ever seen—a man thoughtful, patient, and forbearing, a Christian inspiration to all who knew him, and a model for his children. And no doubt the children, in their disturbed and guilty state, were almost ready to believe this; he had been remote enough to be anything and, anyway, the shock of the incontrovertible, that it was really our father lying up there in that casket, prepared the mind for anything. His sister moaned and this grief-stricken moaning was taken as corroboration. The other faces held a dark, non-committal thoughtfulness. This was not the man they had known, but they had scarcely expected to be confronted with *him;* this was, in a sense deeper than questions of fact, the man they had not known, and the man they had not known may have been the real one. The real man, whoever he had been, had suffered and now he was dead: this was all that was sure and all that mattered now. Every man in the chapel hoped that when his hour came he, too, would be eulogized, which is to say forgiven, and that all of his lapses, greeds, errors, and strayings from the truth would be invested with coherence and looked upon with charity. This was perhaps the last thing human beings could give each other and it was what they demanded, after all, of the Lord. Only the Lord saw the midnight tears, only He was present when one of His children, moaning and wringing hands, paced up and down the room. When one slapped one's child in anger the recoil in the heart reverberated through heaven and became part of the pain of the universe. And when the children were hungry and sullen and distrustful and one watched them, daily, growing wilder, and further away, and running headlong into danger, it was the Lord who knew what the charged heart endured as the strap was laid to the backside; the Lord alone who knew what one *would* have said if one had had, like the Lord, the gift of the living word. It was the Lord who knew of the impossibility every parent in that room faced: how to prepare the child for the day when the child would be despised and how to *create* in the child—by what means?—a stronger antidote to this poison than one had found for oneself. The avenues, side streets, bars, billiard halls, hospitals, police stations, and even the playgrounds for oneself. The avenues, side streets, bars, billiard halls, hospitals, police stations, and even the playgrounds of Harlem—not to mention the houses of correction, the jails, and the morgue —testified to the potency of the poison while remaining silent as to the efficacy of whatever antidote, irresistibly raising the question of whether or not such an antidote existed; raising, which was worse, the question of whether or not an antidote was desirable; perhaps poison should be fought with poison. With these several schisms in the mind and with more terrors in the heart than could be named, it was better not to judge the man who had gone down under an impossible burden. It was better to remember: *Thou knowest this man's fall; but thou knowest not his wrassling.*

While the preacher talked and I watched the children—years of changing their diapers, scrubbing them, slapping them, taking them to school, and scolding them had had the perhaps inevitable result of making me love them, though I am not sure I knew this then—my mind was busily breaking out with a rash of disconnected impressions. Snatches of popular songs, indecent jokes, bits of books I had read, movie sequences, faces, voices, political issues—I thought I was going mad; all these impressions suspended, as it were, in the solution of the faint nausea produced in me by the heat and liquor. For a moment I had the impression that my alcoholic breath, inefficiently disguised with chewing gum, filled the entire chapel. Then someone began singing one of my father's favorite songs and, abruptly, I was with him, sitting on his knee, in the hot, enormous, crowded church which was the first church we attended. It was the Abyssinia Baptist Church on 138th Street. We had not gone there long. With this image, a host of others came. I had forgotten, in the rage of my growing up, how proud my father had been of me when I was little. Apparently, I had had a voice and my father had liked to show me off before the members of the church. I had forgotten what he had looked like when he was pleased but now I remembered that he had always been grinning with pleasure when my solos ended. I even remembered certain expressions on his face when he teased my mother—had he loved her? I would never know. And when had it all begun to change? For now it seemed that he had not always been cruel. I remembered being taken for a haircut and scraping my knee on the footrest of the barber's chair and I remembered my father's face as he soothed my crying and applied the stinging iodine. Then I remembered our fights, fights which had been of the worst possible kind because my technique had been silence.

I remembered the one time in all our life together when we had really spoken to each other.

It was on a Sunday and it must have been shortly before I left home. We were walking, just the two of us, in our usual silence, to or from church. I was in high school and had been doing a lot of writing and I was, at about this time, the editor of the high school magazine. But I had also been a Young Minister and had been preaching from the pulpit. Lately, I had been taking fewer engagements and preached as rarely as possible. It was said in the church, quite truthfully, that I was "cooling off."

My father asked me abruptly, "You'd rather write than preach, wouldn't you?"

I was astonished at his question—because it was a real question. I answered, "Yes."

That was all we said. It was awful to remember that that was all we had *ever* said.

The casket now was opened and the mourners were being led up the aisle to look for the last time on the deceased. The assumption was that the family was too overcome with grief to be allowed to make this journey alone and I watched while my aunt was led to the casket and, muffled in black, and shaking, led back to her seat. I disapproved of forcing the children to look on their dead father, considering that the shock of his death, or, more truthfully, the shock of death as a reality, was already a little more than a child could bear, but my judgment in this matter had been overruled and there they were, bewildered and frightened and very small, being led, one by one, to the casket. But there is also something very gallant about children at such moments. It has something to do with their silence and gravity and with the fact that one cannot help them. Their legs, somehow, seem *exposed,* so that it is at once incredible and terribly clear that their legs are all they have to hold them up.

I had not wanted to go to the casket myself and I certainly had not wished to be led there, but there was no way of avoiding either of these forms. One of the deacons led me up and I looked on my father's face. I cannot say that it looked like him at all. His blackness had been equivocated by powder and there was no suggestion in that casket of what his power had or could have been. He was simply an old man dead, and it was hard to believe that he had ever given anyone either joy or pain. Yet, his life filled that room. Further up the avenue his wife was holding his newborn child. Life and death so close together, and love and hatred, and right and wrong, said something to me which I did not want to hear concerning man, concerning the life of man.

After the funeral, while I was downtown desperately celebrating my birthday, a Negro soldier, in the lobby of the Hotel Braddock, got into a fight with a white policeman over a Negro girl. Negro girls, white policemen, in or out of uniform, and Negro males—in or out of uniform—were part of the furniture of the lobby of the Hotel Braddock and this was certainly not the first time such an incident had occurred. It was destined, however, to receive an unprecedented publicity, for the fight between the policeman and the soldier ended with the shooting of the soldier. Rumor, flowing immediately to the streets outside, stated that the soldier had been shot in the back, an instantaneous and revealing invention, and that the soldier had died protecting a Negro woman. The facts were somewhat different—for example, the soldier had not been shot in the back, and was not dead, and the girl seems to have been as dubious a symbol of womanhood as her white counterpart in Georgia usually is, but no one was interested in the facts. They preferred the invention because this invention expressed and corroborated their hates and fears so perfectly. It is just as well to remember that people are always doing this. Perhaps many of those legends, including Christianity, to which the world clings began their conquest of the world with just some such concerted surrender to distortion. The effect, in Harlem, of this particular legend was like the effect of a lit match in a tin of gasoline. The mob gathered before the doors of the Hotel Braddock simply began to swell and to spread in every direction, and Harlem exploded.

The mob did not cross the ghetto lines. It would have been easy, for example, to have gone over Morningside Park on the west side or to have crossed the Grand Central railroad tracks at 125th Street on the east side, to wreak havoc in white neighborhoods. The mob seems to have been mainly interested in something more potent and real than the white face, that is, in white power, and the principal damage done during the riot of the summer of 1943 was to white business establishments in Harlem. It might have been a far bloodier story, of course, if, at the hour the riot began, these establishments had still been open. From the Hotel Braddock the mob fanned out, east and west along 125th Street, and for the entire length of Lenox, Seventh, and Eighth avenues. Along each of these avenues, and along each major side street —116th, 125th, 135th, and so on—bars, stores, pawnshops, restaurants, even little luncheonettes had been smashed open and entered and looted—looted, it might be added, with more haste than efficiency. The shelves really looked as though a bomb had struck them. Cans of beans and soup and dog food, along with toilet paper, corn flakes, sardines, and milk tumbled every which way, and abandoned cash registers and cases of beer leaned crazily out of the splintered windows and were strewn along the avenues. Sheets, blankets, and clothing of every description formed a kind of path, as though people had dropped them while running. I truly had not realized that Harlem *had* so many stores until I saw them all smashed open; the first time the word *wealth* ever entered my mind in relation to Harlem was when I saw it scattered in the streets. But one's first, incongruous impression of plenty was countered immediately by an impression of waste. None of this was doing

anybody any good. It would have been better to have left the plate
glass as it had been and the goods lying in the stores.

It would have been better, but it would also have been intolerable,
for Harlem had needed something to smash. To smash something is the
ghetto's chronic need. Most of the time it is the members of the ghetto
who smash each other, and themselves. But as long as the ghetto walls
are standing there will always come a moment when these outlets do
not work. That summer, for example, it was not enough to get into a
fight on Lenox Avenue, or curse out one's cronies in the barber shops.
If ever, indeed, the violence which fills Harlem's churches, pool halls,
and bars erupts outward in a more direct fashion, Harlem and its citizens are likely to vanish in an apocalyptic flood. That this is not likely
to happen is due to a great many reasons, most hidden and powerful
among them the Negro's real relation to the white American. This
relation prohibits, simply, anything as uncomplicated and satisfactory
as pure hatred. In order really to hate white people, one has to blot so
much out of the mind—and the heart—that this hatred itself becomes
an exhausting and self-destructive pose. But this does not mean, on
the other hand, that love comes easily: the white world is too powerful,
too complacent, too ready with gratuitous humiliation, and, above all,
too ignorant and too innocent for that. One is absolutely forced to
make perpetual qualifications and one's own reactions are always can-
celing each other out. It is this, really, which has driven so many people
mad, both white and black. One is always in the position of having to
decide between amputation and gangrene. Amputation is swift but
time may prove that the amputation was not necessary—or one may
delay the amputation too long. Gangrene is slow, but it is impossible
to be sure that one is reading one's symptoms right. The idea of going
through life as a cripple is more than one can bear, and equally unbearable is the risk of swelling up slowly, in agony, with poison. And
the trouble, finally, is that the risks are real even if the choices do not
exist.

"But as for me and my house," my father had said, "we will serve the
Lord." I wondered, as we drove him to his resting place, what this line
had meant for him. I had heard him preach it many times. I had
preached it once myself, proudly giving it an interpretation different
from my father's. Now the whole thing came back to me, as though
my father and I were on our way to Sunday school and I were memo-
rizing the golden text: *And if it seem evil unto you to serve the Lord,*
choose you this day whom you will serve; whether the gods which your
fathers served that were on the other side of the flood, or the gods of the
Amorites, in which land ye dwell: but as for me and my house, we will

serve the Lord. I suspected in these familiar lines a meaning which had never been there for me before. All of my father's texts and songs, which I had decided were meaningless, were arranged before me at his death like empty bottles, waiting to hold the meaning which life would give them for me. This was his legacy: nothing is ever escaped. That bleakly memorable morning I hated the unbelievable streets and the Negroes and whites who had, equally, made them that way. But I knew that it was folly, as my father would have said, this bitterness was folly. It was necessary to hold on to the things that mattered. The dead man mattered, the new life mattered; blackness and whiteness did not matter; to believe that they did was to acquiesce in one's own destruction. Hatred, which could destroy so much, never failed to destroy the man who hated and this was an immutable law.

It began to seem that one would have to hold in the mind forever two ideas which seemed to be in opposition. The first idea was acceptance, the acceptance, totally without rancor, of life as it is, and men as they are: in the light of this idea, it goes without saying that injustice is a commonplace. But this did not mean that one could be complacent, for the second idea was of equal power: that one must never, in one's own life, accept these injustices as commonplace but must fight them with all one's strength. This fight begins, however, in the heart and it now had been laid to my charge to keep my own heart free of hatred and despair. This intimation made my heart heavy and, now that my father was irrecoverable, I wished that he had been beside me so that I could have searched his face for the answers which only the future would give me now.

robert graves

goodbye to all that

Robert Graves was born in London in 1895, and educated at Charterhouse, in the trenches during the First World War, and at Oxford. Although he has often stated that he regards himself primarily as a poet, he is also a novelist, a classical scholar, a journalist, a critic, an anthologist, and in one form or another has published well over a hundred literary works.

Of all these many books, perhaps none has more intrinsic value than *Goodbye To All That,* Graves's unforgettable memoir of his experiences

in the 1914-1918 war. The very title of his book recalls the lasting shock
of this war upon his generation. Like so many Englishmen of his time,
he was virtually still a boy when he went into the trenches, and the
impact on so young a man of the constant, mechanized and often senseless violence he has described with extraordinary coolness and dramatic
objectivity.

Goodbye To All That is a personal *narrative,* not a "confession" or a
complaint. It flows with incident and dialogue. It is a brilliantly successful description of war because of the easy, casual, almost unbelievably
cheerful tone in which so many horrors and outrages are described.
Graves has invented for this book a loose, drifting narrative tone that
corresponds exactly to the overwhelming sense which these soldiers
had—that the war was only a series of frightful and unrelated accidents.

Although the present selection is a chapter from the middle of
Graves's book, it is self-contained. It can easily be understood and
appreciated for itself; the people described in it, whatever their names
or military titles, are *soldiers.* They are human beings plunged into a
violence which they can neither understand nor control. At the same
time, as Graves so touchingly makes clear, the 1914-1918 war still saw
sufficient instances of old-fashioned chivalry toward the enemy and of
ambition to do honor to one's regiment; hence the attrition of these
ideals, in actual conditions of trench warfare, seems particularly cruel.
"The junior Royal Welch officers complained loudly at our not being
given the honor of leading the attack. . . . Half a mile of communication trench, known as 'Maison Rouge Alley', separated us from the firing line. At half-past five the gas would be discharged. We were cold,
tired, sick, and not at all in the mood for a battle, but tried to snatch
an hour or two of sleep squatting in the trench. It had been raining for
some time." Notice how little actual bitterness there is on the *surface*
of such writing. Graves puts everything he feels, everything he wants to
say, into the details of the experience. It is as if he were saying—not we
but the *war* is the subject, the *war* is what everything was all about. This
is why a passage like the following, which describes the boomeranging
of a clumsy gas attack on the Germans, is so distinct in all its frightful
details:

"The gas-men . . . managed to discharge one or two cylinders; the
gas went whistling out, formed a thick cloud a few yards off in No
Man's Land, and then gradually spread back into our trenches. . . .
Bundles of oily cotton-waste were strewn along the German parapet and
set alight as a barrier to the gas. Then their batteries opened on our
lines. The confusion in the front trench must have been horrible; direct
hits broke several of the gas-cylinders, the trench filled with gas, the gas-
company stampeded."

By the end of August 1915, particulars of the coming offensive against La Bassée were beginning to leak through the young staff officers. The French civilians knew about it; and so, naturally, did the Germans. Every night now new batteries and lorry-trains of shells came rumbling up the Béthune-La Bassée road. Other signs of movement included sapping forward at Vermelles and Cambrin, where the lines lay too far apart for a quick rush across, and the joining up of the sap-heads to make a new front line. Also, orders for evacuation of hospitals; the appearance of cavalry and New Army divisions; issue of new types of weapons. Then Royal Engineer officers supervised the digging of pits at intervals along the front line. They were sworn not to reveal what these would hold, but we knew that it would be gas-cylinders. Ladders for climbing quickly out of trenches were brought up by the lorry-load and dumped at Cambrin village. As early as September 3rd, I had a bet with Robertson that our Division would attack from the Cambrin-Cuinchy line. When I went home on leave six days later, the sense of impending events had become so strong that I almost hated to go.

Leave came round for officers about every six or eight months in ordinary times; heavy casualties shortened the period, general offensive cut leave altogether. Only one officer in France ever refused to go on leave when his turn came—Colonel Cross of the Fifty-second Light Infantry (the Second Battalion of the Oxford and Bucks Light Infantry, which insisted on its original style as jealously as we kept our 'c' in Welch). Cross is alleged to have refused leave on the following grounds: 'My father fought with the Regiment in the South African War, and had no leave; my grandfather fought in the Crimea with the Regiment, and had no leave. I do not regard it in the Regimental tradition to take home-leave when on active service.' Cross, a professional survivor, was commanding the Battalion in 1917 when I last heard of him.

London seemed unreally itself. Despite the number of uniforms in the streets, the general indifference to, and ignorance about, the War surprised me. Enlistment still remained voluntary. The universal catch-word was 'Business as usual'. My family were living in London now, at the house formerly occupied by my uncle, Robert von Ranke, the German consul-general. He had been forced to leave in a hurry on

August 4th, 1914, and my mother undertook to look after the house for him while the War lasted. So when Edward Marsh rang me up from the Prime Minister's office at 10 Downing Street to arrange a meal, someone intervened and cut him off—the telephone of the German consul-general's sister was, of course, closely watched by the anti-espionage section of Scotland Yard. The Zeppelin scare had just begun. Some friends of the family came in one night, and began telling me of the Zeppelin air-raids, of bombs dropped only three streets off.

'Well, do you know,' I said, 'the other day I was asleep in a house and in the early morning a bomb dropped next door and killed three soldiers who were billeted there, a woman and a child.'

'Good gracious,' they cried, 'what did you do then?'

'It was at a place called Beuvry, about four miles behind the trenches,' I explained, 'and I was tired out, so I went to sleep again.'

'Oh,' they said, 'but that happened in France!' and the look of interest faded from their faces as though I had taken them in with a stupid catch.

'Yes,' I agreed, 'and it was only an aeroplane that dropped the bomb.'

I went up to Harlech for the rest of my leave, and walked about on the hills in an old shirt and a pair of shorts. When I got back to France, 'The Actor', a regular officer in 'A' Company, asked me: 'Had a good time on leave?'

'Yes.'

'Go to many dances?'

'Not one.'

'What shows did you go to?'

'I didn't go to any shows.'

'Hunt?'

'No.'

'Sleep with any nice girls?'

'No, I didn't. Sorry to disappoint you.'

'What the hell *did* you do, then?'

'Oh, I just walked about on some hills.'

'Good God,' he said, 'chaps like you don't deserve leave.'

On September 19th we relieved the Middlesex Regiment at Cambrin, and were told that these would be the trenches from which we attacked. The preliminary bombardment had already started, a week in advance. As I led my platoon into the line, I recognized with some disgust the same machine-gun shelter where I had seen the suicide on my first night in trenches. It seemed ominous. This was by far the heaviest bombardment from our own guns we had yet seen. The trenches shook properly, and a great cloud of drifting shell-smoke obscured the German line. Shells went over our heads in a steady stream; we had to shout to make our neighbors hear. Dying down a little at night, the racket began again every morning at dawn, a little louder each time. 'Damn it,' we said, 'there can't be a living soul left in those trenches.' But still it went on. The Germans retaliated, though not very vigorously. Most of their heavy artillery had been withdrawn from this sector, we were told, and sent across to the Russian front. More casualties came from our own shorts and blow-backs than from German shells. Much of the ammunition that our batteries were using was made in the United States and contained a high percentage of duds; the driving bands were always coming off. We had fifty casualties in the ranks and three officer casualties, including Buzz Off — badly wounded in the head. This happened before steel helmets were issued; we would not have lost nearly so many with those. I got two insignificant wounds on the hand, which I took as an omen of the right sort.

On the morning of the 23rd, Thomas came back from Battalion Headquarters carrying a note-book and six maps, one for each of us company officers. 'Listen,' he said, 'and copy out all this skite on the back of your maps. You'll have to explain it to your platoons this afternoon. Tomorrow morning we go back to dump our blankets, packs and greatcoats in Béthune. The next day, that's Saturday the 25th, we attack.' This being the first definitive news we had been given, we looked up half startled, half relieved. I still have the map, and these are the orders as I copied them down:—

'FIRST OBJECTIVE—*Les Briques Farm*—The big house plainly visible to our front, surrounded by trees. To reach this it is necessary to cross three lines of enemy trenches. The first is three hundred yards distant, the second four hundred, and the third about six hundred. We then cross two railways. Behind the second railway line is a German trench called the Brick Trench. Then comes the Farm, a strong place with moat and cellars and a kitchen garden strongly staked and wired.

'SECOND OBJECTIVE—*The Town of Auchy*—This is also plainly visible from our trenches. It is four hundred yards beyond the Farm and defended by a first line of trench half-way across, and a second line immediately in front of the town. When we have occupied the first line our direction is half-right, with the left of the Battalion directed on Tall Chimney.

'THIRD OBJECTIVE—*Village of Haisnes*—Conspicuous by high-spired church. Our eventual line will be taken up on the railway behind this village, where we will dig in and await reinforcements.'

When Thomas had reached this point, The Actor's shoulders were shaking with laughter.

'What's up?' asked Thomas irritably.

The Actor giggled: 'Who in God's name is responsible for this little effort?'

'Don't know,' Thomas said. 'Probably Paul the Pimp, or someone like that.' (Paul the Pimp was a captain on the Divisional Staff, young, inexperienced and much disliked. He 'wore red tabs upon his chest, and even on his undervest.') 'Between the six of us, but you youngsters must be careful not to let the men know, this is what they call a "subsidiary attack". There will be no troops in support. We've just got to go over and keep the enemy busy while the folk on our right do the real work. You notice that the bombardment is much heavier over there. They've knocked the Hohenzollern Redoubt to bits. Personally, I don't give a damn either way. We'll get killed whatever happens.'

We all laughed.

'All right, laugh now, but by God, on Saturday we've got to carry out this funny scheme.' I had never heard Thomas so talkative before.

'Sorry,' The Actor apologized, 'carry on with the dictation.'

Thomas went on:

> 'The attack will be preceded by forty minutes' discharge of the accessory,* which will clear the path for a thousand yards, so that the two railway lines will be occupied without difficulty. Our advance will follow closely behind the accessory. Behind us are three fresh divisions and the Cavalry Corps. It is expected we shall have no difficulty in breaking through. All men will parade with their platoons; pioneers, servants, etc., to be warned. All platoons to be properly told off under N.C.O.'s. Every N.C.O. is to know exactly what is expected of him, and when to take over command in case of casualties. Men who lose touch must join up with the nearest company or regiment and push on. Owing to the strength of the accessory, men should be warned against remaining too long in captured trenches where the accessory is likely to collect, but to keep to the open and above all to push on. It is important that if smoke-helmets have to be pulled down they must be tucked in under the shirt.'

The Actor interrupted again. 'Tell me, Thomas, do you believe in this funny accessory?'

Thomas said: 'It's damnable. It's not soldiering to use stuff like that, even though the Germans did start it. It's dirty, and it'll bring us bad luck. We're sure to bungle it. Look at those new gas-companies—sorry, excuse me this once, I mean accessory-companies—their very look makes

---

* The gas-cylinders had by this time been put into position on the front line. A special order came round imposing severe penalties on anyone who used any word but 'accessory' in speaking of the gas. This was to keep it secret, but the French civilians knew all about the scheme long before this.

me tremble. Chemistry-dons from London University, a few lads straight from school, one or two N.C.O.'s of the old-soldier type, trained together for three weeks, then given a job as responsible as this. Of course they'll bungle it. How could they do anything else? But let's be merry. I'm going on again:

'Men of company: what they are to carry:

Two hundred rounds of ammunition (bomb-throwers fifty, and signallers one hundred and fifty rounds).

Heavy tools carried in sling by the strongest men.

Waterproof sheet in belt.

Sandbag in right tunic-pocket.

Field-dressing and iodine.

Emergency ration, including biscuit.

One tube-helmet, to be worn when we advance, rolled up on the head. It must be quite secure and the top part turned down. If possible each man will be provided with an elastic band.

One smoke-helmet, old pattern, to be carried for preference behind the back, where it is least likely to be damaged by stray bullets, etc.

Wire-cutters, as many as possible, by wiring party and others, hedging gloves by wire party.

Platoon screens, for artillery observation, to be carried by a man in each platoon who is not carrying a tool.

Packs, capes, greatcoats, blankets will be dumped, not carried.

No one is to carry sketches of our position or anything to be likely of service to the enemy.

'That's all. I believe we're going over first with the Middlesex in support. If we get through the German wire I'll be satisfied. Our guns don't seem to be cutting it. Perhaps they're putting that off until the intense bombardment. Any questions?'

That afternoon I repeated the whole rigmarole to the platoon, and told them of the inevitable success attending our assault. They seemed to believe it. All except Sergeant Townsend. 'Do you say, Sir, that we have three divisions and the Cavalry Corps behind us?' he asked.

'Yes,' I answered.

'Well, excuse me, Sir, I'm thinking it's only those chaps on the right that'll get reinforcements. If we get half a platoon of Mons Angels,* that's about all we get.'

'Sergeant Townsend,' I said, 'you're a well-known pessimist. This is going to be a really good show.'

* According to the newspapers, a vision of angels had been seen by the British Army at Mons; but it was not vouchsafed to Sergeant Townsend, who had been there, with most of 'A' Company.

We spent the night repairing damaged trenches.

When morning came we were relieved by the Middlesex, and marched back to Béthune, where we dumped our spare kit at the Montmorency barracks. The Battalion officers messed together in the château near by. This billet was claimed at the same time by the staff of a New Army division, due to take part in the fighting next day. The argument ended amicably with the Division and Battalion messing together. It was, someone pointed out, like a brutal caricature of The Last Supper in duplicate. In the middle of the long table sat the two pseudo-Christs, our Colonel and the Divisional General. Everybody was drinking a lot; the subalterns, allowed whiskey for a treat, grew rowdy. They raised their glasses with: 'Cheerio, we will be messing together tomorrow night in La Bassée!' Only the company commanders were looking worried. I remember 'C' Company Commander especially, Captain A. L. Samson, biting his thumb and refusing to join in the excitement. I think it was Childe-Freeman of 'B' Company who said that night: 'The last time the Regiment visited these parts we were under decent leadership. Old Marlborough had more sense than to attack the La Bassée lines; he masked them and went around.'

The G.S.O. 1 of the New Army division, a staff-colonel, knew the Adjutant well. They had played polo together in India. I happened to be sitting opposite them. The G.S.O. 1 said, rather drunkenly: 'Charley, see that silly old woman over there? Calls himself General Commanding! Doesn't know where he is; doesn't know where his division is; can't even read a map properly. He's marched the poor sods off their feet and left his supplies behind, God knows how far back. They've had to use their iron rations and what they could pick up in the villages. And tomorrow he's going to fight a battle. Doesn't know anything about battles; the men have never been in trenches before, and tomorrow's going to be a glorious balls-up, and the day after tomorrow he'll be sent home.' Then he ended, quite seriously: 'Really, Charley, it's just as I say, no exaggeration. You mark my words!'

That night we marched back again to Cambrin. The men were singing. Being mostly from the Midlands, they sang comic songs rather than Welsh hymns: 'Slippery Sam', 'When We've Wound up the Watch on the Rhine', and 'I Do Like a S'nice S'mince Pie', to concertina accompaniment. The tune of the 'S'nice S'mince Pie' ran in my head all next day, and for the week following I could not get rid of it. The Second Welsh would never have sung a song like 'When We've Wound up the Watch on the Rhine'. Their only songs about the War were defeatist:

I want to go home,
I want to go home.
The coal-box and shrapnel they whistle and roar,
I don't want to go to the trenches no more,
I want to go over the sea
Where the Kayser can't shot bombs at me.
Oh, I
Don't want to die,
I want to go home.

There were several more verses in the same strain. Hewitt, the Welsh machine-gun officer, had written one in a more offensive spirit:

I want to go home,
I want to go home.
One day at Givenchy the week before last
The Allmands attacked and they nearly got past.
They pushed their way up to the Keep,
Through our maxim-gun sights we did peep,
Oh, my!
They let out a cry,
They never got home.

But the men would not sing it, though they all admired Hewitt.

The Béthune-La Bassée road was choked with troops, guns and transport, and we had to march miles north out of our way to circle round to Cambrin. Even so, we were held up two or three times by massed cavalry. Everything radiated confusion. A casualty clearing-station had been planted astride one of the principal cross-roads, and was already being shelled. By the time we reached Cambrin, the Battalion had marched about twenty miles that day. Then we heard that the Middlesex would go over first, with us in support; and to their left the Second Argyll and Sutherland Highlanders, with the Cameronians in support. The junior Royal Welch officers complained loudly at our not being given the honor of leading the attack. As the senior regiment, they protested, we were entitled to the 'Right of the Line'. An hour or so past midnight we moved into trench sidings just in front of the village. Half a mile of communication trench, known as 'Maison Rouge Alley', separated us from the firing line. At half-past five the gas would be discharged. We were cold, tired, sick, and not at all in the mood for a battle, but tried to snatch an hour or two of sleep squatting in the trench. It had been raining for some time.

A grey, watery dawn broke at last behind the German lines; the bombardment, surprisingly slack all night, brisked up a little. 'Why the devil don't they send them over quicker?' The Actor complained.

'This isn't my idea of a bombardment. We're getting nothing opposite us. What little there seems to be is going into the Hohenzollern.'

'Shell shortage. Expected it,' was Thomas's laconic reply.

We were told afterwards that on the 23rd a German aeroplane had bombed the Army Reserve shell-dump and sent it up. The bombardment on the 24th, and on the day of the battle itself, compared very poorly with that of the previous days. Thomas looked strained and ill. 'It's time they were sending that damned accessory off. I wonder what's doing.'

The events of the next few minutes are difficult for me now to sort out. I found it more difficult still at the time. All we heard back there in the sidings was a distant cheer, confused crackle of rifle-fire, yells, heavy shelling on our front line, more shouts and yells, and a continuous rattle of machine-guns. After a few minutes, lightly wounded men of the Middlesex came stumbling down Maison Rouge Alley to the dressing-station. I stood at the junction of the siding and the Alley.

'What's happened? What's happened?' I asked.

'Bloody balls-up,' was the most detailed answer I could get.

Among the wounded were a number of men yellow-faced and choking, their buttons tarnished green—gas cases. Then came the badly wounded. Maison Rouge Alley being narrow, the stretchers had difficulty in getting down. The Germans started shelling it with five-point-nines.

Thomas went back to Battalion Headquarters through the shelling to ask for orders. It was the same place that I had visited on my first night in the trenches. This cluster of dug-outs in the reserve line showed very plainly from the air as Battalion Headquarters, and should never have been occupied during a battle. Just before Thomas arrived, the Germans put five shells into it. The Adjutant jumped one way, the Colonel another, the R.S.M. a third. One shell went into the signals dug-out, killed some signallers and destroyed the telephone. The Colonel, slightly cut on the hand, joined the stream of wounded and was carried back as far as the base with it. The Adjutant took command.

Meanwhile 'A' Company had been waiting in the siding for the rum to arrive; the tradition of every attack being a double tot of rum beforehand. All the other companies got theirs. The Actor began cursing: 'Where the bloody hell's that storeman gone?' We fixed bayonets in readiness to go up and attack as soon as Captain Thomas returned with orders. Hundreds of wounded streamed by. At last Thomas's orderly appeared. 'Captain's orders, Sir: "A" Company to move up to the front line.' At that moment the storeman arrived, without rifle or equipment, hugging the rum-bottle, red-faced and retching. He staggered up to The Actor and said: 'There you are, Sir!', then fell on his face in the thick mud of a sump-pit at the junction of the trench and the siding. The stopper of the bottle flew out and what remained of the three gallons bubbled on the ground. The Actor made no reply. This was a crime that deserved the death penalty. He put one foot on the storeman's neck, the other in the small of his back, and trod him into the mud. Then he gave the order 'Company forward!' The Company advanced with a clatter of steel, and this was the last I ever heard of the storeman.

It seems that at half-past four an R.E. captain commanding the gas-company in the front line phoned through to Divisional Headquarters: 'Dead calm. Impossible discharge accessory.' The answer he got was: 'Accessory to be discharged at all costs.' Thomas had not over-estimated the gas-company's efficiency. The spanners for unscrewing the cocks of the cylinders proved, with two or three exceptions, to be misfits. The gas-men rushed about shouting for the loan of an ad-justable spanner. They managed to discharge one or two cylinders; the gas went whistling out, formed a thick cloud a few yards off in No Man's Land, and then gradually spread back into our trenches. The Germans, who had been expecting gas, immediately put on their gas-helmets: semi-rigid ones, better than ours. Bundles of oily cotton-waste were strewn along the German parapet and set alight as a barrier to the gas. Then their batteries opened on our lines. The confusion in the front trench must have been horrible; direct hits broke several of the gas-cylinders, the trench filled with gas, the gas-company stampeded.

No orders could come through because the shell in the signals dug-out at Battalion Headquarters had cut communication not only be-tween companies and Battalion, but between Battalion and Division. The officers in the front trench had to decide on immediate action; so two companies of the Middlesex, instead of waiting for the intense bombardment which would follow the advertised forty minutes of gas, charged at once and got held up by the German wire—which our artillery had not yet cut. So far it had only been treated with shrapnel, which made no effect on it; barbed wire needed high-explosive, and plenty of it. The Germans shot the Middlesex men down. One pla-toon is said to have found a gap and got into the German trench. But there were no survivors of the platoon to confirm this. The Argyll and Sutherland Highlanders went over, too, on the Middlesex left; but two companies, instead of charging at once, rushed back out of the gas-filled assault trench to the support line, and attacked from there. It will be recalled that the trench system had been pushed forward nearer the enemy in preparation for the battle. These companies were therefore attacking from the old front line, but the barbed-wire entanglements protecting it had not been removed, so that the Highlanders got caught and machine-gunned between their own assault and support lines. The other two companies were equally unsuccessful. When the attack started, the German N.C.O.'s had jumped up on the parapet to encourage their men. These were Jägers, famous for their musketry.

The survivors of the two leading Middlesex companies now lay in shell-craters close to the German wire, sniping and making the Germans keep their heads down. They had bombs to throw, but these were nearly all of a new type issued for the battle. The fuses were lighted on the match-box principle, and the rain had made them useless. The other two companies of the Middlesex soon followed in support. Machine-gun fire stopped them half-way. Only one German machine-gun remained in action, the others having been knocked out by rifle- or trench-mortar fire. Why the single gun survived is a story in itself.

It starts with the privilege granted British colonial governors and high-commissioners of nominating one or two officers from their countries for attachment in wartime to the Regular Army. Under this scheme, the officers began as full lieutenants. The Captain-General of Jamaica (if that is his correct style) nominated the eighteen-year-old son of a rich planter, who went straight from Kingston to the First Middlesex. He was good-hearted enough, but of little use in the trenches, having never been out of the island in his life or, except for a short service with the West India militia, seen any soldiering. His company commander took a fatherly interest in 'Young Jamaica', and tried to teach him his duties. This Company Commander was known as 'The Boy'. He had twenty years' service with the Middlesex, and the unusual boast of having held every rank from 'boy' to captain in the same company. His father, I believe, had been the regimental sergeant-major. But 'Jamaica', as a full lieutenant, ranked senior to the other experienced subalterns in the company, who were only second-lieutenants.

The Middlesex Colonel decided to shift Jamaica off on some course of extra-regimental appointment at the earliest opportunity. Somewhere about May or June, when instructed to supply an officer for the brigade trench-mortar company, he had sent Jamaica. Trench-mortars, being then both dangerous and ineffective, the appointment seemed suitable. At the same time, the Royal Welch had also been asked to detail an officer, and the Colonel had sent Tiley, an ex-planter from

Malaya, and what is called a 'fine natural soldier'. Tiley was chosen because, when attached to us from a Lancashire regiment, he had showed his resentment at the manner of his welcome somewhat too plainly. But, by September, mortars had improved in design and become an important infantry arm; so Jamaica, being senior to Tiley, held the responsible position of Brigade Mortar Officer.

When the Middlesex charged, The Boy fell mortally wounded as he climbed over the parapet. He tumbled back and began crawling down the trench to the stretcher-bearer's dug-out, past Jamaica's trench-mortar emplacement. Jamaica had lost his gun-team, and was boldly serving the trench-mortars himself. On seeing The Boy, however, he deserted his post and ran off to fetch a stretcher-party. Tiley, meanwhile, on the other flank opposite Mine Point, had knocked out all the machine-guns within range. He went on until his mortar burst. Only one machine-gun in the Pope's Nose, a small salient facing Jamaica, remained active.

At this point the Royal Welch Fusiliers came up Maison Rouge Alley. The Germans were shelling it with five-nines (called 'Jack Johnsons' because of the black smoke) and lachrymatory shells. This caused a continual scramble backwards and forwards, to cries of: 'Come on!' 'Get back, you bastards!' 'Gas turning on us!' 'Keep your heads, you men!' 'Back like hell, boys!' 'Whose orders?' 'What's happening?' 'Gas!' 'Back!' 'Come on!' 'Gas!' 'Back!' Wounded men and stretcher-bearers kept trying to squeeze past. We were alternately putting on and taking off our gas-helmets, which made things worse. In many places the trench had caved in, obliging us to scramble over the top. Childe-Freeman reached the front line with only fifty men of 'B' Company; the rest had lost their way in some abandoned trenches half-way up.

The Adjutant met him in the support line. 'Ready to go over, Freeman?' he asked.

Freeman had to admit that most of his company were missing. He felt this disgrace keenly; it was the first time that he had commanded a company in battle. Deciding to go over with his fifty men in support of the Middlesex, he blew his whistle and the company charged. They were stopped by machine-gun fire before they had got through our own entanglements. Freeman himself died—oddly enough, of heart-failure—as he stood on the parapet.

A few minutes later, Captain Samson, with 'C' Company and the remainder of 'B', reached our front line. Finding the gas-cylinders still whistling and the trench full of dying men, he decided to go over too —he could not have it said that the Royal Welch had let down the

Middlesex. A strong, comradely feeling bound the Middlesex and the Royal Welch, intensified by the accident that the other three battalions in the Brigade were Scottish, and that our Scottish Brigadier was, unjustly no doubt, accused of favoring them. Our Adjutant voiced the extreme non-Scottish view: 'The Jocks are all the same; both the trousered kind and the bare-arsed kind: they're dirty in trenches, they skite too much, and they charge like hell—both ways.' The First Middlesex, who were the original 'Diehards', had more than once, with the Royal Welch, considered themselves let down by the Jocks. So Samson charged with 'C' and the remainder of 'B' Company.

One of 'C' officers told me later what happened. It had been agreed to advance by platoon rushes with supporting fire. When his platoon had gone about twenty yards, he signalled them to lie down and open covering fire. The din was tremendous. He saw the platoon on his left flopping down too, so he whistled the advance again. Nobody seemed to hear. He jumped up from his shell-hole, waved and signalled 'Forward!'

Nobody stirred.

He shouted: 'You bloody cowards, are you leaving me to go on alone?'

His platoon-sergeant, groaning with a broken shoulder, gasped: 'Not cowards, Sir. Willing enough. But they're all f—ing dead.' The Pope's Nose machine-gun, traversing, had caught them as they rose to the whistle.

'A' Company, too, had become separated by the shelling. I was with the leading platoon. The Surrey-man got a touch of gas and went coughing back. The Actor accused him of skrimshanking. This I thought unfair; the Surrey-man looked properly sick. I don't know what happened to him, but I heard that the gas-poisoning was not serious and that he managed, a few months later, to get back to his own regiment in France. I found myself with The Actor in a narrow communication trench between the front and support lines. This trench had not been built wide enough for a stretcher to pass the bends. We came on The Boy lying on his stretcher, wounded in the lungs and stomach. Jamaica was standing over him in tears, blubbering: 'Poor old Boy, poor old Boy, he's going to die; I'm sure he is. He's the only one who treated me decently.'

The Actor, finding that we could not get by, said to Jamaica: 'Take that poor sod out of the way, will you? I've got to get my company up. Put him into a dug-out, or somewhere.'

Jamaica made no answer; he seemed paralyzed by the horror of the occasion and could only repeat: 'Poor old Boy, poor old Boy!'

'Look here,' said The Actor, 'if you can't shift him into a dug-out we'll have to lift him on top of the trench. He can't live now, and we're late getting up.'

'No, no,' Jamaica shouted wildly.

The Actor lost his temper and shook Jamaica roughly by the shoulders. 'You're the bloody trench-mortar wallah, aren't you?' he shouted.

Jamaica nodded miserably.

'Well, your battery is a hundred yards from here. Why the hell aren't you using your gas-pipes to some purpose? Buzz off back to them!' And he kicked him down the trench. Then he called over his shoulder: 'Sergeant Rose and Corporal Jennings! Lift this stretcher up across the top of the trench. We've got to pass.'

Jamaica leaned against a traverse. 'I do think you're the most heartless beast I've ever met,' he said weakly.

We went up to the corpse-strewn front line. The captain of the gas-company, who was keeping his head, and wore a special oxygen respirator, had by now turned off the gas-cocks. Vermorel-sprayers had cleared out most of the gas, but we were still warned to wear our masks. We climbed up and crouched on the fire-step, where the gas was not so thick—gas, being heavy stuff, kept low. Then Thomas arrived with the remainder of 'A' Company and with 'D', we waited for the whistle to follow the other two companies over. Fortunately at this moment the Adjutant appeared. He was now left in command of the Battalion, and told Thomas that he didn't care a damn about orders; he was going to cut his losses and not send 'A' and 'D' over to their deaths until he got definite orders from Brigade. He had sent a runner back, and we must wait.

Meanwhile, the intense bombardment that was to follow the forty minutes' discharge of gas began. It concentrated on the German front trench and wire. A good many shells fell short, and we had further casualties from them. In No Man's Land, the survivors of the Middlesex and of our 'B' and 'C' Companies suffered heavily.

My mouth was dry, my eyes out of focus, and my legs quaking under me. I found a water-bottle full of rum and drank about half a pint; it quieted me, and my head remained clear. Samson lay groaning about twenty yards beyond the front trench. Several attempts were made to rescue him. He had been very badly hit. Three men got killed in these attempts; two officers and two men, wounded. In the end his own orderly managed to crawl out to him. Samson sent him back, saying that he was riddled through and not worth rescuing; he sent his apologies to the Company for making such a noise.

We waited a couple of hours for the order to charge. The men were silent and depressed; only Sergeant Townsend was making feeble, bitter jokes about the good old British Army muddling through, and how he thanked God we still had a Navy. I shared the rest of my rum with him, and he cheered up a little. Finally a runner arrived with a message that the attack had been postponed.

Rumors came down the trench of a disaster similar to our own in the brick-stack sector, where the Fifth Brigade had gone over; and again at Givenchy, where men of the Sixth Brigade at the Duck's Bill salient had fought their way into the enemy trenches, but been repulsed, their supply of bombs failing. It was said, however, that things were better on the right, where there had been a slight wind to take the gas over. According to one rumor, the First, Seventh and Forty-seventh Divisions had broken through.

My memory of that day is hazy. We spent it getting the wounded down to the dressing-station, spraying the trenches and dug-outs to get rid of the gas, and clearing away the earth where trenches were blocked. The trenches stank with a gas-blood-lyddite-latrine smell. Late in the afternoon we watched through our field-glasses the advance of reserves under heavy shell-fire towards Loos and Hill 70; it looked like a real break-through. They were troops of the New Army division whose staff we had messed with the night before. Immediately to the right of us we had the Highland Division. Ian Hay has celebrated their exploits on that day in *The First Hundred Thousand;* I suppose that we were 'the flat caps on the left' who 'let down' his comrades-in-arms.

At dusk, we all went out to rescue the wounded, leaving only sentries in the line. The first dead body I came upon was Samson's, hit in seventeen places. I found that he had forced his knuckles into his mouth to stop himself crying out and attracting more men to their death. Major Swainson, the Second-in-command of the Middlesex, came crawling along from the German wire. He seemed to be wounded in lungs, stomach, and one leg. Choate, a Middlesex second-lieutenant, walked back unhurt; together we bandaged Swainson and got him into the trench and on a stretcher. He begged me to loosen his belt; I cut it with a bowie-knife I had bought at Béthune for use during the battle. He said: 'I'm about done for.'* We spent all that night getting in the wounded of the Royal Welch, the Middlesex

---

* Major Swainson recovered and was at the Middlesex Depôt again after a few weeks. On the other hand, Lawrie, a Royal Welch quartermaster-sergeant back at Cambrin, was hit in the neck that day by a spent machine-gun bullet which just pierced the skin, and died of shock a few hours later.

and those Argyll and Sutherland Highlanders who had attacked from the front trench. The Germans behaved generously. I do not remember hearing a shot fired that night, though we kept on until it was nearly dawn and we could see plainly; then they fired a few warning shots, and we gave it up. By this time we had recovered all the wounded, and most of the Royal Welch dead. I was surprised at some of the attitudes in which the dead had stiffened—bandaging friends' wounds, crawling, cutting wire. The Argyll and Sutherland had seven hundred casualties, including fourteen officers killed out of the sixteen who went over; the Middlesex, five hundred and fifty casualties, including eleven officers killed.

Two other Middlesex officers besides Choate came back unwounded; their names were Henry and Hill, recently commissioned second-lieutenants, who had been lying out in shell-holes all day under the rain, sniping and being sniped at. Henry, according to Hill, had dragged five wounded men into a shell-hole and thrown up a sort of parapet with his hands and the bowie-knife which he carried. Hill had his platoon-sergeant there, screaming with a stomach wound, begging for morphia; he was done for, so Hill gave him five pellets. We always took morphia in our pockets for emergencies like that.

Choate, Henry and Hill, returning to the trenches with a few stragglers, reported at the Middlesex Headquarters. Hill told me the story. The Colonel and the Adjutant were sitting down to a meat pie when he and Henry arrived. Henry said: 'Come to report, Sir. Ourselves and about ninety men of all companies. Mr. Choate is back, unwounded too.'

They looked up dully. 'So you've survived, have you?' the Colonel said. 'Well, all the rest are dead. I suppose Mr. Choate had better command what's left of "A" Company; the Bombing Officer will command what's left of "B" (the Bombing Officer had not gone over, but remained with Headquarters); Mr. Henry goes to "C" Company. Mr. Hill to "D". The Royal Welch are holding the front line. We are here in support. Let me know where to find you if you're needed. Good night.'

Not having been offered a piece of meat pie or a drink of whiskey, they saluted and went miserably out.

The Adjutant called them back. 'Mr. Hill! Mr. Henry!'
'Sir?'

Hill said that he expected a change of mind as to the propriety with which hospitality could be offered by a regular colonel and adjutant to temporary second-lieutenants in distress. But it was only: 'Mr. Hill, Mr. Henry, I saw some men in the trench just now with their shoulder-straps unbuttoned and their equipment fastened anyhow. See that this does not occur in future. That's all.'

Henry heard the Colonel from his bunk complaining that he had only two blankets and that it was a deucedly cold night.

Choate, a newspaper reporter in peacetime, arrived a few minutes later; the others had told him of their reception. After having saluted and reported that Major Swainson, hitherto thought killed, was wounded and on the way down to the dressing-station, he boldly leaned over the table, cut a large piece of meat pie and began eating it. This caused such surprise that no further conversation took place. Choate finished his meat pie and drank a glass of whiskey; saluted, and joined the others.

Meanwhile, I took command of what remained of 'B' Company. Only six company officers survived in the Royal Welch. Next day we were down to five. Thomas was killed by a sniper while despondently watching through field-glasses the return of the New Army troops on the right. Pushed blindly into the gap made by the advance of the Seventh and Forty-seventh Divisions on the previous afternoon, they did not know where they were or what they were supposed to do. Their ration supply broke down, so they flocked back, not in panic, but stupidly, like a crowd returning from a cup final, with shrapnel bursting above them. We could scarcely believe our eyes, it was so odd.

Thomas need not have been killed; but everything had gone so wrong that he seemed not to care one way or the other. The Actor took command of 'A' Company. We lumped 'A' and 'B' Companies together after a couple of days, for the sake of relieving each other on night watch and getting some sleep. I agreed to take the first watch, waking him up at midnight. When the time came, I shook him, shouted in his ear, poured water over him, banged his head against the side of the bed. Finally I threw him on the floor. I was desperate for a lie-down myself, but he had attained a depth of sleep from which nothing could rouse him; so I heaved him back on the bunk, and had to finish the night without relief. Even 'Stand-to!' failed to wake him. In the end I got him out of bed at nine o'clock in the morning, and he was furious with me for not having called him at midnight.

We had spent the day after the attack carrying the dead down for burial and cleaning the trench up as best we could. That night the Middlesex held the line, while the Royal Welch carried all the unbroken gas-cylinders along to a position on the left flank of the Brigade, where they were to be used on the following night, September 27th. This was worse than carrying the dead; the cylinders were cast-iron, heavy and hateful. The men cursed and sulked. The officers alone knew of the proposed attack; the men must not be told until just beforehand. I felt like screaming. Rain was still pouring down, harder than ever. We knew definitely, this time, that ours would be only a diversion to help a division on our right make the real attack.

The scheme was the same as before: at 4 p.m. gas would be discharged for forty minutes, and after a quarter of an hour's bombardment we should attack. I broke the news to the men about three o'clock. They took it well. The relations of officers and men, and of senior and junior officers, had been very different in the excitement of battle. There had been no insubordination, but a greater freedom of speech, as though we were all drunk together. I found myself calling the Adjutant 'Charley' on one occasion; he appeared not to mind in the least. For the next ten days my relations with my men were like those I had in the Welsh Regiment; later, discipline reasserted itself, and it was only occasionally that I found them intimate.

At 4 p.m., then, the gas went off again with a strong wind; the gasmen had brought enough spanners this time. The Germans stayed absolutely silent. Flares went up from the reserve lines, and it looked as though all the men in the front trench were dead. The Brigadier decided not to take too much for granted; after the bombardment he sent out a Cameronian officer and twenty-five men as a feeling-patrol. The patrol reached the German wire; there came a burst of machine-gun and rifle-fire, and only two wounded men regained the trench.

We waited on the fire-step from four to nine o'clock, with fixed bayonets, for the order to go over. My mind was a blank, except for the recurrence of 'S'nice S'mince Spie, S'nice S'mince Spie . . . I don't like ham, lamb or jam, and I don't like roly-poly . . .'

The men laughed at my singing. The acting C.S.M. said: 'It's murder, Sir.'

'Of course, it's murder, you bloody fool,' I agreed. 'And there's nothing else for it, is there?' It was still raining. 'But when I sees a s'nice s'mince spie, I asks for a helping twice . . .'

At nine o'clock Brigade called off the attack; we were told to hold ourselves in readiness to go over at dawn.

No new order came at dawn, and no more attacks were promised us after this. From the morning of September 24th to the night of October 3rd, I had in all eight hours of sleep. I kept myself awake and alive by drinking about a bottle of whiskey a day. I had never drunk it before, and have seldom drunk it since; it certainly helped me then. We had no blankets, greatcoats, or waterproof sheets, nor any time or material to build new shelters. The rain continued. Every night we went out to fetch in the dead of the other battalions. The Germans continued indulgent and we had very few casualties. After the first day or two the corpses swelled and stank. I vomited more than once while superintending the carrying. Those we could not get in from the German wire continued to swell until the wall of the stomach collapsed, either naturally or when punctured by a bullet; a disgusting smell would float across. The color of the dead faces changed from white to yellow-grey, to red, to purple, to green, to black, to slimy.

On the morning of the 27th a cry arose from No Man's Land. A wounded soldier of the Middlesex had recovered consciousness after two days. He lay close to the German wire. Our men heard it and looked at each other. We had a tender-hearted lance-corporal named Baxter. He was the man to boil up a special dixie for the sentries of his section when they came off duty. As soon as he heard the wounded man's cries, he ran along the trench calling for a volunteer to help him fetch him in. Of course, no one would go; it was death to put one's head over the parapet. When he came running to ask me, I excused myself as being the only officer in the Company. I would come out with him at dusk, I said—not now. So he went alone. He jumped quickly over the parapet, then strolled across No Man's Land, waving a handkerchief; the Germans fired to frighten him, but since he persisted they let him come up close. Baxter continued towards them and, when he got to the Middlesex man, stopped and pointed to show the Germans what he was at. Then he dressed the man's wounds, gave him a drink of rum and some biscuit that he had with him, and promised to be back again at nightfall. He did come back, with a stretcher-party, and the man eventually recovered. I recommended Baxter for the Victoria Cross, being the only officer who had witnessed the action, but the authorities thought it worth no more than a Distinguished Conduct Medal.

The Actor and I had decided to get in touch with the battalion on our right. It was the Tenth Highland Light Infantry. I went down their trench sometime in the morning of the 27th and walked nearly a quarter of a mile without seeing either a sentry or an officer. There were dead men, sleeping men, wounded men, gassed men, all lying anyhow. The trench had been used as a latrine. Finally I met a Royal Engineer officer who said: 'If the Boche knew what an easy job he had, he'd just walk over and take the position.'

So I reported to The Actor that we might find our flank in the air at any moment. We converted the communication trench which made the boundary between the two battalions into a fire-trench facing right; and mounted a machine-gun to put up a barrage in case the Highlanders ran. On the night of the 27th they mistook some of our men, who were out in No Man's Land getting in the dead, for the enemy, and began firing wildly. The Germans retaliated. Our men caught the infection, but were at once ordered to cease fire. 'Cease fire!' went along the trench until it reached the H.L.I., who misheard it as 'Retire!' A panic seized them and they went rushing away, fortunately down the trench, instead of over the top. They were stopped by Sergeant McDonald of the Fifth Scottish Rifles, a pretty reliable territorial battalion now in support to ourselves and the Middlesex. He chased them back at the point of the bayonet; and was decorated for this feat.

On the 3rd of October we were relieved by a composite battalion consisting of about a hundred men of the Second Warwickshire Regiment and about seventy Royal Welch Fusiliers—all that was left of our own First Battalion. Hanmer Jones and Frank Jones-Bateman were both seriously wounded. Frank had his thigh broken with a rifle bullet while stripping the equipmnt off a wounded man in No Man's Land; the cartridges in the man's pouches had been set on fire by a shot and were exploding.* We went back to Sailly la Bourse for a couple of days, where the Colonel rejoined us with his bandaged hand; and then farther back to Annezin, a little village near Béthune, where I lodged in a two-roomed cottage with a withered old woman called Adelphine Heu.

george orwell

a hanging

George Orwell (1903-1950) was born in India and went to Eton. From 1922 to 1928 he served in the Imperial Police in Burma—an experience, as one can tell from this powerful sketch of the hanging of a native, that made it impossible for him ever again to see imperialism from the traditional point of view of a white "master race." Perhaps as a result of his early experiences as a colonial policeman, Orwell then made a point of living in the poorest and most miserable sections of Paris, and in later years, was a volunteer on the Republican side in the Spanish Civil War, where he was severely wounded. Orwell was so incensed by the treacherous part that the Communists played in the Civil War that he became an increasingly bitter critic of Soviet totalitarianism, and his

* He was recommended for a Victoria Cross, but got nothing because no officer evidence, which is a condition of award, was available.

most famous work, *1984,* is perhaps the most imaginatively powerful indictment of totalitarianism, in a novel, that has been written in our day.

"A Hanging" is an extraordinarily effective piece of writing. It presents the author in his old occupation of policeman as if he were studiously neutral in the business of escorting a Hindu to his death. (No doubt the man was hanged for committing a serious crime, perhaps murder; but it is extraordinary how Orwell manages to suggest that he is being hanged simply because he is a native, a lower order of human being.) Nowhere, until the very end of this sketch, is there any overt complaint on Orwell's part against the ghastly business of seeing a prisoner (whatever his crime) to his death. Yet if you look at the images with which Orwell builds up the atmosphere of the execution, you can see the dismay and even the horror that he actually feels.

The effect of "A Hanging" lies in the difference that Orwell is able to convey between the condemned man and his guards; between the utterly pitiful and wretched man who is described as insignificant and silent and all those others, healthy and cheerful, who can't wait to get the execution over so that they can resume their normal routine. With his brilliant instinct for noticing every possible shade of difference between the condemned man and his guards, Orwell even describes the prisoner, who "was a Hindu, a puny wisp of a man, with a shaven head and vague liquid eyes," being escorted by six tall Indian warders who were guarding him "like men handling a fish which is still alive and may jump back into the water."

The cruelty of existing relationships between man and man has never been presented so graphically. On their way to the gallows, "A dreadful thing had happened—a dog . . . had appeared in the yard . . . it had made a dash for the prisoner and, jumping up, tried to lick his face." "Dreadful" from whose point of view? Obviously from that of authority, from those who wish only to get their prisoner hanged and disposed of forever. But "dreadful," used in this ironic way, also communicates to us Orwell's conviction that the experience he has been describing *is* dreadful. And this awareness, on our part, is the measure of Orwell's achievement. He has succeeded in making us feel what he wants us to feel.

It was in Burma, a sodden morning of the rains. A sickly light, like yellow tinfoil, was slanting over the high walls into the jail yard. We were waiting outside the condemned cells, a row of sheds fronted with

A HANGING: From *Shooting An Elephant And Other Essays* by George Orwell. Copyright 1945, 1946, 1949, 1950 by Sonia Brownell Orwell. Reprinted by permission of Harcourt, Brace & World, Inc., and Martin Secker & Warburg Ltd.

double bars, like small animal cages. Each cell measured about ten feet by ten and was quite bare within except for a plank bed and a pot for drinking water. In some of them brown silent men were squatting at the inner bars, with their blankets draped round them. These were the condemned men, due to be hanged within the next week or two.

One prisoner had been brought out of his cell. He was a Hindu, a puny wisp of a man, with a shaven head and vague liquid eyes. He had a thick, sprouting moustache, absurdly too big for his body, rather like the moustache of a comic man on the films. Six tall Indian warders were guarding him and getting him ready for the gallows. Two of them stood by with rifles and fixed bayonets, while the others hand-cuffed him, passed a chain through his handcuffs and fixed it to their belts, and lashed his arms tight to his sides. They crowded very close about him, with their hands always on him in a careful, caressing grip, as though all the while feeling him to make sure he was there. It was like men handling a fish which is still alive and may jump back into the water. But he stood quite unresisting, yielding his arms limply to the ropes, as though he hardly noticed what was happening.

Eight o'clock and a bugle call, desolately thin in the wet air, floated from the distant barracks. The superintendent of the jail, who was standing apart from the rest of us, moodily prodding the gravel with his stick, raised his head at the sound. He was an army doctor, with a grey toothbrush moustache and a gruff voice. "For God's sake hurry up, Francis," he said irritably. "The man ought to have been dead by this time. Aren't you ready yet?"

Francis, the head jailer, a fat Dravidian in a white drill suit and gold spectacles, waved his black hand. "Yes sir, yes sir," he bubbled. "All iss satisfactorily prepared. The hangman iss waiting. We shall proceed."

"Well, quick march, then. The prisoners can't get their breakfast till this job's over."

We set out for the gallows. Two warders marched on either side of the prisoner, with their rifles at the slope; two others marched close against him, gripping him by arm and shoulder, as though at once pushing and supporting him. The rest of us, magistrates and the like, followed behind. Suddenly, when we had gone ten yards, the procession stopped short without any order or warning. A dreadful thing had happened—a dog, come goodness knows whence, had appeared in the yard. It came bounding among us with a loud volley of barks, and leapt round us wagging its whole body, wild with glee at finding so many human beings together. It was a large woolly dog, half Airedale, half pariah. For a moment it pranced round us, and then, before any-one could stop it, it had made a dash for the prisoner and, jumping up, tried to lick his face. Everyone stood aghast, too taken aback even to grab at the dog.

"Who let that bloody brute in here?" said the superintendent angrily. "Catch it, someone!"

A warder, detached from the escort, charged clumsily after the dog, but it danced and gambolled just out of his reach, taking everything as part of the game. A young Eurasian jailer picked up a handful of gravel and tried to stone the dog away, but it dodged the stones and came after us again. Its yaps echoed from the jail walls. The prisoner, in the grasp of the two warders, looked on incuriously, as though this was another formality of the hanging. It was several minutes before someone managed to catch the dog. Then we put my handkerchief through its collar and moved off once more, with the dog still straining and whimpering.

It was about forty yards to the gallows. I watched the bare brown back of the prisoner marching in front of me. He walked clumsily with his bound arms, but quite steadily, with that bobbing gait of the Indian who never straightens his knees. At each step his muscles slid neatly into place, the lock of hair on his scalp danced up and down, his feet printed themselves on the wet gravel. And once, in spite of the men who gripped him by each shoulder, he stepped slightly aside to avoid a puddle on the path.

It is curious, but till that moment I had never realized what it means to destroy a healthy, conscious man. When I saw the prisoner step aside to avoid the puddle I saw the mystery, the unspeakable wrongness, of cutting a life short when it is in full tide. This man was not dying, he was alive just as we are alive. All the organs of his body were working —bowels digesting food, skin renewing itself, nails growing, tissues forming—all toiling away in solemn foolery. His nails would still be growing when he stood on the drop, when he was falling through the air with a tenth-of-a-second to live. His eyes saw the yellow gravel and the grey walls, and his brain still remembered, foresaw, reasoned— reasoned even about puddles. He and we were a party of men walking together, seeing, feeling, understanding the same world; and in two minutes, with a sudden snap, one of us would be gone—one mind less, one world less.

The gallows stood in a small yard, separate from the main grounds of the prison, and overgrown with tall prickly weeds. It was a brick erection like three sides of a shed, with planking on top, and above that two beams and a crossbar with the rope dangling. The hangman, a grey-haired convict in the white uniform of the prison, was waiting beside his machine. He greeted us with a servile crouch as we entered.

At a word from Francis the two warders, gripping the prisoner more closely than ever, half led half pushed him to the gallows and helped him clumsily up the ladder. Then the hangman climbed up and fixed the rope round the prisoner's neck.

We stood waiting, five yards away. The warders had formed in a rough circle round the gallows. And then, when the noose was fixed, the prisoner began crying out to his god. It was a high, reiterated cry of "Ram! Ram! Ram! Ram!" not urgent and fearful like a prayer or cry for help, but steady, rhythmical, almost like the tolling of a bell. The dog answered the sound with a whine. The hangman, still standing on the gallows, produced a small cotton bag like a flour bag and drew it down over the prisoner's face. But the sound, muffled by the cloth, still persisted, over and over again: "Ram! Ram! Ram! Ram! Ram!"

The hangman climbed down and stood ready, holding the lever. Minutes seemed to pass. The steady, muffled crying from the prisoner went on and on, "Ram! Ram! Ram!" never faltering for an instant. The superintendent, his head on his chest, was slowly poking the ground with his stick; perhaps he was counting the cries, allowing the prisoner a fixed number—fifty, perhaps, or a hundred. Everyone had changed color. The Indians had gone grey like bad coffee, and one or two of the bayonets were wavering. We looked at the lashed, hooded man on the drop, and listened to his cries—each cry another second of life; the same thought was in all our minds: oh, kill him quickly, get it over, stop that abominable noise!

Suddenly the superintendent made up his mind. Throwing up his head he made a swift motion with his stick. "Chalo!" he shouted almost fiercely.

There was a clanking noise, and then dead silence. The prisoner had vanished, and the rope was twisting on itself. I let go of the dog, and it galloped immediately to the back of the gallows; but when it got there it stopped short, barked, and then retreated into a corner of the yard, where it stood among the weeds, looking timorously out at us. We went round the gallows to inspect the prisoner's body. He was dangling with his toes pointed straight downwards, very slowly revolving, as dead as a stone.

The superintendent reached out with his stick and poked the bare brown body; it oscillated slightly. *"He's* all right," said the superintendent. He backed out from under the gallows, and blew out a deep breath. The moody look had gone out of his face quite suddenly. He glanced at his wrist-watch. "Eight minutes past eight. Well, that's all for this morning, thank God."

The warders unfixed bayonets and marched away. The dog, sobered and conscious of having misbehaved itself, slipped after them. We walked out of the gallows yard, past the condemned cells with their waiting prisoners, into the big central yard of the prison. The convicts, under the command of warders armed with lathis, were already receiving their breakfast. They squatted in long rows, each man holding a tin panikin, while two warders with buckets marched round ladling out rice; it seemed quite a homely, jolly scene, after the hanging. An enormous relief had come upon us now that the job was done. One felt an impulse to sing, to break into a run, to snigger. All at once everyone began chattering gaily.

The Eurasian boy walking beside me nodded towards the way we had come, with a knowing smile: "Do you know, sir, our friend [he meant the dead man] when he heard his appeal had been dismissed, he pissed on the floor of his cell. From fright. Kindly take one of my cigarettes, sir. Do you not admire my new silver case, sir? From the boxwalah, two rupees eight annas. Classy European style."

Several people laughed—at what, nobody seemed certain.

Francis was walking by the superintendent, talking garrulously: "Well, sir, all hass passed off with the utmost satisfactoriness. It was all finished—flick! like that. It iss not always so—oah, no! I have known cases where the doctor wass obliged to go beneath the gallows and pull the prissoner's legs to ensure decease. Most disagreeable!"

"Wriggling about, eh? That's bad," said the superintendent.

"Ach, sir, it iss worse when they become refractory! One man, I recall, clung to the bars of hiss cage when we went to take him out. You will scarcely credit, sir, that it took six warders to dislodge him, three pulling at each leg. We reasoned with him. 'My dear fellow,' we said, 'think of all the pain and trouble you are causing to us!' But no, he would not listen! Ach, he wass very troublesome!"

I found that I was laughing quite loudly. Everyone was laughing. Even the superintendent grinned in a tolerant way. "You'd better all come out and have a drink," he said quite genially. "I've got a bottle of whisky in the car. We could do with it."

We went through the big double gates of the prison into the road. "Pulling at his legs!" exclaimed a Burmese magistrate suddenly, and burst into a loud chuckling. We all began laughing again. At that moment Francis' anecdote seemed extraordinarily funny. We all had a drink together, native and European alike, quite amicably. The dead man was a hundred yards away.

s. j. perelman

---

no starch in the dhoti,
s'il vous plaît

S(idney) J(oseph) Perelman was born in Brooklyn in 1904, graduated from Brown University, and is famous as a writer of humor for *The New Yorker* and as the author of the best Marx Brothers comedies.

Perelman is one of the greatest parodists in the English language. He is a master of the mock imitation, of the lampoon that is close enough to the real thing to make the unwitting reader dizzy with apprehension at seeing the familiar text slide away from him. Perelman writes like a demonic master of ceremonies who introduces a writer with so many mock compliments that the poor fellow cannot get to his feet. He is funny, above all, because he has an unerring ability to render ridiculous any kind of prose that has some blatant insincerity at the heart of it—advertising, movie scenarios, political speeches.

This gift for jeering at certain rhetorical statements, by imitating their pomposity almost too well, is Perelman's particular skill. He has an inborn sense, perhaps developed from growing up with a foreign language in an immigrant home, of the absurdity of those who sit a bit too heavily in judgment over the newer stocks in America by always talking a bit too correctly, too pompously. It is significant, perhaps, that so many famous comedians in America—the Marx Brothers, Danny Kaye, Willie Howard, Lou Holtz—have had the same attitude, at once humble and derisive, toward a language which, as children of immigrants, they have had thrust at them by humorless teachers in big-city public schools.

In any event, no contemporary parodist can equal Perelman for imitating some external flourish of style. He has a particular eye for the zany detail, the improbable fact—and then developing it into a sequence which could have made sense only in *Alice In Wonderland*. Think of all the people who read a little item in a magazine, and immediately forgot it—Prime Minister Nehru's father used to send his laundry to Paris! On the slender strength of this report, Perelman has developed the lunatic correspondence between a Hindu nobleman, writing to complain of what has been happening to his shirts—and an obsequious but somehow insanely self-satisfied Parisian laundry-owner!

The situation is hilarious enough—why send your shirts from India to Paris if you don't like the way they do them? Why send shirts to Paris at all? But Perelman, undaunted by a situation that would have frozen with horror any mortal writer but himself, goes on to give the elder Nehru's complaints the unerring style of an eighteenth-century nobleman looking down his nose at a flea—"Enlighten me, my dear fellow, since I have never been a tradesman myself—what passes through your head when you mulct a customer in this outrageous fashion? Is it glee? Triumph? Self-approbation at the cunning with which you have swindled your betters? I ask altogether without malice, solely from a desire to fathom the dark intricacies of the human mind."

Up until recently, I had always believed that nobody on earth could deliver a throwaway line with quite the sang-froid of a certain comedian I worked for in Hollywood during the thirties. You probably don't recall the chap, but his hallmark was a big black mustache, a cigar, and a loping gait, and his three brothers, also in the act, impersonated with varying degrees of success a mute, an Italian, and a clean-cut boy. My respect for Julio (to cloak his identity partially) stemmed from a number of pearls that fell from his lips during our association, notably one inspired by an argument over dietary customs. We were having dinner at an off-Broadway hotel, in the noisiest locale imaginable outside the annual fair at Nizhnii Novgorod. There were at least a dozen people in the party—lawyers, producers, agents, brokers, astrologers, tipsters, and various assorted sycophants—for, like all celebrated theatrical personages, my man liked to travel with a retinue. The dining room was jammed, some paid-up ghoul from Local 802 was interpreting the "Habanera" on an electric organ over the uproar, and, just to insure dyspepsia, a pair of adagio dancers were flinging themselves with abandon in and out of our food. I was seated next to Julio, who was discoursing learnedly to me on his favorite subject, anatomical deviations among showgirls. Halfway through the meal, we abruptly became aware of a dispute across the table between several of our companions.

"It is *not* just religious!" one was declaring hotly. "They knew a damn sight more about hygiene than you think in those Biblical days!"

"That still don't answer my question!" shouted the man he had addressed. "If they allow veal and mutton and beef, why do they forbid pork?"

"Because it's unclean, you dummy," the other rasped. "I'm trying to tell you—the pig is an unclean animal!"

"What's that?" demanded Julio, his voice slicing through the alterca-

NO STARCH IN THE DHOTI, S'IL VOUS PLAIT: From *The Road to Miltown.* Copyright 1955 by S. J. Perelman. Reprinted by permission of Simon and Schuster, Inc., New York.

tion. "The pig an unclean animal?" He rose from his chair and repeated the charge to be certain everyone within fifty feet was listening.
"The pig an unclean animal? Why, the pig is the cleanest animal there
is—except my father, of course." And dropped like a falcon back into
his chow mein.

As I say, I'd gone along for years considering Julio pre-eminent in
tossing off this kind of grenade, and then one Sunday a few weeks ago,
in the *Times* Magazine, I stumbled across an item that leaves no doubt
he has been deposed. The new champ is Robert Trumbull, the former
Indian correspondent of the paper and a most affable bird with whom
I once spent an afternoon crawling around the Qutb Minar, outside
New Delhi. In the course of an article called "Portrait of a Symbol
Named Nehru," Mr. Trumbull had the following to say: "Nehru is
accused of having a congenital distaste for Americans because of their
all too frequent habit of bragging and of being patronizing when in
unfamiliar surroundings. It is said that in the luxurious and gracious
house of his father, the late Pandit Motilal Nehru—who sent his laundry to Paris—the young Jawaharlal's British nurse used to make caustic
remarks to the impressionable boy about the table manners of his
father's American guests."

It was, of course, the utter nonchalance of the phrase "who sent his
laundry to Paris" that knocked me galley-west. Obviously, Trumbull
wasn't referring to one isolated occasion; he meant that the Pandit
made a practice of consigning his laundry to the post, the way one used
to under the academic elms. But this was no callow sophomore shipping his wash home to save money. A man willful and wealthy enough
to have it shuttled from one hemisphere to another could hardly have
been prompted by considerations of thrift. He must have been a con-
summate perfectionist, a fussbudget who wanted every last pleat in
order, and, remembering my own Homeric wrangles with laundrymen
just around the corner, I blenched at the complications his overseas
dispatch must have entailed. Conducted long before there was any air
service between India and Europe, it would have involved posting the
stuff by sea—a minimum of three weeks in each direction, in addition
to the time it took for processing. Each trip would have created problems of customs examination, valuation, duty (unless Nehru senior
got friends to take it through for him, which was improbable; most
people detest transporting laundry across the world, even their own).
The old gentleman had evidently had a limitless wardrobe, to be able
to dispense with portions of it for three months at a time.

The major headache, as I saw it, though, would have been coping
with the *blanchisseur* himself. How did Pandit Motilal get any service

or redress out of him at such long range? There were the countless vexations that always arise: the missing sock, the half-pulverized button, the insistence on petrifying everything with starch despite the most detailed instructions. The more I thought about it, the clearer it became that he must have been enmeshed in an unending correspondence with the laundry owner. I suggest, accordingly, that while the exact nature of his letters can only be guessed at, it might be useful—or, by the same token, useless—to reconstruct a few, together with the replies they evoked. Even if they accomplish nothing else, they should help widen the breach between East and West.

> *Allahabad,*
> *United Provinces,*
> *June 7, 1903*

Pleurniche et Cie.,
124, Avenue de la Grande Armée, Paris.

MY DEAR M. PLEURNICHE:

You may be interested to learn—though I doubt that anything would stir you out of your vegetable torpor—that your pompous, florid, and illiterate scrawl of the 27th arrived here with insufficient postage, forcing me to disgorge one rupee three annas to the mailman. How symbolic of your character, how magnificently consistent! Not content with impugning the quality of the cambric in my drawers, you contrive to make me *pay* for the insult. That transcends mere nastiness, you know. If an international award for odium is ever projected, have no fear of the outcome as far as India is concerned. You can rely on my support.

And à propos of symbols, there is something approaching genius in the one that graces your letterhead, the golden fleece. Could any trademark be more apt for a type who charges six francs to wash a cummerbund? I realize that appealing to your sense of logic is like whistling an aria to the deaf, but I paid half that for it originally, and the Muslim who sold it to me was the worst thief in the bazaar. Enlighten me, my dear fellow, since I have never been a tradesman myself—what passes through your head when you mulct a customer in this outrageous fashion? Is it glee? Triumph? Self-approbation at the cunning with which you have swindled your betters? I ask altogether without malice, solely from a desire to fathom the dark intricacies of the human mind.

To revert now to the subject of the drawers. It will do you no good to bombinate endlessly about sleazy material, deterioration from pounding on stones, etc. That they were immersed in an acid bath powerful enough to corrode a zinc plate, that they were wrenched through a mangle with utmost ferocity, that they were deliberately spattered with grease and kicked about the floor of your establishment, and, finally, that a white-hot iron was appliquéd on their seat—the whole sordid tale of maltreatment is writ there for anybody to see. The motive, however, is far less apparent, and I have speculated for hours on why I should be the target of vandalism. Only one explanation fits the facts. Quite clearly, for all your extortionate rates, you underpay your workmen, and one of them, seeking to revenge himself, wreaked his spite on my undergarment. While I sympathize with the poor rascal's plight, I wish it understood that I hold you responsible to the very last sou. I therefore deduct from the enclosed draft nine francs fifty, which will hardly compensate me for the damage to my raiment and my nerves, and remain, with the most transitory assurances of my regard,

Sincerely yours,
PANDIT MOTILAL NEHRU

Paris,
July 18, 1903

Pandit Motilal Nehru,
Allahabad, U.P., India.
DEAR PANDIT MOTILAL:

I am desolated beyond words at the pique 1 sense between the lines in your recent letter, and I affirm to you on my wife's honor that in the six generations the family has conducted this business, yours is the first complaint we have ever received. Were I to list the illustrious clients we have satisfied—Robespierre, the Duc d'Enghien, Saint-Saëns, Coquelin, Mérimée, Bouguereau, and Dr. Pasteur, to name but a handful —it would read like a roll call of the immortals. Only yesterday, Marcel Proust, an author you will hear more of one of these days, called at our *établissement* (establishment) to felicitate us in person. The work we do for him is peculiarly exacting; due to his penchant for making notes on his cuffs, we must observe the greatest discretion in selecting which to launder. In fine, our function is as much editorial as sanitary, and he stated unreservedly that he holds our literary judgment in the highest esteem. I ask you, could a firm with traditions like these stoop to the pettifoggery you imply?

You can be sure, however, that if our staff has been guilty of any oversight, it will not be repeated. Between ourselves, we have been zealously weeding out a Socialist element among the employees, malcontents who seek to inflame them with vicious nonsense about an eleven-hour day and compulsory ventilation. Our firm refusal to compromise one iota has borne fruit; we now have a hard core of loyal and spiritless drudges, many of them so lackluster that they do not even pause for lunch, which means a substantial time saving and consequently much speedier service for the customer. As you see, my dear Pandit Motilal, efficiency and devotion to our clientele dominate every waking thought at Pleurniche.

As regards your last consignment, all seems to be in order; I ask leave, though, to beg one trifling favor that will help us execute your work more rapidly in future. Would you request whoever mails the laundry to make certain it contains no living organisms? When the current order was unpacked, a small yellow-black serpent, scarcely larger than a pencil but quite dynamic, wriggled out of one of your *dhotis* and spread terror in the workroom. We succeeded in decapitating it after a modicum of trouble and bore it to the Jardin d'Acclimatation, where the curator identified it as a krait, the most lethal of your indigenous snakes. Mind you, I personally thought M. Ratisbon an alarmist—the little émigré impressed me as a rather cunning fellow, vivacious, intelligent, and capable of transformation into a household pet if one had leisure. Unfortunately, we have none, so fervent is our desire to accelerate your shipments, and you will aid us materially by a hint in the right quarter, if you will. Accept, I implore of you, my salutations the most distinguished.

Yours cordially,

OCTAVE-HIPPOLYTE PLEURNICHE

Allahabad, U.P.,
September 11, 1903

DEAR M. PLEURNICHE:

If I were a hothead, I might be tempted to horsewhip a Yahoo who has the effrontery to set himself up as a patron of letters; if a humanitarian, to garrote him and earn the gratitude of the miserable wretches under his heel. As I am neither, but simply an idealist fatuous enough to believe he is entitled to what he pays for, I have a favor to ask of you, in turn. Spare me, I pray, your turgid rhetoric and bootlicking protestations, and be equally sparing of the bleach you use on my shirts. After a single baptism in your vats, my sky-blue *jibbahs* faded to a ghastly greenish-white and the fabric evaporates under one's touch. Merciful God, whence springs this compulsion to eliminate every trace of color from my dress? Have you now become arbiters of fashion as well as littérateurs?

In your anxiety to ingratiate yourselves, incidentally, you have exposed me to as repugnant an experience as I can remember. Five or six days ago, a verminous individual named Champignon arrived here from Pondichéry, asserting that he was your nephew, delegated by you to expedite my household laundry problems. The blend of unction and cheek he displayed, reminiscent of a process server, should have warned me to beware, but, tenderhearted ninny that I am, I obeyed our Brahmin laws of hospitality and permitted him to remain the night. Needless to say, he distinguished himself. After a show of gluttony to dismay Falstaff, he proceeded to regale the dinner table with a disquisition on the art of love, bolstering it with quotations from the Kamasutra so coarse that one of the ladies present fainted dead away. Somewhat later, I surprised him in the kitchen tickling a female servant, and when I demurred, he rudely advised me to stick to my rope trick and stay out of matters that did not concern me. He was gone before daylight, accompanied by a Jaipur enamel necklace of incalculable value and all our spoons. I felt it was a trivial price to be rid of him. Nevertheless, I question your wisdom, from a commercial standpoint, in employing such emissaries. Is it not safer to rob the customer in the old humdrum fashion, a franc here and a franc there, than to stake everything on a youth's judgment and risk possible disaster? I subscribe myself, as always,

Your well-wisher,
PANDIT MOTILAL NEHRU

Paris,
October 25, 1903

DEAR PANDIT MOTILAL:

We trust that you have received the bundle shipped five weeks since and that our work continues to gratify. It is also pleasing to learn that our relative M. Champignon called on you and managed to be of assistance. If there is any further way he can serve you, do not hesitate to notify him.

I enclose herewith a cutting which possibly needs a brief explanation. As you see, it is a newspaper advertisement embodying your photograph and a text woven out of laudatory remarks culled from your letters to us. Knowing you would gladly concur, I took the liberty of altering a word or two in places to clarify the meaning and underline the regard you hold us in. This dramatic license, so to speak, in no way vitiates the sense of what you wrote; it is quite usual in theatrical advertising to touch up critical opinion, and to judge from comment I have already heard, you will enjoy publicity throughout the continent of Europe for years to come. Believe us, dear Pandit, your eternal debtor, and allow me to remain

Yours fraternally,
OCTAVE-HIPPOLYTE PLEURNICHE

Allahabad,
November 14, 1903

DEAR M. PLEURNICHE:

The barristers I retained immediately on perusing your letter—Messrs. Bulstrode & Hawfinch, of Covent Garden, a firm you will hear more of one of these days—have cautioned me not to communicate with you henceforth, but the urge to speak one final word is irresistible. After all, when their suit for a million francs breaks over you like a thunderclap, when the bailiffs seize your business and you are reduced to sleeping along the *quais* and subsisting on the carrot greens you pick up around Les Halles, you may mistakenly attribute your predicament to my malignity, to voodoo, djinns, etc. Nothing of the sort, my dear chap. Using me to publicize your filthy little concern is only a secondary factor in your downfall. What doomed you from the start was the bumbling incompetence, the ingrained slovenliness, that characterizes everyone in your calling. A man too indolent to replace the snaps he tears from a waistcoat or expunge the rust he sprinkles on a brand-new Kashmiri shawl is obviously capable of any infamy, and it ill becomes him to snivel when retribution overtakes him in the end.

Adieu then, *mon brave,* and try to exhibit in the dock at least the dignity you have failed to heretofore. With every good wish and the certainty that nothing I have said has made the slightest possible impression on a brain addled by steam, I am,

Compassionately,

PANDIT MOTILAL NEHRU

e. m. forster

what i believe

E. M. Forster (1879-   ), the famous English novelist, is also one of the most intelligent and most charming of all twentieth-century essayists. He is a writer who personifies the best of that cultivated, urbane and liberal civilization which to many people seems to be perishing under the onslaught of totalitarianism.

In this now-famous essay, "What I Believe," Forster manages with characteristic suppleness and ease to make his style the very echo of his thought. When a man begins, "I do not believe in Belief," he has already succeeded in communicating to us, by a gentle pun, the fact that he regards individual personality as a higher value than the powerful creeds that now divide the world. And in fact Forster does believe in the individual, in personal relationships, in the preeminence of love, exactly to the same degree that he does *not* believe in Belief, or even in Faith. "Faith, to my mind, is a stiffening process, a sort of mental starch, which ought to be applied as sparingly as possible. I dislike the stuff. I do not believe in it, for its own sake, at all."

This kind of writing has a relatively unusual and even unpopular thesis to maintain. How many of us could say, with Forster—". . . I hate the idea of causes, and if I had to choose between betraying my country and betraying my friend, I hope I should have the guts to betray my country"? And since Forster is the last person in the world to make an angrily lonely and defiant cause out of anything, he must depend entirely on his ability to disarm you and to charm you—in a word, to appeal to the reader wholly as a private individual, and thus to his essential humanity. Forster does not say that he could betray his country; if he had "to choose between betraying my country and betraying my friend," he *hopes* he should have *the guts* to do precisely what is most difficult for him to do. This is a perfect example, in the living thought that style really is, of Forster's refusal of all extreme and over-positive views. Forster's prose itself succeeds perfectly in persuading us that he is as liberal and easy and good-humored as he wishes to be. Rarely has that well-known disguise of strong feelings, the British gift of understatement, the national gift for "playing it down," been used to such good effect in such an important instance. "This is such a difficult moment to live in, one cannot help getting gloomy and also a bit rattled, and perhaps short-sighted."

I do not believe in Belief. But this is an age of faith, and there are so many militant creeds that, in self-defence, one has to formulate a creed of one's own. Tolerance, good temper and sympathy are no longer enough in a world which is rent by religious and racial perse-cution, in a world where ignorance rules, and science, who ought to have ruled, plays the subservient pimp. Tolerance, good temper and sympathy—they are what matter really, and if the human race is not to collapse they must come to the front before long. But for the mo-ment they are not enough, their action is no stronger than a flower, battered beneath a military jack-boot. They want stiffening, even if the process coarsens them. Faith, to my mind, is a stiffening process, a sort of mental starch, which ought to be applied as sparingly as possible.

I dislike the stuff. I do not believe in it, for its own sake, at all. Herein I probably differ from most people, who believe in Belief, and are only sorry they cannot swallow even more than they do. My law-givers are Erasmus and Montaigne, not Moses and St. Paul. My temple stands not upon Mount Moriah but in that Elysian Field where even the immoral are admitted. My motto is: "Lord, I disbelieve—help thou my unbelief."

I have, however, to live in an Age of Faith—the sort of epoch I used to hear praised when I was a boy. It is extremely unpleasant really. It is bloody in every sense of the word. And I have to keep my end up in it. Where do I start?

With personal relationships. Here is something comparatively solid in a world full of violence and cruelty. Not absolutely solid, for Psychology has split and shattered the idea of a "Person," and has shown that there is something incalculable in each of us, which may at any moment rise to the surface and destroy our normal balance. We don't know what we are like. We can't know what other people are like. How, then, can we put any trust in personal relationships, or cling to them in the gathering political storm? In theory we cannot. But in practice we can and do. Though A is not unchangeably A or B unchangeably B, there can still be love and loyalty between the two. For the purpose of living one has to assume that the personality is solid, and the "self' is an entity, and to ignore all contrary evidence. And since to ignore evidence is one of the characteristics of faith, I certainly can proclaim that I believe in personal relationships.

Starting from them, I get a little order into the contemporary chaos. One must be fond of people and trust them if one is not to make a mess of life, and it is therefore essential that they should not let one down. They often do. The moral of which is that I must, myself, be as reliable as possible, and this I try to be. But reliability is not a matter of contract—that is the main difference between the world of personal relationships and the world of business relationships. It is a matter for the heart, which signs no documents. In other words, reliability is impossible unless there is a natural warmth. Most men possess this warmth, though they often have bad luck and get chilled. Most of them, even when they are politicians, *want* to keep faith. And one can, at all events, show one's own little light here, one's own poor little trembling flame, with the knowledge that it is not the only light that is shining in the darkness, and not the only one which the darkness does not comprehend. Personal relations are despised today. They are regarded as bourgeois luxuries, as products of a time of fair weather which is now past, and we are urged to get rid of them, and to dedicate ourselves to some movement or cause instead. I hate the idea of causes, and if I had to choose between betraying my country and betraying my friend, I hope I should have the guts to betray my country. Such a choice may scandalize the modern reader, and he may stretch out his patriotic hand to the telephone at once and ring up the police. It would not have shocked Dante, though. Dante places Brutus and Cassius in the lowest circle of Hell because they had chosen to betray their friend Julius Caesar rather than their country Rome. Probably one will not be asked to make such an agonizing choice. Still, there lies at the back of every creed something terrible and hard for which the worshipper may one day be required to suffer, and there is even terror and a hardness in this creed of personal relationships, urbane and mild though it sounds. Love and loyalty to an individual can run counter to the claims of the State. When they do—down with the State, say I, which means that the State would down me.

This brings me along to Democracy, "even Love, the Beloved Republic, which feeds upon Freedom and lives." Democracy is not a Beloved Republic really, and never will be. But it is less hateful than other contemporary forms of government, and to that extent it deserves our support. It does start from the assumption that the individual is important, and that all types are needed to make a civilization. It does not divide its citizens into the bossers and the bossed—as an efficiency-regime tends to do. The people I admire most are those who are sensitive and want to create something or discover something, and do not see life in terms of power, and such people get more of a chance under a democracy than elsewhere. They found religions, great or small, or they produce literature and art, or they do disinterested scientific research, or they may be what is called "ordinary people," who are creative in their private lives, bring up their children decently, for instance, or help their neighbors. All these people need to express themselves; they cannot do so unless society allows them liberty to do so, and the society which allows them most liberty is a democracy.

Democracy has another merit. It allows criticism, and if there is not public criticism there are bound to be hushed-up scandals. That is why I believe in the Press, despite all its lies and vulgarity, and why I believe in Parliament. Parliament is often sneered at because it is a Talking Shop. I believe in it *because* it is a talking shop. I believe in the Private Member who makes himself a nuisance. He gets snubbed and is told that he is cranky or ill-informed, but he does expose abuses which would otherwise never have been mentioned, and very often an abuse gets put right just by being mentioned. Occasionally, too, a well-meaning public official starts losing his head in the cause of efficiency, and thinks himself God Almighty. Such officials are particularly frequent in the Home Office. Well, there will be questions about them in Parliament sooner or later, and then they will have to mind their steps. Whether Parliament is either a representative body or an efficient one is questionable, but I value it because it criticizes and talks, and because its chatter gets widely reported.

So Two Cheers for Democracy: one because it admits variety and two because it permits criticism. Two cheers are quite enough: there is no occasion to give three. Only Love the Beloved Republic deserves that.

What about Force, though? While we are trying to be sensitive and advanced and affectionate and tolerant, an unpleasant question pops up: does not all society rest upon force? If a government cannot count upon the police and the army, how can it hope to rule? And if an individual gets knocked on the head or sent to a labor camp, of what significance are his opinions?

This dilemma does not worry me as much as it does some. I realize that all society rests upon force. But all the great creative actions, all the decent human relations, occur during the intervals when force has not managed to come to the front. These intervals are what matter. I want them to be as frequent and as lengthy as possible, and I call them "civilization." Some people idealize force and pull it into the foreground and worship it, instead of keeping it in the background as long as possible. I think they make a mistake, and I think that their opposites, the mystics, err even more when they declare that force does not exist. I believe that it exists, and that one of our jobs is to prevent it from getting out of its box. It gets out sooner or later, and then it destroys us and all the lovely things which we have made. But it is not out all the time, for the fortunate reason that the strong are so stupid. Consider their conduct for a moment in the Niebelung's Ring. The giants there have the guns, or in other words the gold; but they do nothing with it, they do not realize that they are all-powerful, with the result that the catastrophe is delayed and the castle of Walhalla, insecure but glorious, fronts the storms. Fafnir, coiled round his hoard, grumbles and grunts; we can hear him under Europe today; the leaves of the wood already tremble, and the Bird calls its warnings uselessly. Fafnir will destroy us, but by a blessed dispensation he is stupid and slow, and creation goes on just outside the poisonous blast of his breath. The Nietzschean would hurry the monster up, the mystic would say he did not exist, but Wotan, wiser than either, hastens to create warriors before doom declares itself. The Valkyries are symbols not only of courage but of intelligence; they represent the human spirit snatching its opportunity while the going is good, and one of them even finds time to love. Brünnhilde's last song hymns the recurrence of love, and since it is the privilege of art to exaggerate, she goes even further, and proclaims the love which is eternally triumphant and feeds upon freedom, and lives.

So that is what I feel about force and violence. It is, alas! the ultimate reality on this earth, but it does not always get to the front. Some people call its absences "decadence"; I call them "civilization" and find in such interludes the chief justification for the human experiment. I look the other way until fate strikes me. Whether this is due to courage or to cowardice in my own case I cannot be sure. But I know that if men had not looked the other way in the past, nothing of any value would survive. The people I respect most behave as if they were immortal and as if society was eternal. Both assumptions are false; both of them must be accepted as true if we are to go on eating and working and loving, and are to keep open a few breathing holes for the human spirit. No millennium seems likely to descend upon humanity; no better and stronger League of Nations will be instituted; no form of Christianity and no alternative to Christianity will bring peace to the world or integrity to the individual; no "change of heart" will occur. And yet we need not despair, indeed, we cannot despair; the evidence of history shows us that men have always insisted on behaving creatively under the shadow of the sword; that they have done their artistic and scientific and domestic stuff for the sake of doing it, and that we had better follow their example under the shadow of the aeroplanes. Others, with more vision or courage than myself, see the salvation of humanity ahead, and will dismiss my conception of civilization as paltry, a sort of top-and-run game. Certainly it is presumptuous to say that we *cannot* improve, and that Man, who has only been in power for a few thousand years, will never learn to make use of his power. All I mean is that, if people continue to kill one another as they do, the world cannot get better than it is, and that since there are more people than formerly, and their means for destroying one another superior, the world may well get worse. What is good in people—and consequently in the world—is their insistence on creation, their belief in friendship and loyalty for their own sakes; and though Violence remains and is, indeed, the major partner in this muddled establishment, I believe that creativeness remains too, and will always assume direction when violence sleeps. So, though I am not an optimist, I cannot agree with Sophocles that it were better never to have been born. And although, like Horace, I see no evidence that each batch of births is superior to the last, I leave the field open for the more complacent view. This is such a difficult moment to live in, one cannot help getting gloomy and also a bit rattled, and perhaps short-sighted.

In search of a refuge, we may perhaps turn to hero-worship. But here we shall get no help, in my opinion. Hero-worship is a dangerous vice, and one of the minor merits of a democracy is that it does not encourage it, or produce that unmanageable type of citizen known as the Great Man. It produces instead different kinds of small men—a much finer achievement. But people who cannot get interested in the variety of life, and cannot make up their own minds, get discontented over this, and they long for a hero to bow down before and to follow blindly. It is significant that a hero is an integral part of the authoritarian stock-in-trade today. An efficiency-regime cannot be run without a few heroes stuck about it to carry off the dullness—much as plums have to be put into a bad pudding to make it palatable. One hero at the top and a smaller one each side of him is a favorite arrangement, and the timid and the bored are comforted by the trinity, and, bowing down, feel exalted and strengthened.

No, I distrust Great Men. They produce a desert of uniformity around them and often a pool of blood too, and I always feel a little man's pleasure when they come a cropper. Every now and then one reads in the newspapers some such statement as: "The coup d'état appears to have failed, and Admiral Toma's whereabouts is at present unknown." Admiral Toma had probably every qualification for being a Great Man—an iron will, personal magnetism, dash, flair, sexlessness —but fate was against him, so he retires to unknown whereabouts instead of parading history with his peers. He fails with a completeness which no artist and no lover can experience, because with them the process of creation is itself an achievement, whereas with him the only possible achievement is success.

I believe in aristocracy, though—if that is the right word, and if a democrat may use it. Not an aristocracy of power, based upon rank and influence, but an aristocracy of the sensitive, the considerate and the plucky. Its members are to be found in all nations and classes, and all through the ages, and there is a secret understanding between them when they meet. They represent the true human tradition, the one permanent victory of our queer race over cruelty and chaos. Thousands of them perish in obscurity, a few are great names. They are sensitive for others as well as for themselves, they are considerate without being fussy, their pluck is not swankiness but the power to endure, and they can take a joke. I give no examples—it is risky to do that—but the reader may as well consider whether this is the type of person he would like to meet and to be, and whether (going farther with me) he would prefer that this type should *not* be an ascetic one. I am against asceticism myself. I am with the old Scotsman who wanted less chastity and more delicacy. I do not feel that my aristocrats are a real aristocracy if they thwart their bodies, since bodies are the instruments through which we register and enjoy the world. Still, I do not insist. This is not a major point. It is clearly possible to be sensitive, considerate and plucky and yet be an ascetic too; if anyone possesses the first three qualities, I will let him in! On they go—an invincible army, yet not a victorious one. The aristocrats, the elect, the chosen, the Best People—all the words that describe them are false, and all attempts to organize them fail. Again and again Authority, seeing their value, has tried to net them and to utilize them as the Egyptian Priesthood or the Christian Church or the Chinese Civil Service or the Group Movement, or some other worthy stunt. But they slip through the net and are gone; when the door is shut, they are no longer in the room; their temple, as one of them remarked, is the Holiness of the Heart's Affection, and their kingdom, though they never possess it, is the wide-open world.

With this type of person knocking about, and constantly crossing one's path if one has eyes to see or hands to feel, the experiment of earthly life cannot be dismissed as a failure. But it may well be hailed as a tragedy, the tragedy being that no device has been found by which these private decencies can be transmitted to public affairs. As soon as people have power they go crooked and sometimes dotty as well, because the possession of power lifts them into a region where normal honesty never pays. For instance, the man who is selling newspapers outside the Houses of Parliament can safely leave his papers to go for a drink and his cap beside them: anyone who takes a paper is sure to drop a copper into the cap. But the men who are inside the Houses of Parliament—they cannot trust one another like that, still less can the Government they compose trust other governments. No caps upon the pavement here, but suspicion, treachery and armaments. The more highly public life is organized the lower does its morality sink; the nations of today behave to each other worse than they ever did in the past, they cheat, rob, bully and bluff, make war without notice, and kill as many women and children as possible; whereas primitive tribes were at all events restrained by taboos. It is a humiliating outlook—though the greater the darkness, the brighter shine the little lights, reassuring one another, signalling: "Well, at all events, I'm still here. I don't like it very much, but how are you?" Unquenchable lights of my aristocracy! Signals of the invincible army! "Come along

—anyway, let's have a good time while we can." I think they signal that too.

The Saviour of the future—if ever he comes—will not preach a new Gospel. He will merely utilize my aristocracy, he will make effective the good will and the good temper which are already existing. In other words, he will introduce a new technique. In economics, we are told that if there was a new technique of distribution, there need be no poverty, and people would not starve in one place while crops were being ploughed under in another. A similar change is needed in the sphere of morals and politics. The desire for it is by no means new; it was expressed, for example, in theological terms by Jacopone da Todi over six hundred years ago. "Ordina questo amore, O tu che m'ami," he said; "O thou who lovest me—set this love in order." His prayer was not granted, and I do not myself believe that it ever will be, but here, and not through a change of heart, is our probable route. Not by becoming better, but by ordering and distributing his native goodness, will Man shut up Force into its box, and so gain time to explore the universe and to set his mark upon it worthily. At present he only explores it at odd moments, when Force is looking the other way, and his divine creativeness appears as a trivial by-product, to be scrapped as soon as the drums beat and the bombers hum.

Such a change, claim the orthodox, can only be made by Christianity, and will be made by it in God's good time: man always has failed and always will fail to organize his own goodness, and it is presumptuous of him to try. This claim—solemn as it is—leaves me cold. I cannot believe that Christianity will ever cope with the present world-wide mess, and I think that such influence as it retains in modern society is due to the money behind it, rather than to its spiritual appeal. It was a spiritual force once, but the indwelling spirit will have to be restated if it is to calm the waters again, and probably restated in a non-Christian form. Naturally a lot of people, and people who are not only good but able and intelligent, will disagree here; they will vehemently deny that Christianity has failed, or they will argue that its failure proceeds from the wickedness of men, and really proves its ultimate success. They have Faith, with a large F. My faith has a very small one, and I only intrude it because these are strenuous and serious days, and one likes to say what one thinks while speech is comparatively free: it may not be free much longer.

The above are the reflections of an individualist and a liberal who has found liberalism crumbling beneath him and at first felt ashamed. Then, looking around, he decided there was no special reason for shame, since other people, whatever they felt, were equally insecure.

And as for individualism—there seems no way of getting off this, even if one wanted to. The dictator-hero can grind down his citizens till they are all alike, but he cannot melt them into a single man. That is beyond his power. He can order them to merge, he can incite them to mass-antics, but they are obliged to be born separately, and to die separately, and, owing to these unavoidable termini, will always be running off the totalitarian rails. The memory of birth and the expectation of death always lurk within the human being, making him separate from his fellows and consequently capable of intercourse with them. Naked I came into the world, naked I shall go out of it! And a very good thing too, for it reminds me that I am naked under my shirt, whatever its color.

g. k. chesterton

a defence of rash vows

G. K. Chesterton (1874-1936), the great English essayist, critic and storyteller, wrote many different kinds of books—among them the famous Father Brown detective stories. But his central interest in everything he wrote was to persuade the reader who is likely to be a sceptic in religious matters that Roman Catholicism is the only really sensible and humanly acceptable religion for a man to adopt in modern times.

As a writer, Chesterton was so immensely charming and skillful that he managed to amuse, impress and even move many readers who might not agree with him. He was a master of the essay—a literary form which depends on the ability of the writer to make his voice, his argument, his very personality, as it were, all sufficient to you while you are reading him. An essay like "A Defence Of Rash Vows," for instance, might very well seem to be contradicted by an equally charming essay in praise of scepticism: E. M. Forster's "What I Believe" (p. 302). No matter: when you read Chesterton, you virtually cannot help seeing the world through Chesterton's eyes.

Chesterton's "manner," his style, his tone, his very approach to things —all this somehow helps to make him *seem* authoritative in his wisdom, yet impressive in his warm kindliness. Chesterton is like a magician whose technique engrosses you so completely that you, the audience, don't want his performance to fail. When you read him, the world seems very much what *he* says it is. And the reason Chesterton has this effect is that, starting out from certain fundamental principles which are really acceptable to everybody, he translates them into such dazzling rhythms and phrases that you are swept along by him even if you cannot agree with his "position."

Does Chesterton's final "position" follow from his condemnation of the modern age as unstable? Many people would think not; they would find it perfectly acceptable and indeed most pleasant to agree with the body of his essay—and to disagree with his implied conclusion. They would even say that Chesterton's references to the Middle Ages are entirely romantic and sentimental, based more on this writer's marvelous ability to call up atmosphere than on responsibility to the historical facts.

Yet at the same time Chesterton is so richly aware that human happiness is founded on integrity—*"what shall it benefit a man if he gain the whole world and lose his own soul?"*—that his affirmation of the good sense of the Christian virtues is extraordinarily charming. In the final analysis, this kind of writing is successful not because it is clever but because its cleverness is always at the service of a shrewd awareness of what human beings are really like and what they need for their happiness. To make a "vow," in the medieval sense, is perhaps not the same thing as making a vow to ourselves. To identify the two, as Chesterton does, is a bit of his magician's trick—to make you look at one object while he is pulling the other out of his sleeve. But at the same time, who can deny that to make a "vow" to oneself is more *like* the classic vows than it is unlike them?

Chesterton's key thought here is founded on common sense. "The man who makes a vow makes an appointment with himself at some distant time or place. The danger of it is that he himself should not keep the appointment. And in modern times this terror of one's self, of the weakness and mutability of one's self, has perilously increased, and is the real basis of the objection to vows of any kind."

If a prosperous modern man, with a high hat and a frock-coat, were to solemnly pledge himself before all his clerks and friends to count the leaves on every third tree in Holland Walk, to hop up to the City on one leg every Thursday, to repeat the whole of Mill's *Liberty* seventy-six times, to collect three hundred dandelions in fields belonging to any one of the name of Brown, to remain for thirty-one hours holding his left ear in his right hand, to sing the names of all his aunts in order of age on the top of an omnibus, or make any such unusual undertaking, we should immediately conclude that the man was mad, or as it is sometimes expressed, was 'an artist in life.' Yet these vows are not

A DEFENCE OF RASH VOWS: From *The Defendant*, London 1902. Reprinted by permission of J. M. Dent & Sons Ltd.

more extraordinary than the vows which in the Middle Ages and in similar periods were made, not by fanatics merely, but by the greatest figures in civic and national civilization—by kings, judges, poets, and priests. One man swore to chain two mountains together, and the great chain hung there, it was said, for ages as a monument of that mystical folly. Another swore that he would find his way to Jerusalem with a patch over his eyes, and died looking for it. It is not easy to see that these two exploits, judged from a strictly rational standpoint, are any saner than the acts above suggested. A mountain is commonly a stationary and reliable object which it is not necessary to chain up at night like a dog. And it is not easy at first sight to see that a man pays a very high compliment to the Holy City by setting out for it under conditions which render it to the last degree improbable that he will ever get there.

But about this there is one striking thing to be noticed. If men behaved in that way in our time, we should, as we have said, regard them as symbols of the 'decadence.' But the men who did these things were not decadent; they belonged generally to the most robust classes of what is generally regarded as a robust age. Again, it will be urged that if men essentially sane performed such insanities, it was under the capricious direction of a superstitious religious system. This, again, will not hold water; for in the purely terrestrial and even sensual departments of life, such as love and lust, the medieval princes show the same mad promises and performances, the same misshapen imagination, and the same monstrous self-sacrifice. Here we have a contradiction, to explain which it is necessary to think of the whole nature of vows from the beginning. And if we consider seriously and correctly the nature of vows, we shall, unless I am much mistaken, come to the conclusion that it is perfectly sane, and even sensible, to swear to chain mountains together, and that, if sanity is involved at all, it is a little insane not to do so.

The man who makes a vow makes an appointment with himself at some distant time or place. The danger of it is that he himself should not keep the appointment. And in modern times this terror of one's self, of the weakness and mutability of one's self, has perilously increased, and is the real basis of the objection to vows of any kind. A modern man refrains from swearing to count the leaves on every third tree in Holland Walk, not because it is silly to do so (he does many sillier things), but because he has a profound conviction that before he had got to the three hundred and seventy-ninth leaf on the first tree he would be excessively tired of the subject and want to go home to tea. In other words, we fear that by that time he will be, in the common but hideously significant phrase, *another man*. Now, it is this horrible fairy tale of a man constantly changing into other men that is the soul of the decadence. That John Paterson should, with apparent calm, look forward to being a certain General Barker on Monday, Dr. Macgregor on Tuesday, Sir Walter Carstairs on Wednesday, and Sam Slugg on Thursday, may seem a nightmare; but to that nightmare we give the name of modern culture. One great decadent, who is now dead, published a poem some time ago in which he powerfully summed up the whole spirit of the movement by declaring that he could stand in the prison yard and entirely comprehend the feelings of a man about to be hanged:

> *For he that lives more lives than one*
> *More deaths than one must die.*

And the end of all this is the maddening horror of unreality which descends upon the decadents, and compared with which physical pain itself would have the freshness of a youthful thing. The one hell which imagination must conceive as most hellish is to be eternally acting a play without even the narrowest and dirtiest greenroom in which to be human. And this is the condition of the decadent, of the aesthete, of the free-lover. To be everlastingly passing through dangers which we know cannot scathe us, to be taking oaths which we know cannot bind us, to be defying enemies who we know cannot conquer us—this is the grinning tyranny of decadence which is called freedom.

Let us turn, on the other hand, to the maker of vows. The man who made a vow, however wild, gave a healthy and natural expression to the greatness of a great moment. He vowed, for example, to chain two mountains together, perhaps a symbol of some great relief, or love, or aspiration. Short as the moment of his resolve might be, it was, like all great moments, a moment of immortality, and the desire to say of it *exegi monumentum aere perennius* was the only sentiment that would satisfy his mind. The modern aesthetic man would, of course, easily see the emotional opportunity; he would vow to chain two mountains together. But, then, he would quite as cheerfully vow to chain the earth to the moon. And the withering consciousness that he did not mean what he said, that he was, in truth, saying nothing of any great import, would take from him exactly that sense of daring actuality which is the excitement of a vow. For what could be more maddening than an existence in which our mother or aunt received the information that we were going to assassinate the king or build a temple on Ben Nevis with the genial composure of custom?

The revolt against vows has been carried in our day even to the extent of a revolt against the typical vow of marriage. It is most amusing to listen to the opponents of marriage on this subject. They appear to imagine that the ideal of constancy was a yoke mysteriously imposed on mankind by the devil, instead of being, as it is, a yoke consistently imposed by all lovers on themselves. They have invented a phrase, a phrase that is a black-and-white contradiction in two words—'free-love'—as if a lover ever had been, or ever could be, free. It is the nature of love to bind itself, and the institution of marriage merely paid the average man the compliment of taking him at his word. Modern sages offer to the lover, with an ill-flavored grin, the largest liberties and the fullest irresponsibility; but they do not respect him as the old Church respected him; they do not write his oath upon the heavens, as the record of his highest moment. They give him every liberty except the liberty to sell his liberty, which is the only one that he wants.

In Mr. Bernard Shaw's brilliant play *The Philanderer* we have a vivid picture of this state of things. Charteris is a man perpetually endeavoring to be a free-lover, which is like endeavoring to be a married bachelor or a white negro. He is wandering in a hungry search for a certain exhilaration which he can only have when he has the courage to cease from wandering. Men knew better than this in old times—in the time, for example, of Shakespeare's heroes. When Shakespeare's men are really celibate they praise the undoubted advantages of celibacy, liberty, irresponsibility, a chance of continual change. But they were not such fools as to continue to talk of liberty when they were in such a condition that they could be made happy or miserable by the moving of someone else's eyebrow. Suckling classes love with debt in his praise of freedom.

> *And he that's fairly out of both*
> *Of all the world is blest.*
> *He lives as in the golden age,*
> *When all things made were common;*
> *He takes his pipe, he takes his glass,*
> *He fears no man or woman.*

This is a perfectly possible, rational, and manly position. But what have lovers to do with ridiculous affectations of fearing no man or woman? They know that in the turning of a hand the whole cosmic engine to the remotest star may become an instrument of music or an instrument of torture. They hear a song older than Suckling's, that has survived a hundred philosophies. 'Who is this that looketh out of the window, fair as the sun, clear as the moon, terrible as an army with banners?'

As we have said, it is exactly this back-door, this sense of having a retreat behind us, that is, to our minds, the sterilizing spirit in modern pleasure. Everywhere there is the persistent and insane attempt to obtain pleasure without paying for it. Thus, in politics, the modern Jingoes practically say: 'Let us have the pleasures of conquerors without the pains of soldiers: let us sit on sofas and be a hardy race.' Thus, in religion and morals, the decadent mystics say: 'Let us have the fragrance of sacred purity without the sorrows of self-restraint; let us sing hymns alternately to the Virgin and Priapus.' Thus, in love, the free-lovers say: 'Let us have the splendor of offering ourselves without the peril of committing ourselves; let us see whether one cannot commit suicide an unlimited number of times.'

Emphatically it will not work. There are thrilling moments, doubtless, for the spectator, the amateur, and the aesthete; but there is one thrill that is known only to the soldier who fights for his own flag, to the ascetic who starves himself for his own illumination, to the lover who makes finally his own choice. And it is this transfiguring self-discipline that makes the vow a truly sane thing. It must have satisfied even the giant hunger of the soul of a lover or a poet to know that in consequence of some one instant of decision that strange chain would hang for centuries in the Alps among the silences of stars and snows. All around us is the city of small sins, abounding in back ways and retreats, but surely, sooner or later, the towering flame will rise from the harbor announcing that the reign of the cowards is over and a man is burning his ships.

V

malcolm bradbury

the beats: a very exclusive club

Malcolm Bradbury is a young English college teacher, born in 1932, and is the author of a novel about academic life called *Eating People Is Wrong* and an equally humorous book, *How To Have Class in a Class Society*. Like many Englishmen who have visited the United States—and like many Englishmen who haven't—he regards this country as the wonderland where all material aspirations have come true, and cannot help laughing at the "beats," who deliberately cultivate poverty. As he shows, "the Beat Generation is a component of a highly technologically advanced and rich society," and for this reason, as he says so wittily, "in America if you want to be a failure you have to work much harder at it than if you want to be successful. In Europe the reverse is true."

This is clever writing—it is also very shrewd social analysis. Mr. Bradbury writes out of the age-old feeling of exclusion and injustice that is so natural to young men growing up in the highly class-conscious society of England. He points up the contrast between the English situation and that of the beats—playing at poverty, cultivating fake bohemianism as their only escape from the boredom of material progress.

This lively sense of what really motivates people in our society gives tartness to Mr. Bradbury's prose. No one can miss the contrast between England and America. Saul Bellow's "The Sealed Treasure" (p. 3), also comments on the unexpected difficulties of adjusting to our affluent society, but Bellow can compare America only with itself. Bradbury's view of America, by contrast, is founded on English conditions—and he is free to describe America with the freedom of the satirist. "I have a theory to the effect that people exist when they're alone; but, as all my friends tell me, in America it will never go over." Is it true that Americans dislike being alone—and if so, why? Mr. Bradbury does not question the fact. A whole world of difference between America and England is illuminated by his saying that D. H. Lawrence's famous novel, *Lady Chatterley's Lover,* is misunderstood by Americans. (In that novel the wife of an aristocrat and a gamekeeper have a love affair.) Hence Bradbury's remark that "The English have class the way the Americans have sex, and use it for precisely the same purpose—to find out their identities." Perhaps the finest insight in his essay on the beats stems from the fact that so many of them seem less interested in writing than in *looking* like writers. Hence Bradbury's clever and highly accomplished observation—"As for the literary figures of the Beat movement, they seem to me to be writers who don't write who write. Their work is personal, inchoate, unliterary, and given to euphoria of the strangest kind." *Writers who don't write who write*—this is highly accomplished writing, and it is clever *because* it is so accomplished. But above everything else, it is deeply felt.

When I was a feckless young man in an English provincial city, trying to be a writer against striking odds, I learned that there existed in town a group of persons with literary ambitions who had discovered that it was possible to live without working. Their way of life followed directly from this premise. They spent their days in cafés, eating and talking about Nietzsche and then walking out without paying, and their nights on other people's couches. They considered that they were Supermen and had, without exception, the most interesting life histories of anyone in the world. By working hard at it, they made quite a case. Shiftless, dishonest, and completely untrustworthy, given to stealing (but only food and books), they constituted a kind of phony avant-garde, leading the life of a Villon but not writing a *Testament* because they claimed they were living it instead.

I used to call these persons the Sugar Beet Generation, because the only work that they ever did was on the sugar-beet harvest, in the summer; by working eighteen hours a day for a few weeks they made enough money to cover their expenses for a year. But expenses, really, were not things they had, because they lived off other people (whom they called "steamers" because when they came into port, you unloaded them, and they sailed out again). These parasites were writers who didn't write; they all had great books projected, a compound of phallicism and fascism—pornographic novels to be printed in Italy and smuggled into England in girls' bras. Though they talked about them all the time, they never had a moment to get anything down on paper; the only one who ever really did was Colin Wilson, who in *The Outsider* summed up much of the philosophy of these groups.

After a while, however, something happened in England called the espresso bar, places where you could buy Italian coffee served by a Chinese waitress and listen to Spanish music looking at a French mural, while the English rain poured down outside. Within weeks they were taken up by the middle classes. With these places Bohemianism became easy; anybody could play. Bank clerks combed their hair down over their eyes and came into them to protest, just for the evening. The Sugar Beet Generation eyed these ten-minute Bohemians in dis-

THE BEATS: A VERY EXCLUSIVE CLUB: Reprinted from *The Reporter,* July 9, 1959. Copyright © 1959, The Reporter Magazine Company. By permission of the author.

gust and saw that their *Weltanschauung* was gone. In protest against these fashionable protesters, they got jobs, they got married, they had children—things that none of them would have dreamed of doing before.

I learned that America had its own Sugar Beet Generation when I read Chandler Brossard's *Who Walk in Darkness*. Of course America has long had the ski bum and the beach bum, the hobo and the intellectual vagabond (even the graduate teaching assistant), the studhorse figure, like the hero of *Picnic,* who appears in town, excites a bacchanalia and then lights out again, and the traveler in search of identity, like Mio in *Winterset,* who cries that all he has to leave when he dies is a view of Mount Rainier from the Seattle jail. When I came to America I found that, in university circles at least, it was fashionable to be Beat; and on some campuses the Beats outnumbered the squares (or, as I prefer to call them, normal people), who used to slink about looking embarrassed about their normality. The Beatniks at Yale, a sizable group of guitar players and purveyors of other like forms of protest, were in the habit of meeting in the downstairs john of the Sterling Memorial Library, to plan strategy. Only on rare occasions did they emerge en masse from their warrens—when Gregory Corso, chewing on a bread roll, read his poetry, for instance. Then they all were there, in large quantities, dressed in dirtied-up clothes and old sailors' sweaters (purchased at great expense, and still full of old sailors' sweat), and formidably unwashed. It is, of course, only in America, where everyone has access to washrooms and soap and water, that appearing unwashed can be a form of protest—just as it is only in America that people can voluntarily choose poverty, as Mr. Lipton explains that the Beats do; the point being that in America if you want to be a failure you have to work much harder at it than if you want to be successful. In Europe the reverse is true.

The fact is that the Beat Generation is a component of a highly technologically advanced and rich society. Everywhere else they would not be noticed. While they protest against this kind of society, not at times unreasonably, they are also the products of it. They pose a fair question: How does one live in a society where intellectual things are often scorned and where the intellectual path is considered the path of nonadjustment? Once you have taken this dangerous road in America, there is no turning back—you are forever not one of the group. The answer is to form an opposing group; and the sad thing is that you have to adjust to that. The conformity of nonconformity is as American a phenomenon as its opposite. I have a theory to the effect that people exist when they're alone; but, as all my friends tell me, in America it will never go over.

If you are interested in the Beat Generation, and as a social movement it is immensely important, Mr. Lipton's is by far the best account of it. [Lawrence Lipton, *The Holy Barbarians*] It is written from the inside, and, since Lipton is a Beat himself, he is naturally concerned to make out a case for the Beats, who appear as a strict cabal. Not anyone can join it. It's no good, says Mr. Lipton, just being a juvenile delinquent (the Beat view on this seems to be, quite properly, if you are going to be delinquent, why be juvenile about it?) or a homosexual or a Communist. You may be just a hip square. There is more than one way to overthrow a government. Nor is it enough simply to be in protest against the success ethic of American society; you have to protest in exactly the right way, have the right taste in jazz, be influenced by the proper writers—Henry Miller. Wilhelm Reich, Dylan Thomas, and D. H. Lawrence,* among others. The theme is disaffiliation—they are anti-militarist, anti-business, anti-work, and pro-poverty. They are for sex, Zen, jazz, horse (heroin), and pot (marijuana). Like most cabals, they have a jargon (which, interestingly, is mainly concerned with terms for states of depression and euphoria, and of course the means of access to these all important states; like most good Americans, they place a premium on happiness) which you have to know in order to gain admission. There are periods of initiation, to see whether you're with it. You have, as one of the characters in Mr. Lipton's extremely frank ("Like I *love* sex . . .") case histories puts it, to be "subversive—basically." It is, he says, *we* against *they*. Poverty being protest, the Beats go in for a thing called the New Conspicuous Inconsumption, which consists of not having anything—anything, that is, except a hi-fi *with all the wires showing,* bookcases made from planks and bricks, and a ten-thousand-dollar library packed into a fifty-five-dollar slum apartment. Poverty, says Mr. Lipton, is an art, and like all arts it has to be learned. In some of its phases the attitude is a complete opting out from the purposes of society (here the Beats differ from the so-called Angry Young Men, who think that if society is not right the best way is to try, individually, to do a little something about it) and in others it is frankly suicidal ("If

---

* The American D. H. Lawrence, not the English. I have immense trouble explaining to Americans that his novels—*Lady Chatterley's Lover,* for instance—are not about How to Have Sex. They are about How to Have Class and which class to have. The English have class the way the Americans have sex and use it for precisely the same purpose—to find out their identities.

you love life, despicable is thy name," it says on a wall in the wash-room of a Beat place in Denver).

Like the English writers who didn't write, the Beats live on the fringes of literary and cultural society and claim all the privileges of the avant-garde writer. They are nonliterary expatriates, not to Rome or Paris but to a gas station on Route 66, where you can steal a car. As for the literary figures of the Beat movement, they seem to me to be writers who don't write who write. Their work is personal, in-choate, unliterary, and given to euphoria of the strangest kind. In poetry they have, as Mr. Lipton claims, done a great deal to revive the oral tradition. But it seems to me that the best writer they have pro-duced is Henry Miller, who was around long before the generation. Miller was a true nihilist; given that society was that way, he was its proper opposite. His place was at the very bottom:

A genius looking for employment is one of the saddest sights in the world. He fits in nowhere, nobody wants him. He is maladapted, says the world. With that, the doors are rudely slammed in his face. But is there no place at all for him, then? Oh yes, there is room at the very bottom.

But Miller's was an individual protest, and he was at the bottom because he had to be; the Beats, on the other hand, are socially mobile, *downwards*. While the angry young men are looking for room at the top, the Beats are looking for it at the bottom. And they are looking en masse. They are, indeed, to use Clancy Segal's memorable phrase, Nihilism's Organization Men. For the problem here is what happens to protest when everyone does it. One of the worst things that can happen to a man is to have his ideas put into practice; and the Beats are putting into practice all that writers have been saying for the last 150 years. And it's disturbing. Hearing so many of one's com-plaints on the lips of a whole generation is not pleasing, always. One has to start protesting all over again. Whenever I meet members of the Beat Generation (and when you meet one, you always know), they always make me feel that I've compromised with my destiny; and I haven't, I haven't. My trouble is, I suppose, that I love my mother and father (unlike Mr. Lipton's cases, I never rejected my parents; they rejected me—and when I heard their case, I agreed with them), and haven't sufficient artistic integrity to write books about my friends. It's a block. However, at last, after reading Mr. Lipton's book, I can feel outside something; and what I feel outside is the Beat Generation.

harold rosenberg

---

the orgamerican phantasy

Harold Rosenberg was born in 1906, has studied law, and has published a book of poetry, *Trance Above the Streets,* as well as the essays collected in *The Tradition of the New.* He is a consultant to the Advertising Council in New York. Rosenberg is probably best known for his championship of the so-called "action painters," and he has written with wit as well as enthusiasm about the contemporary painters and poets he admires.

As a critic, Rosenberg has been as much concerned with society as with the arts; in the present selection, taken from *The Tradition of the New,* he challenges, with more intelligence and realism than are usually given to the subject, the increasing belief that our society is losing its old-fashioned individualism and is surrendering to what David Riesman has called "the lonely crowd" and William H. Whyte, Jr., "the organization man."

Rosenberg's complaint is directed against Riesman and Whyte and other sociologists who see no hope of arresting America's drift into a wholly mass society. He charges that they have created a "type," a synthetic model, a "phantasy" of the American as organization man or *orgamerican,* as the author derisively calls it. This type or model serves to keep Americans from thinking hard and honestly about what is really wrong with our society—which is not technology but our failure to apply the benefits of technology to all sections of our population. Not only does Rosenberg refuse to accept Riesman's and Whyte's gloomy prophecies, but he concretely charges that these warnings against the *orgman* make it much more difficult for us to see what is concretely wrong with society. He sharply charges that in such writings "scientific objectivity" has become a disguise for fatalism. The *orgman,* the synthetic monster invented by this school, serves as a device for keeping away confrontation of the real problems, which can occur only to individuals, not to synthetic "masses."

Perhaps the most interesting feature of Rosenberg's essay is his charge that the *orgman* bogeyman has been created by intellectuals who have lost their traditional scepticism and radicalism. Their success in American life has given them a sense of guilt, but they have nowhere to go and so they rail against the image of the American as organization man. "The critics of the new America are disheartened by a revolution won

—their revolution, which can go no farther than the ending of the underground life of the American intellectual mass through economic recognition of the services it has to offer. With his own success achieved the only issue the intellectual can see as remaining for society is 'personality.' "

Rosenberg's essay may seem difficult at first reading; his style is intensely original, and like any good writer, he is concerned with developing his argument rather than with "communicating" it at any price. His style is often harshly condensed, aggressively witty, full of positive statements that force the reader to confront his own experience in a new and more challenging way. But this is contemporary critical writing at its most thoughtful; the pleasant combination of hard-packed thought and a style so informal that it often becomes slangy, gives Rosenberg's essay the effect of illuminating with remarkable directness the society in which we live. Rosenberg's writing is so full of thought, of his own thinking on the problem, that it rises to epigram. "America masks its terrors behind patterns of fact. Here the intolerable discloses its presence not in the grimaces of comedy or tragedy but in the bland citations of the scientific report. Since the War, no novel or play has given body to the larger disturbances of the American consciousness."

America masks its terrors behind patterns of fact. Here the intolerable discloses its presence not in the grimaces of comedy or tragedy but in the bland citations of the scientific report. Since the War, no novel or play has given body to the larger disturbances of the American consciousness. Literature, one hears, is dead, or too enfeebled to risk arduous adventures. Nevertheless, documents keep appearing that touch upon apprehensions equal to any in the history of men: computations of the daily incidence of outlawed sex in America's bedrooms; records of scientific sadism practiced by governments and their programs to transform the will of individuals; estimates by atomic technicians of the flimsiness of the earth and of the natural shape of the human body. When phenomena of this order are explored in a work of the imagination, its author tends to be exiled to the colony of "morbid intellectuals". Given the form of the report or survey, and authorized by the rhetoric of the professions, the most alarming topics overcome the handicap of their profundity and enter into the conversation of solid men of affairs.

Among the grand metaphysical themes of this decade, the one that has proved perhaps most fascinating and persistent has been that of "alienation"—the loss by the individual of personal identity through the operation of social processes. The tone of the post-war imagination was set by Orwell's *1984;* since the appearance of that work, "the de-humanized collective that so haunts our thoughts" (as Mr. William H. Whyte, Jr. calls it in *The Organization Man*) has been a topic for the best-seller lists.

Orwell's melodrama of the pulverized ego was a work of fiction. But Orwell was a Briton; besides, *1984* could be read as a description of life in Stalin's Russia or in a future Labor Party England, rather than of the destiny of America. Of U.S. storytellers who essayed to raise the same spectre, none achieved large public impact. Americans awoke to the menace of robotization when it passed from the fiction-writer's yarn to the testimony of the sociologist and culural anthropologist. Riesman's *The Lonely Crowd,* with its "other-directed" hero-victims of automobile showroows and PTA meetings, left no doubt that the familiar feeling of being someone else was not a mere after-effect of seeing the wrong movie. Spectorsky's *The Exurbanites,* Whyte's *The Organization Man,* Mills' *White Collar,* Packard's *The Hidden Persuaders* filled in important details of personnel, locale and method. Like The Man With The Bomb That Can Blow Up The World, The Creature That Lost Himself ceased to be a reflection of the dream-maker's art, or a literary construction of the philosophical moralist, and emerged as a statistical probability from the file-cards of the social scientist.

It goes without saying that the Other-Directed Man, The Exurbanite, the Organization Man, is a *type,* that is to say, the personification of a behavior system, on the order of, say, Sinclair Lewis' Babbitt. In this respect the difference between the sociologist and the novelist reduces itself to the fact that Riesman explains that he is writing about "social characters" and devotes his book to analyzing what they do, while Lewis trots Babbitt out on the stage and has him do it.

The type or character is deficient in individuality *by definition.* Said Strindberg: "The word 'character' . . . became the middle-class expression for the automaton. An individual who had once for all become fixed in his natural disposition, or had adapted himself to some definite role in life—who, in fact, had ceased to grow—was called a character . . . This middle-class conception of the immobility of the soul was transferred to the stage, where the middle class has always ruled."

Since the immobility or eternal fixedness of the present-day American social type—let us nickname him The Orgman—is presented as something new, in contrast to the dynamism and inwardness of the Inner-Directed Man (Riesman) or the Protestant Ethic Person (Whyte) of the nineteenth century, let us keep in mind Strindberg's point that the image of the person who is identical with his social role has been with us for centuries.

Automata of manners are a feature of traditional literature, as the true automaton, the Golem, Homunculus, Frankenstein, is a familiar figure of mythology and folklore. Most interesting with regard to the type presented by the new American sociology in his relation to the "mechanical man" image conceived by last-century writers as associated with the effects upon human beings of the new machine culture. Poe, in "The Man Who Was Made Up", imagined a person put together from fabricated parts; while Marx built his political philosophy upon the misery and triumph of that human "product of modern industry", the proletariat.

In the current writings, the type that displaces the human person also originates in the productive and distributive machinery of society. The Orgman is further identified with the older literature of industrial alienation by the part of science in his drama. In Marx the key force in historical progress is, of course, science; and it is the scientist of revolution who releases the proletariat upon the world; in *1984* the scientist reappears as the personality-crushing interrogator. Says *The Organization Man:* "The first denominator is scientism;" and goes on to demonstrate the presence in all American institutions of the traditional creator of the mannikin, the "mad scientist", now wearing the guise of the personnel expert, the motivational researcher or some other "soul engineer."

Blood brother to the inhuman "double", the Mr. Hyde, of romantic literature, on the one hand, and to the proletarian of revolutionary socialism, on the other, The Orgman belongs to the latest episode in the saga of the conquest of society by hordes of faceless *directed* men.

Yet the new literature is neither romantic nor revolutionary, and in this lie its most striking characteristics. One no longer hears the metallic lockstep coming closer, like the rising of swarms of beetles or crabs. The enemy of this decade does not come from below. His is neither the face of the ogre over the edge, nor of the ghost behind the window pane. In the muted melodrama of the current sociology, the inhuman does not *invade*. It sits in the living room twisting the TV dial or takes the family for a ride in the two-tone hard-top. It is you.

Recoiling from the outerworld of society's monsters, outcasts and victims, the analysts of contemporary America center their interest on the majority that benefits from the existing social process. With this shift of attention the spectre has shifted too. The alienated man has left the company town for the suburb; the factory for the office, the drafting room, the lecture hall. The presence within him of the socially constructed Other is, by the testimony of each of our authors, the mark of "the new middle class" man. It is to the absorption of this alter-ego that all his education and training are directed. Says Riesman: "The mass media ask the child to see the world as 'the' child—that is, the other child—sees it". To be inhabited by the abstract social person is what is currently meant by the terms "normal" and "socially adjusted".

The charge that all our social behavior stands as a power over and against us *is a more extreme accusation of existing American society than that of the preceding radicalism*. Implicating *everyone*, without distinction as to social class or function, in a single deepening process of dehumanization, such works as *The Lonely Crowd, The Organization Man, The Hidden Persuaders,* communicate in atmosphere, if not in stated concept, the sinister overtones of a developing totalitarianism from which there is no escape. In this literature with its subdued manners of scientific analysis Orwell keeps springing up like a red devil. *The Hidden Persuaders* features Big Brother on the jacket and promises the reader "a slightly chilly feeling along the spine"; an effect which the blurb for Whyte's volume has already delivered through billing its hero as the man who "not only works for the Organization: he belongs to it." The smiling credit manager you spoke to this morning is a piece of company apparatus like the filing case from which he extracts the card that is you; his human appearance is a disguise and his real name isn't Brown but Agent F-362.

With Marx the conversion of the individual's "living time" into lifeless commodities was restricted to the routine of the wage worker. In the current studies no one who participates in any capacity in the system of production and distribution can escape the vampire that drains him of himself. Differences in class functions have ceased to matter. Even the division between labor and leisure has lost its meaning; for the psychic mortification of the individual takes place not only in and through his work but by means of his participation in any form, public or private, of social life, from churchgoing, to cocktail parties, to his relations with his wife and children. Whyte and Mills put the major emphasis on the job as the ground of estrangement; Spectorsky gives mode of employment and style of leisure about equal play, seeing one as the extension (laboratory?) of the other; Riesman regards the externally controlled psyche as a phenomenon of "the consumer age"—and is supported by the evidence of *The Hidden Persuaders* concerning supermarket penetration-assaults and the cold war against the customer by means of the new psycho-sales weapons. All our authors are at one in conceiving the flattening of personality in America as a universal effect of our interrelated economic and social practices.

What the Orgman-critics expose is not a flaw in society but the injurious realities of its normal everyday life. These, however, are presented in a perspective that denudes them of radical implications. Here "scientific objectivity" has become the disguise of a philosophy of fatalism. The emergence of the Orgman is conceived in terms far more deterministic than those of the "historical materialists". Neither Riesman's "age of consumption" nor Whyte's "Organization" was brought into being by the choice, nor even the need, of anyone, whether individual, class, or nation. The "other-directed society" of the first is a manifestation of the population-curve; the new corporate "collectivism" of the second, of an immanent process of expansion and stratification. The vocabularies chosen by Riesman and Whyte of themselves exclude human intervention, in the future as in the past: you cannot re-direct an other-directed period, any more than you can refill an Orgman with "Protestant Ethic". Even if you could, there would be no point in doing so, since other-direction and the ubiquity of the Organization are necessities of our time.

In any case, the histrionic effect of the new criticism is unmistakeable: the bland deadpan of the Objective Observer has definitely replaced the scowl of the radical accuser. For him such words as "capitalist", "class conflict", "profits", "depression" are at once too bulky and needlessly exciting. Since they draw from the same storehouse of material and cultural consumers' goods, all Americans have become "capitalists"; since they are changed into directed beings by their work and social consumption, all have become "proletarianized". On both counts, there is no cause for conflict and a unanimity of interest prevails. All of us, Whyte thinks, will have to revolt. But whatever basis there was for Marx's conception of a metaphysico-political uprising of human machine parts against a minority of opulent personalities has vanished in the universal estrangement.

In the new Organization America there are no fundamental issues, though some old-fashioned people may not yet have gotten rid of the habit of taking sides. To "moralize the flow of words," says Riesman, through which events are apprehended today is a tendency of "the inner-directed person who remains still extant in this period"—which is a marvellously ironical way of saying that you know what is happening only through what you're told about it in the mass media, and that if you care one way or another you merely define yourself as a relic. The deadpan, apparently, is a requisite not only of the analyst of society but of all of us. If Riesman's irony goes unnoticed, as Whyte complains his has, it is because his language is too consistently detached from his subject matter to admit any sense of contrast: Orgprose, too, is dead-pan.

Evoking the sinister concept of man as a tool and as an object, the new writing does so in an oddly disembodied and unpainful way. Its tone is one of injury but of injury unsuffered. It would seem that among the "groups", particularly the better-paid ones, that have re-placed the classes in Orgamerica, the substitution of a corporate iden-tity for one's own is not the unmixed deprivation it might have been for the twelve-hour-a-day factory hand or for the citizen of the slave state. Before the Orgman can feel put upon, it is only fair that he con-sider the advantages gained. "It is not," explains Whyte, "the evils of the organization that puzzle him, but its very beneficence." Strange lit-erature which, assembling the proof of society's subversion of both the will and the intelligence of its members, cries out, like the man in the joke, "But good. But good."

When the fear of the unreal becomes mixed with an idyllic depend-ence on it, a kind of mythic euphoria ensues which is related to the essence of the comic. Chinese folklore is full of the pranks of demons who have shed their awfulness and sit on window-sills and above door-ways minding one's business like so many other-directed neighbors. These every-day fiends may be as spiteful on occasion as one of Whyte's integration-specialists, but their troublemaking only adds gaiety to the way the "system" to which they belong achieves its generous aims. The tale of the Orgman has as much in common with dream farce as with the Orwellian torture phantasy. If its hero suffers, it is in the drugged world of *A Midsummer Night's Dream* laden with bodily pleasures and tremors, where, in the words of *The Organization Man*, "the demands for his surrender are constant and powerful, and the more he has come to like the organization the more difficult does he find it to resist these demands, or even to recognize them."

For both radicalism and conservatism, history is a struggle of win-ners and losers. In the new American scene, everyone has won a fairy-tale luxury and lost himself. The drama of history has been replaced by a pantomime in which, freed of individual or mass conflicts, be-wildered, adjusted beings respond as in a narcosis to mysterious signs, whispers, hints and shocks, which each receives on his Riesman "radar mechanism". The scientific wand-wielder responsible for these psycho-logical pinches and tweaks which inject dream anxieties into their physical serenity is a kind of affable Puck; for even the scientist, since he is necessary, is no longer a real villain; the evil lies rather in his abstract double, "scientism". Riesman and Whyte construct their shadowplay in such a way as to leave no point of resistance. As in Whyte's description quoted above, any struggle against surrender on the part of the individual constitutes a wrestle in a dream. Neither Whyte nor Riesman indicates any direction in which the American person can realize himself in the actual world.

Yet disregarding the nature of the type or "character" as automaton, each holds out the hope that the alter-ego he is describing may some day develop into a human individual. This empty happy-ending is excellent as finale in a farce like *The Three Penny Opera;* as a substitute for protest or for tragic pathos in a portrayal of actual life, such sudden optimism arouses the suspicion of an attempt at ingratiation. Whyte looks forward to a time when "men partially liberated might be tantalized into demanding more"—no doubt by means of mass-persuasion techniques. As for Riesman, he can lift his consumer type out of the trap of "belongingness" only by attaching to him the time-fuse of a self-transforming process: "these developments [the mass distribution of art and literature] suggest to me that the process of taste-exchanging holds the promise of transcending itself and becoming something quite different, and of signally contributing to the development of autonomy in other-directed men." As if one could go from the abstract to the concrete, the automaton to the organism. Our sociologists' remedy for alienation is not "scientism"—it is sorcery.

Extremist but neither radical nor conservative, the Organization criticism is inspired not by a passion for social correction but by nostalgia. A sigh over the lost person mars the phantasy of American unanimity which has supplanted the ideological Passion Plays of Marxian condemnation and conflict. Whyte's memoir on his training in the Vicks Vaporub rugged individualist sales force of "the old days" (the late 'thirties) is the most eloquent and touching passage in this entire literature. The Age of the Giants—alas, gone forever. With Vicks' Richardson extinct, every human degradation may be logically anticipated. Today, the Orgman, the "dominant member of society," still lives among the relics of older types. Tomorrow he will tread the stage alone, in conflict only with himself.

It is the business type of yesterday whom the new social criticism has generalized into its "inner-directed" and "Protestant Ethic" abstraction, and in the name of which it fires its barrages against present-day tendencies. If it takes some daring to bury the boss, it takes less if one also bewails him in public. Especially in a situation where he has much to gain by playing dead. In Whyte's indictment of the human exactions of The Corporation, one hears the voice of the Founder deploring "the drift toward socialization."

Loosed from action, for which it can see no aim, the post-radical criticism often exaggerates its complaints, producing a worse impression of conditions than is warranted by the facts, at the same time that it seeks remedies in the wrong direction. For example, Mills, the most emotionally authentic of these writers, undervalues the personal and social expression of the white-collar worker on the job, with an effect of melancholy that seems unreal when one looks at actual men and women coming out of an office building. On the other hand, the salvation through improvement of taste proposed by Riesman, or through a psychic resistance based on private life (far more impoverished for the clerk than his job) suggested by Whyte, are, as we have seen, equally unreal.

But there is more to the conception of the Orgman than regret for an older social type. As the representative of the new post-War employed intelligentsia, the post-radical critic suffers also a nostalgia for himself as an independent individual. For his former abstract sympathy with a nominal working class, the intellectual of this decade has substituted an examination in the mirror of his own social double as insider of The Organization and The Community. It is what he sees there that has caused him to project a morbid image of society compared with which the old "class struggle" America seems not only naïf but as relatively healthy as a war with rifles and cannons.

For in regard to the misery of alienation, who is a greater victim of what Whyte calls the split "between the individual as he is and the role he is called upon to play" than the member of the intellectual caste newly enlisted *en masse* in carrying out society's functions? As writer, artist, social scientist, he is one with his talents and his education for creative work; in playing his part in the service of the organization he must eliminate any thought of functioning for himself. Through his personal inventiveness he has in the past fifteen years achieved prosperity and social prestige, yet he is the most dependent of wage earners and the most anxiously conscious of his dependence—*The Exurbanites* chronicles this dependence and anxiety to the last installment dollar. (Applying itself to the narrower spectrum of the commercialized intellectuals, *The Exurbanites* is the most realistic of the works we have been considering.)

The intellectual employee also accepts a more total identification with his role than other workers, in that the editorial director, the designer, the copywriter, etc., sells himself more completely in terms of both psychic energy expended and number of hours worked. With him the division between work and leisure, discipline and freedom, has truly been erased. If the free artist or the founder of a great enterprise builds his life exclusively out of the substance of his work, today's intellectual unbuilds his life in order to live his job.†

Besides being the prime victim and exemplar of self-loss in contemporary society, the "organized" professional cannot escape a conviction of guilt for his part in depriving others of their individuality. He has consented to use his capacities as a tool and to approve in practice the proposition recorded by Whyte that "all the great ideas have already been discovered." His skills tend to relate to human management, e.g., writing, image-making, program-forming; even if his specialty is in engineering or the physical sciences, the results of his work directly augment the force by which society is controlled. The intellectual cannot function as Organization Man without also functioning as Organization-Man moulder; as human object he must also affect others as objects; as manipulated act as manipulator. Thus he cannot help but feel himself to be a betrayer of humanity as of his own mind. Helpless to change anything, he is yet the chief culprit of the alienation drama, the driven "scientist", who directs the undermining of the raw individual, whether as motivational expert, inventor of personnel tests, or as preacher of despairing acceptance.

Self-displacement through one's acts is the innermost problem of life in America as of that in all civilized countries. The Social Type has always been among us, of course, despite Riesman's effort to distinguish today's other-directed man from his nineteenth-century counterpart. Tolstoy's Ivan Ilych, who decorated his house entirely according to his own original ideas only to have it turn out exactly like all other houses of his class, is as good an example of automatic "radared" taste-exchanging (Riesman) as can be found in Fairfield County. Tolstoy explicitly insisted that Ilych was a socially made-up man, an "object" guided by public opinion, an example of "dead" living.

In the United States, nineteenth-century literature, whether in the popular stage comedies of manners or in the symbolism of the romantics, centers on society's human abstractions. We mentioned above Poe's hero who owed to industry his movable parts. A contemporary

† The rule quoted by Whyte for corporation executives generally, "You promote the guy who takes his problem home with him," becomes for the intellectual, "You hire the guy who takes his problem to bed with him." His job has a creative side in which his preconscious must also collaborate. Take this into account in computing his average salary, and the difference between the wage-earner of the suburb and of the company town becomes largely a matter of overtime pay. At $2.50 an hour the totally employed intellectual would earn more than $20,000 a year.

of this invention was the ubiquitous Salesman-Preacher, whom Melville, writing in a less unctuous age than ours, named The Confidence Man. Like Whyte, Spectorsky and Packard, Melville saw in this professional who supplied his countrymen with things, ideas and feeling, the outstanding specimen of man as social artifice. As his complement, he set up the brooding inner-directed Indian Fighter, paranoiac Ahab of the prairies; while from the silent recesses of the office files, he drew forth the white-collared tomb deity, Bartleby.

What is new in America is not the socially reflexive person but the presence of a self-conscious intellectual caste whose disillusionment has induced its members to volunteer for the part. The predicament in which these individuals find themselves is what casts a bar sinister over their image of America. The fear-augury that the Orgman will become everyone in a quiet, unopposable totalitarianism is not a conclusion based on social analysis but a projection of the fate they have chosen for themselves. The American landscape has by no means been re-made by the "Social Ethic" compression machine into an electrified Eden set out on porcelain grass. Except in the new suburbs, the physical condition of America's cities, towns and villages is of itself proof enough that decay, shiftlessness, egotism and other forms of popular expressionism are more than holding their own against other-direction. Granted that growth of the supercorporation and the absorption and standardization of small business has changed the independent operator into an agent, at the same time that mechanization has been turning the workman into a technician; granted that Whyte's notation that "the collectivization so visible in the corporation has affected almost every field of work" is indisputable; and that today Orgmen reproduce themselves like fruit flies in whatever is organized, whether it be a political party or a museum of advanced art; given this groundwork for the conquest of America by this "type", still the contention that the nation is, or even might be, subordinated to such a master is at least as ludicrous as it is alarming. The increasing concentration of control and the standardization of work present well-known alternatives which we need not discuss here; but for the individual, the last voice in the issue of being or not being himself is still his own.

The inhabitant of the sacred groves has, however, surrendered all choices. Having accepted self-alienation in trade for social place, the post-radical intellectual can see nothing ahead but other-direction and a corporately styled personality. For him the Orgworld has closed for good. Within these limits the deploring of "conformity" is simply an expression of self-pity. The strategy of fighting the organization through secret resistance behind the outer-shaped mask (Whyte) is, by the measure of the ancient intellectual tradition of denunciation or self-exile, only a dreary professional's ruse for holding on to the best of both worlds. That such a proposal should seem relevant is another proof that the Orgman is, with necessary additions and disguise, none else than the new intellectual talking about himself. Certainly the deft management of the corporate Look which solves things for Whyte would be of no help to the farmer or to the workingman, nor would the boss need to make use of it. The "what to do about it" part of the studies of Whyte and Riesman are clearly sermons for their milieu rather than challenges to history in the name of mankind.

The critics of the new America are disheartened by a revolution won—their revolution, which can go no farther than the ending of the underground life of the American intellectual mass through economic recognition of the services it has to offer. With his own success achieved the only issue the intellectual can see as remaining for society is "personality". Somehow, this seems unattainable in "the dehumanized collective" in the building of which he is taking a leading part. The result is depression—and it is by the power of the depression it generates, in contrast to the smugness of the old-time boosting, that the present sociology is a force against a more radical and realistic understanding of American life.